POVERTY AND PUBLIC POLICY IN MODERN AMERICA

POVERTY AND PUBLIC POLICY IN MODERN AMERICA

Edited by
Donald T. Critchlow,
University of Notre Dame
Ellis W. Hawley,
University of Iowa

The Dorsey Press
Chicago, Illinois 60604

Cover photo: Courtesy of Chicago Historical Society

© RICHARD D. IRWIN, INC., 1989

Sponsoring editor: Casimir Psujek
Project editor: Joan A. Hopkins
Production manager: Carma W. Fazio
Designer: Diana Yost
Compositor: Publication Services, Inc.
Typeface: 10/12 Century Schoolbook
Printer: Malloy Lithographing, Inc.

Library of Congress Cataloging-in-Publication Data

Poverty and public policy in modern America / edited by Donald T.
   Critchlow, Ellis W. Hawley.
      p.   cm.
   ISBN 0-256-06024-X (pbk.)
      1. Public welfare—United States—History.   2. United States-
-Social policy.   I. Critchlow, Donald T., 1948-   . II. Hawley,
Ellis Wayne, 1929-
HV95.P67 1989
361.973—dc19   88–29955
                                                          CIP

Printed in the United States of America
1 2 3 4 5 6 7 8 9 0 ML 5 4 3 2 1 0 9 8

ABOUT THE EDITORS

Donald T. Critchlow, Associate Professor of History at the University of Notre Dame, currently serves as editor of the *Journal of Policy History*. He is the author of *The Brookings Institution, 1916–1952: Expertise and the Public Interest in a Democratic Society* (1985). He is also editor of *Socialism in the Heartland* and (1986) coeditor with Ellis Hawley of *Federal Social Policy: The Historical Dimension* (1988).

Ellis W. Hawley, Department of History, University of Iowa, is the author of *The New Deal and the Problem of Monopoly* (1966) and *The Great War and the Search for a Modern Order* (1979). He is currently working on a study of Herbert Hoover as Secretary of Commerce and President and on a social history of the American people in the 1920s.

Introduction

The modern welfare system of the United States is in large measure a product of twentieth-century developments. It has emerged, in other words, from twentieth-century efforts to solve an American version of the "welfare problem" that began appearing in all major Western nations in the last third of the nineteenth century. All were troubled by the growing inability of their traditional welfare systems to meet the changing or redefined needs of societies that were being rapidly transformed, primarily by the new technologies and changes in resource usage that the workings of commercial markets and capitalist processes were now selecting. New institutions, many came to believe, had to be established. And in the twentieth century, as this belief became widespread among those with the power and resources to act on it, a new complex of welfare institutions and arrangements has taken shape and has generally been regarded, both in the United States and elsewhere, as one of the alterations produced by a larger process of social "modernization."

The reality of this larger pattern, however, should not obscure the fact that the "modern" welfare systems thus produced have differed and continue to differ from each other. History has mattered, both in the sense that heritages from the past have been determinants of what could and could not be done and in the sense that choices existed and were made by historical actors. In the United States as elsewhere, the new welfare system was created by people acting within the context of what had been created by their forebears. And it is to the historical record of these actions and the contexts in which they were taken that one must turn for any adequate understanding of how and why the American system has taken the form that it has. What follows in this collection is intended to illuminate that record, make it more accessible, and facilitate, through expcerpts from both historical actors and scholars, the achievement of a historically grounded understanding of America's modern welfare system and the ongoing debates concerning it.

Such an understanding, we would contend, must logically begin with what the historical record tells us about the traditional system used to meet American welfare needs in the nineteenth century. The core of this, as Chapter 1 discusses in some detail, was rooted in the triple heritage of the English poor law, churchly benevolence, and traditional family and kinship responsibilities. But each of these had been adapted to a society in which individualism and free-market ideology had gained exceptionally strong footholds. And around this core, other arrangements and institutions had grown up. These included a complex of specialized charity organizations and individual philanthropies, an overlay of specialized asylums for dependent and deviant populations, and an accretion of politicized benefits dispensed through political machines, party patronage, and the military pension system. What had failed to grow up, in marked contrast with developments abroad, were arrangements through which the bureaucratic component of the traditional state had assumed new welfare functions. Bureaucratically speaking, nineteenth-century America lacked a genuine "state," and such bureaucratic impulses as could be found in its welfare system were limited mostly to private-sector institutions and to the establishment of a few professionalized public health and charity boards at the state level.

Historians have differed as to why the nineteenth-century system had these particular components. Some have stressed the nation's peculiar governmental structure and political culture; others have assigned a larger role to the workings of a new humanitarianism; and still others have emphasized the workings of a quest for instruments of social control. But most would agree that America did share in the late–nineteenth-century discovery of a "welfare problem." Many Americans came to believe that their traditional system was working badly. The evidence could be found not only in mounting social distress and disharmony but also in wastage of human resources and in the spread of political corruption and discontent. And as many analyzed the situation, the system was likely to become even more unworkable in the future. The economic and demographic changes under way were widening the gap between welfare needs and the capacity of families, churches, poorhouses, and the other components of the traditional system to meet them.

As America entered the twentieth century, moreover, it did share in the general experimentation with new welfare agencies that would lead eventually to the creation of modern welfare states. A variety of welfare reformers began offering prescriptionns for solving the "welfare problem," and within a few years the outlines of what would be continuing debates were becoming relatively clear. One question concerned the effects of the reform projects and their creations on a business system that most Americans wanted to preserve. Another concerned the potential effects on individual character and civic virtue. A third had to do with the role of trained and credentialed experts in a workable system. And a fourth related to the possibility of finding a uniquely American substitute for the statist bureaucracies that were becoming the core of the new welfare systems in Europe. It was and continued to be argued that America could have a workable system without saddling itself with such bureaucracies. Alongside the efforts to build a new state with social service capacities, there also developed a persisting line of efforts to forge a nonstatist alternative, either by drawing the needed system from the group life and power centers of the private sector or by constructing it from modernized community units capable of acting in concert to meet national needs.

In the United States this experimentation with and debate over new welfare agencies began in earnest in the quarter century prior to World War I, a period which both contempories and subsequent historicans have called the "progressive era." In practice, "progressivism" as applied to the "welfare problem" meant the establishment of a wide array of new welfare agencies through which an increasingly professionalized group of social workers could apply new techniques for rehabilitating the dependent and deviant, for preventing the wastage of human resources and for reducing the distress and disharmony inherent in economic and demographic change. Among such agencies, to cite only the most prominent, were juvenile courts, settlement houses, community centers, child welfare stations, charity federations, physical and mental hygiene units, and corporate welfare departments. In addition, progressivism in practice, as Chapters 2 and 3 of this collection make clear, meant new forms of protective legislation for economically vulnerable groups, the establishment of workmen's compensation and mother's pensions as the first tentative steps toward a new social insurance system, and an extensive effort to unite community activism with technical expertise through the formation of new "social units." In all of these respects, the "progressives" helped to lay some of the foundations for the system that would become America's counterpart to the welfare states being erected abroad.

What "progressive" America still lacked and still failed to develop, however, was a national welfare bureaucracy comparable to those in nations like Germany and Britain. The inherited structure of government, the continuing appeal of antistatist ideology, the fear that public-sector programs would be captured by corrupt and inefficient political spoilsmen, and an optimistic faith in what could be done through voluntary action and individual adjustment all worked to prevent the proposals for such a bureaucracy from being implemented. So did the belief that viable communitarian or privatist alternatives could be developed; and by 1920 some opponents of foreign welfare "imports" were pointing to the achievements of community organization work, corporate welfare programs, and welfare association building as constituting a promising start toward realizing these envisioned alternatives and making them part of a superior "American way." It was primarily to these approaches, it was argued, that America had turned in dealing with the social dislocations caused by the mobilization of 1917 and 1918. During the war they had demonstrated a potential that, if adapted to peacetime needs and fully realized, could go a long way toward solving the nation's larger welfare problem.

In the so-called new era of the 1920s, the subject of the readings in Chapter 4, this view that America was pioneering a "new way" rather than "lagging behind" other nations became still more firmly established. In America, it was widely believed, the future need not include either a

Prussian-style "state" or a wasteful and demoralizing British "dole." The answer could come through a system of responsible private groups and local communities, especially if these could be equipped with social expertise and national perspectives and could be linked to the new capacities of modern business for social and community leadership. It was this answer that became the professed goal of Herbert Hoover's Commerce Department and other federal agencies with welfare missions. Its presence, moreover, when taken in conjunction with the period's resurgent individualism and heightened faith in therapies stressing individual adjustment, worked to thwart further attempts to give the United States a comprehensive system of national social insurance. Although much of the earlier progressive handiwork did survive, the central thrust in policy making was toward reducing its public-sector component, erecting new legal barriers against governmental action, and assigning more of the welfare task to what was allegedly being created in the private sector.

The great test of this "new era" solution to modern welfare needs would come with the onset of the Great Depression. As president from 1929 to 1933, Herbert Hoover tried his best to make it work. But the result of his efforts was to discredit the claims made for the system, convince Americans that adequate welfare could not be had without a larger role for the federal government, and pave the way for the innovations of the New Deal. The depression crisis, discussed in the selections for Chapter 5, became in this sense a major force for change, altering not only the prevailing view conerning private-sector capacities but also the willingness to change established structures of government, reconsider established notions about what government could and should do, and set aside long-standing fears about political spoilsmen, welfare parasites, and alienated businessmen. From it came policies assigning new welfare tasks to federal agencies, initially in efforts to rescue the existing system with transfusions of federal resources, but eventually involving direct provision of new welfare services. By 1939 the United States could be said to have a "welfare state"—an "incomplete" one, to be sure, in comparison with those abroad, but still one in which an expanding public-sector bureaucracy, energetically engaged in creating and administering national systems of old age insurance and assistance, unemployment compensation and relief, aid to dependent groups, and fair labor standards, had now become a central component of American welfare provision.

In the evolution of America's modern welfare system, the social legislation and programs associated with Franklin D. Roosevelt's New Deal stand as major landmarks. The policy choices that produced them have not been undone. On the contrary, they have had long-range impacts, both in blocking alternatives and in begetting an institutional apparatus with a built-in proclivity for "completing" what had been started. But as the discussion in Chapter 6 makes clear, the system in existence as the New Deal came to an end also retained much that had its roots in the pre-

New Deal era. In particular, it had preserved important roles for local, state, and private agencies, retained institutional formations dating from the progressive period or the business-dominated New Era, and incorporated a culture in which the "dole," the "state," and the "reliefer" still had generally negative images. In addition, its retained the kind of jerrybuilt quality that had been characteristic of the American system prior to the 1930s. And while conservative opponents saw it as an un-American move toward governmental paternalism, it could be strongly criticized for its inadequacy of benefits and coverage, its reliance on regressive taxation, its sacrifice of national standards to local pressures, and its failure to include such features as national health insurance and an economic bill of rights. Its real purpose, some charged, was to help maintain an oppressive and unjust social order, and this had been a continuing theme in critiques from the left.

The return of good times after 1940 significantly reduced the amounts spent on federal relief. But by that time the political bases for retaining the New Deal's programs of social insurance had been firmly established. In the era of economic growth, rising expectations, and security consciousness that followed Word War II, a process of "incrementalism" involving little economic or political pain kept adding more benefits and areas of coverage. This was a feature both of Harry Truman's "fair deal" and Dwight D. Eisenhower's "modern republicanism." Yet while incrementalism kept expanding America's welfare state, those who would fill its programmatic gaps or give it a more egalitarian bias were unable to secure the reforms that they advocated. As detailed in Chapters 7 and 8, the attempts to establish national health insurance, "full employment" mandates, firmer and better observed national standards, and special programs for impoverished groups all failed. Not only were they widely perceived as "socialistic" and subversive of the social good, they were also seen as steps along a path for which America was once more developing a superior alternative. Appearing again, to some extent during Truman's administration and more so during Eisenhower's, was the notion that the private sector was acquiring new capacities to meet welfare needs and that these private developments, of public/private "partnerships" linked to them, could deal with what remained or America's "welfare problem."

Such views were not subjected to the test of another great depression. But in the late 1950s and early 1960s a growing group of social critics, reminiscent of those helping to set the stage for progressivism, were creating new perceptions of a welfare system that was failing the tests of modernity and leaving major needs unmet. The evidence, it was said and widely believed, lay in deteriorating city cores and dehumanized workplaces, in cultural forms that impoverished rather than enriched their consumers, and particularly in a "hidden poverty" that was now being brought to light. Among liberals the conviction grew that new public-sector programs were badly needed. And with the return of the Democrats to power and of liberals to dominance in Congress, an outcome attributable both to a liberal resurgence and to the impact of a new conservative activism on the Republican party, a number of the proposed additions were made. By 1966 the United States, although still without national health insurance, had added new systems of Medicare for the aged and Medicaid for the poor. It had transformed and greatly expanded its program of Aid to Families with Dependent Children. And, amid much fanfare, it had declared "war on poverty" and established an elaborate complex of antipoverty programs engaged in treating the structural unemployment, feelings of powerlessness, and personal, family, and cultural disorders thought to explain the persistence of poverty in an affluent society. These additions are examined in detail in the selections of Chapter 9.

As Chapter 9 also makes clear, however, some of these innovations failed to establish the political bases needed to make them continuing and accepted parts of the American welfare system. In particular, the AFDC program and the "war on poverty" became involved in practices that alienated middle-class support while failing to generate much support in other quarters. Soon these programs had become the subjects of widespread criticism reaching across the political spectrum and linking them to such phenomena as price inflation, administrative mismanagement, cultural disharmony, elitist manipulation, and rioting in the ghettos. They were producing a "welfare mess" rather than a "great society." And the growth of such a view, when taken in conjunction with other liberal setbacks in the late 1960s, helped to enhance the credibility of broader critiques in which the welfare state itself became the problem rather than the solution. As brought out in Chapter 10, the 1960s were a period in which traditional conservatives, new leftists, and neolibertarian rightists were all developing and articulating variations of this argument.

In the 1970s, moreover, the argument did have important effects on policy making. It did not, to be sure, lead to any major questioning of the established "entitlements" provided through the social security system. On the contrary, these were made more generous and more secure through legislation providing for cost-of-living adjustments, income supplements, and governmental guarantees of private-sector pension contracts. But there was continued questioning of the programs for the poor and the dependent, questioning which insisted that they were not working as intended and which tended to become more pronounced as the nation worried about the purported breakdown of the traditional family and entered an era of economic stagflation, lagging productivity, and loss of markets to foreign competitors. Politicians and scholars talked about a "welfare crisis" involving bureaucratic institutions that were "overloaded," dysfunctional, and "out of control." And increasingly, as discussed in Chapter 11, "welfare reform" came to be viewed not as assigning more welfare tasks to a social worker bureaucracy but rather as implementing schemes that would reduce reliance on such expertise, substitute a guaranteed minimum income for "case work" and "social engineering," and link assistance to stronger systems of work incentives. Such was the thrust of the "family assistance plan" considered during the Nixon years, the Carter administration's reform efforts, and a variety of other schemes put forth by conservatives and liberals alike.

As the 1970s drew to a close, such "reform" had brought relatively few changes. The Nixon and Carter plans were never adopted. They failed because advocates of the principles involved could not agree on particulars. Also, in the limited experimentation with "workfare" that was undertaken, notably under the Talmadge amendments to the AFDC law and in the state systems of Massachusetts and California, the results were disappointing. Yet the continuing "reform" agitation had kept the remaining advocates of a "more complete" welfare state on the defensive, ready for the most part to settle for holding the line or at best for a bit of incrementalism. And beyond this, the continuing call for reform had helped to create the context in which a popular president embracing antiwelfare positions and symbols would succeed in putting through major cuts in federal social expenditures. Again, to be sure, social insurance remained firmly in place. In this area, the widely publicized reforms of 1983 amounted essentially to minor adjustments in benefits. But, beginning in 1981, the Reagan administration did implement policies under which federal outlays for public assistance programs were substantially reduced and much of the responsibility for such assistance was, in theory, turned back to the states and the private sector. As some critics saw it, the new president had replaced the war on poverty with a war on welfare, which in their view would lead not to a clearing away of the "welfare mess" but to the promotion of a new structure of poverty and to what could well be a permanent "underclass."

Also prominent in the 1980s, again with links to what had happened in the 1970s, was the continuing experimentation with and debate over "workfare," discussed in the selection in Chapter 12. Despite meager results from previous efforts to require work or training for assisted "employables," many Americans now seemed convinced that a "harder," better administered, and properly supplemented "workfare" was the real route to a better society. By the mid-1980s, numerous states had adopted programs based on this idea. Furthermore, in some proposals for altering national policy, the goal had become a "work ethic state" in which publicly provided "work" would take the place of most public assistance programs; those able but refusing to work would be left to survive in the world of in-kind shelters, charities, and food dispensaries. This, its proponents argued, would replace pathological cultural forms with socially desirable ones, but to critics it seemed more like a modern equivalent of the "workhouse."

As America approached the last decade of the twentieth century, it had acquired its own counterpart to the modern welfare states emerging elsewhere. It had done so through a series of intellectual, political, and institutional responses to a continuing "welfare problem" posed by changing or redefined social needs, a problem that in a broad sense resembled those to which other nations had responded. Yet the counterpart thus produced clearly had its own distinctive characteristics, its own peculiar arrangement of structural and cultural underpinnings, its own special tangle of historical roots reaching back to differing eras, and its own particular mix of what was acceptable and what was still debatable and unsettled. It was difficult to understand apart from its history and the historical contexts in which each of its components had emerged. And from the study of this history, we would argue, one can gain not only a fuller understanding of its form and developmental direction but also of the choices that have been made and those yet to come.

Contents

CHAPTER 11
Nixon to Reagan   *287*

CHAPTER 12
Postscript   *319*

CHAPTER 1

The Origins of Modern Social Policy

INTRODUCTION

"The chief distinguishing characteristic of the American political system before 1861," political scientist Walter Dean Burnham observed, "is that *there was no state*." Similarly, in the late nineteenth century the major federal social welfare program of the time was the pension system for Civil War veterans, a highly politicized system that by the turn of the century provided two out of every three native white persons over the age of sixty with a federal pension. The political abuses of this system only heightened a general distrust of federal involvement in social policy.

As a consequence, social policy remained localistic, private, and primarily centered around the poorhouse and charity organizations that sought to imbue the values of work among the poor. Americans imparted an intensity to this ideology of work by their insistence that relief of the poor was primarily the domain of private organizations. This antistatist prejudice among Americans was encouraged by a view that local officials were best able to check abuses of relief by "loafers," while harnessing the energies of the unemployed and instilling self-respect among the "deserving poor." Although "outdoor relief" in the form of food baskets and fuel coupons was necessitated at times, most charity workers preferred to provide institutional care for the most helpless—the insane, the handicapped, orphans, widowed mothers, and the indigent elderly.

At the center of this system stood the poorhouse. Charity workers promoted the poorhouse not for its cost-saving features, but for its ability to instill the virtues of labor among the poor. In turn, charity workers claimed that outdoor relief encouraged indiscriminate relief and eroded the will to work. Poorhouses were seen as tools to transform the behavior and character of inmates, while allowing organized charities to distinguish between the able-bodied poor and the "impotent" poor.

The belief in the superiority of private over public relief was held by most private charity organizations, even though the lines between private and public charity were often blurred throughout the nineteenth century. Those concerned with the abuses of outdoor relief sought to have it abolished, and these "reform" efforts indeed proved successful in Brooklyn, New York City, Baltimore, Philadelphia, Washington D.C., St. Louis, Kansas City, and San Francisco.

The misuse of public funds by big city political machines only reinforced this sentiment against public relief efforts. City bosses such as James Michael Curley and Martin Lomasney of Boston built highly personalized political machines that aided constitutents by dispensing cash, food, fuel, credit, and municipal jobs to the unemployed. In a period when municipal payrolls were growing rapidly, bosses such as Lomasney and Curley provided steady and secure work. Curley was able to obtain about 500 jobs a year for residents of his Boston district. With unemployment affecting an estimated 30 percent of all Massachusetts workers during any given year in the last two decades of the nineteenth century, the importance of political jobs to party machines appeared all too apparent to reformers who decried the abuse of democratic government. As Seth Low, a reformer and later mayor of New York, reported, "Outdoor relief was attacked primarily because it was prostituted to political ends and was demoralizing in its administrations."

Even as charity workers remained distrustful of public relief and political influence, the very development of specialized institutions for dealing with crime, poverty, disease, mental illness, and other afflictions marked a profound shift in social policy away from care in the home to public, albeit local, institutions. The development of these institutions coincided with the emergence of experts who offered specialized knowledge as to the care and management of their clients. Throughout the late nineteenth century, these experts sought a variety of ways to improve and rationalize the institutional care of the poor, the afflicted, and the social deviant. The creation of Boards of State Charities following the Civil War marked a key effort to coordinate and rationalize public welfare on the local level. Further centralization of local relief occurred in the last decade of the nineteenth century with the enactment of the Indiana Reform Law of 1895, which established a central state office to oversee local programs. This law became a model for other states to follow in their efforts to eliminate political influence on the municipal level by bringing nonpartisan control to the administration of relief.

In his essay "Origins of the Institutional State," Michael B. Katz examines the emergence of the modern institutional state as embodied in mental hospitals, school systems, reformatories, and penitentiaries. He asks, "Why did the institutional state emerge at the time and in the manner it did?" In answering this question he challenges two other explanations concerning the origins of the institutional state, offered by David Rothman and Gerald Grob, historians who have written widely on social welfare in the United States. Rothman traces the origins of social institutions such as prisons, mental hospitals, and poorhouses to fears of social disorder on the part of reformers who witnessed widespread economic change and social dislocation brought about by industrialization, immigration, and urbanization of the United States early in the nineteenth century. Through the establishment of poorhouses, asylums, and penitentiaries, reformers sought to isolate deviants in institutions designed to imbue their inmates with the virtues of industry, temperance, and good citizenship. Contrary to Rothman's view, Gerald Grob finds the origins of these institutions in enlightened and humanitarian impulses that grew out of religious revivals and scientific concerns.

Katz offers an alternative to these two perspectives—an interpretation that stresses the changing social character of capitalism in the late nineteenth century. For Katz, the key to understanding the emergence of new social institutions is the changing nature of advanced capitalism. The growth of dependent populations, the breakdown of traditional ways of caring for dependents, and the creation of new types of dependents forced the social order to find new ways to control and address the social problems of a capitalistic order.

The second reading, Joseph Kirkland's "Among the Poor of Chicago," provides a contemporary account of the changing social order in Chicago in the late 1890s. Kirkland was a well-known lawyer and author of two widely read novels of the day, *Zury, the Meanest Man in Spring County* and *The McVeys*. Kirkland's lengthy essay chronicles his search for the very poor, "the deserving poor," in Chicago. In his search he comes across Italians, Irish, Chinese, Jews, and others who live on the fringes of society. Throughout his essay he emphasizes the values of hard work and sobriety, and he finds that most of the poor are given to drink and self-indulgence. Only those hard-working poor in the western neighborhoods of Chicago seem deserving of occasional charity. Kirkland's descriptions of the various ethnic groups combine objective insights as well as biases of the day. In his rich tour through Chicago, he also discusses the emergence of settlement houses, Jane Addams's Hull House, the Shelter House, and a variety of other benevolent institutions "whose very number and variety preclude description." He notes that the city directory contains the addresses of 57 asylums and hospitals, 28 infirmaries and dispensaries, 41 missions, 60 temperance societies, and 37 columns of secret benevolent associations, camps, and lodges. The very number and range of these institutions suggest that however one explains the emergence of the institutional state, at the very least, the nineteenth century should be seen as an age of experimentation.

Further Readings

Robert H. Bremner, *Up From the Depths: The Discovery of Poverty in the United States* (New York: New York Univ. Press, 1956).

Gerald N. Grob, *Mental Institution in America: Social Policy to 1875* (New York: Free Press, 1973).

Michael B. Katz, *In the Shadow of the Poorhouse: A Social History of Welfare in America* (New York: Basic Books, 1986).

James Leiby, *A History of Social Welfare and Social Work in the United States* (New York: Columbia Univ. Press, 1978).

David J. Rothman, *The Discovery of the Asylum: Social Order and Disorder in the New Republic* (Boston: Little Brown, 1971).

Walter I. Trattner, *From Poor Law to Welfare State* (New York: New York Univ. Press, 1984).

Origins of the Institutional State

Michael B. Katz

We live in an institutional State. Our lives spin outwards from the hospitals where we are born, to the school systems that dominate our youth, through the bureaucracies for which we work, and back again to the hospitals in which we die. If we stray, falter, or lose our grip, we are led or coerced towards the institutions of mental health, justice, or public welfare. Specialists in obstetrics, pediatrics, education, crime, mental illness, unemployment, recreation, to name only some of the most obvious, wait in the yellow pages to offer their expertise in the service of our well-being. Characteristically, we respond to a widespread problem through the creation of an institution, the training of specialists, and the certification of their monopoly over a part of our lives.

We accept institutions and experts as inevitable, almost eternal. That, after all, is the way the world works. It is hard—almost impossible—for us to recall that they are a modern invention.

In North America prior to the nineteenth century few experts of specialized institutions existed. The sick, the insane, and the poor mixed indiscriminately within relatively undifferentiated almshouses. Criminals of all ages and varieties remained in prison for fairly short periods awaiting trial. If guilty they were punished, not by long incarceration but by fine, whipping, or execution. Dependent or troublesome strangers did not receive much charity; they were simply warned out of town. Children learned to read in a variety of ways and attended schools irregularly. In short, families and communities coped with social and personal problems traditionally and informally.

Everything changed within fifty to seventy-five years. By the last quarter of the nineteenth century, specialized institutions were dealing with crime, poverty, disease, mental illness, juvenile delinquency, the blind, the deaf and dumb, and the ignorant. Institutions proliferated so rapidly that by the 1860's some states began to create Boards of State Charities to coordinate and rationalize public welfare.

The treatment of crime, poverty, ignorance, and disease repeated the same story with different details. Institutions suddenly came to dominate public life in a radical departure in social policy. Aside from their sudden creation, most new public institutions experienced a similar cycle of development during their early histories: a shift from reform to custody. Mental hospitals, school systems, reformatories, and penitentiaries began

SOURCE: Michael B. Katz, *Marxist Perspectives I*, no. 4 (Winter, 1978), pp.6–22.

optimistically with assumptions about the tractability of problems and the malleability of human nature. Early promoters expected them to transform society through their effect upon individual personalities. In some instances, as in the case of early mental hospitals or the first reformatory for young women, the optimism appeared justified for a few years. However, institutions, as even their supporters soon came to admit, could not work miracles. Rates of recovery remained low, recidivism high; school systems did not eliminate poverty and vice; ungrateful inmates even, on occasion, set their institutions on fire.

The public had invested heavily in new institutions that a reasonable person might conclude were failures. Nonetheless, the newly created institutional managers did not intend either to admit faiure or to abandon the intricate hierarchical professional worlds they had created. Instead, they altered their justification: mental illness and crime frequently arose from heredity and were incurable; lower-class children were incorrigible; paupers genetically unable and unwilling to work. Institutions existed to keep deviants off the streets; to prevent a glut on the labor market; to contain, not cure, the ills of society. This shift from reform to custody characterized the history of reformatories, mental hospitals, prisons, and school systems within the first two or three decades of their existence.

Social historians disagree about the impulse underlying institutional development. Why did the institutional State emerge at the time and in the manner it did? The question is straightforward, the answer complex and elusive. Actually, two sets of events must be explained: the origins and founding of institutions and the shift from reform to custody. Here, I shall consider only the former and attempt to show a connection between the origins of institutions and the early history of capitalism in North America.

First, consider the pattern and timing of institutional development. The new institutions of the early nineteenth century divide into various groups. Those on which historians have focused most sharply treated deviance: mental hospitals, poorhouses, reformatories, penitentiaries. The first mental hospital, the private McLean's opened in 1818, followed by the first state hospital in Worchester, Massachusetts, in 1835. The first reformatory, also a private corporation, the New York House of Refuge, opened in 1825; the first state reform school incarcerated its first boys in 1848. Both Massachusetts and New York established a network of poorhouses in the 1820s as a result of the famous Quincy and Yates reports which urged the virtual abolition of outdoor relief. In Ontario the Provincial Penitentiary opened in 1835 and the Lunatic Asylum in 1850.

New institutions were not solely residential nor did they serve only those whom we today label deviant. The most notable of the nonresidential institutions designed to service a clearly defined sector of more ordinary people was the public school. Nineteenth-century educational promoters equated ignorance with deviance and both with poverty, but they intended public schools to serve a broader portion of the population than the children of the slums. And public schooling became especially popular among the middle classes. Tax-supported schools of sorts certainly had existed for centuries. The novelty during the nineteenth century rested in the creation of systems of public education—age-graded, finely articulated, nominally universal institutions presided over by specially trained experts and administrators. In New York City the system of public schools began with the organization of the Free School Society in 1805. The first state board of education was established in Massachusetts in 1837 and the Superintendency of Public Instruction in the Provinces of Canada in 1841. By 1880 elaborate, hierarchical educational systems existed in most urban centers.

New or novel institutions served other groups as well. Private boarding schools for the children of the rich developed in the antebellum period in the United States. The most influential of them, according to their historian, was St. Paul's, started in Concord, New Hampshire, in 1855. Indeed, it is fascinating to observe the parallels between private academies and other institutions. In their educational philosophy, organizational ideal, and theory of human nature, early reform schools resembled nothing so much as academies for the poor.

Within New York City, as Alan Horlick has shown, merchants developed a series of institutions to control and socialize the incoming hordes of young, aggressive, and undeferential clerks. This effort gave rise during the early nineteenth century to the YMCA, the Mercantile Library Association, and similar organizations.

The first general hospitals opened in 1752 in Philadelphia, in 1792 in New York City, and in 1821 in Boston. Construed primarily as charities, early hospitals were supposed to cure both the physical and moral afflictions of the poor who composed their patient populations. As with schools, prisons, or reformatories, the purposes of early hospitals included the reformation of character, and, like the sponsors of other institutions, hospital supporters compounded poverty, crime, ignorance, and disease into a single amalgam. Hospitals proved no more able than schools, prisons, or reformatories to uplift social character, and by the 1870s their purpose narrowed to the treatment of specific diseases. At the same time the internal development of hospitals traced a path similar to that followed in other institutions; a growth in size and complexity accompanied by an emphasis upon professional management increasingly divorced from lay influence.

At the most intimate level even the family reflected the thrust of institutional development in more public spheres. Decreasingly the place of both work and residence, with boundaries more tightly drawn between itself and the community, and decreasingly the custodian of the deviant and deficient, the family—the workingclass as well as the middle-class family— became a sharply delimited haven, a specialized agency for the nurture of the young. Within families sex-roles became more clearly defined, and by the middle nineteenth century Catherine Beecher, among others, was attempting to certify the institutionalization of the home through the conversion of domesticity into a science.

In sum, the institutional explosion did not issue directly or solely from state sponsorship, nor were institutions directed only towards deviance or solely asylums. More accurately, institutional development during the early and middle nineteenth century should be described as the creation of formal organizations with specialized clienteles and a reformist, or character-building, purpose.

Institutions were not in themselves novel. Poorhouses had existed in colonial New England. Indeed, Foucault labels the seventeenth century the age of the great confinement. Nonetheless, the use of institutions as deliberate agencies of social policy, their specialization, and their emphasis upon the formation or reformation of character represented a new departure in modern history.

Most major social institutions originated in a two-stage process. They commenced as private corporations to serve public purposes but within a few decades were imitated, superseded, augmented, or expanded by the State. The transition from voluntarism to the State did not represent a simple evolution. Certainly, the magnitude of the problems undertaken by early voluntary corporations—the alleviation of poverty, mental illness, delinquency, ignorance—strained private resources. Financially, voluntary corporations, however, did not rely solely, or, in many cases, at all, upon private contributions. Rather, they commonly received public funds. The assumption of primary responsibility for the operation as well as the funding of institutions, consequently, represented a shift in generally acceptable models for public organization. Elsewhere, I have called this shift the transition from paternalistic and corporate voluntarism to incipient bureaucracy. Voluntarism upheld an ideal of organizations controlled by self-perpetuating corporations of wealthy, enlightened, and public-spirited citizens, essentially limited in size, staffed by talented generalists. The shift to the State reflected a belief that public funding required public control, a commitment to expansion of scale, and an emphasis upon the importance of specialized, expert administration.

The shift from voluntarism to the State appears in the New York House of Refuge, the McLean Hospital, the New York Free School Society, and another interesting variant, the Boston Primary School Committee. When these voluntary corporations went public they often altered their purpose as well as their form. In the case of mental hospitals, the entrance of the State meant the extension of service from the well-to-do served by McLean's to the poor treated at Worcester; in the case of public schools the opposite occurred, as school promoters sought to incorporate the children of the affluent into the free schools, which in their early years had suffered from their association with pauperism and charity. Both the mental hospitals and the public schools illustrate an attempt to broaden the social composition of public institutions.

The early history of hospitals formed an instructive, if partial, exception to the shift away from corporate voluntarism. The great early hospitals in Philadelphia, New York, and Boston, to name three, remained under the control of private, nonprofit corporations. When public representatives wanted hospitals to expand their size, role, or scope, they could not bring them under State control. Rather, they sometimes had to establish parallel institutions. In Boston in the 1860s the Board and staff of the Massachusetts General Hospital fought against the creation of Boston City Hospital, which they explicitly viewed as an institution more "democratic" and more accessible to public influence in such important ways as admission procedures and internal routines like visiting hours. The social group that wanted Boston City was not the very poor served by Massachusetts General but the skilled workers, petty proprietors, and clerks who were less welcome at the older hospital yet unable to afford easily the cost of medical care at home. The reason that hospitals remained under private control probably rests in their relation to the medical profession. Often, physicians instigated the founding of hospitals and played the principal roles not only in a strictly professional capacity but also in institutional design and administration. Hospitals differed from other major social institutions in that a prestigious, prosperous, and generally cohesive corps of professionals preceded their establishment. By contrast, mental hospitals and schools, to take two examples, created two new professions. The founding of mental hospitals and school systems, therefore, much more than that of general hospitals, depended upon lay support, and they consequently remained much more susceptible to public influence during their early years.

Although private hospitals did not go public, they still reflected one process that characterized other institutions; the shift in the social origins of their clientele. For years hospital supporters had tried to broaden the social composition of the patient population, but, as in the case of early public education, the aura of charity clung to hospitals. In sharp contrast to public schools, however, hospitals were unable to shed that aura until a series of demographic changes and medical advances coalesced during the late nineteenth and early twentieth centuries. The transition from home to hospital care by the affluent was symbolized dramatically by the construction of the expensive and luxurious Phillips House as a branch of the Massachusetts General in 1917.

The supersession of corporate voluntarism reflected the increasingly sharp distinction between public and private, which formed part of a larger theme in social development: the drawing of sharp boundaries between the elements of social organization; the separation of family and community; the division of community into discrete and specialized functions.

The connection that exists between the emergence of modern society and the expansive specialization of both public and private institutions remains open to interpretation. How are we to account, in this case, for the origins of public institutions? What, precisely, did they signify?

Historians currently offer two principal, competing interpretations, which, put crudely, can be called the fear of social disorder versus the humanitarian impulse. The most notable exponent of the former is David Rothman, of the latter, Gerald Grob. Here I must risk some violence to their complex and subtle work in order to highlight the central point in contention and the problems left unresolved. Although Grob has attacked Rothman, the two share much common ground, as Rothman points out in a review of Grob's most recent book. Both tell a similar story and even stress many of the same factors, but they differ in the interpretation they give to events and, ultimately, in the meaning they assign to American history in the formative years between the Revolution and the Civil War.

Rothman argues that the fear of disorder arising from the breakdown of traditional communal controls spurred the discovery of the asylum. He writes, "The response in the Jacksonian period to the deviant and the dependent was first and foremost a vigorous attempt to promote the stability of the society at a moment when traditional ideas and practices appeared outmoded, constricted, and ineffective ... all represented an effort to insure the cohesion of the community in new and changing circumstances." Elsewhere he asserts, "under the influence of demographic, economic and intellectual developments, they [Americans] perceived that the traditional mechanisms of social control were obsolete."

Grob emphasizes the individualist philosophy and humanitarian impulses that arose from the Second Awakening. Although he cannot deny the pervasive fear of social disorder or the manifest influence of class in the social origins of reformers, he argues:

> Since the absence of broad theoretical models relating to public policy made it difficult to gather or to use empirical data in a meaningful way, policy often reflected external factors such as unconscious class interests or similar social assumptions that were never questioned. This is not to imply that mid–nineteenth century legislators and administrators were deficient in intelligence or malevolent in character. It is only to say that lack of theory and methodology often led to the adoption of policies that in the long run had results which were quite at variance with the intentions of those involved in their formulation.

Grob's arresting and partly true statement rests on the assumption that knowledge—hard data—scientific in character and free from bias does in fact exist and awaits discovery by students of deviance and dependence. It assumes further that the acquisition of scientific knowledge automatically leads to rational, humanitarian solutions framed in the best interests of the people to which they were directed. The history of social and behavioral science should make us skeptical.

Five problems, which appear in varying degrees in different accounts, underlie most formulations of both the social disorder and humanitarian interpretations, the very problems that appear in most attempts to explain early nineteenth-century social reforms and institutional creation.

First, most interpretations do not provide a link between institutions created for deviants and the other institutional developments of the time. An adequate interpretation must encompass not only the asylum, not only prisons, mental hospitals, and poorhouses, but also public schools, academies, the YMCA, and, ultimately, the family. Striking parallels exist between the timing, theory, and shape of those developments which affect deviants, dependents, children, adolescents, and families. An understanding of any of them depends upon an exploration of their interconnection.

Second, definitions of disorder usually remain loose. Scholars invoke industrialization and urbanization, but these broad concepts mask as much as they reveal. What was it, exactly, about the development of cities that created social disorder? What type of mechanisms broke down, when, and why? The arrival of hundreds of thousands of impoverished immigrants might explain a heightened concern with poverty or account for some of the nervousness on the part of genteel natives, but it assists little in an attempt to comprehend the origins of academies or even the special attention paid to the mentally ill.

Third, the way in which historical context intersects with the perception of people differentially situated in the social order usually remains unclear. The exact relation between the periodization of socio-economic and institutional development rarely is made explicit, and the identity of institutional sponsors and opponents—and opposition did exist—remains unclear in most accounts. We are left with David Rothman's "Americans," surely a category within which significant differences of opinion existed. But which Americans wanted the asylum? How did their perceptions influence public policy?

There are, however, few, if any, historical subjects more treacherous that human motivation—thus, the fourth problem with existing interpretations. They simplistically use models of individual behavior. They confuse, that is, the analysis of individual motivation with the analysis of class. Class analysis does not deny that individuals believe they do good works. It regards individual sincerity as irrelevant. Class analysis concerns the actions of groups and the relation between activity and class position. It does not deny the role of religion or tradition in the formulation and expression of class action. The theory of class is neither crudely reductionist nor contradicted by the existence of deeply felt humanitarian conviction. To argue that institutional promoters believed they were acting in the best interests of the poor, the criminal, the mentally ill, or the ignorant, and to leave the argument there, is not to refute a class analysis but merely to finesse it.

   The reluctance to probe the interconnections between social context, social position, ideology, and policy underlies the fifth problem. Most accounts of institutional development and social reform uncritically accept the interpretation of problems offered by institutional promoters and social reformers. They fail to question the description of crime, poverty, mental illness, or illiteracy offered in official sources. Thus, Grob simply accepts the proposition that immigrants were more prone than others to insanity and does not probe the social characteristics shaping definitions of mental illness. Other historians similarly accept the proposition that crime increased disproportionately in early nineteenth-century cities, that industrialization eroded the stability of the lower-class family, or that, as Oscar Handlin has written, the Irish were degraded.

   The acceptance of official descriptions of reality ignores important considerations. First, deviance is at least partly a social or political category and cannot be defined as a universal. It is the product of prevailing laws, customs, and views. Second, institutional promoters sometimes gauged popular sentiments inaccurately. The poor occasionally used new institutions in ways that violated the purposes and perceptions of their sponsors. For example, parents themselves provided the largest source of commitments to reform schools. The workingclass family, however, was not breaking down. Rather, poor parents turned to reform schools, which had not yet acquired their present stigma, precisely as other and more affluent parents turned to academies as places that would remove their refractory children from trouble and educate them at the same time. Other poor parents used reform schools in difficult periods as places in which children could stay safely during episodes of family crisis. The people at whom institutions were directed were not inert or passive. The image of degradation and helplessness that emerges from institutional promoters must be treated, always, with skepticism. Indeed, wherever historians have looked with care—and the recent historiography of slavery has been especially rich in this regard—severe disjunctions emerge between official perception of client populations and their actual behavior.

   Thus, a new interpretation of the origin of the institutional State should be set within a revised framework for North American social development between the late eighteenth and the middle nineteenth century. In particular, it should rest on a substitution of a three-stage for the more familiar two-stage paradigm that underlies much of North American history. The focus of the revised framework should be the spread of wage-labor and the values associated with capitalism rather than urbanization and industrialization.

   Most North American history rests on a simple two-stage paradigm— a shift from a preindustrial to an industrial society or from rural to urban life—which obscures the relationship between institutions and social change. For, though the transformation of economic structures and the creation of institutions did take place at roughly the same period, attempts to construct causal models or to develop tight and coherent explanations usually appear mechanistic or vague.

When a three-stage paradigm replaces the two-stage one, the connection between social change and institutional creation becomes tighter. In the three-stage paradigm North America shifted from a peculiar variety of a mercantile-peasant economy to an economy dominated by commercial capital to industrial capitalism. Though the pace of change varied from region to region and stages overlapped each other, the most important aspect of the late eighteenth and early nineteenth centuries was not industrialization or urbanization but, rather, the spread of capitalism defined, in Maurice Dobb's words, as "not simply a system of production for the market...but a system under which labour-power had itself become a commodity and was bought and sold on the market like any other object of exchange." Capitalism was the necessary, though conceptually distinct, antecedent of industrialization.

Consider the following as reflections of the spread of capitalist relations prior to industrialization. Between 1796 and 1855, prior to industrialization, the most striking change in New York City's occupational structure, according to Carl Kaestle's figures, was the increase in the proportion of men who listed themselves simply as laborers—an increase from 5.5% to 27.4%. Moreover, apprenticeship, whose emphasis on bound labor is incompatible with capitalism, had ceased to function with anything like its traditional character well before industrialization. In both Buffalo, New York, and Hamilton, Ontario, prior to their industrialization, there were about eleven skilled wage workers and several semiskilled and unskilled ones for every independent master or manufacturer. From a different point of view one historian recently has pointed to an unmistakable increase in the wandering of the poor from place to place in late eighteenth-century Massachusetts. The expansion of commerce in this period has been documented extensively, and it was in this era that state governments exchanged their essentially mercantilist policies for a reliance upon competition and private initiative to regulate the economy.

The problem, thus, becomes one of formulating the connection between the development of capitalism and the spread of institutions. The drive towards institutional development preceded the industrial take-off in the Northeast. Any interpretation based upon industrialization must fall simply upon considerations of time. A much better temporal connection exists between institutional origins and the spread of capitalist relations of production.

The most profound statement of the relation between capitalism and the institutional State occurs in the remarkable book by the late Harry Braverman, *Labor and Monopoly Capital*. It is worth considering in detail:

> The ebbing of family facilities, and of family, community, and neighborly feelings upon which the performance of many social functions formerly depended, leaves a void. As the family members, more of them now at work away

from home, become less and less able to care for each other in time of need, and as the ties of neighborhood, community and friendship are reinterpreted on a narrower scale to exclude onerous responsibilities, the care of humans for each other becomes increasingly institutionalized. At the same time, the human detritus of the urban civilization increases, not just because of the aged population, its life prolonged by the progress of medicine, grows ever larger; those who need care include children—not only those who cannot "function" smoothly but even the "normal" ones whose only defect is their tender age. Whole new strata of the helpless and dependent are created, or familiar old ones enlarged enormously: the proportion of "mentally ill" or "deficient," the "criminals," the pauperized layers at the bottom of society, all representing varieties of crumbling under the pressures of capitalist urbanism and the conditions of capitalist employment or unemployment. In addition, the pressures of urban life grow more intense and it becomes harder to care for any who need care in the conditions of the jungle of the cities. Since no care is forthcoming from an atomized community, and since the family cannot bear all such encumbrances if it is to strive for action in order to survive and "succeed" in the market society, the care of all these layers becomes institutionalized, often in the most barbarous and oppressive forms. Thus understood, the massive growth of institutions stretching all the way from schools and hospitals on the one side to prisons and madhouses on the other represents not just the progress of medicine, education, or crime prevention, but the clearing of the marketplace of all but the "economically active" and "functioning" members of society. . . .

Note that Braverman isolates three processes that link capitalism and insitutions: (1) the absolute growth of a dependent population through underemployment, accidents, and other means; (2) the end of traditional ways of caring for dependents; (3) the creation of new types of dependents— not just the sick, poor, or criminal, but all who are economically unproductive and, as a consequence, put out of the way and out of sight. In fact, all three processes can be shown clearly at work in late eighteenth- and early nineteenth-century North America. Take some examples:

First, the rise in transiency. By the early nineteenth century a highly mobile class of wage-laborers, cut off from close ties with any communities, drifted about and between cities. Living for the most part in nuclear families, with no personal or communal resources for the periods of recurrent poverty or frequent disaster that disfigured their lives, they swelled the dependent class.

The recognition that transiency had become a widespread way of life impelled the reform of the poor laws called for by the Quincy and Yates reports in Massachusetts and New York during the second decade of the nineteenth century. Previously, counties had retained legal responsibility for their own poor almost wherever they wandered. Poor strangers were warned out of town or shipped back to the communities from which they came. But after a point who could claim that any particular community could be considered home for the poor who wandered through it? The upsurge in population movement made obsolete the concept of a community of origin, and the very size of the problem meant that the customary practice would produce an endless stream of poor people shipped back and forth between counties. The sensible solution appeared to be to end the traditional practice and to require each county to support the poor within its boundaries, whatever their place of origin, in a new network of poorhouses strung out across the state.

The problem of the poor illustrates both the growth of dependency and breakdown of traditional ways of coping with poverty. Other developments underscore another process—the creation of new categories of dependency. One of these categories was youth. In earlier times the life-cycle of young people had followed a clear and well-defined sequence. At no point in their lives were they uncertain how they should spend their time or in what setting they should live. But the erosion of apprenticeship and, contrary to popular belief, the lack of wage-work for young men in the early phase of capitalist development, occurred before the creation of any set of institutions to contain or instruct them. In consequence, young people in the nineteenth-century city faced a crisis that cut across class lines. In the 1820s, for instance, a group of Boston merchants gathered at the home of William Ellery Channing to discuss their anxieties about their sons, no longer needed in the counting-house or on shipboard at the age of fourteen. The result of that meeting was Boston English High School. In Hamilton, Ontario, the rapid creation of a public school system with special provisions for adolescent students followed the period in which the crisis of idle youth became almost acute. Similarly, the disruption of traditional career patterns and living arrangements for young men in New York City provoked worried merchants to create new institutions to guide their behavior and refine their manners.

The nineteenth century's institutionalized population represented the casualties of a new social order: landless workers exposed without buffers to poverty and job-related accidents; men broken by the strain of achievement in a competitive, insecure work; women driven to desperation by the enforced repression inherent in contemporary ideals of domesticity; or even children—casualties on account of their age. But how did institutions assume the shape they did? Why did the response to problems take the form not simply of institutions but of ones specialized in organization and reformist in intent?

Peter Dobkin Hall offers an answer applicable to the early, voluntarist stage of institutional development. After the Revolution, he argues, merchants sought to expand the scope of their activities. To do so, they had to increase specialization, pool risks, create joint-stock corporations, and accumulate capital outside of family firms:

> The disengagement of capital from family firms was achieved through two fundamental innovations in the means of wealth transmission: the testamentary trust and the charitable endowment. Under testamentary trusts it became possible for testators to entirely avoid the partible division of their estates....

The charitable endowment was also a kind of trust. Through it moneys could be left in perpetuity to trustees or to a corporate body for the accomplishment of a variety of social welfare purposes—most of which had, in Massachusetts, been traditionally carried out through families. Once the merchants began to search for means of disengaging capital from familial concerns, they quickly recognized the usefulness of charitable endowments both for the accumulation of capital and for relieving their families from the burdens of welfare activity.

The specialization in mercantile life between institutions for credit, insurance, wholesaling, retailing, warehousing, and other activities reflected the division of labor that characterizes capitalist development. That division, as Marx observed, takes opposite forms in social life and in industry. Within manufacuring the division of labor results from the combination of previously distinct operations into one process. By contrast, the social division of labor requires the decomposition of tasks—all originally performed by the family—into separate organizations. "In one case," wrote Marx, "it is the making dependent what was before independent; in the other case the making independent what was before dependent." Equally, with cotton mills, foundries, or shoe factories, new social institutions—schools, penitentiaries, mental hospitals, reformatories—exemplified in their own way the division of labor as the dynamic organizational principle of their age.

The spread of what Christopher Lasch called the "single standard of honor" accompanied the early history of capitalism in North America. By that standard the unproductive became more than a nuisance; they became unworthy. In an attempt to raise their usefulness, the unproductive were swept into massive brick structures that looked distressingly like factories and there taught those lessons in social and economic behavior which, it was hoped, would facilitate their reentry into real workplaces. The depressing sameness about the look of schools, prisons, mental hospitals, and factories belied the sentimentality of the age. The romantic proclamation of the child's innocence, purity, and potential masked the disdain and exasperation that designed urban schools or reformatories. As in the case of children, a transmutation of disdain into purity justified the confinement of women in the institution called home. Indeed, the unwillingness to acknowledge confinement as nasty proved a remarkable feature of early nineteenth-century institutional promotion. But promoters protested too much: their love for, or at least neutrality towards, those they would incarcerate sounds hollow when echoing through the halls of a nineteenth-century mental hospital, prison, or school. We do no better today, though our particular specialty is perhaps the aged. We construct ghettos for the aged, ostensibly because they want them. In fact, we want to have them out of the way. The single standard of honor remains our legacy and our trademark.

Early capitalist development was experienced by the immediate heirs of the Enlightenment and the Revolution—by people swept simultaneously by optimistic theories of human nature and evangelical religion. Their intellectual and religious heritage composed complex lenses through which people filtered their perceptions of social and economic change. The refraction undoubtedly contributed to their interpretation of crime, poverty, mental illness, ignorance, and youth as conditions of character. Imbued with a belief in progress and committed to either a secular or spiritual millenium, institutional promoters approached their work optimistically, defining their task as the shaping of souls. Nonetheless, characters were to be shaped to a standard with clear components: sensual restraint, dependability, willingness to work, acquiescence in the legitimacy of the social order, and acceptance of one's place within it—all serviceable traits in early capitalist America.

One example sums up the problem of character, its relation to social institutions, to cultural definitions of deviance, and to the personal strain exacted by early capitalism: the trouble with the first patient admitted to the New York State Lunatic Asylum when it opened on January 14, 1843. He thought he was Tom Paine.

Among the Poor of Chicago

Joseph Kirkland

Chicago's plague-spots are rather red than black; blotches marking excess rather than insufficiency. Vice and crime are more characteristic of a new, young, busy, careless, properous city than is any compulsory, inevitable misery. An English philanthropist who visited Hull House (Rev. Mr. Barnett, Warden of Toynbee Hall) remarked, in taking his leave, that the prevalent dirt and flagrant vice in Chicago exceeded anything in London; but that he had seen scarce any evidence of actual want.

The West is the paradise of the poor. "And the purgatory of the rest of us," adds some fine lady who agonizes over the servant problem. Well, even if this were true (which it is not), it would be better than the reverse. The paradise of the rich, based on the purgatory of the poor, has endured long enough in the older lands.

"How the other half lives," in Chicago, is "pretty much as it chooses." Americans born, and the better natures among the foreign (supposing them to have physical strength), can select their own kind of happiness. If they choose the joy which springs sobriety, they can have it in plenty. If they prefer the delight of drink, that also is abundant. A solid devotion to work and saving gives a house and lot, a comfortable and well-taught family, and a good chance for children and grandchildren, who will take rank among the best, employing laborers of their own, and perhaps, alas! looking back with mortification on their laboring ancestors. An equally solid devotion to drink gives vice, crime, want, and (what we should call) misery; but this is a free country. The latter class, like the former, are exercising their inalienable right of self-government. They absolutely do not want our cleanliness, our savings-accounts, our good clothes, books, schools, churches, society, progress, and all that, unless they can have them without paying the price—temperance; and they cannot so have them. Half of the "other half" belong strictly to the first-named class, a tenth to the last-named, and the rest pursue a middle course. Some rise from the middle to the upper; the others live along, having ups and downs and furnishing the recruits to keep up the numbers of the lower, the "submerged tenth" which, happily, has not the faculty of maintaining itself by direct reproduction.

The city has no "East End," "Whitechapel," or "Mulberry Street" region; no locality given over to great hives of helplessness, since there is no quarter which was built up for fine residences or business blocks and afterward deserted and turned over to baser uses. The most ancient house

SOURCE: Joseph Kirkland, in *The Poor in Great Cities,* ed. Robert Woods (New York: Charles Scribner's Sons, 1895; repr. New York: Arno Press, 1971), pp. 195–235.

in town (but one) is not fifty years old, and the average scarcely twenty. Therefore "the tenement-house evil," as it is known in New York and London, shows almost no trace in the new, spacious mart on the edge of the Grand Prairie. Rooms are sublet to individuals and families, yet it is not in tall, huge rookeries built for the purpose, but in smaller, lower structures, outside the limits of the Great Fire, which destroyed the whole middle district—cleared it of weeds to make way for a sturdier and healthier growth. If ever the time comes when the sky-scraping structures of today are deserted by the uses for which they are now occupied because they are in the geographical and business centre of the city, then there may be in Chicago gigantic human hives of wretchedness such as exist in London and New York. But as Chicago can spread north, south, and west, it is difficult to imagine a state of things when the present business district shall not be what it is.

The "lay of the land" is against local congestion. The river, with its main stem running east and west and its sprawling branches running north and south, trisects the whole plain into North Side, South Side, and West Side. These in turn are dissected into smaller patches by the railways, which come to the very centre of population, and radiate thence in all directions except due east, where the lake maintains a glorious ventilation, moral and material.

There is no "Sailors' Quarter," no place where Jack ashore hastens to spend in a week the savings of a year; gets drunk as soon as possible, and stays drunk as long as possible, to balance his weeks or months of enforced abstinence. The sailors here have only a week or less afloat at one stretch, and they spend, every winter, several months on shore, when they go mining or lumbering or pursuing whatever calling suits their fancy. Many of them are family men—good, sturdy fellows, not distinguishable from the average of intelligent tradesmen.

For depth of shadow in Chicago low life one must look to the foreign elements,[*] the persons who are not only of alien birth but of unrelated blood—the Mongolian, the African, the Sclav, the semitropic Latin. Among them may be found a certain degree of isolation, and therefore of clannish crowding; also of contented squalor, jealous of inspection and interference. It is in the quarters inhabited by these that there are to be found the worst parts of Chicago, the most unsavory spots in their moral and material aspects.

---

[*]Of Chinamen there are about two thousand in Chicago, living, as a general rule, in one quarter of the city—South Clark Street, adjoining the line occupied by the Lake Shore and eastern Illinois Railways, running eastward and southward, and the Rock Island, running westward. Of Italians Chicago has many thousands, part of whom live in the South Clark Street neighborhood, and a larger number only a few squares away, on the West Side, across the south branch of the river. Besides the light common labor of street-cleaning, scavengering, etc., they control, practically, all the great fruit-business of the city, and

Twelfth Street is encumbered by a long viaduct, reaching from Wabash Avenue, westward, across the south branch of the river, ending on the west side very near the starting-point of the Great Fire of 1871. The viaduct nearly fills the street, and from it one looks into the second stories of the taller houses, and over the roofs of the shorter. One has there the advantages for observation possessed by the fabled "devil on two sticks." This is the habitation of the Italian proletariat.

To get to the main floors of these squalid habitations one must climb down many steps; hence the name of the locality, "The Dive." I once saw men carrying into one of the darkened entrances here an immense bunch of green bananas, which hung down between them like the "grapes of Eshcol" in the old primer. One can only fancy the atmosphere in which this wonderful fruit would hang to ripen, and hope that the ripening process is one of exhalation, not of inhalation, during the week or more which must elapse before it appears, yellow and mellow, to be sold from the wayside fruit-stand, or be dragged slowly about the streets in the wagons attended by the dark-skinned pedlers as they troll forth, in the sonorous Italian tones, "Banano-o! Fi, Ri, Banano-o-o-o!"

A bad state of things exists under the shadow of this viaduct, and under the inclined planes by which the traffic of each street it crosses is raised to its level. This is easy to believe, but it is hard to imagine just how filthy, how squalid, how noisome, how abhorrent it all is. Walking along between inhabited houses and the brick abutments of the raised way is like walking between the walls of a sewer—like it to every sense—sight, smell, hearing, and feeling.

The adjacent buildings are mostly of wood—small, low, rotten, and crowded. In no case have I found one family occupying more than two rooms—often only one. Here and there would be seen an attempt at cleanliness of floor and bedclothing, but nowhere even a pretence of sweeping of halls and stairways, or of shovelling out of gutters and other foul conduits.

---

some of them are getting rich at it. Yet all homes of the majority are among the most lowly and squalid in the city. Educated Italians of the upper classes are handsomely housed in some of the fashionable streets. The Poles and Bohemians inhabit a southwestern quarter, where their impossible names occupy the sign-boards and their unbeautiful faces strike the eye and haunt the memory. They are hard workers and not extravagant, and though crowded they are not congested, though poor they are not in want. The colored people have done and are doing remarkably well, considering the disadvantages and discouragements under which they live. They are not largely the supporters of the grog-shops. Their besetting sin is gambling. They are industrious rather than hard-working, docile rather than enterprising, and economical rather than acquisitive. There are impediments to any accumulation such as their white neighbors engage in. For instance, suppose one of them chooses to invest his savings in a "Building Society," he would find, when his lot was ready for him, that he would be unwelcome to his neighbors of a lighter skin. Even as a renter he is only acceptable in regions devoted to his race. As one of them said to me: "Nobody thinks a colored man fit for anything above being a porter." Still, as I said, there is a very perceptible advance in the race; and it shows but little of poverty or dependence, and still less of crime.

What squalor, filth, crowding! The constant feeling of the visitor is, "how dreadfully wretched these people—ought to be."

Ought to be, but are not. They are chiefly the lower class of Italians, born and bred, probably, to the knowledge of actual hunger, which here they must rarely feel. I went among them recently; there were scarcely any men visible; the swarms were chiefly of women and children. The men were away, largely, no doubt, attending to the fruit business and scavenger work which have been mentioned. The women were universally caring for their innumerable children, and these latter, especially the boys, played, shouted, careened about the halls and stairways, yards and roofs, in uncontrolled freedom and gayety. Two or three of them had found a great turnip, or some such vegetable, and split it in pieces, which they displayed in a row on a board beside a gutter; no pretence of having any customers— it was merely the exhibition of an inherited instinct for keeping an Italian fruit-stand!

In the corner of a squalid hallway, just outside of the maternal door (there not being an inch of spare room within), a bright-eyed little girl had arranged a quite respectable imitation of a floor-bed (both coverlet and stuffing being rags), and on it lay a dirty, dilapidated, flaxen-haired doll. The girl's instinct, too, was showing itself. Within the room the mother, with head bound up, as is the universal custom of her kind, was attending to some duties; a child of two or three years sat staring at the intruder, and on the floor stood a wash-tub over which was bending (and really working) a mite of a girl not more than six years old. Her little arms could scarcely reach the grimy liquid in the bottom of the tub, but she did the best she could, and up and down the tin wash-board sounded her tiny knuckles, handling some dingy, dripping stuff or other, she scarcely pausing to look up and notice who had opened the door.

Here were a few men, more women, and most children; but no young unmarried women. One wonders where are the grown girls. They are not in service in private families; such a thing is unknown here; and they are not adapted to the business of shop-girls. It is to be hoped that they are engaged in the innumerable handicrafts that prevail; paper-box and paper-bag makers, tobacco-handlers, book-folders and stitchers, etc. The Hull-House ladies say that they marry early in their teens, and that many of them do bits of plain sewing—the mere finishing of trouser-legs, etc.—at wonderfully low rates, and wonderfully large quantities, often in the so-called "sweat-shops" of the tailoring trade. The clothing of all has been (apparently) bought at Chicago second-hand clothing stores; or, if imported from Italy, has a common and familiar aspect, which anew illustrates the levelling and averaging hand of modern commerce and intercourse, whence it comes that all man-kind is growing to look alike—each individual to be a "composite photograph" of all the rest.

Every person, of whatever sex or age, is clothed sufficiently for decency and for warmth; and seems to be provided with all food necessary to sustain life, though perhaps not the rudest health.

Emerging on a second-story balcony at the back on one of these Italian houses one comes upon a long vista of house rears and tumble-down backsheds, squalid beyond conception. Neighboring windows are filled with faces peering out with interest and amusement at the stranger. Here and there are bits of rope stretched from one nail to another—from house to shed, from fence to banister, from window-sill to door-post—carrying forlorn arrays of washed clothing. Each is the effort of some lowly woman to preserve a little cleanliness in the garments of herself and her household. At least a forlorn hope is keeping up the battle against vileness.

On a hot summer night every roof and every balcony in sight is covered with sleeping men, women, and children, each with only a single blanket or coverlet for all purposes of protection and decency. All winter the cook-stove of each family supplies warmth to the little household. (The cheapest coal is always to be had at $3 a ton or less.)

"The Bad Lands" is a quarter more repellent because more pretentious than "The Dive," but, being the abode of vice and crime rather than of poverty, it can be properly omitted here. Women of the town are not molested so long as they stay within doors, except on occasion of the frequent rows, fights, robberies, and murders. The men about are, if possible, more repulsive than the women. Some have showy clothes, more are "bums," wrecks of humanity; slouching, dirty, sneaking, hangdog tramps. They do not want work, could not get it if they wanted it, and could not do it if they got it. All they want is a dime a day. With that they can get a great big "schooner" of beer and a chance at the free-lunch counter. They sleep on the floor till the place closes up and then crawl into some doorway or hallway, or go to the police station for a bunk.

One recognizes Chinatown by the curious signs over the shops. The Chinese are industrious and economical and peaceable—never molest anybody who lets them alone. Opium they take just as our people take whiskey, and it does not seem to hurt them any more. But when the police find them taking in whites as well as Chinamen, they "run them in." It is death, and worse than death, to the others, especially to women. In a typical Chinese shop all is scrupulously neat and clean. It seems as if, by some magic, the smoky, dusty atmosphere of Chicago had been excluded from this unique interior, which looks like the inside of a bric-à-brac cabinet, with bright colors, tinsel, and shining metals. On the walls are colored photographs, showing the proprietors beautifully dressed in dove-colored garments. In a kind of shrine stands a "Joss table" or altar, with what is probably a Confucian text hanging over it, and lying on it some opuim pipes. In a room behind the shop a "fan-tan" game is going on upon a straw-matted table, around which gather interested Celestials three deep. In the shop is a freshly opened importation, barrels and boxes of Chinese delicacies, pickled fish of various kinds, with the pungent odor which belongs to that kind of food the world round and the seas over. The men are clothed in heavy, warm cloth, cut in Chinese fashion—great, broad cloaks, loose trousers, felt-soled shoes, etc.—but in American felt hats.

At 406 Clark Street, in the very midst of all that is alien to our better nature, rises the Clark Street Mission.* Here are daily gathered, in a free kindergarten, some scores of the little unfortunates whom a cruel fate has planted in this cesspool. It is a touching sight; they are so innocent as yet, mere buds springing up in the track of a lava-stream. There is a creche here as well as kindergarten, and tiny creatures, well fed and cared for, swing in hammocks, or sit, stand, walk, or creep all about in charge of kind, devoted young women. Curiously enough, many of the little ones are born of Arabian mothers. There are some hundreds of Arabs housed near by. The attendant thinks they are Christian converts, in charge of church folk who were formerly missionaries in Arabia. The women are occupied in peddling small wares and trinkets, which they carry about in packs and baskets.** In the same hall are evening and Sunday religious meetings; and not long ago there was a series of midnight prayer-meetings held here, with how much success I do not know.

The whole enterprise is in charge (and at the charge) of the great Woman's Christian Temperance Union. This is an institution of wonderful strength and beauty; a giantess, throned in intelligence and honor; stretching her strong hands toward the weak, sinking thousands of the "submerged tenth," and all who are on the edge of the submergence. The W.C.T.U. numbers more that 200,000 members in all, of whom 16,000 are in Illinois, and their activity is tireless, their ability wonderful. It is one of the phenomena marking the elevation of the sex under the sunshine of Western freedom and prosperity. The building, planned, erected, and paid for by this body, is the most perfect and (as it should be) the most sightly of all Chicago's new "sky-scrapers." It is named "Temperance Temple;" its cost was $1,100,000. Its spare room is fully occupied, and it will earn rentals amounting to $200,000 a year.

The Pacific Garden Mission has a large hall, opening directly on Van Buren Street, within five hundred feet of the Grand Pacific Hotel, yet within a scarcely greater distance of some of the worst of the "bad districts" of the city. "The Dive" is only half a mile south of it, and "The Levee," "The Bad Lands," "Chinatown," etc. are still nearer. The single big room is vast and dingy—the latter characteristic inseparable from every apartment in Chicago which is not the object of constant, laborious cleaning and renovation. The walls are covered with Scripture texts in large letters, "Blessed are ye poor, for yours is the kingdom of God," etc. "Welcome," "God is love," and other cheering mottoes are embossed in Christmas greens over the platform. A little collection of hymns is upon each seat, and notices of the hours of services are suspended in various places, among the rest some announcing the Salvation Army meetings. No effort at ornament for

---

*The mission is now on Wabash Avenue, between Fourteenth and Fifteenth Streets.

**A year ago I met a party of Arabians on the San Juan River, in Nicaragua, and they too were peddling trinkets carried in packs and baskets.

ornament's sake appears anywhere; nor any outward gayety to suggest inward joy and peace. Colonel Clark* is the moving and controlling spirit of the Mission, as well as its chief money supporter. The meetings on Sunday are often full to the doors; a few front seats being filled by the "workers" and particular friends, and the rest by the chance-comers, gathered from adjacent slums to hear the music and look on at the devotional exercises. It is one of the simply religious efforts to elevate the debased and reform the bad, by offering to them "Christ and him crucified;" by the direct interposition of heaven it must succeed, but without such miracle it cannot. The "news of salvation" no longer surprises and charms the world, for the world has ceased to fear the opposite. One is reminded of the plaint made two hundred years ago by the French missionaries sent to the savages of this very region (their skin was red in those days) when they said, in effect: "Surely we are in nowise to be compared with the Holy Apostles; yet the world must have changed since they went forth among the heathen who heard them gladly, and rejoicing to receive the glorious news of salvation, flocked forward, one and all demanding baptism. Here we sail the floods and scale the mountains in pursuit of one poor savage, if haply we may prevail to save him from the wrath to come, and in most cases his salvation is changed to backsliding as soon as our backs are turned." To the same general effect is the conclusion reached by the religious workers of today, who say "these beings are in nowise fit subjects for a merely religious ministry."

I once told a young musician (a Scandinavian) at the Pacific Garden Mission that I was then in search of the very poor and miserable, the helplessly wretched, and asked him where they were to be found. He asked where I had been, and on telling him that I came fresh from "The Dive," "The Bad Lands," "Biler Avenue," "Niggertown," "Chinatown," etc., he asked if these were not poor enough. I said they were rather vicious, drunken, and depraved than poor; that I wanted to find the poverty that springs from misfortune rather than that from drink. To this he impulsively gave the pregnant answer: "There is none. You might find one or two others in five hundred, but it is drink in the case of all the rest."

And so it goes. Such is the evidence of the experts, the philanthropists, the missionaries, and the senses themselves. There are sixty saloons in two blocks of this dreadful Dismal Swamp. Each saloon pays $500 a year of city license alone; pays its United States Government license for selling spirits, beer, and tobacco; pays for all its stock in trade, its rent, its wages, and expenses—thrives like a Canada thistle on the barren soil of its environment. Five hundred dollars for license, $500 for rent, $1,000 for wages and expenses, and $1,500 for stock in trade makes $3,500. The sums paid by these "poor" must reach $4,000 a year, on the average, to

---

*Since Colonel Clark's death the work has been ably carried on by Mrs. Clark.

each saloon; and sixty saloons gives $240,000 a year, all in one street, within a distance of two squares. Verily the savings of the rich are as nothing compared with the wastings of the poor. Beer is the alleviation and perpetuation of poverty.

I also asked the young musician about the condition of his fellow-Scandinavians, where their poor could best be studied. He replied that there were none. Individual helplessness was cared for by individual charities and the churches. That is what might be expected. The Scandinavian immigration has been, on the whole, the finest addition to the northwest. They are largely agriculturists, are temperate, industrious, strong, frugal, and hardy. Not seldom do great colonies of them go on cheap excursions back to visit the Fatherland. They pass through Chicago—men, women, and children—with bands playing and flags flying; they cross the sea and spend some time at the old home, spreading the news of Western freedom and plenty, and then return with many recruits and with fresh relish for the Greater Scandinavia they are building among us. Those who do remain in the cities are helpers worth having. The girls make the best house-servants—strong, intelligent, respectful, and self-respecting; and the men, though not blameless in the matter of drink, yet are not among the willing slaves to it. On the whole, they see the alternative presented to them— the two kinds of happiness already spoken of—and make what seems to us the wisest choice between them. The servants, as cooks and "second girls," earn from three to five or six dollars a week besides their board and lodging, and the demand for such as have anything like a fair knowledge of their business is always ahead of the supply. They dress well, save money, and spend immense sums in helping their friends here and in the Fatherland.

In the "North Division," near the great gas-works, exists a large colony which of old earned the name of "Little Hell," and which presents features of deep shadow with gleams of growing light—a dark cloud with a silver lining. Many of the men are gas-work laborers, doing hard duty, earning large wages, and drinking deep draughts. They are of three races—Irish, German, and Scandinavian—the first-named the most able and the most turbulent. The wages earned since the works were started, if they had been wisely used, would have bought the entire plant; would have vested every dollar of the vast and profitable stock in the workers. The latter would now be the capitalists. But that is a mere truism. The wage-earners of the whole country would be the capitalists if it were not that they have preferred to take their joy drop by drop.

The bright lining of the dark cloud hovering about the gas-works is the Unity Church Industrial School and Boys' Club near by, and the Saint James's Church and Central Church Missions, not far away. The former (which I happen to know most about) was started in 1876 by the women of Robert Collyer's church, in an effort to do something for the poorest and most neglected children, the difficulty being that this class was soon supplanted by a better class, less in need of help—"people more anxious for what they could get than what they could learn." The others, children of the drunken and vicious, were always hardest to reach and to keep hold of.

From this grain of mustard-seed has grown a great tree. The excellent and benevolent Eli Bates bequeathed to the enterprise $20,000, which was used for the construction of a brick building having all the appliances for an industrial school, and there the worthy Unity Church people spend time and money to good purpose. There are classes in various branches, and a large and well-kept creche.

A noticeable feature of this "lay mission" is the Boys' Club, where, for several months every year, meetings have been held on several evenings each week to give the youth of the neighborhood rational and wholesome fun with some incidental instruction. The boys range from eight to six-teen years old, and were at the start a "hard lot." Yet they always had some traits of good feeling. The young women teachers always found them easier to manage than did the men. And even when discipline had to be maintained by force, the majority was sure to be on the side of law and order. As far as possible, the boys are made to manage their own games and exercises, showing sometimes a good deal of ability. They number, on ordinary evenings, about sixty, the "picnic aggregate" reaching to a hun-dred and fifty. The older boys are workers during the daytime; the younger, attendants on public and parochial schools.

There is but little want among the families. Their houses are small and not crowded together; but the households occupy generally only two or three rooms each.

Whether influenced by the various missions near by, by the paving and improvement of streets, or by other causes, or partly by the one and partly by the others, the place is losing its old character, and even its ugly sobriquet is almost forgotten.

In Chicago the "fashion" and the larger part (though not by any means all) of the wealth of the city are on the "South Side" and "North Side," where also the deepest poverty and degradation are to be found. On the great "West Side" are the industrious and prosperous workers, with their tens of thousands of labor-bought homes. It may be a new idea to the denizens of older cities that laborers should, can, and do own their dwelling-places, both land and building. Far more than half the homes in Chicago are so owned and occupied. The chief part of real-estate speculation is the buying of suburban acres and sub-dividing and selling them in lots to thrifty workmen. Purchase for the sake of putting up houses to rent as dwellings (except in the case of flats) is now extremely rare. The chief agent in this homestead movement is to be found in the numerous "building societies," wherein the mechanic deposits his savings as they accrue, and then when he wishes to build his home he draws from the society whatever he may have laid up, and borrows from it what he may need in addition, paying a premium in addition to the usual interest. (This premium and interest inure to the benefit of the other depositors.) Membership in a building society, and the hope of a bit of ground all his own, are wonderful incentives to temperance in the man and economy in the wife. And when the lot is selected, how he clings to it! Beer and whiskey are forgotten. Even schooling and some other good and proper cares are apt to be postponed. A city of such homes is safe from anarchy. As for any wielder of torch and dynamite, as soon as he steps forth into the light of the humble private fireside, and the "lamp in the window," he is in peril of his life.

On the West Side are also, especially in winter, the unemployed; some of whom could not find work if they would, some would not if they could, and some, when they can and do work, make the omnipresent saloon their savings-bank; a bank which takes in good money but pays out only false tokens.

I accompanied one of the "Volunteer County Visitors" on her walk in search of the people who should be helped by charity, public or private. We walked through a half-mile of street lined with the crowded habitations of the poor. At the farther end of it are visible the moving trains of the Fort Wayne Railway, and above and beyond these the masts and funnels of shipping. Being just outside the old "burnt district," its houses are of wood, ancient, squalid, dilapidated. There is not more than about one saloon to every street corner, therefore this is far from an "infested" region. It is chiefly occupied by Italians, who are not, as yet, the sots and terrors of the social system, and do not seem likely ever to become so. Groups of them are idling about, well enough dressed, but low-browed, looking with apparent surliness on visitors come to spy out the nakedness of the land. Within the houses we find the families crowded into two small rooms each, or thereabouts; and in those two rooms are all operations of existence to be carried on in each case. Sleeping, eating, cooking, washing, ironing, sickness, child-bearing, nursing, living, dying, and burying—these considerations force themselves on the mind and suggest dismal pictures as one fancies a life so spent.

Yet as to mere room, warmth, shelter, dryness, and convenience, the inhabitants are better accommodated than is the campaigning soldier in his tent, having no furniture, clothing for night or day, or other appliances for comfort, except those he can carry with him from camp to camp in addition to his arms and accoutrements. But women and children are not soldiers. Camp miseries would kill them; one who has suffered such privation can scarcely feel the proper degree of pity for these creatures—warm, dry, fat, clothed, safe, at leisure and at liberty.

The poorest and most wretched household we found that day was that of an old soldier, a gray-haired man of education and (at some time) of intelligence, once a lieutenant in a volunteer regiment. He was wounded at the battle of Fair Oaks. There he lies, grimy and vermin-infested, in a filthy bed, with a young grandchild beside him in like condition, and a drunken virago of a woman, ramping and scolding in the two rooms which constitute the family abode. She is quite the most repulsive being yet met with. A little inquiry develops the fact that this man was in the Soldiers' Home at Milwaukee (and could return there to remain, if he wished), well fed, clothed, and cared for, and that he left there because: "You see you can't stand it to be kept down all the time, and moved back and forth, and here and there, whether you like it or not." And he moved his black paws back and forth, and here and there, on the dingy bedclothes, to indicate how the Home deprived him of his freedom—his "liberty" to pass his time in the living death which his present condition seems to the onlooker.

Chicago's "Hull House" is already widely known as the "Toynbee Hall" of the West, though the parallelism between the two institutions is far from absolute and complete. In the first place, Hull House was started and is carried on by women, with only the occasional and exceptional help— welcome though it is—of the other sex. Then, too, the system is as different as are the conditions in which the two institutions are placed. Its best service in stimulating the intellectual life of the neighborhood has been in the establishment of its college-extension classes, which have grown into what is practically an evening college, with thirty courses weekly and a membership of one hundred and fifty to two hundred students of a high order.

In a widely different sphere is its strictly philanthropic work. Yet, even here, Hull House is not a mission, since no especial religion is inculcated and no particular social reform is announced as the object of its being. If people in the humbler classes of its visitors learn there to live good, clean, temperate lives, it is through the demonstration of the enduring beauty and gayety of such a life as contrasted with the lurid and fleeting joys of the other. Hull House parlors, class-rooms, gymnasium, library, etc., are the rivals of the swarming grog-shops. Nobody, not even the ornaments of the college-extension classes, is more welcome than the poor fellow who has begun to feel that he can no longer struggle against poverty and drink, and nobody is less pointed at, preached at, or set upon than he. The choice is open to him, right hand or left hand as he sees fit, and it surely seems as if no sane human being could hesitate. At least the boy growing up with the choice before him, and the light shining on the parting of the ways, will take—is taking—the one those devoted young women are making so inviting to his footsteps.

It is not charity that Hull House offers, any more than it is precept. True, there are some cases which arise, outside the business of the House, where public or private beneficence is turned toward deserving helplessness. But that is not strictly Hull House work. The latter consists in bestowing friendship and sympathy, the sisterly heart, hand, and voice, on all who are willing to come within its sweet and pleasant influence.

With characteristic wisdom and good feeling the Board of the grand Chicago Public Library (free to all) has placed one of its sub-stations in the reading-room of Hull House; and in that large, handsome, well-lighted apartment applications for books are taken, and the books are delivered and returned, all quite without expense of any kind to the reader.

The building which contains the library and reading-room has been added to the Hull House structures by the liberality of Edward B. Butler. The same building contains a studio in which drawing-classes are held each evening, and an admirably fitted art-exhibit room in which some of the best pictures in Chicago are shown from time to time. The humanitarian side of the Hull House activity is maintained by the Nursery, the Kindergarten, the Diet Kitchen, the District Nursing, and the Industrial Classes. Its activities are multiform that they may meet the needs, not alone of the enterprising nor yet the poor, but of its neighborhood as a whole. That it has met such a need is shown by the fact that the weekly membership of its club and classes is nine hundred.

The Creche, or Day Nursery, is surely as bright, sunny, and pretty a room as any ever devoted to that angelic purpose. Two little, low tables, two dozen little, low chairs, each holding a pathetic little figure, dear to some mother's heart, and a young lady as busy (and sometimes as puzzled) as a pullet with a brood of ducklings—these are the *dramatis personae*. It is luncheon-time, and with much pains the babes have been brought to reasonable order, side by side, each restless pair of hands joined in a devotional attitude far from symbolic of the impatient being behind them. One small creature remains rebellious, and stands against the wall in tearful protest. The guardian angel explains that the small creature misses its mother, whereupon a visitor lifts it in his arms, and all is peace.

The Creche has flourished greatly. The numbers vary from twenty-five to thirty, being governed by a curious law—the prevalence of house-cleaning! When many mothers can find jobs of scrubbing (which, by the way, earns a dollar and a half a day), then many babies are the helpless beneficiaries of the good offices of Hull House. But the benefit is not a gift; Hull House gives out no alms; every child is paid for at five cents a day.

The Sewing-Class is, if possible, a still more beautiful sight. Twenty or thirty little girls are gathered about low tables sewing away for dear life, and sitting among them are several young "society" women, guiding the immature hands and thoughts. It is proudly said that no social pleasures are allowed to stand in the way of this philanthropic duty.

From an admirable pamphlet entitled "Hull House: A Social Settlement," I condense the following sketch of labors and efforts:

Monday Evenings: Social Club, thirty girls. Debating Club, thirty young men. (The two clubs join later in the evening.) Athletic Class.

Drawing Class. Greek Art Class. Mathematics Class. English Composition Class.

Tuesday Evening: Working People's Social Science Club. (Addresses and discussions led by judges, lawyers, and business men.) Gymnasium. Drawing Class. Cooking Class. American History. Reading Party. Caesar. Latin Grammar. Political Economy. Modern History.

And so on through the week. The noticeable varieties of interest include (besides the branches already named) Singing, Needlework, Diet Kitchen, Biology, Shakespeare, Lilies and Ferns, Victor Hugo, German Reception, Chemistry, Electricity, Clay Modeling, English for Italians, Women's Gymnastics, etc. This vast curriculum is only for the evenings; the mornings and afternoons and the Sundays have their own programmes; and it may well be imagined that no business establishment goes far beyond this beehive of benevolence in orderly bustle and activity.

Hull House is fairly supplied with means. The use of the property it occupies was freely and generously bestowed upon it by Miss Helen Culver, to whom the property was devised by the late Charles J. Hull, whose old family residence it was. Then, too, the needs of the institution are wonderfully small compared with the ever-widening and deepening sphere of its influence.

Miss Jane Addams and Miss Ellen Gates Starr are the young women whose hearts conceived it, whose minds planned it, and whose small hands started it and have managed it thus far.

One of the young women had some private means of her own; and such is the sway of their gentle influence among those who know them that when they are told that money must come, lo! it appears. And, what is more, when they are forced to admit that their strength—unfortunately not superabundant—has reached its limit, other young helpers are at hand and the work never flags.

There exist in Chicago other benevolent institutions whose very number and variety preclude description. The City Directory contains the addresses of 57 asylums and hospitals, 28 infirmaries and dispensaries, 41 missions, 60 temperance societies, lodges, etc., and *thirty-seven columns* of secret benevolent associations, camps, lodges, circles, etc. The city is honeycombed with philanthropic associations in all magnitudes, shapes, and forms, from the ancient and honorable "Relief and Aid" (which won deathless fame after the Great Fire) down to the latest "Working-Girls' Luncheon Club," the Ursula, instituted by the graduates of an advanced school to provide and furnish, at cost, mid-day meals in the business districts for their toiling sisters. (There are several such clubs, and more are forming.) Everyone of the hundreds of churches is a centre of charitable effort. It becomes a net-work so all-pervading that one wonders that any should slip through, after all, and perish of want, as occasionally happens, nevertheless.

What is known as the "Poor Jews' Quarter" (as contra-distinguished from the splended homes of their richer co-religionists) lies near the western end of Twelfth Street Bridge, and to the southward of the West Side Italian quarters already spoken of. Certainly it is not the abode of ease, luxury, and elegance; its odors are not those of flowery meads, its architecture is not marked by either massiveness or ornamentation, its streets and alleys are not grassy (though they look as if they might be fertile under proper cultivation), and its denizens are more remarkable for number than for attractiveness. On the other hand, the region is still less suggestive of a "Ghetto," according to any prevailing tradition of those abodes. Children, ranging from infancy to adolescence, and from invalidism to rude health, throng the sidewalks. Many of these children have never seen a tree or a blade of grass. "In our summer country excursion," said a lady of Hull House, "we have much pleasure in watching them—they kneel down sometimes so as to study the grass and feel it with their hands." Yet the sidewalk seems to furnish a tolerable substitute for the grass-plat, and the passer-by has to edge close to street or fence to keep clear of the flying rope, turned by two girls, while a little string of others are awaiting their turn to jump, each one who "trips" taking the place of one of the turners— just as is done by their richer fellow-mortals, better fed and better dressed, but perhaps not more joyous and unregretful.

In the midst of this swarming colony rises—tall, large, handsome, and solid—the "Jewish Training School," under the management of a strong band of the solid Israelites of the city (representing, of course, solid millions of money) and the superintendency of Professor Gabriel Bamberger. Fifty thousand dollars a year is wisely and economically expended here, and eight hundred children and youths, of both sexes, *and all races and religions*, are taught and cared for. The classes in drawing and clay-modeling are especially notable.

Not far away is the "Shelter House" of the "Society in Aid of Russian Refugees." There the members of this unfortunate class find surcease of their woes and persecutions in a blessed harbor of temporary refuge, whence they are scattered to various employments and chances to earn an honest living, free from imperialsm, officialism, priestcraft, and military service. They are a sturdy-looking set, and will not be long in learning that their greatest ill-treatment is turned to their greatest good luck when they arrive at the "Shelter House." They are "submerged" no longer.

When the back streets of Chicago are undergoing their spring cleaning, the mass of mud collected for removal in this quarter is incredible. The piles along the street-side are as high as they can be made to stand erect, and as close together as they can be. This is the accumulation of the months of December to March inclusive—the months when snow, frost, and short days impede the work so that a dollar laid out does perhaps not forty cents' worth of good. Then, too, the cold renders the vile deposit less hurtful to health, and the moisture and the frost keep it from flying about in the form of dust. The main streets are cleaned even when there is snow on the ground.*

One characteristic development of business-like philanthropy in Chicago is in the "Liberty Bell" and "Friendship" buildings for the accommodation of working-men. They are not germane to the subject of poverty, except to show its absence, prevention, or alleviation. The first-named was an experiment in the direction of furnishing to working-men good accommodations at rates almost nominal. A man is there offered a bath, a shave, and the use of a laundry (both provided with hot and cold water and soap), and a clean bed in a clean and ventilated room, all for ten cents. The whole main floor is devoted to a waiting-room with chairs and tables. In this room one sees from fifty to one hundred men, old and young, talking, smoking, reading newspapers, and the place is filled with the hum of conversation. In one corner is a group discussing work and wages; in another the younger fellows have made their newspapers into balls which they toss one to another. There is no drinking, no singing, and no boisterous mirth. "They take their pleasure sadly, according to their wont," as Froissart remarks concerning their far-away ancestors.

From the profits earned by the "Liberty Bell" the "Friendship" has been built. There things are more handsomely done. Not only are there no beds in tiers, as at the other place; but each is entirely inclosed in a locked space, eight feet high, and protected by charged electric wires, so that the tenant and all his belongings are safe from intrusion or theft. The same accommodations (in more elegant form) are offered as in the former place, and the entire charge is fifteen cents. The originator of the pleasant and profitable scheme is now abroad, looking for further knowledge wherewith to provide further improvements.

At each place a good meal is served, in a restaurant attached, at an additional charge of ten cents. The savings of the men are accepted and cared for by the concern, and they amount to a very considerable sum. The men are largely dock-workers, sailors waiting for the opening of the lakes, mechanics out of a job, workers at light trades and callings about town, etc. All are comfortably clothed and quite free from any marks of want.

This is a pleasant aspect of the labor situation; but it is to be remembered that here we have only the able-bodied single men, the class which is last to feel the griping hand of poverty. Women and children, the difficult and distressing element in the social problem, are in all this left out of the account. The dock-laborers among these men—the largest class—earn from twenty to twenty-five cents an hour.

---

*Even in well-swept London the streets are neglected in winter. "In one street is the body of a dead dog, and near by two dead cats, which lie as though they had slain each other; all three have been crushed flat by the traffic which has gone over them, and they, like everything else, are frozen and harmless."—Labor and Life of the People, vol.ii., p. 96, London, 1892.

On the North Side (255 Indiana Street) is the "Home for Self-supporting Women," which, as its name implies, does a service for the other sex somewhat similar to that offered to men at the "Friendship." For obvious reasons the difficulties in dealing with the stronger sex are greatly magnified when the weaker is in question. Yet, great or small, those difficulties are braved, and, to a large extent, conquered. Better entertainment must be (and is) provided; larger charges must therefore be imposed, and that on individuals whose wages are smaller. Still the enterprise is nearly self-supporting, and when kindly fate shall inspire some rich and benevolent friend of woman to pay off a $10,000 mortgage on the realty of the Home, then its net income will overtake its outgo, and even in time exceed it, making its devoted ministers (all women) able to extend its influence in an ever-increasing ratio. Meantime the annual reports are written in an admirable style of good-humored *naivete* which shows that work and worry cannot daunt or sadden those whose hearts are in their business. It is a most worthy and successful effort at the best kind of help; but it still leaves untouched the problem of family helplessness—the soft, elastic, unbreakable bond which binds the hands and feet of mothers.

Near the centre of business are two institutions for the care of homeless newsboys, bootblacks, and other young street workers, the "Waifs' Mission and Training School" and "Newsboys' Home." The former has a school, a dining-room and kitchen, a dormitory with fifty beds, a bath-room, a gymnasium, a printing office, etc., and its plan includes military drill (with a brass band formed among the boys themselves), instruction in the printing business, and the finding of places for boys old enough to enter steady employment. Its patrons and managers include judges of court, business men and capitalists, and a board of charitable women. The number of boys accommodated is limited to the number of beds.

An institution somewhat analogous to this is the "Illinois School of Agriculture and Manual Training for Boys," placed on three hundred acres of farming land at Glenwood, not far south of the city limits. Until this school was started (1887) there was absolutely no place to which a boy could be sent who was thrown upon the world by any of the lamentable casualities to which every community is subject—orphanage, desertion, forced separation from drunken or criminal parents. The courts of certain counties make use of this as a refuge for such boys, and allow a certain small monthly stipend for each; but this is necessarily far short of the absolute requirements of proper subsistence, clothing, and education, and more money than the school has yet received could be well used in it. The boys are provided with homes, chiefly with farmers, and the average outlay for each, up to the time when he is so provided for, is only about $60. The future life of the boy is kept in view and recorded; almost always with results that justify the efforts.

The Newsboys' and Bootblacks' Home is the oldest of the institutions of its class. It cares for some fifty or sixty boys, giving them decent sustenance and protection at lowest cost, and also providing for their amusement when circumstances permit. Some philanthropic persons object to these refuges of the human waifs and strays on the ground that they encourage boys to run away from their families. To this there seem to be two possible answers—first, that every lodge, circle, hospital, asylum, and refuge runs to some extent against the family relation, not even excepting the fashionable club-houses; next, that the boys in the missions have perhaps found a better home than they left; that the change for them is a step upward, not downward. As far as one can see, it is a change from the gutter to the mission.

The *sweat-shop* is a place where, separate from the tailor-shop or clothing-warehouse, a "sweater" (middleman) assembles journeymen tailors and needle-women, to work under his supervision. He takes a cheap room outside the dear and crowded business centre, and within the neighborhood where the work-people live. Thus is rent saved to the employer, and time and travel to the employed. The men can and do work more hours than was possible under the centralized system, and their wives and children can help, especially when, as is often done, the garments are taken home to "finish." (Even the very young can pull out basting-threads.) This "finishing" is what remains undone after the machine has done its work, and consists in "felling" the waist and leg-ends of trousers (paid at one and one-half cent a pair), and, in short, all the "felling" necessary on every garment of any kind. For this service, at the prices paid, they cannot earn more than from twenty-five to forty cents a day, and the work is largely done by Italian, Polish, and Bohemian women and girls.

The entire number of persons employed in these vocations may be stated at 5,000 men (of whom 800 are Jews), and from 20,000 to 23,000 women and children. The wages are reckoned by "piece-work," and (outside the "finishing") run about as follows:

Girls, hand-sewers, earn nothing for the first month, then as unskilled workers they get $1 to $1.50 a week, $3 a week, and (as skilled workers) $6 a week. The first-named class constitutes fifty per cent of all, the second thirty per cent, and the last twenty per cent. In the general work men are only employed to do button-holing and pressing, and their earnings are as follows: "Pressers," $8 to $12 a week; "underpressers," $4 to $7. Cloak operators earn $8 to $12 a week. Four-fifths of the sewing-machines are furnished by "sweaters" (middlemen); also needles, thread, and wax.

The "sweat-shop" day is ten hours; but many take work home to get in overtime; and occasionally the shops themselves are kept open for extra work, from which the hardest and ablest workers sometimes make from $14 to $16 a week. On the other hand, the regular work-season for cloakmaking is but seven months, and for other branches nine months, in the year. The average weekly living expenses of a man and wife, with two children, as estimated by a self-educated workman named Bisno, are as follows: Rent (three or four small rooms), $2; food, fuel, and light, $4; clothing, $2, and beer and spirits, $1.

The first matter complained of is the wretchedness of the quarters. The proposed remedy for this is the establishment by clothiers of outlying workshops which shall be clean, light, and ventilated—in other words, not "sweat-shops." A city ordinance enacts that rooms provided for workmen shall contain space equal to five hundred cubic feet of air for each person employed; but in the average "sweat-shop" only about a tenth of that quantity is to be found. In one such place there were fifteen men and women in one room, which contained also a pile of mattresses on which some of the men sleep at night. The closets were disgraceful. In an adjoining room were piles of clothing, made and unmade, on the same table with the food of the family. Two dirty little children were playing about the floor.

The second complaint regards the public good. It is averred, with apparent reason, that clothing should not be exposed to contamination and possible infection in rooms not set apart for working-rooms, especially in private houses, where members of the family, young and old, may quite possibly be ill of dangerously contagious fevers and other complaints. The danger of contagion from the hands of the workman himself is multiplied in proportion as the tenement is crowded where the garments are taken for work.

Another complaint, urged with much feeling, is that when the workers set up a "Union" shop of their own, where they did the very best work at prices as low as those charged at the "sweat-shops," but (by saving the profits of a middleman) were able to give more to the workers, they were deliberately and confessedly "frozen out" by the withholding of patronage by the clothing firms, and this after having been in prosperous and peaceable operation for two years. The "sweaters" could not force down wages as low as they wished, because the workers in the "Union" shops were doing so well. Therefore they got the employing firms to refuse work to the men's own establishment, and throw it all into the middleman's hands. A firm of employers for whom the association had worked two years were instrumental in this incredible cruelty. It is said by the workmen that they were driven to their action by others in the business, for when the little cooperative concern applied for work, they were referred to an association of the employing firms, and were there absolutely refused.

The "sweating system" has been in operation about twelve years, during which time some firms have failed, while others have increased their production tenfold. Meantime certain "sweaters" have grown rich; two having built from their gains tenement-houses for rent to the poor workers. The wholesale clothing business of Chicago is about $20,000,000 a year.

Mr. Bisno, the workman to whom I have alluded, has been led by his reading toward Socialism (very far from Anarchism), and he thinks that poverty and drink are parent and child—poverty the parent. A talk with him would be an enlightenment to any person who had not already adequate knowledge of the meaning of the short phrase "A good day's work." He would get a new idea of the unusual ability, mental and manual, the unflagging speed, the unwearied application which go to make the earning of a day's wages of the higher grades. He thinks that he could not maintain such speed without some liquid stimulus, in which other equally good workers think he is mistaken. (At the same time he is extremely moderate.) He says that beer is sold at five cents the measured pint (yielding two-and-a-half glasses), and that it is freely brought into the "sweat-shops," wherein, in fact, the workers are entirely independent of personal control, their work alone being subject to inspection and criticism. The inspection is close and constant, and failure entails the doing over of the job. Spoiling (such as tearing while ripping spoiled seams) leads to deductions from pay. The latter is very rare.

Division of labor is good; scattering of workers from great groups into smaller groups is good; employment of women in their own homes is good; prevention of theft is good, and cheapness of garments is good.

Unwholesome atmosphere, moral and material, is bad; insufficient wages is bad; possibility of infection is bad, and child-labor is (usually) bad. How shall the good be preserved and bad cured or alleviated?

At the head-quarters of the West Side police one is in the near neighborhood of the "Anarchist Riot" of 1886. In that building the police force was mustered and formed for its march out to the anarchist meeting-place, 500 feet distant; and there 67 of the police, killed and wounded, were laid when brought back a few minutes later. The messenger in attendance is one of the severely wounded, now too much shattered to do more than light tasks about the station. Conversation with some of the men at this station has led me to a new appreciation of the magnitude of the issues then and there fought out, and the finality of the settlement arrived at. A lieutenant of police recently said to me:

"The whole thing is played out. They will never make another experiment. There is no interest in anarchy or socialism any more, and no meetings to speak of. They do get together, some of them, at Twelfth Street Turner Hall, but you'd never know that they had ever planned a riot or loaded a bomb. No; they have no connection with hardship and poverty. They can always get their beer, and that's the main thing with them."

These quiet and unassuming officers of law and order know that they did their duty, and think that their success was a foregone conclusion. They do not know that though other "stronger" governments could have put down anarchy by force of arms, and hanged or shot the insurgents by martial law, yet this is perhaps the only government on earth which could have met such a movement by the ordinary police power, and then have given the guilty a long public trial before "a jury of their peers," and have relied on a verdict of conviction, a judgment of death, and the deliberate execution of that judgment.

Mr. Joseph Greenhut (himself a Socialist, somewhat out of sympathy with the alleviation of poverty, its absolute cure being in his view, possible by changes in the constitution of society), furnishes many statistics showing the ruling rates of wages earned in some hundreds of trades and callings, from which the following are selected:

	Per diem.	
Bricklayers, stone-cutters, and stone-masons	$4 00	
Plasterers	3 50 to	$4 00
Carpenters	2 50 to	2 80
Bridge-builders	2 50 to	3 25
Ship-carpenters and caulkers	2 00 to	3 50
Machinists, blacksmiths, and wagon-makers	2 00 to	2 50
Pattern-makers and horse-shoers	2 75 to	3 50
Engineers	2 00 to	5 00
Grain-trimmers	2 75 to	3 50
Lumber-shovers	3 00 to	6 00
Sewer-builders	2 00 to	3 00
Plumbers, gas-fitters, painters, photographers, printers, etc	2 00 to	3 50
Boot- and shoe-makers, cigar-makers, millers, stereotypers and electrotypers, copper, tin, and sheet-iron workers, brass finishers, upholsterers, etc	1 75 to	3 00
Iron and steel mill-workers, japanners, etc	1 50 to	6 00
Tailors and suit-makers	1 00 to	3 00
Type-founders, furriers, bookbinders, furniture-workers, distillers, brewers, etc	1 50 to	3 00
Sailors (with board)	1 50 to	2 00
Farmers	1 50 to	3 00
Coopers, fish-packers, gravel-roofers, freight-house men, laundry-men, makers of iron and lead pipe, wire-goods, vault-lights, etc.	1 50 to	2 50
Brick-makers	1 00 to	3 00
Planing-mill hands	1 25 to	2 25
Harness-makers, musical instrument-makers	1 25 to	3 00
Market-men, ice-wagon men, etc	1 50 to	2 75
Packing and slaughter-house men, etc	1 25 to	4 00
Lumber-yard hands	1 25 to	1 50
Dock-laborers	1 00 to	2 00
Confectioners, millinery and straw-goods makers, hair-workers, etc.	1 00 to	3 00
Female clerks	1 00 to	2 75
Glove and mitten-makers	60 to	3 00

	By the week.	
Drug clerks	$12 00 to	$25 00
Telegraph and telephone operators	10 00 to	20 00
Bakers and barbers	10 00 to	14 00
Stablemen	9 00 to	15 00
Teamsters	9 00 to	12 00
Dressmakers	6 00 to	15 00
Office stenographers and typewriters	6 00 to	20 00

Mr Greenhut estimates the immigrant nationalities (including their children) composing Chicago as follows: Germans, 400,000; Irish, 210,000; Sclavonians, 100,000; Scandinavians, 110,000; English, Scotch, and Welsh, 80,000; French Canadians, 15,000; Italians, 15,000; French, 5,000; Colored, 13,000; and Chinese, 2,000.

No one doubts but that the drink-bill of Chicago—estimated at $1,000,000 a week, of which three-fourths comes from the pockets of the poor—would change into prosperity, practically, all the adversity of the unfortunate classes, just as the drink-bill of Russia—$1,000,000 a day—would supplant famine by abundance. Much poverty comes from drink that does not come from drunkenness. A man may spend in drink the total profit on his earnings, the total surplus above necessary outgoes, and it may—usually does—amount to an insurance fund which, well invested, would form a respectable fortune during his prosperous years. Then, when old age, sickness, or accident befalls, he is penniless. His poverty springs from drink; no matter if he never was drunk in his life. The man who drinks up what he might save is as short-sighted as the husbandman who should needlessly eat up his seed-wheat.

"Paying off" is often done in saloons, in which the paymaster may or may not be interested. It is a vile and hurtful practice. A late article in a Chicago paper contains the following words on this theme:

Contractor Piatkiewicz said some of his workmen habitually spent for liquor half their earnings, and that on one pay-night, several years ago, he recollected that out of a total of $480 due his men, the chips in the basket gave to the saloon-keeper $200. To add to this, he said that as many "treats all around" were made as there were men in the saloon. From a large number of sources it was learned that it is the custom with the Polish laborers—the violation of which means disgrace—for each man on pay-night to treat all his fellows, the bartender and contractor included, and for the two latter, when it comes their turn, to treat the men. It is needless to say that the contractor and bartender rarely have to pay for what they "set up" to the crowd.

The possible remedy for this state of things—if there be any remedy—is outside the province of the present essay. Suffice it to say here, that the non-expert observer, however sympathetic, is prone to feel that any effort at relief of the "chosen miseries," which does not strike at the cause of the choice, is futile.

A late issue of the Chicago *Tribune* had the following suggestive paragraph:

WORK WAITING FOR UNEMPLOYED
THE STATEMENT ABOUT CHICAGO'S
ARMY OF IDLE MEN REFUTED.

"The statement that there are 30,000 to 50,000 laboring men out of employment today in Chicago is false," said Oscar Kuehne yesterday. Mr. Kuehne is the General Agent of the German Benevolent Society and is in position to know. "I could have furnished," he continued, "during the month of March, employment to 300 to 400 more men than I did, if I had had the men to fill the applications that came into my office. Farmers from within a radius of thirty miles of Chicago come to me to supply them with farm-laborers, and when I tell them that I haven't men for them, and can't get the sort of men they want, they ask in surprise where these 50,000 unemployed in Chicago are. At one o'clock this afternoon there were thirty farmers in my office after laborers. They would have employed fifty men, but I had to disappoint them. The truth of the matter is that there is no excuse for the idleness of an energetic young man who is not married. He can get work if he wants it. For a married man there is more excuse. He is not free to move about as the unmarried man is, and is more limited in his choice of occupations. We find it more difficult to get work for men of families."

There is some chosen poverty which is not necessarily connected with drink. Many instances arise in the minds of men and women who are trying to do their philanthropic duty.

The pitiable man is he who cannot get work to do, and in so far as this article on poverty in the West does not present the harrowing pictures of want elsewhere, it must be accounted for in the same way as was the shortness of the celebrated chapter on "Snakes in Iceland." Work and wages, seed-time and harvest, have not yet failed in the land. And the art of making the wise choice of possible joys, though not yet fully learned, is gaining ground.

The overwhelming tendency of modern life is toward the cities. It almost seems as if they would have to be walled about in order to keep in the country the proportions—four-fifths at least—which must remain there in order to provide food for all. Everything done "to alleviate the condition of the poor in great cities" works in the direction of bringing more into them; and no argument or persuasion, or more solid consideration of betterment, prevails to get them out after once immersed in the pleasurable excitement of gregarious existence; they would rather starve in a crowd than grow fat in quietude—especially if the "crowd" is sprinkled with aromatic "charity."

Humanity, like other semifluids, moves in the line of least resistance and most propulsion. Idleness drifts toward where commiseration and alms-giving are most generous and unquestioning; love of drink toward where beer and liquor are most plentiful. The free soup-kitchen is a profitable neighbor for the saloon. Labor is a blessing—in disguise; and a free gift is often a disguised curse.

Then is a part of the prevalent philanthropic feeling, though coming from the noblest part of our nature, tainted with sentimentality and sensationalism? Is it, to a certain extent, the vagary of good men and women who, consciously or unconsciously, regard physical labor as only a necessary evil? Is it part of the new creed which sees in drink not the cause but the consequence of want and misery? *Quien sabe?* At any rate, if any statement should be made of the Western aspect of the matter, as it appears to men who regard duly paid toil as the condition of well-being, which statement did not present this possibility as at least an obtruding suspicion, it would be false and defective.

"In the sweat of thy face shalt thou eat bread" was not a curse but a blessing, and so shall be until a dreary Utopia prevail, competition giving place to combination, mankind being beaten up into an omelet, and excelling and excellence no more.

CHAPTER 2

Progressivism
In Action, I

INTRODUCTION

The clear division between private and public charity efforts came slowly and would only be more sharply delineated with the New Deal. A turning point came gradually as charity workers, churchmen, social scientists, and reformers began to see the poor as victims of the new industrial system.

Symbolizing this shift was the movement to "save" the children of the poor. "Childsaving" emerged as a movement that drew a diverse collection of reformers together into a loose but effective coalition. James E. West, chief executive of the Boy Scouts of America, himself an orphan, proved to be an important figure in organizing the movement on behalf of child welfare, which culminated in Theodore Roosevelt calling a White House Conference on the Care of Dependent Children in 1909. This conference drew national attention to the plight of poor children. As a consequence, attitudes toward the poor and the state and federal government's responsibility toward them began to change.

Three years after the White House Conference, Congress enacted legislation that established the Federal Children's Bureau. At this same time state legislatures began to establish mothers' aid laws that provided dependent mothers with state "pensions" on the assumption that children should not be separated from their mothers. Missouri and Illinois established the first mothers' pensions systems in 1911, and over the next two years 20 other states followed suit. By 1919 nearly all of the states had such laws, although it should be noted that relief and coverage remained small, inadequate, and allotted to a limited number of those eligible for pensions. Moreover, legislation on the state level further restricted coverage and adequacy of the system. In 1913 Illinois ruled divorced women ineligible for assistance, and other state legislatures placed strict standards on residence, behavior, and proof of destitution. Still, public welfare expenditures increased dramatically in these years, although per capita spending on welfare remained relatively low.

These developments marked significant changes in caring for the poor, but they should not be mistaken for a transformation in social policy in America. Even as workmen's compensation plans and new assistance programs for the blind, the elderly and the widowed were instituted, out-door relief still remained an anathema to the public and to the policy-makers. Only three states—North Carolina, Missouri, and Minnesota—even allowed for the possibility that the county should administer outdoor relief, and in no case was a state agency given the right to supervise outdoor relief. Most states had established industrial compensation programs for injured workers, but attempts to enact health insurance, unemployment insurance, or social insurance on the federal level had failed before World War I.

In this chapter's first reading Mark H. Leff traces the development of mothers' pensions in the Progressive era. He shows that a general consen-sus emerged in this period concerning the state's responsibility to assist mothers. Led by moral reformers, women's clubs, labor unions, and certain settlement workers, the movement for mothers' pensions became a power-ful force that imparted new responsibilities to the state in providing assis-tance to the poor. Underlying this movement, Leff maintains, was a strong sensibility that the woman's place was in the home.

Many social workers and private charities, however, continued to oppose outdoor relief. These interests particularly worried that government was already too involved in their affairs through the enactment of new state laws regulating orphanages and children's homes throughout many midwestern states in the last decade of the nineteenth century. This growth of government involvement in areas once the domain of private charities led a small group of reformers to ask, "If government could regulate pri-vate social institutions, why couldn't government assume greater responsi-bility for the widows and mothers of poor children?" At the urging of these reformers, many state governments moved to provide education and home care assistance to dependent children. This activity, Leff explains, culmi-nated in the White House Conference on the Care of Dependent Children, called by President Theodore Roosevelt in 1909.

Although the conference expressed a preference for private and volun-taristic care of dependent children, the result of the meeting was to rally support for public funding of mothers' pensions. Juvenile reformers, includ-ing Judge E. E. Porterfield in Missouri, Judge Merritt Pinckney of Illinois, and Judge Ben Lindsey of Colorado, played key roles in the movement for public-funded mothers' pensions.

Still, many continued to oppose public assistance programs. Settle-ment workers and charity workers were divided on the issue, as Edward Devine, Josephine Shaw Lowell, and Mary Richmond denounced the pen-sion system. They were joined by more traditional conservatives who saw the increased government role in this area as a step toward socialism. These opponents of mothers' pensions faced stiff opposition from such lead-ing political figures as Theodore Roosevelt, Robert LaFollette, and Louis Brandeis, as well as from womens' clubs, child labor reformers, and pro-gressive journalists. The call to protect widows and poor children easily won the hearts of the public.

The second reading in this chapter provides an illustration of Theodore Roosevelt's role in galvanizing national support for some measure of public care for dependent children. His message to Congress describes the problems and concerns of the Conference on the Care of Dependent Children held in Washington, D.C. in early 1909. The keynote of the conference, Roosevelt observes, was expressed in the sentiment that "Home life is the highest and finest product of civilization. Children should not be deprived of it except for urgent and compelling reasons." Roosevelt's message shows the important role a president can play in social reform. His message also suggests that traditional values relating to home, family, and motherhood can have progressive and profound implications in policy debates.

Further Readings

Leroy Ashby, *Saving the Waifs: Reformers and Dependent Children, 1890–1917* (Philadelphia: Temple University Press, 1984).

Priscilla Clement, *Welfare and the Poor in The Nineteenth Century City: Philadelphia, 1800 to 1854* (Rutherford, N.J.: Fairleigh Dickenson University Press, 1985).

Sidney Fine, *Laissez-Faire and the General Welfare State: A Study of Conflict in American Thought, 1865–1901* (Ann Arbor: University of Michigan Press, 1956).

Nathan I. Huggins, *Protestants against Poverty: Boston's Charities, 1870–1900* (Westport, Conn.: Greenwood Publishing Corp., 1971).

James T. Patterson, *America's Struggle against Poverty, 1900–1980* (Cambridge, Mass.: Harvard Univ. Press, 1981).

Walter I. Trattner, *Crusade for the Children: A History of the National Child Labor Committee and Child Labor Reform in America* (Chicago: Quadrangle Books, 1970).

Consensus for Reform:
The Mothers'-Pension Movement in the Progressive Era

Mark H. Leff

Scoring its first statewide victory in Illinois in 1911, the mothers'-pension movement swept forty states in less than a decade. No plank of the social-justice platform, with the possible exception of workmen's compensation, mustered a better legislative record. Drawing upon historic American concerns with children, widows, and the home, mothers' pensions incorporated the major strains of progressivism. Moral reformers and economic-efficiency buffs, women's clubs and labor unions, middle-class do-gooders and relief recipients, New Freedom advocates and New Nationalism partisans, all jumped onto the bandwagon. Their clash with unconvinced charity workers and half-dormant conservatives was a mismatch.

The startlingly narrow scope of this consensus highlights the economic and social limitations of early-twentieth-century reform. Mothers' pensions (also called widows' pensions or mothers' aid) were paltry long-term cash provisions for children without employable fathers, contingent upon their mothers' acceptance of middle-class behavioral norms. The program thus promised to be cheap and morally uplifting, while raising no specter of dissolute male misfits lining up for their monthly liquor money.

In 1935, the aid-to-dependent-children provisions of the Social Security Act tendered federal guidelines and financial support to state mothers'-aid agencies. This program has earned as great a consensus in its opposition as had formerly been secured in its favor. Yet popular principles regarding welfare have changed little; they still encompass reliance upon local administration, the rejection of a right to public aid, and the imposition of "suitable home" criteria. Today's "welfare mess" is, in no small part, a product of yesterday's welfare maxims.

THE DEVELOPMENT OF MOTHERS' PENSIONS

The case for mothers' pensions was airtight in terms of contemporary concerns. Seeing in children "infinite possibilities for good," Progressives believed that "in the child and in our treatment of him rests the solution of the problems which confront the State and society today." But interest in children was not unique to progressivism. In the 1860s and 1870s, sym-

SOURCE: Mark H. Leff, *Social Service Review* 47, no. 3 (September 1973), University of Chicago Press, pp. 397–415. ©1973 by the University of Chicago. All rights reserved. Reprinted with permission.

pathy for war orphans, supplemented by a belief in the value of differential treatment of children and adults, had resulted in state campaigns to remove orphans and other children from almshouses and to place them in institutions. By the turn of the century, dissatisfaction with the "products" of orphanages, combined with objections to institutional regimentation, artificiality, and inability to dispense individual care, elicited substantial popular opposition. "Even a very poor home," it was said, "offers a better chance for [a child's] development than an excellent institution." By 1909, children's-home societies in twenty-eight states furthered the foster-home movement.

The widow, too, was an object of public sympathy. She could scarcely be held accountable for the death of her husband; yet the disintegration of the extended family in urban America often left her with pitifully little to fall back on. While it was expected that married women would not be gainfully employed (only 5–10 percent of them were), almost one-third of all widows found it necessary to hold jobs. It became a cliché to warn that "to be the breadwinner and the home-maker of the family is more than the average woman can bear." The results, it was said, were that "the home crumbles" and that "the physical and moral well-being of the mother and the children is impaired and seriously menaced." Aid to prevent this disintegration was distinguished from other relief because it buttressed traditional family roles: "Women and children ought to be supported, and there is no sense of degradation in receiving support."

The role of government in public relief aroused more controversy. Late in the nineteenth century, social workers and private charities challenged public outdoor-relief programs, and succeeded in abolishing or curtailing them in most major cities. Yet, by 1900, new state laws regulating private children's institutions reasserted the government position. Boards of public welfare were established in a number of midwestern cities, beginning in Kansas City in 1908 and reaching Chicago soon thereafter. Their proponents asserted that relief was a public responsibility rather than a private service, that relief needs had grown too large to be met by private resources, and that public agencies could apply the lessons of efficiency and scientific philanthropy as competently as private ones.

Many private agencies thus came to fear a preemption by government. Realizing that their failure to preserve the home was the chink in their armor, they established nurseries, along with job-placement services for widows. However, they still encouraged many widows to send some of their children to orphanages in order to provide adequate family support. A few charity institutions (particularly Jewish ones) disregarded the admonitions of scientific philanthropy that assured relief would be pauperizing, and began to give regular monetary aid to widows. Other organizations pointed out that regular private charity showed little commitment to meeting this need, and focused their efforts on widows' pensions alone.

Around the turn of the century, public aid for dependent children in their own homes had been proposed as an alternative to public outdoor relief and private charity. In 1898, the New York legislature passed a bill granting widowed mothers in New York City an allowance equal to the state expenditure for institutionalizing their children. However, the mayor of New York City, pressured by the interests of private charity, convinced the governor not to sign the bill. In 1906, the juvenile courts in some California counties liberally interpreted laws to furnish county aid to children in their own homes, and in 1910 the attorney general of New Jersey took a similar step. Oklahoma in 1908 established "school scholarships," paid from educational funds to children of widows; and in the early months of 1911 Michigan enacted a comparable law for indigent children. None of these laws explicitly recognized state responsibility for support of dependent children in their own homes. Nevertheless, it is clear that the public distinguished widows' aid from other public relief.

Probably the greatest spur to the subsequent passage of mothers'-pension laws was the 1909 Conference on the Care of Dependent Children. President Roosevelt opened the conference by discussing the plight of the widow unable to support her children. "Surely in such a case," he urged, "the goal toward which we should strive is to help that mother, so that she can keep her own home and keep the child in it; that is the best thing possible to be done for that child. How the relief shall come, public, private, or by a mixture of both, in what way, you are competent to say and I am not." In the debate that followed, several members called for public mothers' pensions. In rebuttal, a vocal minority desperately defended children's institutions. The fourteen conference resolutions, which reflected the most advanced ideas on child welfare of the time, laid the foundation for several future reforms. The creation of the Children's Bureau, for example, was one result of this conference. But the resolution relating to mothers' pensions attracted the most attention:

> Home life is the highest and finest product of civilization. It is the great molding force of mind and of character. Children should not be deprived of it except for urgent and compelling reasons. Children of parents of worthy character, suffering from temporary misfortune and children of reasonably efficient and deserving mothers who are without the support of the normal breadwinner, should, as a rule, be kept with their parents, such aid being given as may be necessary to maintain suitable homes for the rearing of the children. This aid should be given by such methods and from such sources as may be determined by the general relief policy of each community, preferably in the form of private charity, rather than of public relief. Except in unusual circumstances, the home should not be broken up for reasons of poverty, but only for considerations of inefficiency or immorality.

This resolution, though expressing a preference for privately funded mothers' pensions, catalyzed the drive for public legislation. Soon a stream of people declared their advocacy of pensions for mothers. With the passage of the first mothers'-pension laws, this stream became a flood.

The legislative breakthrough came with the passage of two mothers'-pension provisions in 1911. Missouri's statute, confined to Kansas City, was sponsored by Judge E. E. Porterfield of the Jackson County (Kansas City) juvenile court. The statewide law in Illinois benefited from lobbying efforts by the Chicago-based National Probation League (a recently formed organization primarily geared toward probation as an alternative to prison or reformatories for child and adult offenders); it also drew support from Judge Merritt Pinckney of the Cook County juvenile court, whose participation in the 1909 conference had reinforced his interest in mothers' pensions. As judges, both men had found it distasteful to separate children from their unsupported mothers on grounds of poverty, and they believed that many delinquent children became "bad" because their working mothers could not care for them.

Although 1912 was an off year for most state legislatures, momentum gathered in a Colorado referendum victory led by Denver juvenile court judge Ben Lindsey, and in several municipal and county ordinances adopting mothers' pensions. In 1913, the floodgates burst. Of the forty-two state legislatures in session, twenty-seven considered mothers'-pension legislation and seventeen passed it. Twenty states, sixteen of them in the West or Midwest, had now enacted mothers'-pension laws (see Table 1). By 1915, the number had grown to twenty-nine; in 1919 it reached thirty-nine, plus Alaska and Hawaii. By this point, the mothers'-pension movement ceased to be a national concern. The next fifteen years were a mopping-up operation that gathered in the two remaining western and New England states, the District of Columbia, and five of the seven remaining southern states.

This "wildfire spread of widows' pensions," many commentators contended, exceeded that of any other social or humanitarian idea of their era. Mothers'-pension provisions usually carried by near-unanimous tallies; opposition successes depended on preventing the bills from coming to a vote. Referendums, too, proving no contest, won by majorities of more than two to one in both Colorado and Arizona.

The enactments resulting from this popular upsurge exhibited broad similarities. Funding and administration of the laws was locally based. Administrative duties usually fell to juvenile courts, a recent Progressive Era attainment. Their existing bureaucracy and responsibility for dependent children, along with their dissociation from both outdoor relief and private charity, made them a natural choice for this function. Almost every statue established a maximum allowable monthly pension, which ranged from nine dollars to fifteen dollars a month for the first child and four dollars to ten dollars a month for additional children. To be eligible to receive this pension, a mother had to be "a proper person, physically, mentally and morally fit to bring up her children." Pensions could usually be granted only for children under the age of fourteen or sixteen. The state-residency requirement was one to three years; two states required the mother to be a United States citizen. Most states did not restrict eligible recipients

TABLE 1 Passage of Mothers'-Pension Laws, by Time Period and Region

Time Period	Region			
	Northeast	Central	South	West
1911–13	Massachusetts New Hampshire New Jersey Pennsylvania	Illinois Iowa Michigan Minnesota Missouri Nebraska Ohio South Dakota Wisconsin		California Colorado Idaho Nevada Oregon Utah Washington
1914–19	Connecticut Maine New York Vermont	Indiana Kansas North Dakota	Arkansas Delaware Florida Maryland Oklahoma Tennessee Texas Virginia West Virginia	Alaska Arizona Hawaii Montana Wyoming
1920–31	Rhode Island		Alabama District of Columbia Kentucky Louisiana Mississippi North Carolina	New Mexico

to widows alone; pensions were occasionally authorized for women whose husbands had deserted them, were confined to mental hospitals or prisons, or were physically or mentally incapacitated. Only Michigan specifically included unmarried or divorced mothers, though several laws were general enough to include fathers. Rarely, however, were such opportunities exploited, since they were usually the result of legislative imprecision or fear that the law would otherwise be declared unconstitutional. All states required proof of extreme poverty, along with an agreement to cease or limit employment upon receipt of a pension.

But the rudimentary measures instituted between 1911 and 1919 had already forged one of the major contributions of the social-justice movement to the New Deal's formulation of the welfare state.

THE FORMATION OF THE CONSENSUS

The alignment of forces contesting mothers'-pension proposals was unique in the history of American reform. Even persistent conservative foes of social-justice legislation muted their criticism. In their stead, the vanguard of the social-justice movement itself rose in opposition to mothers' pensions. Swept aside by a movement that had advanced beyond their original reform intentions, a phalanx of prominent charity workers turned against many of their colleagues and most of their disciples.

Charity-worker opposition to widows'-pension legislation emanated from the perceived threat to the agencies that employed them and to their cult of scientific philanthropy. Only in the 1920s did mothers' pensions gain widespread social work support. By that time, as administrators, social workers had molded the program to suit their casework approach.

The social service profession polarized over what has been called "the well-nigh universal disagreement between settlements and organized charity on the question of widows' pensions." Nowhere was this better illustrated than in New York City, where every major private charity in the state opposed the 1913 widows'-pension bill, while the Association of Neighborhood Workers, which represented the settlement houses of New York City, publicly favored it. Settlements had always been more prone than private charities to attribute individual problems to social ills and to seek government aid to make necessary economic and environmental changes.

Some advocates of mothers' pensions, such as Robert Hebbard and Jacob Billikopf, held positions on boards of public welfare or in other governmental relief organizations that were less likely to resent an expanded public-aid role. The failure of private charity to find adequate funding for widows'-aid experiments led charity workers such as Hannah Einstein and Homer Folks to favor a mothers'-pension law. A number of social work leaders, such as Mary Simkhovitch, Lillian Wald, Jane Addams, and Florence Kelley, counted themselves among the early proponents of pensions for mothers, as did the Abbott sisters and Julia Lathrop to a lesser extent. (All seven of these women were either former or active settlement workers.) Yet this support was usually tempered by fear of reversion to pre-scientific-philanthropy methods. Thus, no spokesman for this group emerged, and most of these social welfare leaders played minor or inactive roles in widows'-pension campaigns.

Most leading charity workers felt keenly threatened by the attack upon private philanthropy's hegemony. "Who are these sudden heroes of a brand new program of state subsidies to mothers?" asked Edward T. Devine, general secretary of the New York Charity Organization Society and the most vocal antagonist of mothers' pensions. "Who are these brash reformers who so cheerfully impugn the motives of old-fashioned givers, of the conscientious directors of charitable institutions, of pious founders of hospitals and all manner of benefactions?" Opposition to widows' pensions permeated almost every private charity agency and orphanage in the country. Charity-organization societies contributed the four major opponents of mothers' pensions: Edward Devine, Josephine Shaw Lowell, Frederic Almy, and Mary Richmond. Charity workers led the attack in New York, Massachusetts, Pennsylvania, and other states with strong charity interests. (The latter did not include the western and midwestern states, which were to be the most fertile ground for the new laws.)

In their assault upon mothers' pensions, charity workers used two main lines of argument: a defense of orphanages and private charity and a restatement of the truths of scientific philanthropy. Especially in the debates on mothers' pensions in the 1909 conference, social workers such as Edward Devine and directors of children's institutions had acclaimed the benefits of institutional care for even nondelinquent children whose parents supported them but were not a "pure, moral influence." This argument had little currency in later mothers'-pension debates. But numerous social workers defended private charity throughout this period, contending that few children were separated from their parents on grounds of poverty alone ("inefficiency" of the mother, for example, might be the justification), and that private charity could finance wider private widows'-pension programs if they did not have to compete against government (one problem, though not stated explicitly, was that impoverished widows and children were good drawing cards for funds).

The philosophy of scientific philanthropy underpinned the case against public grants for dependent children. Opposition was particularly fierce in cities that had succumbed to intense private-charity pressure to dismantle their public outdoor-relief systems. The widow's plight had served as a justification for the maintenance of government relief; the reemergence of this image thus presented a special threat. Defending their hard-won position, charity workers depicted mothers' pensions as "a step backward, a reversal of policy." Government was deemed incapable of learning the lessons of scientific philanthropy: it would be subject to corruption and political interference; it would fail to realize the importance of attracting competent trained administrators; and it would not provide adequate supervision. Combined with the subversive and fiercely assailed belief that certain forms of regular relief were a right, the result would be "pauperization," a "pathological parasitism" that would "inevitably create a new class of dependents." It was a scandalous mistake to give recipients cash rather than certain basic necessities; with pensions averaging twenty-three dollars a month for some families, "temptations come to spend money recklessly or foolishly." Moreover, mothers' pensions were "an insidious attack upon the family, inimical to the welfare of children and injurious to the character of parents." Not only did pensions encourage desertion in those few states that granted them to deserted families, but they failed to invoke the "great principle of family solidarity, calling upon the strong members of the family to support the weak."

Few detractors of widows' pensions emerged outside the social service community. A number of social-insurance advocates (many of whom were charity workers who rallied to this alternative as the mothers'-pension movement gained momentum) expressed their fear that the pension campaign would divert interest from more basic reforms. This opposition, however, derived from different assumptions than might be supposed. These workers were leery of the imputation of a primary governmental responsibility for the alleviation of poverty. Social insurance many of them felt, was "only a cooperative form of self-help"; no "self-respecting worker" would want it to become "a subsidy either from employers or from consumers."

Unlike much social legislation, mothers'-pension programs were neither expensive nor disruptive to productive efficiency. They thus posed no threat to wealthy conservatives, who were disinclined anyway to exert their political muscle on the wrong side of motherhood. The infrequent public attacks trod familiar ground. Widows'-pension expenditures, it was predicted, would irrepressibly soar. Poor widows from other countries or other states would descend upon states with new laws to make a quick pittance. The greatest danger, of course, was socialism. It was warned that the guiding philosophy of mothers' pensions was "not alms, but their right to share"—a principle that "represses the desire for self-help, self-respect, and independence," and leads to old-age pensions, free food for the unemployed, and state socialism. But such objections seldom surfaced. Some conservative newspapers led campaigns against such laws, but, except for the referendum fight in Colorado, these too seem to have been rare. Even the large number of juvenile-court judges who opposed aid to dependent children chose the strategy of nonenforcement in preference to public disputes with their reformist colleagues.

Support for mothers' pensions was neither so limited nor so reticent. Approval was widespread despite the polycentricity of the mothers'-pension movement, which had no national coordinating committee or national leader.

Juvenile-court judges had initially spearheaded widows'-pension drives. They had been pivotal in the passage of the first three state mothers'-pension laws, and they were important advocates of later dependent-children provisions in New York, Wisconsin, and California. But the role of these judges in legislative campaigns waned as the growing strength of the movement was catalyzed by the first few state laws.

Progressive politicians played a less readily definable role. Many consider the years from 1911 to 1915 to be the pinnacle or culmination of progressivism. Especially in those western and midwestern states that proved the most fertile ground for widows' pensions, this legislation was frequently accompanied by statutes on child labor, working conditions and minimum wages for women and children, or workmen's compensation, which drew more upon a concern for women and children than is now generally realized. Mothers' pensions dovetailed neatly with other reformist drives: they compensated certain families inadequately protected by accident-insurance laws, and they made child-labor restriction and compulsory education less onerous to families of widowed mothers.

Yet mothers' pensions were not a central political concern. The belief that public aid and other social services were a local responsibility rendered them a dead issue on the national level. Before the 1930s, the scattered mothers'-pension bills proposed in Congress (starting in 1914) received little consideration, while aid-to-dependent-children planks emerged in the national platforms of only two minor parties. Despite the widespread Progressive support for mothers' pensions, which transcended party boundaries, this program rarely even merited mention in the party platforms of states that enacted such laws. In Wisconsin, where a mothers'-pension provision was urged in the 1912 Republican state platform, proposed in 1913 by a Republican governor, and overwhelmingly passed later that year by a Republican legislature, this law ranked near the bottom of the Republicans' list of accomplishments in their 1914 state platform. More typically, state platforms did not advocate mothers'-pension legislation until its enactment; the follow-up was either continued silence, self-congratulation, or calls for its expansion and support.

Political figures, however, were not divorced from the widows'-pension movement. Mothers'-pension partisans claimed support from Theodore Roosevelt, Robert LaFollette, and Louis Brandeis. A 1923 campaign biography cited Calvin Coolidge's past support for mothers' pensions as evidence of his Progressive nature. In his December 1925 message to Congress, Coolidge proposed an aid-to-dependent-children law for the District of Columbia—a belated action that Congressman La Guardia termed "the only human touch in the President's message." Alfred E. Smith was perhaps more deserving of the credit he received on this score in his campaign biographies, for he delivered a heart-rending 1915 widows'-pension speech, which received wide coverage in New York newspapers, and he helped guide the law through the legislature. Some gubernatorial messages dealt with mothers' pensions, and some state legislators publicly discussed their advocacy of pensions, but on the whole, politicians remained followers rather than molders of public opinion.

Progressive newspapers and magazines participated more actively in the mothers'-pension movement. Beginning in 1907 with the arrival of Theodore Dreiser as its editor, the *Delineator*, a crusading mass-circulation women's fashion magazine, had championed foster homes as an alternative to institutional care for dependent children. By 1912, the *Delineator* became a forceful advocate for mothers' pensions and even sent a lecturer around the country to promote this cause. William Hard, a young Rooseveltian Progressive who had formerly headed the Northwestern University Settlement House, turned the *Delineator's* regular column on women and children into a journalistic campaign for mothers'-pension laws. Hard was also a member of the heavily packed New York commission whose 1914 report was probably the most uncompromising defense of mothers' pensions and the most forthright attack on the ineffectiveness of private charity ever delivered by a public body.

Another member of this commission was Sophie Loeb, a thirty-seven-year-old staff reporter for the *New York Evening World*, a Democratic paper with strong ties to the Wilson administration. Loeb launched a personal crusade, through her columns and through lobbying efforts, to secure a New York child welfare law. To her belongs much of the credit for both the appointment of the previously mentioned New York mothers'-pension commission and the 1915 passage of the mothers' pension law. She soon became president of the board that administered this law, and later used her position as president of the Child Welfare Committee of America to foster the passage of dependent children laws and to urge their funding and enforcement.

Other Progressive newspapers and magazines, though not so intimately involved in the activities of the mothers'-pension movement, contributed to its success. The Scripps-McRae and Hearst chains both conducted editorial campaigns for widows' pensions, as did a number of locally based papers. The legislation found acceptance throughout the spectrum of Progressive magazines; it received endorsement from such journals as *Outlook, Nation,* and *Public.*

Labor also gave some encouragement to mothers'-pension laws. In the early 1900s, the concept of widows' pensions had been associated, rightly or wrongly, with labor interests. In 1911, the American Federation of Labor endorsed a federal mothers'-pension resolution. However, only in the middle 1920s, when it supported a mothers'-aid bill for the District of Columbia, did the AFL Executive Council play an active role in promoting mothers'-pension legislation.

Labor's slighting of mothers' pensions was more a matter of priority than of neutrality. Certain state federations of labor testified in favor of proposed mothers'-pension statutes, and a number of supporters of these laws (such as Secretary of Labor Wilson and the Socialist party) could be classified as sympathetic to labor. Other social-justice legislation, such as workmen's compensation and child labor, was of greater importance to labor, but mothers' pensions did not pass unnoticed.

Social-insurance advocates who were not charity workers were also likely to favor mothers' pensions. By asserting a public responsibility that entailed an enlarged government-welfare role, and by picturing private charity as an inadequate and improper repository for this function, the mothers'-pension movement borrowed and reinforced two of the main pillars of the case for social insurance. Thus, a number of social-insurance proponents, such as Ben Lindsey and Issac Rubinow, held that these pensions would "prove at least a good entering wedge for those social and industrial-insurance laws that must come in time as the public is educated to their necessity." There was a difference in emphasis among these advocates, however. Those directly involved in the mothers'-pension campaign, such as William Hard and the New York widows'-pension commission, averred that comprehensive social insurance lacked sufficient support to be adopted in the near future, and contended that mothers' pensions might prove an essential part of a social-insurance package anyway. Those less involved in the movement decried the meagerness of the grants, and contended that the law's reliance on requirements of moral "fitness" and the means test betrayed it as a prisoner of charity concepts. Yet both groups looked forward to building upon the success of what they considered to be at least a partial corrective for an existing social ill.

Women made up the principal component of the mothers'-pension movement. Around the turn of the century, women's organizations began to flourish under leadership that helped to direct the latent energies of middle-class women into reform channels. The politicization of the woman's role built upon society's concession of feminine expertise on child welfare matters; women were thus ritualistically appointed to mothers'-pension commissions, and occasional statutes even required their appointment as administrators.

The United States traveled a solitary road in its halting and hazardous trek to the welfare state. Although mothers'-pension adherents occasionally referred to European social-insurance schemes, they cited them more as precedents than as models. No other major industrial nation had such a special concern for its children and such a fear of providing assistance to indigent men. Thus, the United States was the world leader in mothers' pensions and a world laggard in social insurance.

The legacy of the mother's-pension movement, though, went beyond the passage of one unique piece of child welfare legislation. It laid a foundation for later contentions that government had the responsibility to establish welfare as a right, independent of the compassion, altruism, and paternalism of the "better" members of society. It shattered the view of income support as a mere adjunct to more direct programs of social control. It undermined the prestige of private charities to such an extent that they never again so confidently asserted their prerogative to define the government-welfare role. The United States had reached a preliminary recognition of poverty as a public problem requiring governmental remedies.

Special Message on Dependent Children

Theodore Roosevelt

To the Senate and House of Representatives:

On January 25–26, 1909, there assembled in this city, on my invitation, a conference on the care of dependent children. To this conference there came from nearly every State in the Union men and women actively engaged in the care of dependent children, and they represented all the leading religious bodies.

The subject considered is one of high importance to the well-being of the nation. The Census Bureau reported in 1904 that there were in orphanages and children's homes about 93,000 dependent children. There are probably 50,000 more (the precise number never having been ascertained) in private homes, either on board or in adopted homes provided by the generosity of foster parents. In addition to these there were 25,000 children in institutions for juvenile delinquents.

Each of these children represents either a potential addition to the productive capacity and the enlightened citizenship of the nation, or, if allowed to suffer from neglect, a potential addition to the destructive forces of the community. The ranks of criminals and other enemies of society are recruited in an altogether undue proportion from children bereft of their natural homes and left without sufficient care.

The interests of the nation are involved in the welfare of this army of children no less than in our great material affairs.

Notwithstanding a wide diversity of views and methods represented in the conference, and notwithstanding the varying legislative enactments and policies of the States from which the members came, the conference, at the close of its sessions, unanimously adopted a series of declarations expressing the conclusions which they had reached. These constitute a wise, constructive, and progressive programme of child-caring work. If given full effect by the proper agencies, existing methods and practices in almost every community would be profoundly and advantageously modified.

More significant even than the contents of the declarations is the fact that they were adopted without dissenting vote and with every demonstration of hearty approval on the part of all present. They constitute a standard of accepted opinion by which each community should measure the

SOURCE: Theodore Roosevelt, delivered to the United States Senate, *Proceedings of the Conference on the Care of Dependent Children, held at Washington, D.C.* (Washington, D.C., 1909), pp. 5–8.

adequacy of its existing methods and to which each community should seek to conform its legislation and its practice. The keynote of the conference was expressed in these words:

> Home life is the highest and finest product of civilization. Children should not be deprived of it except for urgent and compelling reasons.

Surely poverty alone should not disrupt the home. Parents of good character suffering from temporary misfortune, and above all deserving mothers fairly well able to work but deprived of the support of the normal breadwinner, should be given such aid as may be necessary to enable them to maintain suitable homes for the rearing of their children. The widowed or deserted mother, if a good woman, willing to work and to do her best, should ordinarily be helped in such fashion as will enable her to bring up her children herself in their natural home. Children from unfit homes, and children who have no homes, who must be cared for by charitable agencies, should, so far as practicable, be cared for in families.

I transmit herewith for your information a copy of the conclusions reached by the conference, of which the following is a brief summary:

1. *Home care.*—Children of worthy parents or deserving mothers should, as a rule, be kept with their parents at home.

2. *Preventive work.*—The effort should be made to eradicate causes of dependency, such as disease and accident, and to substitute compensation and insurance for relief.

3. *Home finding.*—Homeless and neglected children, if normal, should be cared for in families, when practicable.

4. *Cottage system.*—Institutions should be on the cottage plan with small units, as far as possible.

5. *Incorporation.*—Agencies caring for dependent children should be incorporated, on approval of a suitable state board.

6. *State inspection.*—The State should inspect the work of all agencies which care for dependent children.

7. *Inspection of educational work.*—Educational work of institutions and agencies caring for dependent children should be supervised by state educational authorities.

8. *Facts and records.*—Complete histories of dependent children and their parents, based upon personal investigation and supervision, should be recorded for guidance of child-caring agencies.

9. *Physical care.*—Every needy child should receive the best medical and surgical attention, and be instructed in health and hygiene.

10. *Cooperation.*—Local child-caring agencies should cooperate and establish joint bureaus of information.

11. *Undesirable legislation.*—Prohibitive legislation against transfer of dependent children between States should be repealed.

12. *Permanent organization.*—A permanent organization for work along the lines of these resolutions is desirable.

13. *Federal children's bureau.*—Establishment of a federal children's bureau is desirable, and enactment of pending bill is earnestly recommended.

14. Suggests special message to Congress favoring federal children's bureau and other legislation applying above principles to District of Columbia and other federal territory.

While it is recognized that these conclusions can be given their fullest effect only by the action of the several States or communities concerned, or of their charitable agencies, the conference requested me, in section 14 of the conclusions, to send to you a message recommending federal action.

There are pending in both Houses of Congress bills for the establishment of a children's bureau, i.e., Senate bill No. 8323 and House bill No. 24148. These provide for a children's bureau in the Department of the Interior, which

> shall investigate and report upon all matters pertaining to the welfare of children and child life, and shall especially investigate the questions of infant mortality, the birth rate, physical degeneracy, orphanage, juvenile delinquency and juvenile courts, desertion and illegitimacy, dangerous occupations, accidents and diseases of children of the working classes, employment, legislation affecting children in the several States and Territories, and such other facts as have a bearing upon the health, efficiency, character, and training of children.

One of the needs felt most acutely by the conference was that of accurate information concerning these questions relating to childhood. The National Government not only has the unquestioned right of research in such vital matters, but is the only agency which can effectively conduct such general inquiries as are needed for the benefit of all our citizens. In accordance with the unanimous request of the conference, I therefore most heartily urge your favorable action on these measures.

It is not only discreditable to us as a people that there is now no recognized and authoritative source of information upon these subjects relating to child life, but in the absence of such information as should be supplied by the Federal Government many abuses have gone unchecked; for public sentiment, with its great corrective power, can only be aroused by full knowledge of the facts. In addition to such information as the Census Bureau and other existing agencies of the Federal Government already provide, there remains much to be ascertained through lines of research not now authorized by law; and there should be correlation and dissemination of the knowledge obtained without any duplication of effort or interference with what is already being done. There are few things more vital to the welfare of the nation than accurate and dependable knowledge of the best methods of dealing with children, especially with those who are in one way or another handicapped by misfortune; and in the absence of such knowledge each community is left to work out its own problem without being able to learn of and profit by the success or failure of other communities along the same lines of endeavor. The bills for the establishment of the children's bureau are advocated not only by this conference, but by a large number of national organizations that are disinterestedly working for the welfare of children, and also by philanthropic, educational, and religious bodies in all parts of the country.

I further urge that such legislation be enacted as may be necessary in order to bring the laws and practices in regard to the care of dependent children in all federal territory into harmony with the other conclusions reached by the conference.

LEGISLATION FOR THE DISTRICT OF COLUMBIA

Congress took a step in the direction of the conclusions of this conference in 1893, when, on the recommendation of the late Amos G. Warner, then superintendent of charities for the District of Columbia, the Board of Children's Guardians was created, with authority, among other things, to place children in family homes. That board has made commendable progress, and its work should be strengthened and extended.

I recommend legislation for the District of Columbia in accordance with the fifth, sixth, seventh, and eighth sections of the conclusions of the conference, as follows:

1. That the approval of the Board of Charities be required for the incorporation of all child-caring agencies, as well as amendments of the charter of any benevolent corporation which includes child-caring work, and that other than duly incorporated agencies be forbidden to engage in the care of needy children. This legislation is needed in order to insure the fitness and responsibility of those who propose to undertake the care of helpless children. Such laws have long been in satisfactory operation in several of the larger States of the Union.

2. That the Board of Charities, through its duly authorized agents, shall inspect the work of all agencies which care for dependent children, whether by institutional or by home-finding methods, and whether supported by public or private funds. The state has always jealously guarded the interest of children whose parents have been able to leave them property by requiring the appointment of a guardian, under bond, accountable directly to the courts, even though there be a competent surviving parent. Surely the interests of the child who is not only an orphan but penniless ought to be no less sacred than those of the more fortunate orphan who inherits property. If the protection of the Government is necessary in the one case, it is even more necessary in the other. If we are to require that only incorporated institutions shall be allowed to engage in this responsible work, it is necessary to provide for public inspection, lest the state should become the unconscious partner of those who either from ignorance or inefficiency are unsuited to deal with the problem.

3. That the education of children in orphan asylums and other similar institutions in the District of Columbia be under the supervision of the

board of education, in order that these children may enjoy educational advantages equal to those of the other children. Normal school life comes next to normal home life in the process of securing the fullest development of the child.

4. That all agencies engaged in child-caring work in the District of Columbia be required by law to adopt adequate methods of investigation and make permanent records relative to children under their care, and to exercise faithful personal supervision over their wards until legally adopted or otherwise clearly beyond the need of further supervision; the forms and methods of such investigation, records, and supervision to be prescribed and enforced by the Board of Charities.

I deem such legislation as is herein recommended not only important for the welfare of the children immediately concerned, but important as setting an example of a high standard of child protection by the National Government to the several States of the Union, which should be able to look to the nation for leadership in such matters.

I herewith transmit a copy of the full text of the proceedings.

THEODORE ROOSEVELT.

THE WHITE HOUSE, *February 15, 1909.*

CHAPTER 3

Progressivism
In Action, II

INTRODUCTION

In the years following the Depression of 1893, the city became a focus of reform activity for settlement workers, social activists, progressive businessmen, and new professionals who called for the reorganization of municipal government and municipal services. With this reform activity, a new breed of social worker emerged who decried the fictive boundaries of private versus public relief and the repressive attitudes held by the older generation of charity workers. They called for the professionalization of social work through the introduction of higher education standards, better training, and the formation of national social work associations. At the same time, many of these reform-minded social workers suggested new approaches for addressing the problems of the urban poor and the newly arrived immigrants who flooded the city in these years. These new approaches included the establishment of settlement houses, modeled after the famous Toynbee House in London, and an attempt to organize neighborhoods through activist citizens' groups.

The "crisis of the city" in late–nineteenth-century America gave natural impetus to reform efforts. The rapid growth of the urban population following the Civil War disrupted city life, its politics, services, housing, and traditional social life. The urban population jumped from 6.2 million in 1860 to 42 million by 1910. In the first two decades following the Civil War, most of the urbanization can be accounted for by a migration of people from rural areas in the United States to the cities. After 1880, immigration accounted for most of this growth. Many of these immigrants were from southern and eastern Europe. Both social conservatives and reformers were quick to observe that by 1910 children of immigrants outnumbered the children of natives in most large cities (population over 100,000). Moreover, the economy of the city was transformed with industrialization. Unlike the factories of the antebellum period, which were usually placed in rural areas along waterways, most factories now could be found in cities.

This rapid growth in population and industry simply overwhelmed the capacity of local city governments. Under the onslaught of population growth, cities witnessed the breakdown of services for water, electricity, health care, police, education, and welfare. Social order itself seemed to be threatened under these circumstances. Fearing social chaos, business-men joined with new professionals to institute new administrative stan-dards and accounting principles in local governments. Municipal reformers called for nonpartisan government, civil service reform, a strong executive branch, and centralized administrative agencies to correct the severe prob-lems faced by the American city. Increasingly, civil engineers, city plan-ners, school superintendents, public health officials, housing experts, and professional social workers were called upon to manage the modern city.

City charities also came under review as public spending on charities soared in the period from 1912 through 1930. With these soaring costs, many officials sought new ways to control and manage public welfare in their cities. The establishment of a central Board of Public Welfare in Kansas City in 1913 became a model for other city governments. By 1918 over fifty such boards had been established throughout the Midwest and West.

Social reformers also sought new ways of dealing with the day-to-day problems of the urban poor, especially the newly arrived immigrant. One of the most innovative approaches appeared in the form of the settlement house. Samuel A. Barnett and Arnold Toynbee founded the first settlement house, Toynbee Hall, in East London in the 1880s. Toynbee Hall attracted university men to the slums of London to improve the lives of the poor. By 1910, over forty such settlements had been established throughout Great Britain.

Toynbee Hall became a model for reform-minded, idealistic, young Americans who had traveled to London to visit this unique experiment in bridging the lives of the rich and the poor. Stanton Coit, a follower of Felix Adler's Ethical Culture Society, established the first settlement house in America in August 1886 in a New York City tenement on the Lower East Side. Through his widely read book *Neighborhood Guilds* (1891), he promoted his vision of social settlements and the good society. Other settlement houses soon followed, including Vidda Scudder's College Set-tlement and Lillian Wald's Henry House in New York City and Robert Woods's South End House in Boston. The most famous settlement house was Jane Addams's Hull House in Chicago. By 1910 there were more than 400 settlement houses throughout the United States.

The settlement houses were designed to provide practical help to the poor and the immigrants who lived in the neighborhood. A house offered a range of educational, cultural, and vocational activities. In addressing the problems of the neighborhood, settlement workers inevitably became involved in larger issues relating to city politics, tenement housing reform, child labor laws, and community services.

Settlement houses became a training ground for a group of key men and women who were to dominate and shape social work as a profession, including Julia Lathrop, first director of the U.S. Children's Bureau; Edith Abbot, founder of the Univeristy of Chicago School of Social Service Administration; consumer advocate Florence Kelley; philosopher John Dewey; historian Charles Beard; Gerard Swope, president of General Electric and prime mover in corporate welfare programs; John Collier, a leading advocate of Indian rights; and Francis Perkins, secretary of labor in the New Deal.

These men and women shared a common faith in the value of expert and professional opinion in the field of social welfare. These reformers, as social activists and social scientists, hoped to restore political order and representative government to American society through the intervention of nonpartisan expertise in community affairs. In these years, social work became professionalized through the establishment of specialized training programs and the formation of professional associations such as the National Conference of Social Work, the precursor to the National Conference on Social Welfare.

This movement, which sought to combine expertise and community democracy, found its clearest articulation in Wilbur C. Phillips's Cincinnati Social Unit Plan and Neighborhood Association, established in 1918 to bring health professionals to the local community. Patricia Mooney Melvin discusses this remarkable experiment in the first reading of this chapter. Her story shows one kind of Progressivism in action.

Wilbur C. Phillips's plan grew from his experiences in community reform in New York City and Milwaukee. As secretary of the New York Milk Committee, an organization aimed at lowering infant mortality by providing "clean" (tuberculosis-free) milk to New York's poor children, Phillips realized that high rates of infant mortality resulted as much from poor maternal education as from distributing impure milk to children. He saw that mothers needed to be educated concerning proper maternal care and health care principles. He envisioned a system in which health professionals could be integrated into local neighborhoods to provide such infant health care and maternal education.

In 1911, Phillips was given an opportunity to apply his vision for educating the community when he was offered the position to organize a child welfare program in Milwaukee. As secretary of the Child Welfare Commission, he attempted to construct a program that brought health care professionals to local residents. He organized a community infant health service in St. Cyril's Parish, but a change in city administration brought his efforts to a close. He returned to New York where he drew up a plan for a cooperative health care program structured around what he called the "social unit plan." Based on neighborhood units, the plan was designed to bring health care professionals together with local neighborhoods through elected councils. By 1915 Phillips had attracted the support of leading reformers, including the editor of the *New Republic*, Herbert Croly. Soon after their establishment of the National Social Unit Organization, they received offers from sixteen cities to host a demonstration program. They finally decided on Cincinnati as a model city, and by the summer of 1917, Phillips had established his social unit plan in the Mohawk-Brighton neighborhood, a lower-middle-class neighborhood near the center of the city.

Phillips's experiment in health care proved a short-lived success. Both health care professionals and local residents actively participated in the preventive health care program. A health center and a visiting nurse program, which made more than 5,000 visits to 500 babies, were established. By 1919 the program offered prenatal care, general bedside nursing, medical examinations for all preschool children, and postnatal examinations. The program became a major force in combating the influenza epidemic in the fall of 1918. Yet for all of its successes the program fell victim to the Red Scare in 1919 and to bureaucratic infighting on the part of the city public health administration. As a result, Phillips soon withdrew from Cincinnati. Later attempts to carry on his experiment were prevented by lack of financial support.

The Outlook article, written in 1919, captures the excitement this project held for reformers. The experiment demonstrated the feasibility of bringing "specialists" and "citizens" together to care for the health and welfare of the nation's children. *The Outlook* was a leading advocate of the settlement house movement in the United States. This journal exerted an important influence on the social reformers in this period. This article projects a hope that the social unit plan would spread across the nation.

The settlement house movement and the social unit plan suggest the great faith these reformers placed in voluntarism on the community level and nonpartisan expertise in public affairs. The faith continued to find expression in the post–World War I years, even as the Progressive movement faltered. The greatest advocate of voluntarism was Herbert Hoover.

Further Readings

Roy Lubove, *The Progressives and the Slums: Tenement House Reform in New York City, 1890–1917* (Pittsburgh: University of Pittsburgh Press, 1962).

Roy Lubove, *The Professional Altruist: The Emergence of Social Work as a Career, 1880–1930* (New York: Atheneum, 1980).

Judith Ann Trolander, *The Settlement Houses and the Great Depression* (Detroit: Wayne State University Press, 1975).

Judith Ann Trolander, *Professionalism and Social Change: From the Settlement House Movement to Neighborhood Centers, 1886 to the Present* (New York: Columbia University Press, 1987).

A fascinating documentary record of settlements is provided in Allen F. Davis and Mary Lynn McCree, eds., *Eighty Years at Hull House* (Chicago: Quandrangle Books, 1980).

A fine account of the English side of the settlement movement is found in Standish Meacham, *Toynbee Hall and Social Reform, 1880–1914: The Search for Community* (New Haven, Conn.: Yale University Press, 1987).

"A Cluster of Interlacing Communities": The Cincinnati Social Unit Plan and Neighborhood Organization, 1900-1920

Patricia Mooney Melvin

The "urban crisis" of the 1960s generated concern about the urban environment as a whole as well as its component parts. Part of this concern manifested itself in a fascination with utilizing the neighborhood as a "testing ground" for solutions to contemporary problems. As part of Lyndon Johnson's War on Poverty, numerous "community action programs," designed to stimulate resident participation in neighborhood affairs and to foster "working relationships" among the different groups active in the neighborhood, sprung up in a variety of American communities. But interest in the neighborhood as a base to promote "maximum feasible participation" is not new; its roots reach back to the first decades of the twentieth century. During those years, individuals concerned about urban conditions labored to involve all neighborhood residents in local organizations that promised fuller services as well as the potential for social change. Adopting the organic analogy that was popular in descriptions of society, activists viewed the city as an interdependent system of complementary parts. Guided by a biological conception of interdependence, they sought to translate their beliefs into a workable system of urban organization. Their attempt to organize cities and neighborhoods along the lines of interdependence and cooperation constitutes the first community organization movement.

Late-nineteenth-century America experienced extraordinary urban growth, geographic specialization of land use, and high rates of internal migration. The convergence of these trends "disrupted" society, and stimulated many Americans to search for a way to cope with the "new society." They wanted a conceptual resolution for what they perceived as a lack of harmony between the different groups and interests jockeying for secure positions. They began to look for an organized body of ideas through which to understand and to direct society. By the 1880s, the notion of interdependence had captured their imagination.

SOURCE: Patricia Mooney Melvin, in *Community Organization for Urban Social Change: A Historical Perspective,* eds. Robert Fisher and Peter Romanofsky (Westport, Conn.: Greenwood Press, 1981), pp. 59–88. ©1981 by Robert Fisher and the Estate of Peter Romanofsky. Reprinted with permission.

Interdependence, generally expressed in terms of an organic analogy, soon dominated turn-of-the century thought. While not everyone championed the new beliefs, many Americans began to accept the idea that no part of life could be viewed in isolation, and that all parts were interrelated in a larger whole.

Students of urban areas began to see the city as an organically inter-dependent unit as well. They groped for a new image or definition of the urban landscape to replace the older and seemingly inapplicable image that described urban areas as collections of amorphous groups of individuals. They abandoned the notion of the city as a residential community composed of congeries of densely settled individuals joined together by a "quest for economic expansion and social improvements," and began to see the city as an interdependent system of differentiated but complementary parts. While each of these parts, or neighborhoods, exhibited differences, propo-nents of the organic view stressed the existence of a symbiotic relationship between the local units and the city as a whole. According to Boston's South End House director, Robert A. Woods, the organic city was

> a cluster of interlacing communities, each having its own vital ways of expres-sion and action, but all together creating the municipality which shall render the fullest service through the most spirited participation of all its citizens.

Insisting that the well-being of the whole depended upon the health of the parts, numerous groups, among them public-health activists, settlement workers, and community organizers, attempted to organize neighborhoods and to establish systems designed to facilitate communication between the city and its constituent parts.

Advocates of the organic, or interdependent, city believed that city life could not be understood, nor its problems met, unless the process began in the neighborhood. Just as the city was seen as a distinct unit within a larger organic society, it was also viewed as being composed of a "bunch of communities," or units. As the fundamental social unit, the neighborhood was seen as an "elaborate nexus of interrelations, needs and ambitions." Sufficiently small enough to be comprehensible to and manageable for the average citizen, it was at the same time large enough "to include, in essence, practically all the problems of the city, state, and nation." As epitomes of the city, the neighborhoods were believed to provide "handy laboratories for social inquiry."

Those working in the neighborhoods, arguing that once Americans "knew how to be one neighborhood they would then know how to be one nation," championed a variety of programs designed to develop more fully the neighborhood as a vital part of the city, and to foster a high degree of concern for the city and, ultimately, the nation as a whole. These programs, which were loosely covered by the term "community organization," repre-sented an attempt to effect the "reconstruction, expansion, and integration" of neighborhood and community life. The activities all sought resident participation in discovering and solving neighborhood problems, and included the establishment of settlement houses, school centers, community councils, and social unit organizations.

Of all the activities that focused on organizing neighborhoods, Wilbur C. Phillips's Social Unit Organization represents the quintessential example of the attempt to organize neighborhoods "to function properly as a part of the city." More than most of his contemporaries, Phillips tried to bring the neighborhood into the "stuff of American life," and to provide residents with the potential to better the community. On the basis of his experiences with the New York Milk Committee and the Milwaukee Child Welfare Commission, Phillips devised an organizational scheme built around grouping experts and citizens on the neighborhood level in order to foster the continual interaction between the "forces of democracy" and those of "specialism." He proposed to divide the neighborhood into occupational and citizen groups that would meet regularly to ascertain needs and allocate community resources to meet those needs, making the neighborhood unit into a "well-constituted community" within the larger city. From 1917 to 1920, Phillips attempted to demonstrate the feasibilty of organizing neighborhood residents in this way, as citizens and experts, in the Mohawk-Brighton district of Cincinnati.

Phillips first began his neighborhood work in New York City with the New York Milk Committee (NYMC). As secretary of the organization from 1906 to 1911, he helped to mobilize community resources for a campaign against infant mortality. Like many others who were active in the early twentieth-century crusade against infant mortality, Phillips found that programs that focused narrowly on cleaning up the physical environment in which milk was produced failed to bring down the high rates of infant mortality. He began to look beyond the physical environment, and started to concentrate on the people within that environment. Once he realized that infant mortality resulted from more than "dirty milk," Phillips transferred his emphasis from "milk to motherhood."

Stressing social, personal, and environmental aspects of community health, under Phillips's direction, the NYMC infant milk stations not only dispensed "clean" milk, but also offered maternal education in the principles of child hygiene. The work in the NYMC's milk depots exemplified the shift from milk to motherhood, and helped to publicize the fact that concerted programs focusing both on the environment and on the child could help in lowering the infant death rate and in promoting infant health and welfare. The activities undertaken in the milk stations in the fight for human welfare pointed to the interdependence of the environment and the child.

But Phillips soon became restive working within the confines of the New York Milk Committee. Unfortunately for Phillips, the committee's program consisted of more than the milk depot work; it also included cleaning up the milk environment, which required Phillips to devise programs for securing a pure and inexpensive milk supply and for regulating milk standards. Because of this twofold program, the committee could not divert all its resources to the milk depots. As a result, and despite the new direction taken in the stations, the NYMC's work fell short of Phillips's growing expectations.

While caring for those infants whose mothers sought help or who were accidently brought to the attention of the depot workers, the New York Milk Committee failed to seek and reach every mother and every baby in the areas served by each milk station. Phillips wanted the depot personnel to contact every mother and infant and to attack infant health problems on the basis of the community rather than by focusing only on random individual cases. If it were able to establish a close and continuing relationship with the mothers, Phillips believed, the depot would grow into a social center and, as he told members of the Child Welfare Conference for Research and Development in 1909, would "radiate the influences of education and social betterment," thus improving the whole environment of the child. On the basis of his work with the NYMC, he also looked beyond efforts in a single neighborhood. He felt that such work, if duplicated in neighborhoods across the city, would provide the base for a thorough, city-wide child-welfare program. Each part of the city would contribute to the well-being of the larger whole.

When an opportunity came to organize a child-welfare program in Milwaukee in 1911, Phillips left the New York Milk Committee and traveled west. In Milwaukee, as secretary of the Child Welfare Commission, a semiprivate organization under the aegis of the municipal government, Phillips attempted to construct a child-welfare program that more closely matched his desire for a "total" child-health program. Building upon the lessons learned in New York City, Phillips sought to organize a neighborhood—St. Cyril's Parish—for community-oriented infant-health services. This service operated from the commission's baby station located in the heart of the parish. He and his corps of local doctors, nurses, midwives, and residents tried to bring knowledge of proper infant care into every home, to coordinate the activities of the numerous organizations that touched on child welfare in the neighborhood, and to involve the local residents in planning their own health programs. No other agency in the country provided such intensive preventive care as did the health center in St. Cyril's Parish. A change in the municipal administration, however, resulted in the creation of a Division of Child Welfare under the auspices of the Health Department and in the dissolution of the Child Welfare Commission. Phillips returned to the East, reviewed his experiences, and pondered the possibilities and techniques of both health and community organization.

On the basis of his experiences with the New York Milk Committee and with the Child Welfare Commission, Phillips developed his theory of community organization. In his 1914 treatise, entitled "The Plan for Social

Organization or the Unit Method of Gradually Building Up a Complete System for Studying and Meeting Social Needs," Phillips laid out his organizational scheme. The plan centered around the establishment of a "democratic" structure through which citizens could participate directly in the control of community affairs while at the same time making use of the highest technical skills available. According to Phillips's plan, this structure was to be set up first in "the basic unit of national life, the neighborhood." He visualized the nation as a grand union of neighborhoods, which, when linked together, comprised cities, counties, states, and ultimately, the nation as a whole. Learning to function "intelligently" and democratically within the confines of the neighborhood allowed Americans to understand society, to participate more fully in its operation, and to enjoy the fruits of living in a democracy. Believing, as did many of his contemporaries, that the neighborhood was small enough to be manageable and comprehensible, and large enough to reflect the needs of the entire community, Phillips devised a system that utilized the neighborhood as a "laboratory unit" to coordinate needs and resources for all.

Although the organization Phillips proposed in his Social Unit Plan was more developed than those of many of his contemporaries, the thrust of his proposals reflected a general fascination, among Progressive reformers, with the notion of a cooperative society. During the early twentieth century, political theorists, most particularly Herbert Croly, argued that the American political system failed to meet the American citizens' particular needs while at the same time remaining, in a general fashion, responsive to their collective wishes. Most people had only sporadic and superficial contact with their chosen leaders; there existed little interaction between the representatives and their constituents. In addition, Croly, like Phillips, believed that most legislators did not base many of their decisions upon "technical knowledge," voting, instead, on the basis of "interests." As a result, those in power failed to provide the basis for real social "progress."

Croly argued for cooperation most persuasively in *Progressive Democracy,* published in 1915. His general theme in this treatise was cooperation and participation. "Democracy," he wrote,

> implies and needs some method of representation which will be efficient and responsible enough a . . . policy but which does not imply the delegation of its ultimate discretionary power to any [fixed] body of men or law.

Active, popular participation created responsible and creative citizens, who then relayed their needs to experts capable of devising suitable programs. Such a communion between the citizens and the experts constituted, according to Croly, a "fundamentally whole and sound society."

From his Milwaukee experience, in particular, Phillips arrived at similar conclusions about the importance of cooperative interplay between citizens and experts. He found that if he generalized about the people he worked with, he was dealing with two groups in the social structure: those who supplied human service, such as the doctors and the nurses, and those who sought service, the consumers of health and social programs. The Social Unit Plan represented an attempt to formulate a method for resolving these two "separate but complementary forces of supply and demand." Because Phillips believed that everything was "inextricably related to and dependent upon each other," he wanted his system to provide for the expression of all people, be they producers or consumers.

But, in order to effect such interaction, there had to be complete and continuous contact between both groups. Cooperation demanded some mechanism that encouraged the collection of all necessary information concerning consumer needs, and then provided for its transmission to the experts for resolution. Again, on the basis of his experience, Phillips believed that the neighborhood represented the ideal arena for this interchange between consumers and producers.

Based on neighborhood units, the plan depended upon four fundamental instruments designed to stimulate people to define and meet their own needs and to interact as consumers and producers. These integral components were the Block Councils, the Citizens' Council, the Occupational Council, and the General Council. In essence, the plan called for subdividing the neighborhood into block associations to promote face-to-face contact among the residents. Then, to provide vehicles for the expression and resolution of block ideas, needs, and aspirations, Phillips set up a Citizens' Council and an Occupational Council. Representatives from each Block Council sat on the Citizens' Council to advance the needs of the locale, and representatives from the area's professional sector sat on the Occupational Council to suggest ways to meet neighborhood needs. And finally, Phillips wanted both groups to meet together regularly to seek, through consensus, practical resolutions of the neighborhood's needs. (See figure 1.)

Phillips believed that the formulation of a sound program necessitated a well-grounded knowledge of each neighborhood and its needs. In order to secure more than just nominal representation, Phillips thought that it was essential to reach all neighborhood residents and to solicit their ideas and demands. Based on his work in St. Cyril's Parish, where a group of eight residents assisted the doctors and the nurses of the child-welfare station, Phillips felt that if the resident group were expanded, it would provide an ideal way to secure information about neighborhood residents' needs. But, instead of merely being adjuncts to the health station's staff, as were the eight residents in St. Cyril's Parish, the neighborhood residents, under the Social Unit Plan, would actually be part of the work team. They would be "representatives of the people." Thus, Phillips reasoned, "nothing could be done in their neighborhood that they [the residents] didn't want."

Phillips selected the block as the unit to represent the neighborhood residents. Those over eighteen years of age in each block were to meet together and select first a Block Council and then a block worker. After

FIGURE 1 Phillips's Social Unit Plan

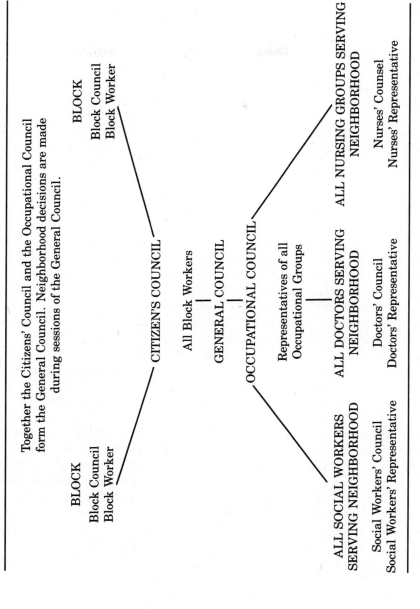

Together the Citizens' Council and the Occupational Council form the General Council. Neighborhood decisions are made during sessions of the General Council.

BLOCK
Block Council
Block Worker

BLOCK
Block Council
Block Worker

CITIZEN'S COUNCIL

All Block Workers

GENERAL COUNCIL

OCCUPATIONAL COUNCIL

Representatives of all Occupational Groups

ALL SOCIAL WORKERS SERVING NEIGHBORHOOD

Social Workers' Council
Social Workers' Representative

ALL DOCTORS SERVING NEIGHBORHOOD

Doctors' Council
Doctors' Representative

ALL NURSING GROUPS SERVING NEIGHBORHOOD

Nurses' Counsel
Nurses' Representative

some instruction by the "directors" of the plan, each block worker would serve as an educational agent who instructed the residents of his or her block about the work and the principles of the Social Unit Plan. Phillips wanted each worker to establish a friendly acquaintance with all the residents of the block. Then, each block worker was to solicit the concerns of his or her constituents and, after "neighborly" discussion, compile information concerning the needs of the area. One fact collector, known to the residents of each block, could secure more information and explain its importance far better, Phillips believed, than all the volunteers and paid agents from numerous organizations who combed the city making intimate inquiries and duplicating both questions and services. The block worker, as Courtenay Dinwiddie, a Cincinnati Social Unit Organziation executive, said later, "was in the best sense of the word a neighbor familiar with the conditions and needs and responsive to the wishes of other residents."

The block worker represented his or her block in the Citizens' Council, and presented the problems and needs of their respective blocks at regular meetings. The council then studied the data presented by the various block workers. From this information, the Citizens' Council prepared complete and accurate statements outlining the needs of the neighborhood residents. Phillips, in a 1919 outline of the Social Unit Plan, compared the relationship between the block workers and the Citizens' Council to the nervous system of the human body. Just as the "body has a system which notifies every part of it as to what the needs of the body are," the block workers were to serve as the nerves of the district, knowing whenever a need existed, and then transmitting that need to the central node of the system—the Citizens' Council—making the need felt until it was satisfied.

The third component of the Social Unit Plan was the Occupational Council. Comprised of representatives from the "skilled groups," or "experts" such as doctors, nurses, and social workers who served the neighborhood, the members of the Occupational Council were charged with the formulation of "sound and efficient" programs for meeting the needs discerned by the Citizens' Council. In theory, each skilled group in the neighborhood organized and elected from its number a representative to serve on the Occupational Council. If the Citizens' Council desired a plan to meet a need identified by the block workers, the council contacted the Occupational Council. Once the need was presented to the Occupational Council, all groups that were able to provide supportive services collaborated on the plan, which was sent back to the Citizens' Council for consideration and, hopefully, for adoption. Phillips believed that this collaboration would develop a well-rounded program that would cover all aspects of a need. By studying new opportunities for better and wider service to meet the needs disclosed by the Citizens' Council, Phillips felt that the neighborhood would be able to have at its disposal the "skill, judgement and experience of the service sector of the population."

To ensure a close relationship between those who possessed specialized knowledge and those who needed expert service, Phillips capped his plan with a General Council. Based on the premise that citizen participation, combined with expert analysis, produces a "working democracy," the General Council represented the union of the people (the Citizens' Council) and the experts (the Occupational Council). With individuals separated according to their special activities into occupational and citizens' groups, the General Council provided the arena where the experts and the people worked together to develop practical plans for meeting neighborhood needs. In such a way, all groups would work together to solve the problems of the neighborhood and promote, by implication, a healthy society.

Once this plan was functioning in neighborhoods throughout the city, Phillips hoped to achieve intracity cooperation. He wanted each neighborhood to send delegates to a citywide Citizens' Council and a citywide Occupational Council. These groups were to articulate city needs and strategies for action, the actual programs to be decided upon in joint meetings of the two bodies at the citywide General Council. Phillips envisioned the eventual reproduction of this organizational form at the county, state, and federal levels. He felt that such a structure permitted more group participation in the decision-making process, provided a sense of order throughout the city, and trained neighborhood inhabitants to be responsible citizens. It was to be a total plan for community betterment.

By late 1915, Phillips had interested a number of people, such as the *New Republic* editor, Herbert Croly, Dr. Richard Cabot of the Massachusetts General Hospital, Dr. S. S. Goldwater, former health commissioner of New York City, and John L. Elliott, head worker of the Hudson Guild, a New York City settlement house, in backing his plan. Together, they established the National Social Unit Organization (NSUO), with headquarters in New York City, and voted to sponsor a three-year demonstration of Phillips's social unit scheme, focusing on a preventive health program for young children to illustrate the plan's feasibility. Soon after the announcement, sixteen cities offered to host the NSUO's demonstration. In November 1916, following a vigorous campaign led by Courtenay Dinwiddie, superintendent of the Cincinnati Tuberculosis League, and Dr. John Landis, health officer of Cincinnati and chairman of the Municipal Tuberculosis Committee, the NSUO selected Cincinnati as the host city for the social unit experiment. According to the NSUO, Cincinnati possessed the best facilities of all the interested cities for carrying out the social unit demonstration. These included a high degree of enthusiasm displayed by the general public in the Social Unit Plan; the promise by Cincinnati's social- and public-health agencies to support the experiment, and to relinquish their own work within the section of the city selected for the demonstration; and the pledge of $15,000 per year to help finance the operation. At the end of December, Phillips left New York City and arrived in Cincinnati on January 2, 1917, ready to "set to work."

Phillips spent all of 1917 working with Cincinnatians to select a district, or neighborhood, for the social unit demonstration, and then to organize the area following the Social Unit Plan guidelines. First, Phillips concentrated on explaining the plan to the public through a series of public lectures, and on laying the necessary groundwork for a Cincinnati Social Unit Organization. Such an organization, Phillips believed, composed of "representative citizens," would stimulate competition among the various neighborhoods, and would allow those areas of the city not involved in the experiment to familiarize themselves with the general principles of social unit organization. On March 22, 1917, at a meeting held in Exchange Hall at the Chamber of Commerce, over six hundred people gathered to vote the Cincinnati Social Unit Organization (CSUO) into existence. This organization, composed of a Citizens' Council and an Occupational Council, was to oversee the social unit experiment, to advise the unit laboratory, and, at the conclusion of the experiment, to assist the NSUO in the evaluation of the demonstration. The CSUO's first task, after its formation, was to select an appropriate neighborhood for the social unit demonstration.

For the next two months, the CSUO concentrated on choosing the experimental district. It announced in the daily newspapers that it intended to select as the laboratory district the neighborhood of the city that proved most eager for the plan. From May 14 through May 21, all the major newspapers carried a daily column on "What the Social Unit Experiment Means for You and Your Neighborhood." Randall J. Condon, superintendent of Cincinnati's public schools, authorized the distribution of five thousand ballots throughout the public-school system to collect information concerning neighborhood interest in the demonstration.

By the beginning of June, five neighborhoods emerged as leading contenders. Residents in these areas sent the CSUO numerous petitions and letters urging the selection of their neighborhood as the social unit district. At a meeting held in Exchange Hall on June 7, 1917, the CSUO announced that it had selected Mohawk-Brighton as the demonstration neighborhood and that organization of the neighborhood would begin at once.

This Cincinnati neighborhood lay slightly west of the center of the city. Described by Phillips as "a picturesque area that lay both at the foot and the side of one of those many hills of Cincinnati," Mohawk-Brighton was part of the "Zone of Emergence," a term used by Robert A. Woods and Albert J. Kennedy for that area of the city inhabited by city residents who "had emerged from the slum into the mainstream of American life." It nestled between the belt of land surrounding the central business district, which contained the central city slums, and the fashionable hilltop suburbs of Cincinnati. With the movement of industries up the Millcreek Valley in the late-nineteenth century, and the rapid settling of the peripheral area of the old walking city, Mohawk-Brighton, like most areas in the zone, emerged as both a residential and an industrial neighborhood. By the turn of the century, it had grown into an "industrial beehive," containing perfumeries, brass founderies, machine shops, and a flour mill. A wide variety of small enterprises, such as tobacconists, groceries, dry goods shops, and saloons, located primarily along Central Avenue, the main artery into Mohawk-Brighton, provided the necessary services to the neighborhood residents. And the majority of these residents, whether laborers or small entrepreneurs, were predominatly first- or second-generation Germans or Irish.

While it remains unclear precisely why Mohawk-Brighton residents sought the Social Unit Plan so strenuously, one peculiarity of the zone perhaps provides a general reason for the interest of Mohawk-Brighton in securing the social unit demonstration. By definition, the Zone of Emergence consisted of people with only marginal economic security who feared engulfment or reengulfment by the slums. To combat this threat, one characteristic of most of the areas comprising the Zone of Emergence was the "penchant for organization." Residents of zone neighborhoods tended to be "joiners" and organization builders. By banding together in groups, whether social, economic, or religious, "zone residents sought to realize their aspirations," however imprecisely defined, and "to control their community." The other four neighborhoods in the social unit competition, all part of the Zone of Emergence, exhibited different levels of organization-making in their attempt to secure the unit demonstration. While Mohawk-Brighton residents set up a 145-member committee to canvass all the blocks in their neighborhood, and to sponsor public meetings about the unit plan, the other neighborhoods only established "small" committees that were relatively inactive. Evidently, the residents of Mohawk-Brighton, and more particularly the neighborhood leaders of this community on the cutting edge of the slums, were more interested in pursuing an activity that they viewed as an opportunity for neighborhood betterment.

Once Mohawk-Brighton had been selected as the experimental district, the committee in charge of the campaign to secure the unit met and voted to remain active as a Temporary Organizing Committee for the neighborhood. The committee turned its attention first to the establishment of definite boundaries for the social unit area. It constructed a spot map showing the residences of all who had signed petitions urging the selection of Mohawk-Brighton. Then, since the NSUO budget only allowed for a district of fifteen thousand people, the committee "fixed the geographical center and eliminated those blocks on the border of the district which contained the smallest number of petitioners." Emming Street bounded this area on the north; Liberty Street, on the south; West and Colerain avenues, on the west; and Linn, Renner, Manchester, and Central streets, on the east. The committee divided this area into thirty-one blocks, with approximately five hundred people per block.

Once the district was divided, the committee began to set up Block Councils by visiting supporters from each block and securing their help. After a series of talks by committee members and by Phillips with block residents, each Block Council elected a block worker as representative to the Citizens' Council. Without exception, all the block workers were women. According to Phillips, the committee urged the selection of women for two reasons: first, the initial service planned for the social unit district, an infant health program, directly affected women as mothers; second, Phillips, as well as the committee, believed that men would not have the time to devote the "kind of attention" necessary during the initial organizational phase of the Social Unit Plan. Once the blocks selected their representatives, the committee and Phillips worked tirelessly with them. They acquainted the women with the plan of organization, outlined their duties as block representatives, and placed them on the social unit payroll. Because Phillips strongly believed in the importance of the block workers' role as block representatives, the women received $8.00 a week to compensate them for the time spent on social unit activities.

Concurrent with the formation of the Block Councils, Phillips worked with the Temporary Organizing Committee to organize groups to be represented on the Mohawk-Brighton Occupational Council. They approached various occupational groups in the neighborhood and attempted to familiarize them with the plan's basic ideas. Because the NSUO recommended that the initial program undertaken by the selected district focus on child welfare, Phillips and the committee concentrated primarily on organizing physicians, nurses, and social workers. However, they also spent time with teachers, businessmen, and clergymen, acquainting them with the plan, and enlisting their help in encouraging neighborhood participation and in disseminating information about the Social Unit Organization's activities. Once it was organized into a council, each occupational group elected an executive to serve on the neighborhood Occupational Council, through which they would contribute their special knowledge or skill to the community.

The three most active councils during the life of the social unit demonstration were those of the physicians, the nurses, and the social workers. The Physicians' Council consisted of nine men who represented the twenty-six physicians active in Mohawk-Brighton. The Nurses' Council included a representative from each of the four nursing organizations active in Mohawk-Brighton and a nursing aide to handle the paperwork. The Social Workers' Council organized in a similar fashion. Most of the social-service agencies active in Mohawk-Brighton assigned workers to the social unit district, and these workers constituted the Social Workers' Council.

By the middle of September 1917, as a result of the organizational activities carried on by the Temporary Organizing Committee and by Phillips, the residents of Mohawk-Brighton grew impatient for action. On September 27, the committee called a meeting to discuss the neighborhood's progress. Those who attended the meeting voted for the creation of the Mohawk-Brighton Social Unit Organization (MBSUO), consisting of a neighborhood Citizens' Council, an Occupational Council, and a General

Council. Immediately, the MBSUO General Council established a neighborhood bulletin to serve as a "medium for the expression of the community's thought" and to assist in the exchange of information between the various groups active in the neighborhood organization. The council then announced the location of the headquarters for the district operation and explained the NSUO's projected budget for 1918, which consisted of the funds raised by the NSUO from private donations plus the $15,000 promised by various Cincinnati social and health organizations.

During the next six weeks, the block workers held block meetings to discuss the proposed budget, and the General Council held several general informational sessions. On December 4, 1917, the residents approved the neighborhood budget of $35,049, which represented approximately three-fourths of the total money collected by the NSUO. This budget covered the rental of the headquarters, the health-center physicians' fees, the salaries of the executives and their assistants, the salaries of the block workers, all operating expenses, and a number of miscellaneous expenses. At a meeting in early December, following the wishes of the NSUO, the MBSUO adopted a preventive child-health program as its pilot project. On December 17, 1917, the MBSUO launched its infant-welfare program.

After the preparatory training sessions on the importance of preventive health care, the block workers held a number of discussions with the members of their blocks on the subject of infant health care. Then they canvassed their blocks, house by house, to locate the infants in their area. Nurses followed the block workers, met with each infant's mother, and encouraged her to attend the examination sessions. The health center soon became very popular. As babies were born, they automatically came under the station's care. By the end of 1918, the nursing staff had made 5,388 visits to 576 babies, and of the 576, over two-thirds had received full medical examinations. By 1919, there existed in Mohawk-Brighton, one observer noted, "a markedly greater interest and intelligence about child care."

The success of the postnatal medical service affected the medical and nursing services offered at the health station. The enthusiasm of the MBSUO's staff, and the apparent success of the infant-health campaign, heightened the neighborhood mothers' receptiveness to the advantages of preventive health care. During 1918, block workers reported an increasing number of requests to extend health programs. By 1920, in response to this demand, the MBSUO offered prenatal care, general bedside nursing, medical examinations of all preschool children, and supervision of local tuberculosis cases, in addition to postnatal examinations.

Two unforeseen events in 1918 tested the efficiency of the Social Unit Organization: the Children's Year campaign and the influenza epidemic. Early in 1918, the U.S. Children's Bureau announced its decision to sponsor a nationwide campaign, Children's Year, to direct public attention to the problem of correctible defects and to the advantages of periodic medical examinations. In cooperation with the Women's Committee of the Council of National Defense, the Children's Bureau launched its campaign on April 6, 1918, to weigh and measure as many preschool children as possible. After discussing the national program with their block members, block workers announced their support for the Children's Year crusade. To generate even more enthusiasm for the weight and measurement program, and to promote the goal of 100 percent participation in preschool examinations, the MBSUO General Council sponsored a Children's Year Parade, complete with ponies, marching bands, and floats. Because of the enthusiasm generated by the festivities, and the familiarity of the block workers with their constituents, the MBSUO was able to send a complete list of the district's preschool population to the Children's Bureau by the end of April. By July, 1,075 of the 1,173 children under six had received medical examinations. And, in accordance with the social unit's attempt to work with the doctors of the neighborhood, the 640 children who were found to have physical difficulties were referred to their family physicians for the proper treatment.

The outbreak of the influenza epidemic in the fall of 1918 provided the second opportunity for the MBSUO to demonstrate the efficiency of its organizational apparatus. Influenza first appeared in a mild form in the East during the spring. By the beginning of September, Massachusetts health officers noted an increasing number of cases of "Spanish influenza" in Boston. Following the main east-west lines of transportation, the virus soon began to spread throughout the rest of the country. Before the epidemic officially hit the Midwest, the block workers and the nurses had reported to the MBSUO health station an alarming increase in the number of colds and sore throats. On the advice of the Nurses' and Physicians' councils, the General Council decided to initiate preventive measures against the influenzalike symptoms before the virus "officially" hit Cincinnati. The Nurses' and Physicians' councils drafted a handbill announcing the possible danger of an outbreak of influenza in the Cincinnati area, giving instructions on the prevention and treatment of grippe and stressing the importance of prompt medical attention.

Within twenty-four hours, the block workers delivered a copy of the handbill to each family in the Mohawk-Brighton district. Armed with this information, the neighborhood residents were better prepared than were most Cincinnatians when the epidemic struck the Queen City in late September. After a study of all the influenza cases reported to the Health Department, the social unit's medical and nursing staffs found that the "percentage of cases per thousand population was great, if not greater, in the Mohawk-Brighton district than in the city as a whole." But, despite the large number of cases reported in the social unit neighborhood, the area had a lower death rate than that of the city as a whole. The mortality rate from influenza and pneumonia per thousand population for the rest of the city of Cincinnati for the months of October, November, and December stood at 4.10 per thousand compared with 2.26 per thousand for the social unit district. Although the medical and nursing staffs recognized that they could not say with absolute certainty that the unit organization was responsible for the lower death rate, the fact that the district organization "proved to be more efficient in the prompter and more complete reporting of cases, in the quick dissemination of information about the epidemic, and in the care provided by the nurses, block workers and physicians indicated that the neighborhood organization, if nothing else, certainly facilitated the saving of lives."

During 1918 and 1919, the Mohawk-Brighton Social Unit Organization established one of the most comprehensive neighborhood health-care programs in the country. From the establishment of its initial infant-health service, the neighborhood Social Unit Organization brought trained health personnel into a "working relationship" with the citizens of the district and stimulated a "local health consciousness." The MBSUO demonstrated that geographical localization and administrative coordination, complemented by the social organization of the neighborhood, resulted in a health-care program that could meet the needs of a community. By focusing on the interaction between health experts and the "people," the MBSUO fostered nearly 100-percent health care and revealed the importance of mobilizing the entire community in the pursuit of health and, more broadly, social welfare.

By nourishing the interaction between medical and social-welfare personnel and residents, the MBSUO helped to improve significantly the overall health of the Mohawk-Brighton district. Courtenay Dinwiddie and Dr. A. G. Kriedler, head of the MBSUO's Physicians' Council, concluded that the "unusual features" of the social unit's health-care operation were responsible for the improved level of neighborhood health care. According to Dinwiddie and Kriedler, the fact that the necessity for many of the services offered at the social unit center was not determined "by an outside group," but rather by neighborhood-based medical and social-welfare personnel in conjunction with neighborhood residents, increased local participation in the social unit's programs. In addition, because the nurses and the physicians spent a great deal of time explaining the nature of the services offered and their expected effect on the health of the community, many residents understood and appreciated the importance of preventive health care.

In his study of the health programs offered by the MBSUO, Haven Emerson, a former health officer of New York City, found that the neighborhood organization had produced a number of "tangible accomplishments." Emerson noted that the MBSUO provided necessary prenatal advice to a very high percentage of expectant mothers and supervised all babies born in the district. He found that the physical examinations of the neighborhood preschool population uncovered a number of "correctible defects," and that many of the children with the "defects" received corrective treatment. Emerson reported that during the influenza epidemic, the "prompt and efficient nursing service" of the MBSUO helped to reduce the number of deaths from the virus. In general, he concluded that the mothers and fathers of the district had become "educated to an alertness, an understanding, and an interest in the relation of health and its maintenance to their children's welfare, and that the medical needs of the district had been better met than before."

But, despite the social unit's success in the area of neighborhood health care, it failed to survive the antiradical hysteria that followed World War I. In March 1919, Cincinnati's mayor, John Galvin, accused the MBSUO of expressing an alien political philosophy and declared that, as such, it represented "a menace to our municipal government and was but one step removed from Bolshevism." Investigations by the Council of Social Agencies and the Helen S. Trounstine Foundation, made during the previous summer when Director of Public Welfare James White questioned the "Americanism" of the social unit experiment, exonerated the MBSUO of these charges. At the same time, Cincinnati's health officer, William Peters, after observing the work of the social unit health center, feared that the health programs sponsored by the MBSUO would undercut the work of the Health Deparment. Peters withdrew his support from the social unit experiment and campaigned actively against the expansion of this type of health-care program. These charges slowed the neighborhood work as the MBSUO battled for its existence. Despite the favorable outcome of a referendum held to determine support for the plan in Mohawk-Brighton, the city withdrew its support. Without increased expenditure forthcoming from the NSUO, the MBSUO could not survive. Despite a gallant effort on the part of the residents to raise enough money to support the MBSUO health center, in November 1920, the Babies Milk Fund Association, an agency concerned with the reduction of infant mortality, assumed control of the MBSUO's headquarters, equipment, and infant health work.

When Phillips left Cincinnati, he did not abandon the social unit idea. The National Social Unit Organization remained intact, and Phillips began to work closely with the NSUO in New York City to promote the establishment of more social unit-style community organizations. In December 1919, the NSUO entered into an agreement with the New York City Community Councils (New York City's reorganized Community Councils of National Defense) and made plans to establish another social unit laboratory in New York City. But, within little more than a year, both the New York City Community Councils and the NSUO disbanded after a series of financial disagreements. The dissolution of the NSUO and of the New York City Community Councils in 1921 represented more than just the end of an experiment; it marked the beginning of a major shift in community organization practice from democratic, collaborative neighborhood schemes to task-oriented, problem-solving activities led by professionals.

The Social Unit Organization illustrated, according to social-welfare historian Roy Lubove, "community organization in the years when its exponents believed literally in the possibility of a social harmony that transcended the fragmentation of American life." It represented that part of the larger community organization movement that constituted, according to Eduard C. Lindeman, a prominent social-welfare theorist,

> a conscious effort on the part of the community to control its affairs democratically and to secure the highest service from its specialists, organizations, agencies and institutions by means of recognized interrelatedness.

Like other community organizations of that period, such as the settlements, the school centers, and the Community Councils of National Defense, the social unit theory of organization rested upon two basic premises: the "wholeness of the environment," and the importance of "neighborhood in nationbuilding." Community organizers during the first two decades of the twentieth century stressed the totality of the world around them. And, like others who promoted community organizing during that period, Phillips based his plan on the belief that "America was made up of the sum total of thousands of neighborhoods," and that "neither the city nor the nation could be understood nor their problems met" unless the process began in the neighborhood. Moreover, they emphasized not what the social technician could do for the citizen but, instead, the joint responsibility of the citizen and the specialist in discerning local needs and meeting them through consultation and cooperation. Theoretically, the city and its neighborhoods represented a "cluster of interlacing communities."

Of all the attempts to organize communities during the first two decades of the twentieth century, Phillips's Social Unit Plan represents the most celebrated attempt to facilitate communication and cooperation between the "interlacing communities," despite the fact that the experimentation period proved too short to yield conclusive results. Probably in no other community were plans and policies for the neighborhood so painstakingly submitted in advance to the people of a neighborhood. Most decisions rested on public understanding and approval. The residents of Mohawk-Brighton studied some of their own problems, determined community needs, and conducted the proposed services themselves. The unit organization stimulated local initiative so that, as the life of the unit progressed, the establishment of some of the services, such as the prenatal service and the bedside nursing program, was not initiated by the founders of the plan.

In theory, the experiment sought to demonstrate the feasibility of cooperation between "specialists" and "citizens" and to illustrate the practicality of democratically run health services. The novel feature of the organization, the division of function between the Occupational Council and the Citizens' Council, made it possible for various elements of the community to make substantial contributions. The Citizens' Council encouraged a general community consciousness and neighborhood spirit. The block workers developed an ability to diagnose needs and then to direct, when called upon, the implementation of the programs. And the Occupational Council brought together the skilled groups in the area and fostered an understanding of the interrelatedness of their services. It eliminated duplicated efforts and overlapping services and tended to elevate the standards of service rendered to the community.

In operation, however, the social unit fell short of success. The project had some serious deficiencies. The Block Councils, while supporting the block workers, failed to operate as an effective part of the organizational machinery. The councils rarely assumed responsibility for carrying out policies for the block workers. For the most part, the block workers bypassed the councils and dealt directly with the residents of their block. This only added to the block workers' inordinately heavy burden, which included canvassing the neighborhood and developing programs and policies in the Citizens' Council. On the occupational side, not all groups were as well integrated into the organizational structure as were the physicians, nurses, and social workers. The project never achieved widespread acceptance. Cooperation was hampered, especially near the end of the experiment, by those groups, such as the Health Department, that felt threatened by social unit-style activities. Ultimately, and most importantly, the unit organization failed to sustain itself financially.

Despite these and other organizational problems, the Social Unit Organization demonstrated that it was possible to democratically organize a neighborhood to facilitate the identification and resolution of local needs. Residents did discover neighborhood problems and did participate in the solutions of those problems as never before. The social unit stands as a "bold effort" to achieve neighborhood organization through the nurturing of an "organic" relationship between the citizen and the specialist, and it attemped, although with mixed success, to foster a civic consciousness that identified with and yet transcended the neighborhood and incorporated it into the whole of the American experience.

The Social Unit Plan

Robert A. Woods

A plan of community organization which has been on trial for two and a half years in what is known as the Mohawk-Brighton district of Cincinnati, Ohio, may be extended to other districts and cities or applied throughout one municipality in 1920 if plans under discussion by the National Social Unit Organization mature.

Mr. Franklin K. Lane, of President Wilson's Cabinet, who recently became chairman of the National Social Unit Organization, describes the social unit as "a plan for bringing Government closer to people's lives, developing the neighborhood as a unit of the city, State, and Nation, and creating for the people the municipal and civic life fulfilling their desires."

This the Organization seeks to do by creating a neighborhood administration representative, first, of all of the people, divided geographically into units of a hundred families, with elected "block committees" and "block executives," and second, of the various skilled groups, federated together into a planning body for the community, initiating programmes, submitting them to the people for ratification or rejection, and putting them into effect through the intimate block organization. Representatives of the blocks and representatives of the skilled groups join in a central community council. It is claimed for this system of neighborhood administration that it provides for the utilization of the highest type of expert skill, and tends to secure the constant participation of an increasingly large number of people in the conduct of their own affairs.

In the plan as it has been tested in the Mohawk-Brighton district every block has been organized and block committees and representatives elected by a very fair proportion of the entire adult citizenship. Physicians, social workers, teachers, nurses, trade-union representatives, business men, recreation workers, and clergymen have come together as groups, and have elected representatives to the "Occupational Council," a body co-operating with the representatives of the blocks. Together these bodies have planned and carried out a remarkably comprehensive programme of preventive health work, have vitalized recreation, made a beginning in the establishment of a unique and significant system of collecting community statistics, started a community newspaper edited and controlled by an elected editorial board, improved housing conditions, and brought into activity scores of people hitherto passive in community affairs. Simultaneously there has been a marked increase in attendance at night schools, attendance at school social centers has increased, and representatives of agencies which had been working in the district, both before and after the community orga-

SOURCE: Robert A. Woods, *The Outlook,* vol. 122 (July 23, 1919), pp. 460, 462.

nized, agree that neighborliness and general community pride and intelligence have noticeably increased. The most clear-cut demonstration of the value of this form of organization in carrying out a complete programme in any field has been made in public health. Local physicians have opened a diagnostic clinic, and through the co-operation of the block organization have given medical examinations to over eighty percent of all children of pre-school age in the district. Nurses, backed by an organized community and assisted by lay representatives in the blocks, have put every baby under nursing care. During the influenza epidemic the district organization demonstrated its superiority over the rest of the city both in the prompter and more complete reporting of cases, and in a markedly lowered death rate—less than half that of the immediately contiguous territory and of the city as a whole. When the community took cases of tuberculosis under its general nursing system, the number under care increased four hundred percent, and it has been possible through this organization to reach a remarkably large proportion of all expectant mothers.

The plans of the National Social Unit Organization include the rounding out of the Mohawk-Brighton experiment, the building up of a large National membership representative of territories and skilled groups, the valuation of the results accomplished in the experimental period, and the holding of a National conference at which plans for extension shall be made.

CHAPTER 4

New Era Thought and Policy

INTRODUCTION

In the decade of the 1920s, Republicans promised a "New Era" in which economic prosperity and social betterment was to be brought to all Americans. Enlightened businessmen, responsible labor representatives, knowledgeable experts, and governmental leaders, all working together, would fulfill the promise of American life.

The clearest advocate of this philosophy was Herbert Hoover, who stood in this decade as a genuine American hero. He represented the fulfillment of the American dream: orphaned at the age of eight, Hoover rose to become a millionaire in his own right through hard work and good investments in international mining conglomerates. World War I brought Herbert Hoover to the public's attention. After heading the Belgium Relief program, Hoover returned to the United States in 1917 to accept President Woodrow Wilson's appointment to head the United States Food Administration. At the war's end, Hoover further enchanced his reputation as a humanitarian and a progressive when he directed the American Relief Administration, which saved post-Armistice Europe from chaos by providing vast quantities of food to the continent.

Hoover's name was already a household word when he entered the Warren Harding administration in 1921 as Secretary of Commerce. As Secretary of Commerce, Hoover articulated a progressive vision of the federal government's role in promoting economic and social advancement for the nation. Hoover envisaged the federal government as playing an active, but not dominant, role in facilitating cooperation within American industry and between business and labor. He maintained that one central task should be that of bringing expertise to bear on the social and economic problems of the day. Hoover's conception of the federal government, described by historians as the "associative" state, was that of an umpire and regulator, encouraging cooperation and acting when necessary to maintain equal opportunity. He stated that "government can and must cure abuses," and that government would do best to "encourage and assist in the creation and development of institutions controlled by our citizens and evolved by themselves from their own experience and directed in a sense of trusteeship of public interest." While Hoover projected a different role for the federal government than had been held by nineteenth-century conservatives, he continued to maintain a profound faith in traditional American values of individualism, self-reliance, and voluntarism.

Hoover's social philosophy found expression throughout his tenure as Secretary of Commerce (1921–1928) and the first years of his presidency. In 1921 he invited the nation's business, agricultural, and labor leaders to an economic conference in Washington, D.C. to address the severe problems of unemployment caused by wartime demobilization and a postwar depression. Following the conference, state and local committees were organized throughout the country to solicit relief funds, encourage public work projects, and maintain employment within industry. In subsequent years, Hoover called over three thousand such conferences or committees to address economic, social, and industrial problems.

Hoover's accomplishments were impressive. His progressive voice in the Harding and Coolidge administrations enhanced his reputation as the good humanitarian, the great engineer, and the visionary cabinet officer. He spoke in favor of private unemployment insurance, a child labor amendment, and shorter work hours in the steel industry. He promoted the development of the Railway Labor Mediation Board, created by Congress in 1926. He took an active interest in the housing question and played a key role in organizing the American Child Health Association. In the spring of 1927, Hoover rushed to the Mississippi Valley to organize relief for the victims of one of the great floods in the nation's history. He mobilized federal, state, local, and private agencies to provide relief for the thousands whose lives had been washed away in the flood.

His vision for the New Era, however progressive in its sentiment, embodied a deep belief in traditional American values of individualism, voluntarism, and local initiative. As a consequence, Hoover maintained a profound conviction that the federal government's role in social policy should be limited to that of a coordinator of industry, labor, and local efforts. His widely read *American Individualism,* published in 1922, spoke eloquently of the need to preserve American liberty through government self-restraint. What made the American system so unique was its faith in the balance of powers, a division in powers between federal government and state government, and in local initiative.

For these reasons, Hoover became a major force in the community chest movement of the 1920s. Within a decade, community chests multiplied from 40 cities in 1919 to nearly 350 cities by 1929. The movement promoted local fundraising efforts while offering a means to rationalize the distribution of charitable funds. The federal government's role in social policy remained relatively small. The government provided small matching grants for vocational rehabilitation and for maternity and infant hygiene under the Sheppard-Towner Act of 1921. This measure, however, was to lapse in 1929 when Congress refused to appropriate the necessary funds for the program.

As a consequence, social welfare remained for the most part local, private, and voluntaristic.

In the 1920s, large corporations were assigned the responsibilty for establishing pension plans, safety and health insurance benefits, and stable employment. "Welfare capitalism," as it would be called, was designed to stabilize a work force that before the war had experienced high rates of labor turnover and shortages of skilled, experienced workers. In the 1920s, large corporations experimented with various employee plans to ensure a loyal work force.

In these years, most social workers believed private philanthropic services were more efficient than government. Social workers expected the government to provide assistance primarily to the permanently dependent, while the social workers' role was to investigate the poor and to offer individual counseling to those groups needing assistance. Influenced by recent trends in psychiatry, many social workers expressed new awareness of individual adjustment to social problems. Given these views—progressive action on the local level and limited fereral involvement in social policy—it wasn't surprising that most social workers, including Jane Addams, endorsed Herbert Hoover's presidential nomination in 1928.

Edward D. Berkowitz and Kim McQuaid explore the rhetoric and the practice of social policy in the 1920s through the federal government's efforts to fund state vocational rehabilitation programs. They maintain that in these years the federal government placed a heavy emphasis on "efficiency" as a criterion for judging the success of social programs. Distinctions between private and public welfare programs continued to be made throughout the decade, usually in favor of private programs. The federal government therefore provided only modest matching funds to support child health and vocational rehabilitation programs on the state level. Private groups continued to act as the chief providers of welfare in the United States. Federal support of vocational rehabilitation programs, Berkowitz and McQuaid argue, shows the clear limitations of social policy in the 1920s, as most states did little more than set up small pilot demonstration programs.

In "Public Welfare and Our Democratic Institutions," Joseph K. Hart, an editor of *The Survey*, articulates the case for maintaining local control of welfare programs. Although he accepts the government's role in maintaining "the general welfare," he feels that not every welfare program is compatible with America's democratic institution. He states that "humanitarian" public welfare programs can "seriously obstruct the application of scientific knowledge to the solution of the problems of social and racial survival." Moreover, he argues, centralized control of welfare will subvert democracy by "saving the unfit." Movements for centralizing public welfare, Hart concludes, must be offset by movements for "decentralizing intelligence, opportunity, and individual responsibility." Hart's essay captures the argument for "scientific" applications to public welfare and for localism and voluntarism in social policy.

Further Readings

Guy Alchon, *The Invisible Hand of Planning: Capitalism, Social Science, and the State in the 1920s* (Princeton: Princeton University Press, 1985); and Donald T. Critchlow, *The Brookings Institution, 1916–1952: Expertise and the Public Interest in a Democratic Society* (DeKalb, Ill.: Northern Illinois University Press, 1985).

Loren Baritz, *The Servants of Power: A History of the Use of Social Science in American Industry* (New York: Wiley, 1965).

Herbert Hoover and the faith placed in expertise in these years are explored in Ellis W. Hawley, *The Great War and the Search for a Modern Order: A History of the American People and their Institutions, 1917–1933* (New York: St. Martins Press, 1979).

The promotion of corporate welfare programs in this period is discussed by Stuart D. Brandes, *American Welfare Capitalism, 1880–1940* (Chicago: University of Chicago Press, 1976), and Edward D. Berkowitz and Kim McQuaid, *Creating the Welfare State: The Political Economy of Twentieth-Century Reform* (New York: Praeger, 1980).

Bureaucrats as "Social Engineers": Federal Welfare Programs in Herbert Hoover's America

Edward D. Berkowitz and Kim McQuaid

At the end of World War I, federal administrators faced an uncertain future. Mobilization had demonstrated the possibilities of non-market management of the nation's economy, but the Wilson administration proved unwilling to transfer wartime planning into peacetime settings. Washington bureaucrats resumed established roles as expediters and coordinators of actions initiated by states, localities, or private groups—notably businessmen.

In the decade following the Versailles Peace Conference, however, federal officials cautiously expanded their social welfare responsibilities. Under the terms of legislation passed during and immediately after the war, modest amounts of federal "matching funds" were supplied to the states to maintain the health of children; to rehabilitate disabled workers; and to create vocational education programs. Previously, war veterans and Indians had been the only recipients of federal funds on a regular basis. The 1920s witnessed a growth in federal willingness to supply public monies, through the states, to new welfare clienteles.

The resulting federal welfare programs were administered by tiny bureaucracies of fiscal control. Handfuls of federal officials dispensed funds to illustrate the effectiveness of a small number of welfare activities which were legitimized as profitable investments which increased social efficiency and decreased waste. These new programs did not displace private groups as the chief welfare providers in America's industrial society. In fact, they furthered cooperation between such groups and the State.

Herbert Hoover's career exemplified the cooperative aspects of federal welfare efforts in the 1920s. Paradoxically, Hoover saw himself as both a "planner" and as an anti-statist. His idea of the federal government's proper role resembled the administration of an airport hotel and convention center. Private citizens from across the country met at the hotel, discussed their problems, and flew home with the solutions in their briefcases. The government ran the hotel, encouraged people to attend meetings, but was not responsible for interests left unattended. In this manner, public power helped businessmen and others arrive at—and depart with—private understandings.

SOURCE: Edward D. Berkowitz and Kim McQuaid, *American Journal of Economics and Sociology*, Vol. 39, No. 4 (October 1980), pp. 321–34.

Hoover, then, believed that the federal government should "serve as a midwife to a new, non-statist commonwealth" composed of private interest groups. The private parties involved in the process would then create new organizations and techniques to spread enlightened ideas. These "socially responsible" standards they created would serve as the key element in defining an American social welfare system.

FEDERAL WELFARE PROGRAMS

Unlike many of his fellow citizens, Herbert Hoover lived in a logically complete—even insulated—world. Yet even he believed that the federal government owed special obligations to well-defined disadvantaged groups, children and disabled workers in particular. Hoover supported unsuccessful efforts to pass a constitutional amendment banning child labor in the 1920s and assisted the implementation of federal vocational rehabilitation, vocational education, and infant and maternal health programs. These programs represented more than institutional manifestations of Hoover's personal emotions; they also interfaced neatly with the political and ideological environment of the post-war era.

Vocational education was the first of the new federal programs. Created by the passage of the Smith-Hughes Act of 1917, federal support of vocational education reflected a longstanding concern to provide training which meshed with industry's growing importance in America's occupational structure. Vocational education, indeed, was generally conceived of by its supporters as a public sector counterpart to the managerial training provided by increasing numbers of corporations and universities in the private sector.

As was the case with many reforms successfully advocated during the Progressive Era, the vocational education movement depended upon a coalition of business and labor interests for its success. Both the National Association of Manufacturers and the American Federation of Labor cooperated with a pre-war Commission on National Aid to Vocational Education whose very existence owed much to their efforts. The Commission's report, published in 1914, stressed that vocational education conserved labor and contributed to overall economic "efficiency." As such, it was a legitimate recipient of federal funds.

The major sticking point in carrying out the Commission's recommendations concerned the propriety of using federal money to finance what many still regarded as a local welfare function. Despite a long tradition of granting federal lands for public schools and agricultural colleges, some congressmen saw federal grants-in-aid as a real threat to local self-sufficiency. They feared (rightly, as it turned out) that creation of an ongoing program of federal grants would be a first step in effecting a permanent shift from local to federal control within the American welfare system.

World War I, however, facilitated the passage of vocational education legislation. Emergency mobilization and a cessation of immigration from Europe heightened the need for trained manpower and made enhanced vocational training programs seem more urgent than ever before. With the strong backing of organized America, Congress legislated federally-subsidized vocational education. War had legitimized an important welfare innovation.

The other two components of the federal welfare system of the 1920s, vocational rehabilitation and infant and maternal hygiene, also owed their existence to a wartime political environment. Civilian vocational rehabilitation marked an extension of state-run workers compensation programs into new areas at federal expense. The argument for rehabilitation programs as a necessary adjunct to workers compensation began with the notion that modern medical technology and vocational training techniques made it possible to do more than compensate the victims of industrial accidents. Much of an injured person's productive capacity could be restored through the use of rehabilitation procedures. Since the injured worker and society at large would reap the benefits of rehabilitation, its costs would be charged to society, or the injured themselves, instead of to the employers—who paid the costs under workers compensation. The injured, however, were likely to be in relatively poor economic condition at the time that their rehabilitation was initiated. So, vocational rehabilitation programs required new sources of public funds.

The founding of the International Association of Industrial Accident Boards and Commissions (IAIABC) in 1913 provided state workers compensation officials with a forum to lobby for public funds for rehabilitation. States responded to these efforts. In 1918, for example, Massachusetts authorized its State Industrial Accident Board to provide vocational training and job-placement services for the industrially disabled. Not satisfied with such scattered efforts, the IAIABC began lobbying for a national industrial rehabilitation law.

War facilitated such endeavors. In 1918, Congress passed a rehabilitation law for veterans. Veterans, who had long enjoyed federal "workers compensation" payments in the form of disability pensions, would now receive vocational training from a new Federal Board for Vocational Education and "physical restoration" services from medical agencies designated by the U.S. Surgeon General's Office.

On July 1, 1918, the two full-time employees of the new Federal Board of Vocational Education awaited the first injured veterans. The veterans tore the doors down. By December, 1919, 21,000 were involved in federally-funded vocational training. By August of 1921, this number had risen to 113,000. A total of 296,940 veterans had been declared eligible for such training.

The veterans' experience provided the lobbyists of the IAIABC with the opportunity to argue that if federal rehabilitation services were being provided to veterans, they should also be given to those who had served their nation on the home front. Observing the veterans' rehabilitation act in operation, the International Association noted that although the war had shocked the nation into rehabilitating traditional recipients of federal welfare services, an even greater need existed to restore "industry's cripples." This logic proved persuasive enough to enable Congress to initiate a policy of federal grants-in-aid to state bureaus of vocational education to establish vocational rehabilitation programs.

A year after ratifying a civilian vocational rehabilitation law in 1920, Congress passed an infant and maternal health program in the form of the Sheppard-Towner Act. This was the last of the three federal welfare programs created during the 1920s. Infant and maternal health was less a product of wartime emergency than either vocational education or vocational rehabilitation; it was a political response to a new force in American politics: women. Sheppard-Towner's provision of federal grants-in-aid for state projects designed to decrease infant and maternal mortality demonstrated congressional responsiveness to its newly-enfranchised constituents.

The three new welfare programs undertaken by federal administrators were modest in scope. In 1924, four physicians, a nurse, an accountant, a secretary, and a stenographer composed the entire staff of the Washington office of the infant and maternal health program. As late as 1928, 96 percent of total federal welfare expenditures went to war veterans. The remaining 4 percent of expenditures—totalling $30,000,000—represented "less than 6 percent of the comparable [public welfare] spendings of the country as a whole." In 1928, federal bureaucrats disbursed only $1,585,000 to promote vocational rehabilitation and infant and maternal health combined. A federal government which spent nine *cents* per capita on civilian welfare expenditures in 1913, spent only 25 cents per capita fifteen years later.

Barriers to the expansion of direct federal welfare activities remained strong. All the welfare programs created during the 1920s operated on the principle of federal grants-in-aid to the states. This meant that state governments, which had to match federal grants dollar-for-dollar, spent the increased welfare appropriations. Each of the programs involved state provision of services to welfare recipients. These people received advice or training from a professional counsellor or teacher, not money from the federal government. Further, all federal welfare programs relied on private labor markets for their ultimate effectiveness. Welfare recipients could remain on the rolls of programs such as vocational rehabilitation for only a limited time period. No expectation existed that the federal government would provide continuing protection against life's hazards. In fact, federal programs did not even guarantee that all who could benefit from them would do so. Federal programs served more to demonstrate the social effectiveness of a particular welfare activity, such as rehabilitation or the pasteurization of milk for infants, rather than to provide permanent federal support for these activities.

With all these limitations, the new programs did escalate the level of Washington's social welfare responsibility. No longer would the federal government be limited to supervising state minimum standard laws or providing for its own wards such as soldiers and Indians. Beginning in the 1920s, Washington began to become a source of funds for states to initiate new welfare activities.

THE FEDERAL PROGRAMS IN ACTION

The new federal programs, then, occupied a unique place within America's social welfare system. The twin elements of cooperation and efficiency characterized government welfare activities and linked federal programs with the informal web of activities undertaken by trade associations and other private interest groups. Federal vocational education officials worked with organized business to improve the efficiency of employees. The infant and maternal health program, for its part, brought officials of private public health associations to communities to explain the latest in medical and sanitary technique. Federal rehabilitation administrators urged their peers in the states to undertake "organized cooperation" to "secure in each community, city, or county, some clearing agency which will take the responsibility of locating, reporting, and investigating cases." State agencies might establish rehabilitation councils and place "the president or secretary of a manufacturers association, a Rotary, or a Kiwanis Club" in charge of them.

Along with such cooperative activity, each of the federal programs struggled to meet the decade's standards of efficiency in conducting its internal affairs and external activities. The well-run public program was perceived to resemble the well-conducted business: it performed its operations at the least possible cost, and created products society valued. This desire for program efficiency through businesslike administration was the characteristic which most clearly defined the 1920s style of public welfare.

In the case of vocational rehabilitation, the drive for efficiency on the part of public administrators was so influential that it transformed the program into something quite different from the public service envisioned by its creators. As the program became more and more committed to efficient administration, it moved further and further away from its original mission of cooperating with state-run workers compensation agencies to rehabilitate industrial accident victims. By the end of the 1920s, indeed, workers compensation and vocational rehabilitation had evolved into completely separate programs. Their separation illustrated the differences between Progressive Era and New Era social welfare programs.

When the vocational rehabilitation program began in 1920, federal and state administrators stated its objectives in both humanitarian and economic terms. The program's virtue lay precisely in the fact that it combined the humanitarian and the cost-effective rationales for the treatment of the disabled. It cost less to cure a disability than to support one; and rehabilitation promoted a "fitness to work" which was one of the preconditions of both economic efficiency and personal satisfaction.

Within a few years, however, the rhetoric used to justify the vocational rehabilitation program changed. The efficiency objective was more explicitly emphasized. Program officials now argued that the "efficiency problem" should determine the course of social policy. This view meant that program activities should be considered in terms of "securing the greatest social return for a dollar expended."

The triumph of a cost-benefit approach caused growing friction between the workers compensation and vocational rehabilitation programs. This phenomenon occurred despite the fact that workers compensation officials in IAIABC, more than any other group, had pressured Congress to start a federal vocational rehabilitation program. The vocational rehabilitation law, in fact, mandated that each state furnish a plan of cooperation between its rehabilitation and compensation agencies as a precondition for receiving federal aid. The Federal Board for Vocational Education, which administered the rehabilitation program, reiterated that "the work of vocational rehabilitation is supplementary to that of compensating injured workers."

In one of the Federal Board's annual reports, it illustrated how the relationship between vocational rehabilitation and workers compensation should proceed. A piece of wood flew into a young carpenter's eye, blinding him in that eye. Since the accident occured at work, the carpenter received medical treatment for his injured eye through workers compensation. At the same time, the state's rehabilitation agency helped the carpenter retain the vision in his remaining eye and counselled him on ways to adjust to his impairment. The Federal Board found the carpenter's case "particularly interesting" since it demonstrated "where the work of the bureau of rehabilitation takes up what is left incomplete by the workmen's compensation bureau."

But a part of the Federal Board of Vocational Education's interest in the carpenter stemmed from his uniqueness. Few other workers compensation recipients made such a smooth transition from compensation to rehabilitation. If, for example, the carpenter had been injured in Georgia in 1921 he would have had to come to the attention of one of the state's two vocational rehabilitation caseworkers—only one of whom worked full time. The process of rehabilitation itself was a painstaking matter of direct interviews between the client and the counsellors. "There is no such thing as rehabilitation in general," the federal office noted, "It is always rehabilitation in particular." Because of rehabilitation's nature, each counsellor could handle only 75 to 100 cases at any one time. In Georgia the two counsellors managed to see only 207 people in fiscal year 1921. If the carpenter was one of the lucky 207, he was still faced with formidable barriers before actually receiving rehabilitation. The counsellors might tell him that he was "not susceptible" of rehabilitation (as they told five other people that year), or that he was not eligible for program services.

In fact, of the 207 people who managed to see the State of Georgia's rehabilitation counsellors in fiscal 1921, only 12 received some form of vocational training and only three eventually obtained a job as a result of that training. In fiscal 1922 the story was the same. The same two counsellors saw 66 new cases. Three of these were deemed not eligible; eight were deemed not susceptible; and twenty decided to reject the agency's services. Despite the cooperation of private charities, the Red Cross, the State Board of Health, and the Georgia Industrial Commission, the Georgia rehabilitation program hardly made a dent in dealing with the disability problem in the state—whether such disabilities originated from industrial accidents or from any other souce.

The situation was not much different in other states. The State of New York depended upon two full-time directors and ten other employees to run its rehabilitation program. In fiscal 1921, they closed 46 cases. Four of these cases rehabilitated themselves; 17 cases rejected the agency's services; and five were declared not eligible for services. In the nation as a whole, state vocational rehabilitation programs consistently rehabilitated less than a third of the people who applied for their services.

Federal welfare bureaucrats tried to put an optimistic gloss on affairs. By the end of the 1920s, they simply stopped issuing statistics on the numbers of people turned away by state rehabilitation agencies. The statistics concentrated instead on the number of people such agencies had successfully rehabilitated. During the 1920s, this annual calculus of felicity reached a high of 5,852 cases in 1925. By the Federal Board's own admission, this accomplishment came at a time when between 50,000 and 70,000 potential rehabilitation cases were being created every year.

Because of limited staff, funds, and influence, the Washington office of the federal rehabilitation program could do little to improve the situation. An average of six people worked in this office during the 1920s—five of whom spent most of their time on the road. One federal regional supervisor was in charge of overseeing program operations in the states of Massachusetts, Connecticut, New York, New Jersey, Pennsylvania, and Virginia. The chief responsibilities of the federal office for vocational rehabilitation were to inform Congress of the program's progress in the states and to fight to maintain its small congressional appropriation.

Even these modest tasks proved difficult to accomplish for a program which, throughout the decade, never managed to spend all its annual allotments. This failure stemmed from the requirement that states receiving federal grants for vocational rehabilitation match Washington's contributions dollar-for-dollar. As the federal office explained: "There are some states in which the rehabilitation program has not been sufficiently developed to require the expenditure of all available funds." Congress became so annoyed that in the first half of fiscal 1925 it simply failed to appropriate any money at all for rehabilitation. Federal rehabilitation officials, however, refused to intervene in state programs in order to get them to put up more money. "Each state," the Washington office announced, "has its own problems and must establish its own policies and procedures in order to deal with its problems effectively."

The vocational rehabilitation program, therefore, reached so few people and was conducted on such a small scale that each successful rehabilitation resembled a demonstration or pilot project more than it formed part of an ongoing social process. Rehabilitation was not conceived of as a social service in which the federal government helped finance the nation's disabled citizens; it was a sporadic, widely dispersed activity which rationed its available resources to dramatize its welfare potential. Through the vocational rehabilitation program, state and federal bureaucrats publicized an efficient way of dealing with welfare problems in much the same way as the Department of Commerce publicized a new production technique. In both cases, the private sector had the obligation, a moral obligation reinforced by its cost-reducing, efficiency-promoting possibilities, to spread this technique across the entire spectrum of the nation's industrial order.

THE "PROFITS" FROM GOVERNMENT "INVESTMENT"

It was precisely this pilot project, efficiency-oriented nature of the vocational rehabilitation program which obliterated any chances for a cooperative relationship between it and the workers compensation programs established during the Progressive Era. In the states of California and Ohio, for example, workers compensation officials viewed the arrival of vocational rehabilitation optimistically—in the belief that rehabilitation would serve an adjunct role in improving compensation procedures. The California workers compensation bureau dumped 1,580 cases into the new rehabilitation agency's lap. Of these, only 280 reached the stage of vocational training. Meanwhile, Ohio workers compensation authorities were having their own troubles. Data that they accumulated on the origins of rehabilitation clients in their state showed that only a third of the caseload in Ohio's rehabilitation bureau came from the workers compensation agency. National statistics told the same story of declining interest in compensation clients on the part of rehabilitation agencies. Less than half the individuals successfully rehabilitated in 1927, 1928, 1929, and 1930 had disabilities which originated in employment accidents.

The growing separation between the caseloads of workers compensation and vocational rehabilitation agencies reflected important differences between Progressive Era and New Era welfare practices. Like other Progressive Era programs, workers compensation asked private employers to meet a set of industrial standards and to pay for the increased costs, if any, themselves. By contrast, vocational rehabilitation spent money from the general revenue of the public sector to demonstrate rehabilitation's utility. Workers compensation functioned automatically as a no-fault insurance fund. An injured employee received his compensation with little or no state intervention. Rehabilitation, however, depended for its effectiveness on intensive interaction between a state official and a disabled person. Rehabilitation, in short, was intrinsically a matter of state intervention; workers compensation was not. Not limited by the level of public appropriations, workers compensation programs could expand to encompass all industrial activity. Tightly bound by state and federal budgets, rehabilitation agencies could only go as far as their program funds allowed them to go. Unlike workers compensation, vocational rehabilitation programs had to demonstrate that they put the taxpayers' money to good use. Vocational rehabilitation programs were deemed "efficient" because, in the long run, they returned more to society than they cost. Despite the best intentions of Congress and government officials, therefore, the very structures of vocational rehabilitation and workers compensation programs doomed them to become isolated from one another.

Once separated from workers compensation, vocational rehabilitation developed its own image: one which underlined the close ideological fit between public and private sector welfare activities throughout the 1920s. According to the ideology that justified the vocational rehabilitation program, it generated economic returns by acting like a profit-making loan company. Vocational rehabilitation agencies loaned a disabled person vocational training. The person then repaid the loan in the form of taxes which reflected his or her new productivity. A similiar analogy was applied to vocational education by the public bureaucrats involved in financing it. The infant and maternal health program was rationalized in only slightly different terms: by preventing babies from dying and by preserving the health of their mothers, public officials were strengthening the nation's reserves of human capital and, by only a slight extension in reasoning, increasing total national output as well. Although each of the three federal welfare programs created during the 1920s cost government money in the short run, they saved the public money in the long run. As such, these federal welfare programs exemplified smart business practice.

The cost-benefit approach undertaken by public authorities demonstrated the strength of the link between the welfare operations of private businesses and the federal and state governments. To show how large the government's profits were under New Era welfare programs, officials in Washington and various state capitals adopted private sector accounting techniques. The efforts of W. F. Faulkes, a director of the State of Wisconsin's vocational rehabilitation program, proved particularly memorable. Faulkes refined his calculations down to the penny. The program that he administered cost $11,659.36, increased total earning power by $1,722,419.76, and produced a net gain of $1,610,760.40 for the state.

For the entire nation, the gains were equally impressive. The average weekly wage of all persons rehabilitated in fiscal 1924 was $26.07. These rehabilitants would live, on the average, for at least twenty years. In those twenty years, they would collectively earn $147,004,000. In order to generate the impressive sum of 147 million dollars in additional national income, the federal and state governments had spent only $1,124,500. The vocational rehabilitation program for fiscal 1924, therefore, had reaped returns of over 10,000 percent on investment—not bad even by 1920s standards.

These fulsome statistics possessed a darker side. The clear desire of many vocational rehabilitation program adminstrators to turn a profit for society held important implications for the sorts of persons they accepted as rehabilitation clients. It influenced the age, sex, race, level of education, and physical characteristics of the caseload; and it meant that the public sector would provide special help for precisely that group of people with the best chances of receiving help from the private sector.

Like any loan company, in short, government had to take the best risks. People who gave "irrefutable evidence of the economic benefits of rehabilitation" were "young persons with academic training of at least eight years." These same young people had the most productive years remaining to pay off the loan, and young people with education already had a lot invested in their future. It also helped, of course, if the young person being considered for rehabilitation were white and male—since that person would encounter the least prejudice in the job market. Blacks and females, among others, faced a restricted labor market and would have a comparatively hard time paying off loans.

Finally, it helped if the person's disability was comparatively mild. Severely disabled persons were bad rehabilitation risks because they cost more to train and were more restricted in their physical capabilities even after such training. In 1927, for example, one rehabilation supervisor instructed his employees not to spend money on "shut-in cases" or people confined to wheelchairs, but to concentrate on "better material." One observer in Illinois noted in 1929 that the vocational rehabilitation program there "appears especially desirous of working with young persons and does not wish to take chances on cases in which success is improbable." Such was the New Era welfare system.

CONCLUSION

Depression wiped out the ideological rationale for the social welfare system of the 1920s. The system suffered from the fact that the level of return on the public sector's welfare investment no longer justified spending money on vocational rehabilitation, vocational education, or maternal health. The once-splendid cost-benefit demonstrations undertaken by federal and state bureaucrats now showed, in a depressed economy, that the cost of educating, rehabilitating, or treating welfare clients exceeded the benefits returned to society through these peoples' participation in the labor force. By 1933 the vocational rehabilitation program neared extinction. The Roosevelt administration saved it, but only by diverting emergency funds to "rehabilitate" people on relief. In the first year of the New Deal, it took nearly a million federal dollars to keep solvent the program that had once "paid for itself."

Between 1933 and 1938, federal bureaucrats worked to replace the "social engineering" of the 1920s with different welfare strategies. The process was slow and far from straightforward—as we have shown elsewhere. But by 1937 New Deal officials had created a distinctively public approach to social welfare problems and regarded themselves as administrators of welfare programs which provided federal services directly to the people. Federal bureaucrats even composed an agenda of federal welfare initiatives which included health and disability insurance.

Although war delayed the passage of key elements of this new federal welfare system, the public sector's approach to social welfare problems changed substantially between the New Era and the New Deal. After 1937, federal bureaucrats would no longer confine themselves to providing demonstration projects to interested observers in corporations, trade associations, localities, and states. They would, with increasing success, create a world of their own. In this world, New Era equations of welfare and efficiency occupied but a modest place.

Public Welfare and Our Democratic Institutions

Joseph K. Hart

When, more than a century ago, "our fathers brought forth, on this continent, a new nation," that new nation was "conceived in liberty and dedicated to the proposition that all men are created equal." All men are equal! The various concepts and activities now subsumed under the term "public welfare" can have little place in a society of equals. And the term, itself, had little place in the thought of those who conceived the new nation, or in the thought of their time.

It is true that the preamble to the constitution of the new nation mentions the "general welfare;" and in Section 8, of Article 1, one of the duties laid upon Congress was to "provide for . . . the general welfare." But we are likely to read into that phrase more than its authors had in mind. A study of the conditions under which this phrase got into the constitution reveals two facts:

First, that almost all the statesmen of the times identified the term "general welfare" with the term "common defence," the whole clause in Section 8, of Article 1, reading, "to provide for the common defence and the general welfare." Both contemporaneous and modern authorities hold that the second phrase merely defines the first.

Second, that those few leaders, who, like Gouverneur Morris, wanted the term "general welfare" to mean something more, thought of nothing more than making it a justification for certain public improvements, "erecting piers for the protection of shipping in winter and to preserve the navigation of harbors." No one seems to have suggested that the government should engage in the activities now labeled "welfare." Democratic institutions were to make all such activities unnecessary.

As a matter of fact, the constitution-makers definitely refused to authorize certain border-line activities. Some good men wanted Congress to be authorized to undertake "internal improvements" on the large scale, such as building roads and canals. This proposal, with the exception of the provision of post roads, was definitely rejected, and all such undertakings on the part of the general government have had to find their warrant in indirect ways. Again, there were those who wanted the national government to handle the whole question of public education. But this subject was reserved to the states, with the exception that there was a general feeling that a great national university, free from religious distinctions, should be set

SOURCE: Joseph K. Hart, *The Annals* of the American Academy of Political and Social Science, vol. 105 (January 1923), pp. 31–35. ©1923 by the American Academy of Political and Social Sciences. All rights reserved. Reprinted with permission.

up. Authority to do this was, however, held to be included in the power of congress over the seat of the national government, as it was agreed that such an institution, if built, should be located at the capital.

THE SPIRIT OF THE AGES

In short, the mind of the age did not think of government in relation to public welfare in any modern way. The trend was in an opposite direction. In 1776, American statesmen proclaimed the "equality of all men" before the law. That proclamation did not establish the doctrine. In the same year, Adam Smith proclaimed the equality of all men, women and children before the job. This proclamation did not accomplish the fact. But in both cases, the minds of men were given a direction from which escape was long impossible. For nearly a century, the *Wealth of Nations* dominated the economic and hence the political thinking of the western peoples. Political equality and economic equality became so completely identified and fused in the thinking of political and industrial leaders that very few of them have, even yet, been able to escape from the confusion. We must see this a little more clearly.

The economic point of view that dominated the latter part of the eighteenth century and the early nineteenth served as justification for every political activity or lack of activity. The Industrial Revolution had severely shaken the older economic thinking of the mercantilists. Adam Smith laid the foundations of the new economic structure. Trade, he maintained, is an elaborate and varied network of mutual services, within which any sort of governmental regulations must do more harm than good, because they interfere with that "obvious and simple system of natural liberty" which, left to itself, would assure to each of us what he deserves. The state, therefore, cannot protect the worker. An unimpeded, uncontrolled industry is the best protection he can have.

Growing out of this, immediately, is the doctrine that employers cannot really injure their workers. The argument is simple: The profit of the employer depends upon the fullest productivity of the workers. He wants that profit. He will, necessarily, do anything that will secure him that profit. Hence, he will inevitably see to it that the workers have proper food, clothing, housing, in fact, all that they need to make them more effective. Failure to see to these things falls most heavily upon the employer, himself. Hence, whatever the employer does must necessarily be for the benefit of the workers. Governmental interference can but upset the workings of a mechanism that is normally so favorable to the workers.

THE ATTITUDE TODAY

These doctrines are not wholly unknown to us today. But we have gone still further. Since Adam Smith, Malthus has taught us that poverty is inevitable, that some must die of starvation, and many must live ever on the verge of subsistence. And Ricardo has explained how all economic matters are governed by the iron laws of supply and demand, which men can no more circumvent by legislation than they can raise themselves by their bootstraps. All these doctrines have, in the course of the century, been assimilated to our so-called democratic institutions; or, perhaps, the reverse has been the case. At any rate, Professor Giddings has described the results in the following terms:

> By sheer individual effort and individually controlled organizations, Americans have created . . . the greatest aggregations ever seen of industry and graft, of capital and wreckage, of toil and luxury, of comfort and misery, of sanctification and crime.

Here are positive achievements, about which we love to boast; here are disagreeable items which we should like to forget. There are those who argue that all the positive achievements of America are to be credited to our beneficent democratic institutions, while all the disagreeable developments are to be charged to congenital defects in the individuals concerned. But that explanation is too simple to be acceptable. Democracy is now engaged in a general survey of institutions for the purpose of determining what reconstructions, what eliminations, what additions are necessary in the light of twentieth-century industrial and political conditions. That survey has not yet gone far, and it is opposed by all who hold that our institutions are above criticism or examination. But little by little, that examination will be accomplished. It is not inconsistent with our American ideals. America was founded on the principle that the people shall make their own institutions. Democracy means that, and democracy will live or fall upon the keeping or the losing that right.

IS PUBLIC WELFARE CONSISTENT WITH DEMOCRACY?

Hence, the advocates of "public welfare" developments are fully within the limits of the spirit of democratic institutions. The only problem involved is as to whether such programs are, in their various items, consistent with the complete program of democracy. The problem is difficult, because these various public welfare programs exhibit a wide variety of items and proposals in various parts of the country. In general, however, we may say that they propose to organize under a unified governmental control a considerable range of services, some now a part of governmental activity, some still under private control, some scarcely organized at all, but all having to do with the weak, the defective, the ineffective, the ignorant and the incorrigible elements of the community, for the most part; although, since accidents, epidemics and disasters are likely, at any time, to render any or all of us temporarily helpless, public welfare programs may have to be made so flexible and comprehensive as to be capable of rendering service to whole communities at times.

The question here at issue is as to whether such a program is consistent with the desirable future developments of our social life and institutions. The advocacy of such a program, or of any program, is consistent with democracy. But the adoption of the program is another matter. The question is: Will the adoption of such a program further the democratic aims we strive for, or will its adoption confuse, diffuse and eventually defeat those aims? The answer is not on the surface.

Indeed, the question cannot be answered *en bloc*. It seems obvious that no such program should be set up in its own right, under the protecting mantle of "public welfare," and ignoring its relationships to all our other social institutions and relationships. Every such program should be torn to pieces with a pitiless logic for the purpose of determining whether each item in it is distinctly for the public welfare or opposed to it. The analogy with education is likely to mislead us. Education is a natural need of all of us. We are all born ignorant, naturally ignorant. Hence, the more intelligent our civilization becomes, the more education we shall probably provide for all individuals. But charity, on the other hand, is not a natural need of all of us. And there are those who envisage a day and a social order in which it shall be the need of none of us. Hence, the argument can be made that while more education will indicate the growth of our civilization, more charity will indicate the opposite.

Evidently then, every public welfare program must consent to the strictest criticism and analysis, for the purpose of determining which elements proposed therein are democratically constructive and which are not. Labelling will not suffice, and should not be permitted to control. Let one further illustration indicate the problem.

PUBLIC WELFARE AND INDUSTRIAL CONDITIONS

Consider the problem of public welfare in relationship to industrial conditions. At present large numbers of our population are industrially ineffective: they are objects of public welfare. Are these always to remain "cases"? Are some of them now dependent because, somewhere, back along their lives, industry or education or the courts failed to serve them in the most constructive fashion? Will these same institutions fail them and others like them again in the future? Shall we, therefore, make up for the deficiencies of these existent social instruments by establishing a public welfare department to take care of their failures? That is to say, will the present institutionalizing of public welfare, in an uncritical way, accept, approve and institutionalize the deficiencies and failures of some of our other departments and institutions? And should such a department, having ing to justify itself to the taxpayers, be entitled to as many "cases" as it can handle? And to additional equipment and appropriations so that it can handle more? Where will the "cases" come from?

Suppose that education should turn out fewer persons who must lead incompetent lives. Suppose industry were to break and eliminate fewer men. Suppose the courts should send fewer people to jail. Suppose that all our social institutions were to undertake a democratic revival and a great scientific campaign for the reorganization of themselves and the community, for the purpose of reducing the number of misfits. Would the department of public welfare be entitled to claim that it was being unfairly treated? That is to say, will a proper development, in terms of scientific knowledge and democratic spirit, of our community life mean more room or less room for public welfare activities?

Perhaps we can see that there is an angle from which the development of public welfare activities and programs will be not only consistent with our democratic aspirations but distinctly stimulating to those aspirations. Any development that introduces a larger degree of intelligence into our communities and our social organization is, other things being equal, desirable and democratic. All our social efforts need more light. Governments are largely working in the dark. Our schools are caught in the whirr of great machineries. Our industries are bound up with the traditions of individual success and profits. Carried along by the general drift, none of our institutions knows how properly to criticise itself and its activities. The introduction of public welfare activities can be made the occasion for bringing effective critical intelligence to bear on all these somewhat laggard instruments of our social life; and that same critical intelligence will help to define and organize the work of public welfare itself.

INTERFERENCE WITH AMERICAN DEMOCRACY

Two considerations call for a brief final mention in this all too limited discussion of the subject. There are two respects in which public welfare activities may seriously interfere with the development of our American democracy. In the first place, the humanitarian program of public welfare may seriously obstruct the application of scientific knowledge to the solution of the problems of social and racial survival. Scientists are now greatly concerned about the future of the race. They fear the progressive elimination of the fit and the survival of the unfit. They urge that for every effort expended in the care of the unfit individual, equal effort must be intelligently expended toward the eventual elimination of the unfit stock which produced that unfit individual. Will public welfare programs help or hinder this effort in behalf of a better race? This question is fundamental to the democracy of the future.

In the second place, most friends of democracy are seriously disturbed today by the current drifts toward centralization in government and that consequent bureaucracy which promises to be neither scientific nor democratic. They are saying that democracy cannot stand too much of this centralizing drift, even in the interest of a humanitarian program. Centralization of social activity in governmental bureaus is just another method of saving the unfit. Hence, every movement in the direction of a more complete centralization of power and authority and prestige must be offset by quite as complete a movement in the direction of decentralizing intelligence, opportunity, and individual responsibility.

Upon public welfare proponents rests, at present, a peculiar responsibility, as well as a great opportunity. Democracy must think more about all its problems, including all the problems subsumed under the term *public welfare*. But the whole thinking of democracy must not be done by governmental officials. A society in which govermental officials do all the thinking will not long remain a democracy. The thinking of democracy must be done by all the people; it must be shared by all the people. Nor may the officials be careless as to whether the people are thinking or are prepared to think. Decentralization of education, of intelligence, of understanding of governmental processes is a necessary part of any future development of governmental authority. Democratic officials, including public welfare officials, must be as greatly interested in the one movement as in the other. Democracy will be safe, no matter what programs are undertaken, no matter how effective the central government may become, if along with every increment of centralized power, authority and prestige, there shall go a correlative increment of intelligence, understanding and critical effectiveness to the individual citizen, wherever he may be. Without this, democracy, however humanitarian, will probably fail.

The traditions of the eighteenth and nineteenth centuries, so emphatically individualistic, were right in one respect at any rate: in the long run, our democracy will be tested, not by the humanitarian movements that we foster, important as these are, but by the extent to which we succeed in eliminating the occasions for humanitarian effort. All our institutions need reconstruction with this objective in view. As an integral part of the democratic determination to achieve this human civilization (as distinct from a humanitarian world), public welfare activities will have a real place in the social programs of the future.

CHAPTER 5

The Depression Crisis

INTRODUCTION

The Great Depression shattered prevailing notions of the federal government's role in social policy. Despair stalked American cities, as well as the nation's farmlands, which had experienced depressed conditions throughout the 1920s. In New York unemployment was estimated at 800,000 persons, while in Chicago an estimated 600,000 were without jobs. Overall unemployment in American cities stood at between 13 million and 17 million. The overwhelming numbers of unemployed quickly overtaxed private and local sources, thereby forcing many to reevaluate their views of the federal government. Nonetheless, Herbert Hoover remained steadfast in his belief that primary responsibility for the unemployed should remain the domain of local, state, and private agencies. The scale and magnitude of the industrial collapse and ensuing unemployment finally forced the reluctant Hoover to involve the federal government in areas once restricted to private and local agencies.

The collapse of the financial markets and the erosion of municipal tax bases due to unemployment quickly forced many city governments to call for federal assistance in meeting their relief loads. In turn, private philanthropic and voluntary community agencies simply could not keep up with the great demands placed upon them. During the winter of 1929–30, following the stock market crash in October 1929, private agencies attempted to conduct business as usual. Their funds were soon exhausted; many did not survive the year. In New York City alone, nearly four hundred private agencies disappeared within a three-year period from 1929 to 1932. Those that remained opened often had to close their rolls to any further applicants. Private social workers joined the chorus calling for federal intervention. New York social worker Lillian Wald bitterly observed, "It is almost unbelievable, the misery of the jobless masses."

At the outset of the depression many Americans expected Herbert Hoover, the great engineer and great humanitarian, to duplicate his past feats when he had prevented Europe from starving. From these earlier experiences Hoover held fast to his belief that voluntary cooperation and community effort would address the problems of the emergency. He pursued the path he had traveled in the downturn of 1921, when he called the nation's business and labor leaders to Washington, D.C. In October

1930, he appointed an Emergency Committee for Employment, headed by an ex-police commissioner of New York, Colonel Arthur Woods. By January 1931, the members of the Woods committee were admitting defeat. They too joined the cry for federal intervention through a public works program. With nearly all of his committee's proposals rejected or ignored, Arthur Woods finally submitted his resignation in April 1931. In August, Hoover appointed a new President's Organization on Unemployment Relief headed by Walter S. Gifford, president of the Charity Organization Society. Without funds to aid local relief efforts, and without a clear mandate from the president as to its responsibilities, the Gifford Committee also failed.

By the summer of 1932, under pressure from Congress and a distressed citizenry, Hoover finally accepted a relief bill that allowed the Reconstruction Finance Corporation—initially established to lend money to banks, insurance companies, building and loan associations, and similar enterprises—to lend $1.8 billion to states and municipalities for relief and public works. Still, even as new directions were undertaken for aiding the unemployed, Hoover continued to insist that federal money should not undermine local relief efforts and American individualism.

Andrew Achenbaum examines the social context that led to the increased involvement by the federal government in social policy, culminating in the establishment of the Social Security system in 1935. Achenbaum begins by noting that the census of 1930 showed that over 58 percent of all men and over 8 percent of all women over 65 worked. Those who retired mostly relied on lifetime savings because retirement pensions were limited to a small percentage of America's labor force. Indeed, American cities had pioneered in establishing pensions for firemen, police officers, and school teachers. Only in 1920 did the federal government establish a Civil Service Retirement System. In the 1920s large corporations sought to establish private pensions plans, but by 1930 only 15 percent of the labor force was eligible for benefits. The failure of nearly 5,000 banks (with deposits exceeding $3.2 billion) and the closing of 90,000 businesses brought ruin to the elderly. As Achenbaum notes, "Insecurity pervaded the land. The Depression called into question perennial notions of self-reliance."

Maurice A. Hallgren captures the despair of the nation in "Mass Misery in Philadelphia," published in *The Nation* in the spring of 1932. Hallgren, a radical journalist, employs graphic terms in describing the dire need of an estimated 300,000 Philadelphians who lived in grim poverty, away from the public eye. He shows that the poor had formed their own networks to provide food, fuel, and rent. "In Philadelphia, as in most other cities," he observes, "the poor are taking care of the poor." He finds younger men in these districts remaining secluded in their homes, "visibly ashamed of their misfortune," while middle-aged and elderly workers have given up all hope of work. Hallgren warns that "now misery has greatly increased, there is no telling what might happen."

The presidential campaign of 1932 brought into sharp contrast Hoover's view that he had provided leadership to a country in crisis and a Democratic view that the federal government should be doing more to provide relief for the unemployed and to ensure economic recovery to the nation. Hoover's address in Cleveland, delivered shortly before the election, summarized his record as president. He reviews his leadership in establishing the Woods and Gifford committees. He points out that only after the resources of local communities and the states appeared to be exhausted had he authorized the Reconstruction Finance Corporation to loan relief to the states. These and other actions, he declares, presented to the world "a record unparalleled by any other nation in this period." His defense, however, failed to convince the voters. Hoover was overwhelmingly defeated by Franklin D. Roosevelt in November.

Further Readings

William W. Bremer, *Depression Winters: New York Social Workers and the New Deal* (Philadelphia: Temple University Press, 1984).

John A. Garraty, *Unemployment in History: Economic Thought and Public Policy* (New York: Harper & Row, 1978).

Carole Haber, *Beyond Sixty-Five: The Dilemma of Old Age in America's Past* (Cambridge: Harvard University Press, 1983).

Richard Lowitt and Maurine Beasley, eds., *One Third of a Nation: Lorena Hickok Reports on the Great Depression* (Urbana: University of Illinois Press, 1983).

Studs Terkel, *Hard Times: An Oral History of the Great Depression in America* (New York: Pantheon Books, 1970).

A comprehensive social history of unemployment during the Depression remains to be written. However, a number of fine books offer excellent accounts of social life in the Depression years, including Robert S. McElvaine, *The Great Depression: America, 1929–1941* (New York Times Books, 1984).

Changes in thinking about the poor in this time are discussed in Roy Lubove, *The Struggle for Social Security 1900–1935* (Cambridge: Harvard University Press, 1968).

Social Security: The Early Years

W. Andrew Achenbaum

It took the Great Depression to launch social security in the United States. Every major European country had already embraced the logic of social insurance. But the rationale for a public income security program did not take root here until the Progressive period, when social insurance was promoted as a way to prevent and combat "the three fears" that plagued workers—unemployment, poverty in old age, and ill health. Social insurance proponents also sought to promote "social efficiency"—to advance the well-being of some of the nation's more vulnerable citizens without infringing on middle-class ideals of self-reliance and prudence.

Compulsory social insurance gained support among American Progressives, but it also met stiff opposition. Business associations worked tirelessly against old-age assistance and public retirement benefits, denouncing proposals for federal social insurance as "alien" to the American way of life. Union leaders advanced their own reasons for opposing social insurance. Grassroots labor organizations lobbied for old-age relief at the state level, but Samuel Gompers argued that a federal program would threaten the viability of trade-union pensions and divert attention from the need to increase wages and improve working conditions.

The Depression, however, made it clear that economic misfortune was not always the consequence of individual irresponsibility or failure of character. The notion that economic insecurity was a *social* risk predates the 1930s. But there was insufficient popular and elite pressure for protection against the hazards of unemployment and old-age dependency until Franklin Roosevelt decided to act. Common sense—not an elaborate new theory about the role of the state—was the catalyst. America's leaders were convinced that the human and economic costs of doing nothing would rapidly mount, and would have to be paid for later.

It was one thing to call for governmental action, but quite another to enact legislation mutually acceptable to business leaders, radicals, the aged, fiscal conservatives, states-rights advocates, union officials, constitutional experts, and a confused, anxious middle class. Social security legislation required an amalgam of familiar and innovative responses to a multifaceted problem. Was it Washington's responsibility to prevent as well as relieve destitution? Should there be a single federal system to provide cradle-to-grave coverage? Or should government's approach be more selective? How could current operating costs and long-term financial commitments be kept in bounds?

SOURCE: W. Andrew Achenbaum, *Social Security: Visions and Revisions*, A Twentieth Century Fund, Inc., Study, Cambridge University Press, 1986, pp. 13–18. Copyrighted, ©1986 Cambridge University Press. Reprinted and used with permission.

The program adopted was designed to defuse a political threat as quickly and sensibly as possible. But in the crisis of the Great Depression, federal policymakers created only the illusion of a coherent program. Four years after the Social Security Act was passed, its assumptions were dramatically changed to favor what some feared was a more "radical" approach. Even then, by leaving the direction of much social insurance to private industry and state officials, Roosevelt endorsed traditional American means to cope with the pressing need. His advisors and supporters in Congress increasingly used terms that obfuscated issues they neither fully understood nor could have anticipated. The decisions—as well as the non-decisions and confusions—that emerged during the Depression continue to influence the perception of social security in America profoundly.

THE DEPRESSION MAKES ACTION INESCAPABLE

Prior to the 1930s, working as long as possible and then relying on individual savings was the preferred way to financial independence in later years. Although the elderly's labor-force participation rate had been declining since the latter part of the nineteenth century, the 1930 census reported that 58.4 percent of all men and 8.1 percent of all women over sixty-five were gainfully employed. Few older persons had acquired significant savings or property, but as late as 1936, 15 percent of the noninstitutionalized elderly relied on their assets to make ends meet; savings represented their largest single source of income.

Yet old-age dependency had always been a problem in the United States. Americans dealt with it in time-tested ways. As in Europe, the family was the primary source of support. Ever since the colonial period, local communities had provided food and shelter for the old when there were no kin available or when family members defaulted on their responsibilities. More recent times witnessed a growing number of alternatives to the almshouse. Private old-age homes and charitable relief programs supported about 5 percent of the population over sixty-five. Many elderly people qualified for veterans' benefits: The ever-expanding federal military pension program served as an indirect public means of relieving old-age dependency. There were other ways to provide against disability and the vicissitudes of old age. In 1910, roughly a third of the labor force was insured against accidents and sickness: Private institutions— commercial companies, trade unions, and especially fraternal orders—underwrote most of the coverage. After World War I, proponents of American "welfare capitalism" increasingly offered disability plans and life insurance discounts. Record amounts of disability insurance were sold during the 1920s. Older workers faced with imminent unemployment typically filed disability claims.

Retirement pensions were available to a limited percentage of America's labor force, with the public sector as pacesetter. At the turn of the century, nearly every major American city provided pensions for firemen and police officers; by 1916, thirty-three states had enacted retirement provisions for elementary and secondary-level teachers. During the latter half of the nineteenth century, the federal government instituted "super-annuation" policies for solders, sailors, naval revenue officials, and selected agents working in Alaska and in Indian territories. A federal Civil Service Retirement System was established in 1920.

The development of private pension plans was initially quite slow. Less than 4 percent of the labor force was eligible for existing programs as late as 1915. Changes in the federal tax code during the 1920s, however, induced large enterprises—mainly public utilities, railroads, iron and steel concerns, and firms manufacturing heavy machinery—to create pension funds for their employees. As a result, the proportion of the labor force eligible for benefits rose to 15 percent by 1930. Few such plans required employees to contribute. The typical industrial plan permitted a worker to retire at sixty, sixty-two, sixty-five, or seventy, after completing twenty to thirty years of service. Pensions, generally graduated according to a worker's prior earnings, seldom provided for spouses and dependents.

Once old-age dependency was perceived as a "social problem," more and more state legislatures put helpless senior citizens on relief. By 1933, twenty-one states and Alaska and Hawaii operated such programs; seven other jurisdictions made coverage optional at the county level. None of this was enough; the Depression proved that all existing methods of preventing and reducing old-age dependency were grossly inadequate.

The nation had endured severe economic downturns before. But this time the extent, intensity, and duration of the upheaval were unprecedented. Between October 1929 and June 1932, the common-stock price index dropped from 260 to 90. The nation's real GNP, which had risen 22 percent between 1923 and 1929, fell 30.4 percent over the next four years. Nearly 5,000 banks, with deposits exceeding $3.2 billion, became insolvent; 90,000 businesses failed. Aggregate wages and salaries in 1933 totaled only 57.5 percent of their 1929 value. The gross income realized by farmers was cut nearly in half; the farm-product index took a dive from 105 to 51 between 1928 and 1932. More than a thousand local governments defaulted on their bonds; the rest managed to stay afloat only by firing staff and slashing social services.

Insecurity pervaded the land. The Depression called into question perennial notions of self-reliance. A sizable proportion of middle-class Americans discovered that they were less self-sufficient than they had presumed. Unemployment rose from 3 percent to 25 percent—the highest it has ever been. More than a million adults took to the road. Eighteen million sought public relief in order to subsist. Breadlines formed; shanties were erected on vacant lots. "The sense of the big and out-of-handedness of our contemporary world is neither illusion nor merely another expression of this recurrent restlessness of man in civilization," sociologist Robert S. Lynd observed. "We feel ultimately coerced by larger forces not controllable within our immediate area of personal concentration."

Because misery was not just the lot of the shiftless and improvident, but a threat to everyone, the public became more responsive to the problems of those growing older. The Depression, declared economist (later Senator) Paul H. Douglas in 1936, "increasingly convinced the majority of the American people that individuals could not themselves provide adequately for their old age and that some sort of greater security should be provided by society." The Depression deprived millions of older workers of jobs; it seemed unlikely that they would ever reenter the labor force.

Hard times rent asunder the elderly's "safety net." Bankrupt firms obviously could not honor their pension obligations to superannuated workers: Forty-five plans covering 100,000 employees were discontinued between 1929 and 1932 alone. Indeed, only 10 percent of the programs established before the economic downturn legally obligated employers to honor their promises to employees. Thus, many companies simply decided not to pay retirement benefits; instead, they tapped those pension funds to meet other financial obligations. Managers lacking adequate reserve funds annnounced that they would curtail benefits until the economy recovered. Trade-union pensions fared no better.

More traditional means of support also proved insufficient. Savings were lost when banks collapsed. Intergenerational tensions mounted: Relatives and friends often found it impossible to care for the aged while providing for their more immediate families. Private charities were overwhelmed by the increased demand for assistance. Local relief agencies imposed stringent eligibility criteria, but even then could not help all who qualified. State legislatures, faced with imminent bankruptcy, had reached the limit of what they could do.

Desperate, the elderly wrote to Washington pleading for aid. "Dear Mrs. Roosevelt," a woman from Petersburg, North Dakota, began, "It's hard to be old and not have anything. " A Georgian senior citizen appealed directly to the president:

> I am a old Citizen of West Point and I am about 75 or 6 years old and Have Labored Hard all My Days until depression Came on and I Had no Job in three years and I have a Little Home I Bought when times were good and I managed to Pay my state and County tax But they claim I owe about 15 fifteen dol City tax and going to sell my Little Home for that and will you Please sir Help me out the government Can Have a Lean on the Little House until I Get some way to Pay Back Please Sir do what you Can for me I am to old to be turned out of doors.

Some older applicants stressed that they could not feed, clothe, and shelter their jobless adult children. Middle-aged citizens sometimes wrote on behalf of their parents and the older generation: "Well whither my mother ever gets anything or not, I hope all the other old people that is intilted to it gets it soon, because there is nothing sadder than old people who have struggled hard all there lives to give there family a start in life, then to be forgotten, when they them self need it most."

In this context, millions of Americans seized on utopian schemes promising the aged far greater assistance than was avilable from the states or private charity. Upton Sinclair ran for governor on a pledge to grant $50 pensions to all who had resided in California for at least three years. Senator Huey P. Long's "Share Our Wealth" Society wanted to give $30 per month to every American over sixty with an annual income of less than $1,000 and property valued at not more than $10,000; Long's program would be financed by federal taxes on income, on inheritance, and property exchanges. Dr. Francis E. Townsend rallied support for his proposal that all persons over sixty be given $200 monthly on the condition that they not be gainfully employed and that they spend their pensions within thirty days; this program was to be financed from the proceeds of a new nation-wide tax on transactions. Critics quickly noted serious economic flaws in these radical ideas, but they attracted national attention and gained support in Congress. If these panaceas were not to be enacted, then something else had to be done.

For example, there was new and renewed interest in social insurance. Abraham Epstein's American Association for Old Age Security (founded in 1927) changed its name to the American Association for Social Security in 1933, thus broadening its efforts to protect citizens of all ages. In 1932, the American Federation of Labor reversed its previous stand, endorsed state-funded unemployment insurance, and called for federal old-age relief and insurance. Many business officials also became more supportive of the drive for social security.

During Herbert Hoover's presidency and the initial two years of Roosevelt's first term, Congress considered several prototypes of social security legislation. Roosevelt signed the Railroad Retirement Act in 1934. Some in Washington hoped that a broader program of contributory old-age annuities could be enacted in its wake. But the administration chose neither to initiate nor to support any social insurance measure before the seventy-third Congress. Only after other foundations for a "New Deal" had been laid did the president decide to move ahead in this area.

Mass Misery in Philadelphia

Mauritz A. Hallgren

Philadelphia, February 23, 1932

Soon after he took office last month Mayor J. Hampton Moore declared: "I toured the lower sections of South Philadelphia. I went into the small streets, and saw little of poverty....I have counted automobiles and watched them pass a given point. Rich and poor, white and colored, alien and native-born, all riding by.... There is no starvation in Phildelphia."

To this Mac Parker, investigator for the Phildelphia *Record*, replied:

> Mayor Moore need not have gone into the lower sections of South Phildelphia. He need not have traveled the wide boulevard which is the Parkway. From the porch of his own home at 318 Carpenter Lane, in well-to-do and comfortable Germantown, the Mayor could have flung stones upon the suffering and poverty in his immediate neighborhood.... Behind the lace curtains which the Mayor saw hanging in the windows of "the clean and comfortable homes" lies the picture he didn't see. Gaunt children, sunken eyes, ten-year-olds nineteen pounds under weight. Children in rags, without sufficient clothes to permit their attendance at school. Children without shoes.... Starvation in Philadelphia today is an accumulative starvation; starvation through undernourishment; slow starvation from insufficient food.

A day or two before I arrived in Phildelphia a Negro youth of patently deficient mental powers confessed that he had assaulted and murdered a white girl of seven. The crime took place in an abandoned tenement on North American Street. This narrow and shabby thoroughfare lies near the heart of Phildelphia's "Bandbox District." Here extreme poverty has existed since long before the bull-market crash in 1929. The bandbox tenements are almost all narrow, three-story affairs, one room to a floor. They have no modern heating or plumbing, the majority of them having to depend on outdoor toilets. They are dirty, dingy, and dark, facing upon narrow lanes and courts, some of which are no more than five feet across. Approximately 140,000 people live in the district, in these unsanitary and depressing slum dwellings. In some of the tenements they live two, three, and even four families to a room. What effect such conditions have upon human conduct may be seen from a study recently made of fifteen families that had crowded themselves into nine of these tenements. Over a period of three years there had been reported in the fifteen families thirteen cases of illegitimacy and attacks on girls and women, eleven cases of desertion, three of imbecility, eighteen of communicable diseases, seven of absolute poverty, five of cruelty and

---

SOURCE: Mauritz A. Hallgren, *The Nation* 134 (March 9, 1932), pp. 275–77. ©1932 The Nation Company, Inc. Reprinted and used with permission.

incorrigibility, and five of chronic drunkenness. This offers but a brief picture of what must be happening to many of the other thousands of families in the district.

The Bandbox District was suddenly called to the attention of the social-minded residents of Philadelphia by the murder of Dorothy Lutz. There is now in full swing a campaign to abolish these hideous slums. But, one may ask, what of the larger social problem that has fixed itself upon Philadelphia as a result of unemployment? What of the distress and mass misery to be found in every quarter of the city? Will it take, let us say, a few more murders or perhaps a hunger riot or two, to awaken the good people of the city to the true significance of this problem? There is a distinct connection between the Bandbox District and unemployment in Philadelphia, for under the pressure of unemployment whole sections of the city are sinking into conditions not unlike those obtaining in the slums.

Many of the more fortunate residents of the city, though they know there is unemployment, have really no conception of its extent or severity. I heard it said by more than one person that the mild winter was a blessing, for it meant that the jobless were not suffering! And there are any number of business men and other affluent citizens here who are only too anxious to believe with Mayor Moore that there is no poverty in Philadelphia. They quite obviously think that if this poverty is discovered, something may have to be done about it, and that something would certainly mean an increase in taxes. To the last man these Philadelphians are opposed to higher taxes. Their representatives in Washington say that the federal government must not help because the problem is one for the States and communities. Clinton A. Sowers, machine Republican and a member of the Pennsylvania Legislature representing a Philadelphia district, declared that "Governor Pinchot thinks that all this relief should be distributed from Harrisburg under his personal direction. We think that the neighborhoods of the State know more about the needs of the people than the Governor does." And in this neighborhood the principal public servant, Mayor Moore, declares that "there is no poverty." So the political merry-go-round runs on, while at least 300,000 Philadelphians are in dire need. The poverty and spreading destitution are not thrust under one's nose as one walks along the principal business streets. There are without question thousands of automobiles to be seen daily on the boulevards, and more raccoon coats along Chestnut Street than can be found on any college campus. But just beyond the business section, in the homes of the unemployed on the riverfront, in the Bandbox District, in South and West Philadelphia, one may quickly learn whether there is any actual suffering.

In Philadelphia, as in most other cities, the poor are taking care of the poor. Thousands of small, independent shopkeepers are going bankrupt trying to help their neighbors. The Philadelphia *Record* found any number of these corner grocers, butchers, and bakers, heavily in debt themselves, who had on their books unpaid accounts of customers running in some cases into the hundreds of dollars. John Nigro, a baker, was sued for debt a few days ago. His accounts receivable totaled $5,000. He could collect none of them; he knew when he was letting these bills run up that he was dispensing charity, but he continued to provide relief for his neighbors until he himself went to the wall. In the same neighborhood another shopkeeper, pointing to a bill of $200 that was owed him, said: "Eleven children in that house. They've got no shoes, no pants. In the house, no chairs. My God, you go in there, you cry, that's all. What can you do? Let them go hungry?"

So, too, with many of the landlords. There have been evictions seemingly without end, but inquiry reveals that in most of these cases the landlords own extensive properties. The bulk of the residential property is in the hands of small property-owners, people who own their own homes and perhaps one or two other houses. And untold numbers of these landlords are now destitute or nearly so. Yet they allow their tenants to live on for months without paying rent. In one small area covering a few city blocks I found more than two hundred families who were back in their rent anywhere from six to eighteen months. I visited the home of Mrs. Stout, a widow with a grown son who for months had been without work. She had been buying her home through a building-and-loan association. Some time ago she found it necessary to rent out the second and third floors as separate apartments. Her tenants, like her son, lost their jobs; they stayed on through the summer and fall, paying no rent. The day I was there all three families were destitute. The gas and electricity had been shut off; all three pantries were virtually empty; Mrs. Stout had not a nickel to meet the next building-and-loan payment which was due that evening. She was about to lose her home. Her case was by no means exceptional. There are hundreds of landlords who hang on to the bitter end, letting go only when the mortgage-holder or tax-collector steps in—and then they and their tenants have to double up with relatives or neighbors, or go out into the streets. No fewer than fifteen hundred dwellings are being sold at public auction in Philadelphia every month.

How heavy is the load that these shopkeepers and landlords are carrying can never be measured. But another tremendous load is being borne by the Unemployment Relief Committee, as to whose work statistics are available. The chairman of the organization is Horatio Gates Lloyd, partner in the local branch of Morgan and Company. A year ago Lloyd was typical of his class, a conservative banker, thinking little of the masses. Today he does not hesitate to advocate direct government relief for the unemployed, to support the Costigan-LaFollette bill, to which those of his kind in Philadelphia are bitterly opposed. It may be that Lloyd has been sincerely moved by what he has seen of privation among the workers, or it may be that he is acting out of pure selfishness, knowing that a hungry people will imperil his property and his wealth. But whatever his motive, his committee is doing a remarkable job—with the all too slim resources at its disposal. I say this in all frankness, although I do not believe in the sort of private charity to which Philadephia is having to submit. Lloyd himself has come to acknowledge the limitations of private charity, of the American system of "self-help" concerning which we hear so much from Washington. In a recent statement he pointed out that the average amount of relief expended by his committee per family is $4.38 per week. "While it must be remembered," he said, "that in most instances this was supplemented from such other sources as relatives, churches, wages of minors, and the like, this amount was grossly inadequate. It can best be described as disaster relief, merely enough to maintain existence."

The Lloyd organization began operating last June as a special branch of the Department of Public Welfare. The municipal government borrowed $3,000,000 to pay for the relief to be distributed. Lloyd insisted that the work of distribution be taken out of the hands of the politicians and placed completely in his charge. His organization also took over the relief work of all the private agencies. Thus with one agency dispensing relief, and that agency beholden to no political machine or privileged group, the task so far has been efficiently accomplished with a minimum of overhead expense. In fact, overhead charges, including service and administration supplies and the payroll of the relief workers, have averaged only 6.8 percent of the total outlay of the committee, all the rest of its funds going into food, milk, gas, shoes, and coal for the unemployed. This is probably a better record than can be shown by any similar organization anywhere in the country.

Toward the end of December the city's $3,000,000 was exhausted, and the Lloyd committee had to resort to panhandling on a large scale. In a public subscription drive which began in November, the sum of $10,404,446.71 was raised in cash and pledges. It is hoped that this new fund will last until May, but with the number of families being helped growing daily there is considerable doubt as to this. After that the city may get $2,500,000 from the State—if the State Supreme Court upholds the Talbot Act, which provides for the distribution of $10,000,000 in direct relief to the unemployed. And then? Philadelphia is not thinking, hardly dares think, beyond this point. The municipality is broke and cannot even pay its own employees. The men and women who conducted the United Campaign drive feel certain that very little additional money, if any, can be raised by public subscription. They say that private citizens have just about given their all, or at least those citizens have done so who intend to give anything toward helping the jobless.

And what if the need for relief should continue to grow and the funds now in sight be exhausted before May? There is every likelihood that this will happen. In December, 1930, relief was being extended to 6,590 families by the original Unemployment Relief Committee. This figure grew until in April it reached 24,031; from this point it declined somewhat until August, when it again began to mount. In August there were 23,114 families on the dole; in September, 28,923; October, 31,584; November, 35,595; December, 47,779; and January, 55,643. Last week the total had swelled to 57,126.

Where it will end, it is impossible to forecast. Every day brings new applicants to the relief stations. Of late these prople have been of a distinctly better class, better, that is, in the sense that their standard of living had been much higher than that of the average worker; they had been well paid, had known many comforts and even luxuries, and had never before been in want. They were skilled artisans, professional people, men and women of the white-collar class. They had continued to depend upon the corner grocer, the church, and relatives for help until all these sources of aid had dried up and they had been forced to come to the Relief Committee, begging to be placed on the dole. Most of them had refused to come until every last scrap of bread had been eaten and every last chunk of coal burned. How many more families, too proud to ask for charity, do not come at all cannot even be guessed. Every day dozens of these families are turned up by relief workers in the field, or by neighbors who are too poor themselves to help but who cannot bear to see the people next door go hungry.

What the applicants get in the way of relief is all too meager. Approximately 77 percent of the money expended goes into grocery orders; another 12 percent for food; the remainder, bare pittances, for coal, shoes, and gas. No electric bills are paid, and the Lloyd committee has decided it cannot possibly undertake to meet rent bills, for this, it has been estimated, would add 25 percent to the cost of relief and cut down the food distributed in corresponding measure. It is more essential that the unemployed at least get something to eat. Neither food nor money is directly distributed. Applicants are given grocery orders, the money value of which is determined by the number of persons in each family. The average family every week gets a grocery order worth approximately $4. These orders are honored by most of the stores of the city, who use them in meeting their obligations to the wholesale houses, and the wholesale dealers turn them into the Relief Committee for cash. Families with small children get in addition a weekly milk order. Obviously it takes a great deal of stretching to make $4 cover a week's food for a family of five.

What are the effects of depression—and the dole—on Philadelphia's unemployed? It is perhaps too early to tell; the real consequences may not be known for years, when the children now being brought up on starvation rations reach working age. Nevertheless, close students of the local problem see the physical energy and the nervous resistance of the jobless workers being slowly ground down. Each individual requires more care, more medical attention than he did a year ago. Dr. Jacob Billikopf, who as head of the Jewish Charities has carefully watched the present situation as it developed, is authority for the statement that "the 250,000 persons affected by unemployment today are suffering much more than 300,000 would have suffered a year ago, or 500,000 two years ago."

I could not possibly have talked with all the miserable families in the city. However, in company with different workers attached to the Relief Committee I did visit about thirty homes. Most of the homes were those of normally well-paid mechanics and building workers. I found bewilderment and confusion rather than discouragement or desperation. Not one of the many persons I talked to had really given up hope, but every one of them was rapidly drifting in that direction. All were heavily in debt, had borrowed to the limit on their insurance policies; some had sold much of their furniture, and would have sold more if they could have found buyers. The younger men spent most of their waking hours looking for odd jobs, but the rest were inclined rather to remain in the seclusion of their homes, visibly ashamed of their misfortune or else convinced that it was futile to look for work when there was no work to do. Inquiry revealed that temporary jobs invariably go to the younger men; the middle-aged and older men are simply not given a chance. The most discouraging sign I noted was the total lack of interest in outside activities on the part of all the men I talked with. Although workers for the Relief Committee have repeatedly urged them to seek recreation in study, at the public gymnasiums and playgrounds, or in the free museums and art galleries— printed lists of the various recreation centers, settlement houses, public evening schools, art schools, and museums, which can be attended without charge, have been distributed to the unemployed—these men will not take advantage of the opportunities offered. It seems to be the first instinct of the jobless man to want to withdraw from contact with normal society, in which he feels he no longer has a place. But this, while undoubtedly a result of the depression, cannot be put down as a consequence of the "soul-destroying" dole. I noted little evidence that the dispensation of charity was undermining the character of Philadelphia's unemployed. There was, of course, the man I found lying abed at two o'clock in the afternoon, who clearly felt that so long as other people were feeding him there really was no reason for him to look for work; and there were a number of families who appeared to have lost their sense of responsibility, and who probably would have shown more initiative in fending for themselves had they not known they would get their regular grocery orders at the end of the week.

Again, no positive sign of revolt was discernible, though admittedly it was difficult to get these men to speak frankly. They were afraid that whatever they had to say might prejudice their chances of obtaining continued relief. Nevertheless, an undercurrent of rebellion was noticeable. Strangely enough, most of the grumbling was directed not against the employers or the government, but against the churches. A skilled mechanic by the name of McCollian, a Roman Catholic, complained bitterly that the clergy did not appreciate the extreme plight of their parishioners. Five other families, all Protestants, had given up going to church because, as Mrs. Brown, wife of a cabinetmaker put it, "the church no longer means anything to us." A man named Johnson said that as least half the members of the congregation of his church were continuing to attend only in the hope that the church would be able to help them eke out the slim relief they get from the Lloyd committee. Only one family was openly in revolt. I reached the home of Mrs. Duffy, whose husband is a gardener, about thirty minutes after the constable had been there to serve an eviction notice. Mrs. Duffy cried throughout the interview. Her greatest worry was that her husband and three sons really meant to go out that evening to steal bread for themselves at the point of pistols. They had procured weapons and laid careful plans for their foraging expedition.

But there is no assurance that more Duffys will not turn to robbery, or that other jobless men will not rebel in other ways. Last June, before the city's $3,000,000 fund became available, all relief was suspended for three weeks. The stations were kept open and applications for relief continued to be taken, but toward the end of that period the relief workers in the stations had become seriously alarmed by the rising temper of the applicants. They spoke roughly, demanded food in no uncertain terms, and a few even threatened to take direct action. Should there be another suspension of relief, now that the misery has greatly increased, there is no telling what might happen. In anticipation of trouble the Philadelphia police force is undergoing special training in gas warfare and in the suppression of riots. According to the *Evening Bulletin*, 1,800 policemen have now had sufficient training "and could prove their skill at a moment's notice. The department is always ready for anything, particularly in hard times." So far it has been unnecessary to bring out the gas bombs and riot guns.

Address in Cleveland, Ohio
October 15, 1932

Herbert Hoover

Now, I wish to examine the record and policies of the present administration in their relation to our wage and salary earners, for that record is made. They speak louder than promises. There are 12 major measures and policies which we have put into action and to which I would like to refer.

First, my concern in dealing with the problems of these times, while fighting to save our people from chaos and to restore order in our economic life, has been to avert hunger or cold amongst those upon whom these blows have fallen with heartbreaking severity—that is our unemployed workers.

In the fall of 1930 to meet this situation, I set up the President's Organization for Unemployment Relief[1] under able leadership. Through cooperation of every State, town, and village the forces were organized and mobilized which overcame victoriously the suffering of that winter. In the fall of 1931, we mobilized again, and again with the cooperation of Governors and local communities, all the associations and agencies in the United States, we carried a victorious battle over the winter of 1931–32. Still again, during the past few weeks, I have cooperated with the great national agencies in the remobilization of the voluntary forces of the country for an attack on the forthcoming winter.

But, fearing that the resources of individuals and of local communities and States were being exhausted, I settled with the Congress an authority to be given to the Reconstruction Corporation to loan a total of $300 million to those States whose needs might be found greater than the voluntary associations and local authorities could provide. I had great difficulties with Democratic leaders to prevent this being made a pork-barrel operation rather than one based upon need. Under that authority many millions have already been provided. We have provided, in addition, large quantities of wheat and cotton for the aid of those in distress. There should be no fear or apprehension at any deserving American fireside that starvation or cold will creep within their doors or menace their families and loved ones over the forthcoming winter.

SOURCE: Herbert Hoover, in *Public Papers of the Presidents of the United States, Herbert Hoover, January 1 to March 4, 1933* (Washington, D.C.: U.S. Government Printing Office, 1977), pp. 527–32.

[1]In October 1930, the President's Emergency Committee for Employment was established under the chairmanship of Arthur Woods. In August 1931, the President's Organization on Unemployment Relief was established under the chairmanship of Walter S. Gifford.

With these 3 years of unceasing effort in relief, by the patriotic service of our citizens and our local communities and public officials, and the stimulus and mobilization that we have been able to give by the use of the Presidential office and direct support of the Federal Government, we present to the world a record unparalleled by any other nation in this period. That is a record expressed in technical terms yet interpretable into sheer human sympathy. That record is the information furnished to me constantly by the Surgeon General of the Public Health Service which shows, down to the latest moment, that the adult mortality, the infant mortality are at the lowest rate on record, and that the general health of the Americn people is at a higher level today than ever before in the history of our country. I know that there are exceptions and that there is suffering which always arises in communities where their organization is less efficient than it should be. Even so, no such record could be established if the Nation's unemployed were starving and without shelter. Yet some say that things could not be worse. Had these actions not been taken they would be a thousand times worse.

The second of our actions of interest to the workers was the conference which I called in Washington, in November 1929, of representatives of the leading employers, together with representatives of organized labor, and here we developed certain plans for dealing with this emergency. I believe this can be truly said to have been the first time in history that the Government has taken the leadership to secure an understanding between industry and labor of the complete mutuality of their interest in the face of a national danger.

We worked out on that occasion many purposes.

The first was to uphold the standard of real wages.

The second was to uphold the buying power of our working people until the cost of living had diminished.

The third was to prevent that thing which had happened in every previous depression in our history, and that was an immediate attack upon wages as a basis of maintaining profits. This proposal had the sympathetic support of the employers of the whole country, and for nearly 2 years they maintained the standard of wages in the United States; they maintained them in the face of disappearing profits. As the depression grew more severe there have been readjustments, but these readjustments have come about by agreement between employer and employee after profits were taxed and the cost of living was reduced. As a result of these efforts we have had the astonishing spectacle of a country in which there have been less strikes, less industrial conflict, with all of their bitterness, than even in normal times and where there has been less social conflict than in any other country disturbed by this depression.

The fourth of these undertakings made at that time had to do with the staggering of employment—instead of discharging a portion of workers into complete disaster.

The fifth of the undertakings made on that occasion was that the manufacturers, the railroads, and the utilities would expand their construction of new equipment beyond their immediate need. A vast sum of money was expended in these directions during the first year of the depression. Again some few months ago, I secured the interest of employers in organization of a new campaign to replace obsolete equipment and machinery. That is today resulting in an increase of employment.

As I have said, when history records this depression, it will record no brighter chapter in the whole history of the United States than the approach to this problem by both employers and leaders of labor in a sense of humanity and a sense of social responsibility. To them I pay high tribute. In the face of these results, let no man say that it could not be worse. If it had not been for these actions, this country would have been fired with the flames of bitterness and conflict between workers and employers; millions more would have been without jobs; wages would have been reduced far below their present level.

Now, day before yesterday my opponent announced a plan "to set up in times of prosperity what might be called a nest egg to be used for public works in time of depression." He said, "That is a policy which we should initiate when we get back to good times."

He advocates this apparently as a brand new idea. It will doubtless surprise him to learn that the eggs have not only been laid but they have hatched, long since.

He either ignores or is ignorant of the fact that as far back as 1922, in our unemployment conference of that year under my chairmanship, we developed then the idea of making use of public works to assist in the stabilization of employment in times of depression and laid the foundation for its operation. I do not claim to have invented the notion.

On the breaking out of this depression in November 3 years ago, I announced not only that the Federal Government would speed up its public works, but I requested the States and municipalities to do likewise. During the year 1930 we not only maintained these types of construction work, but we stimulated it to above normal—an amount of $500 to $800 million. The wide extent and pressure of the depression, however, rapidly cut into the construction abilities of many States and municipalities. We, however, have held Federal construction work up to three times its normal, straight through year by year. By the end of this fiscal year we will have expended nearly $2,400 million of Federal money on construction and maintenance work since the depression began. And I ask again, do you think things could not have been worse had these policies not been adopted?

Now, there has proved to be a limitation, however, on this, and that limitation is that the Federal Government should not and must not undertake projects which are not of productive value to the Nation and must not extend its liabilities beyond its ability to maintain a balanced budget. To take money from the taxpayer and thus decrease his ability to employ people himself, and to put it into public works which will never make a real return to the public, is a waste of national wealth and an actual destruction of employment.

Notwithstanding the fact that the Federal Government was carrying a burden of $700 million of public works per annum—the very utmost that its resources permitted and the utmost that could be justified on merit—the Democratic Vice-Presidential candidate introduced, in May of this year, and secured the passage of a bill in the Democratic House of Representatives calling for $1,200 million more of public works. The expenditure of these sums meant unbalancing the budget; it meant the destruction of Government credit.

But, far worse than this, the works upon which it was intended to expend this money were of typical pork-barrel character. In that bill were 3,500 different projects scattered in every community in the country. One list alone would have imposed a maintenance charge on the Government of $15 million a year as against a perfectly efficient service now costing $3 million a year. Lists of the projects in different congressional districts were distributed in the hope that they would appeal to the cupidity of those districts and that I should be forced into the embarrassment not only of appearing to oppose my own policy of speeding up public works, but of depriving thousands of towns and villages of the expenditure of Federal money and myself of votes in this election.

Now, it is a good thing to have a fire in the grate to warm the house, but it is a bad thing to set the house on fire in order to warm your hands.

The Democratic candidate for Vice-President still advocates that bill. He proposes to introduce it in the next session. He proposes it as a part of the policies of the Democratic Party. But, with the responsibility of the President of the United States, I propose to continue to oppose it.

CHAPTER 6

The New Deal and Social Policy

INTRODUCTION

When Franklin D. Roosevelt assumed the presidency in 1933, he faced a social crisis of historic magnitude. Government at all levels simply lacked the administrative apparatus to deal adequately with the problems facing the nation. Only ten states had old-age assistance laws; Mother's Aid laws were not operative at all in New Mexico, Arkansas, and Mississippi; and in forty-two of the states, less than half of the counties were actually administering benefits. More than half the families on unemployment relief were located in eight states, and more than a third were in four states: Pennsylvania, New York, Ohio, and Illinois. In some states one quarter of the population was receiving relief. The percentage of blacks (18 percent) on relief was almost double that of the percentage of whites (9 percent) on relief. Forty-two percent of all persons on relief were children.

With these conditions, federal social policy underwent profound institutional changes which transformed the role of the state, fiscal policy, and private/public social services. Beginning with direct relief programs, the Roosevelt administration moved to public works projects and finally to a social security system in 1935 which profoundly altered welfare policy in this country.

One of Roosevelt's first actions in addressing the unemployment crisis was the passage of the Federal Relief Act in May 1933. The act appropriated $500 million to be allocated to states for relief. The self-liquidating aspects of the Hoover public works program were given up for relief of the unemployed. Headed by Harry Hopkins, a former New York social worker, the Federal Emergency Relief Administration (FERA) initially made no distinction between work relief and direct relief. In the winter of 1933 the Roosevelt administration established an emergency work program, the Civil Works Administration (CWA), to provide additional assistance to the unemployed. At its peak the CWA employed 4.2 million workers, but when criticisms arose that many of these people continued to pass up jobs in the private sector, the program was disbanded.

Both Roosevelt and Hopkins continued to believe that work skills and work values were being undermined by the FERA. The sweep of Democrats into Congress following the elections of 1934 allowed Roosevelt to move in new directions. He moved to enact legislation for a new works program and a social insurance system. As Harry Hopkins told his assistants, "Boys, this is our hour. We've got to get everything we want, a works program, social security, wages and hours, everything. Now or never." Shortly afterwards, at Hopkins's urging FDR disbanded the FERA, bluntly declaring that "The lessons of history, confirmed by the evidence immediately before me, show conclusively that continued dependence upon relief induces a spiritual and moral disintegration fundamentally destructive to the national fibre." FERA was replaced in 1935 by a new program, the Work Progress Administration (WPA).

The WPA was intended to bring the aged, the disabled, the orphaned, and others who could not work—1.5 million such families and individuals—back to state and local welfare agencies. The other 3.5 million "employables" who were receiving direct relief were to be put to work on federal work projects. These projects were to pay a "security wage" which would be higher than relief payments but lower than the prevailing wage scale. The WPA never employed more than 31 percent of the nation's unemployed. Indeed, often between 600,000 and 900,000 WPA-certified workers at any one time were not hired due to budget restrictions.

Following the elections of 1934, Roosevelt acted to establish a social security system. Proposals for a national program for old-age insurance had been around since the turn of the century, but they took on a new urgency with the depression. Francis Townsend, a retired dentist in California, had organized a powerful movement to the left of Roosevelt around a program calling for monthly pensions to the elderly. The success of the Townsend movement, as well as Democratic gains in Congress, led Roosevelt to conclude that the time had come to push social security legislation.

August 14, 1935 marked a major turning point in the history of social welfare in the United States. On that day FDR signed the bill establishing the federal Social Security system. It centered around four major programs: a contributory system that provided those over 65 with pensions; old-age relief for the care of destitute persons over 65 through matching grants from the federal government to state-administered programs; a federal-state system of unemployment insurance; and matching grants-in-aid to states to assist dependent mothers and children, the blind, and public health service. A national Social Security Board was established to oversee and administer the program. Enactment of the Social Security Act signaled a fundamental shift in federal welfare policy in the United States. The Social Security program created the institutional apparatus for further expansion of the federal government into new areas of welfare and health care with the later establishment of Medicare and Medicaid.

The creation of a federal welfare state (or, as Michael Katz has called it, "the quasi-welfare state") created immediate controversy among contemporaries as well as later generations of social scientists. At issue was not whether the Roosevelt social program was good or bad *per se* but more profoundly, how it was affecting the nation's democratic-capitalist order.

Many at the time accused Roosevelt of having gone too far in leading the nation down the road toward socialism; others saw the Roosevelt program as a hoax, largely symbolic in its call for reform. Critics on the right and the left of Roosevelt seemed to agree that the New Deal was primarily a political response by a cunning president whose principal motivation was toward his party and his own reelection. Of course, Roosevelt and his New Deal gained the support of most Americans at the time, and found later defenders (albeit rather critical ones) among scholars who were to write the history of the New Deal.

The readings in this chapter present the clash of judgments concerning the New Deal. Robert H. Bremner, a leading historian of social welfare in the United States, leads our discussion by arguing in his essay that Roosevelt saw the issue of extending aid to the unemployed "not as a matter of charity but as a matter of social duty." Bremner observes that FDR favored work relief over the dole, but he felt that federal aid was justified and sorely needed in the present crisis. Moreover, while Roosevelt opposed a permanent federal employment program, he was willing to go substantially further than any previous president in taking the federal government into new areas of social policy.

In his essay, Bremner does not hesitate to criticize important aspects of the Roosevelt program. He shows that the distinction between "employable" and "unemployable" remained sharper in principle than in application, especially as the Depression continued into the late 1930s. He also observes that federal relief was never adequate, a point made by Harry Hopkins in his book *Spending to Save* (1936). Bremner maintains further that the federal government's policy of returning dependents (the "unemployables") to the states' care meant that they would be provided with inadequate assistance.

For all of his criticisms, Bremner finds much to praise in the Roosevelt program, especially the enactment of the Social Security Act in 1935. Bremner suggests that much of the accomplishment of the legislation was due to such experts as Edwin E. Witte, a Wisconsin economist, who helped draft the act. Witte and his colleagues were able to design a program that earned the support of an array of conflicting interests and addressed such issues as congressional reaction, constitutional issues, and administrative feasibility. When finished the Social Security program stood, as Roosevelt described it, as "a cornerstone in a structure which is being built but is by no means complete." Following the enactment of the bill and the Supreme Court's upholding of the constitutionality of the program, FDR was able to move to advance social reform in other areas. Bremner concludes that the "New Deal response to unemployment relief, economic insecurity, and public assistance was part of, and inevitably influenced by, the general response of the American people to these problems."

In the following essay, Frances Fox Piven and Richard A. Cloward present a radical critique of the New Deal. Piven and Cloward see welfare in modern industrial societies as an instrument to enforce work standards and work values among the laboring classes. Only when social upheaval threatens the system will welfare measures providing unemployment relief be instituted. Such measures are not motivated by humanitarian impulses, but by a need to assuage the discontented. For this reason, welfare benefits remain oppressively low and are never more than necessary to maintain the system.

In their essay, excerpted from their widely read *Regulating the Poor*, Piven and Cloward apply their argument to the Roosevelt program. They maintain that direct relief ran against the American ideology of hard work and private enterprise. Yet as labor and other political groupings became increasingly active following the congressional elections of 1934, Roosevelt promulgated a series of reforms including protective labor legislation, tax reform, the regulation of utilities, social insurance, and work relief. Many of these measures, once enacted however, contained little in substance; they were chiefly of symbolic importance to the Roosevelt administration. Piven and Cloward conclude that the key to understanding the failure of the New Deal to undertake "real" reforms must be seen in the failure of insurgent movements such as Francis E. Townsend's Old People's Movement.

In the final readings of this chapter, Alfred M. Landon, the presidential candidate for the Republican party in 1936, and Franklin D. Roosevelt present their views on the role of the federal government in social policy with a democratic society. Roosevelt set the stage for his election victory in 1936 in his annual address to Congress, January 4, 1935. In this speech, Roosevelt called for new social programs to protect the security and earning opportunities of Americans caught in the Depression. In calling for new programs including unemployment insurance, old-age insurance, and aid to the poor, Roosevelt carefully drew upon traditional American values to frame his social program. He called for the federal government to enter into a new role in protecting the basic needs of its citizens, while at the same time warning that federal relief should not become a permanent feature of American social policy. Roosevelt showed in this speech why his contemporaries and later historians saw him as the master politician.

Alf Landon, in the presidential campaign of 1936, expressed typical Republican opposition to the Social Security Act of 1935. In this speech given to a Milwaukee audience in the final days of the campaign, Landon attacked Social Security as inefficient, paternalistic, and unfair. He maintained that it was arrogant on the part of the federal government to believe that people could not save for their own retirements. This "stern management of a paternal government," he said, revealed a lack of faith in the American people. As a consequence, Landon called for the repeal of compulsory old-age and unemployment insurance. He believed that only the program aimed at providing assistance to the needy elderly should be kept and made the center of the Social Security program. Landon's call for repeal of the Social Security Act marked the last time the Republican party would oppose the program. Within a matter of a few years, Social Security had become a program that neither the Democrats nor the Republicans dared criticize.

Further Readings

For Social Security, W. Andrew Achenbaum offers a readable general history in *Shades of Gray* (Boston: Little, Brown, 1983). Theron F. Schlabach provides a thorough biography of a leading figure in the early years of Social Security in *Edwin E. Witte: Cautious Reformer* (Madison, Wisc.: State Historical Society, 1969). Also of interest is George McJimsey, *Harry Hopkins: Ally of the Poor and Defender of Democracy* (Cambridge: Harvard University Press, 1987).

The best general histories of the New Deal are Arthur M. Schlesinger, *The Crisis of the Old Order* (Boston: Houghton Mifflin, 1957), Schlesinger, *The Coming of the New Deal* (Boston: Houghton Mifflin, 1958), and William E. Leuchtenburg, *Franklin D. Roosevelt and the New Deal* (New York: Harper & Row, 1963). Frances Fox Piven and Richard A. Cloward, *Regulating the Poor* (New York: Random House, 1971) is also an important book.

The New Deal and Social Welfare

Robert H. Bremner

ROOSEVELT'S ATTITUDES TOWARD SOCIAL WELFARE

In August 1931, at a time when President Hoover was seeking to assist the unemployed by mobilizing and coordinating the charitable resources of the nation, Governor Franklin Roosevelt told a special session of the New York state legislature that "aid must be extended [to the unemployed] by Government, not as a matter of charity but as a matter of social duty." Roosevelt acknowledged that in normal times and under ordinary conditions relief of the poor was a function of local government and private agencies. He emphasized that the $20 million he proposed to take from state funds for apportionment among counties and cities was to supplement amounts raised locally. As if to reiterate the extraordinary circumstances that made state action necessary, he proposed the name "Temporary Emergency Relief Administration" for the commission responsible for distributing the fund. Roosevelt made clear his own preference for work relief as opposed to "the dole" and recommended that if local officials were unable to find or provide work for public service, relief should take the form of food, clothing, and shelter. "Under no circumstances," he declared, "shall any actual money be paid in the form of a dole . . . by the local welfare officer to any unemployed [man] or his family."

Early in 1932 Roosevelt commended Senator Robert Wagner for his efforts to get federal appropriations for relief. Federal aid was justified and sorely needed in the present crisis, said Roosevelt, "although it should not be regarded as a permanent Government policy." Roosevelt's speech accepting the Democratic nomination for President had little to say on the subject of relief except that "while now, as ever" primary responsibility rested with localities, the federal government "has always had, and still has a continuing responsibility for broader public welfare." During the closing weeks of the campaign he declared that when states and communities were unable to provide necessary relief "it then becomes the positive duty of the Federal Government to step in to help." This was, in fact, the course reluctantly adopted by the Hoover Administration in the summer of 1932 when the Reconstruction Finance Corporation began to make loans to states for relief and public works. In his inaugural address of March 4, 1933, Roosevelt indicated he was willing to go substantially further, including "direct recruiting" of the unemployed by the federal government

SOURCE: Robert H. Bremner, in *Fifty Years Later: The New Deal Evaluated*, ed. Harvard Sitkoff (New York: Alfred A. Knopf, 1985), pp. 69–91.

for work on "projects to stimulate and reorganize the use of our natural resources."

Scarcely a month after taking office, President Roosevelt signed the executive order establishing the Civilian Conservation Corps (CCC), the first and longest-lived New Deal unemployment relief agency. Within three months the CCC had enrolled 250,000 young unemployed men, 25,000 World War I veterans, and 25,000 experienced woodsmen and put them to work on reforestation, soil conservation, and similar projects in parks and forests at more than 1,400 camps across the nation. In Roosevelt's words, "It was the most rapid large-scale mobilization in our history." Enrollees received $30 a month (of which all but a small allowance was ordinarily sent home to their families), plus food, shelter, clothing, transportation, medical and dental attention, and, after the program had been in operation for some time, the opportunity for general educational and vocational training. During the life of the program enrollees sent a total of $670 million in allotments to their families. After 1937 family need was given less consideration in selection of enrollees and, in 1939, the director of the Corps announced, "The CCC as a monetary relief and job-giving agency has been replaced by the CCC as a work-training agency." When the program came to an end in June 1942 more than 2.5 million youths had served in the CCC; enrollment hit a peak of 500,000 in August 1935 and a low point of 240,000 in March 1937. As late as 1940, more boys entered the Corps each year than entered colleges and universities as freshmen.

In the message to Congress proposing the CCC, Roosevelt also pointed out the need for grants to the states for relief and recommended establishment of an office of Federal Relief Administration "to scan requests for grants and to check the efficiency and wisdom of their use." The Federal Emergency Relief Act, adopted on May 12, 1933 in response to Roosevelt's request, was a landmark in the development of federal-state cooperation in the relief of distress. It authorized outright grants, instead of loans, to the states, transferred administration of the grants from the Reconstruction Finance Corporation to a new social agency, the Federal Emergency Relief Administration (FERA) and, by giving the agency authority to make or withhold grants, allowed the federal government to exert some influence over the kind and quality of relief offered in the states. Roosevelt's remarks on signing the measure emphasized that localities and states must do their utmost to relieve the needy before the federal government would make funds available. In fact, the need for immediate assistance was so well recognized that Harry L. Hopkins, former director of the New York State Relief Commission, approved grants to seven states on the day he took office as head of FERA.

Under Hopkins' leadership, and partly because there were few precedents to follow, the FERA proved one of the most resourceful and innovative of all New Deal executive agencies. In theory it simply supplemented the work of local and state governments, by providing funds dispensed by

local officials with a minimum of federal direction. One of the FERA mandates was that its funds should be spent only through public agencies, a
requirement that strengthened public agencies and, in some communities,
brought them into existence. In addition to making funds available (or
withholding them and thereby stimulating laggard states to bestir themselves), the FERA maintained programs for transients, distributed surplus
commodities supplied by the Agricultural Adjustment Administration to
people on relief, instituted a rural rehabilitation program for the needy in
rural areas, and granted funds to colleges and universities for the employment of students on part-time work projects.

Both Roosevelt and Hopkins vastly preferred work relief to direct cash
relief, which Roosevelt often referred to, always slightingly, as "the dole."
Hopkins recognized that direct relief might tide the unemployed over a
period of a few months or even a year, but he believed that when people
were out ot jobs for a long time, worklessness was as destructive as physical
want. Hopkins also distinguished between work relief of the leaf-raking or
snow-shoveling kind, favored by some local governments, and employment
on a federally financed work project. "To the man on relief," Hopkins
observed, "the difference is very real." He went on to note:

> On work relief, although he gets the disciplinary rewards of keeping fit, and
> of making a return for what he gets, his need is still determined by a social
> worker, and he feels himself to be something of a public ward, with small
> freedom of choice. When he gets a job on a work program, it is very different.
> He is paid wages and the social worker drops out of the picture. His wages
> may not cover much more ground than his former relief budget but they are
> his to spend as he likes.

In November 1933 Roosevelt announced the establishment of the Civil
Works Administration (CWA), a branch of the FERA, which was intended
to take 4 million persons off relief rolls and convert them, for the winter of
1933–34, into "self-sustaining employees" on small public works projects.
During the four and a half months that the CWA operated, Hopkins and
his lieutenants devised 180,000 work projects which, at their peak in mid-
January 1934, employed slightly more than 4 million persons. Most of
the jobs were in construction projects but the CWA also set up projects
for teachers, engineers, architects, artists, nurses, and other white-collar
workers. The total cost of the CWA was just under $1 billion, nearly 80
percent of which went for wages.

Both during and after the CWA experiment with federally controlled
work projects, FERA continued to make grants to states for direct relief
of persons who could not be employed on the work projects. After the
dissolution of the CWA in the spring of 1934, the FERA supported an
Emergency Works Relief Program, transferring to it a number of CWA
projects and employees. The FERA continued efforts begun under the CWA
to adapt work relief to the occupational skills and backgrounds of people
from all walks of life.

In the State of the Union message of January 1935, Roosevelt distinguished between the 1.5 million relief recipients who, for reasons of age or physical or mental incapacity, were unable to maintain themselves independently, and the 3.5 million employable persons then on relief rolls who were victims "of a nationwide depression caused by conditions which were not local but national." Care of the former group, "the unemployables," had traditionally been a local responsibility. In declaring that "the Federal Government must and shall quit this business of relief," Roosevelt signified his intention to return responsibility for their care to local and state officials, justifying the decision by "the dictates of sound administration." "The dictates of sound policy," strongly influenced by the President's reverence for "the moral and spiritual values of work," determined his prescription for the employables: "Work must be found for able-bodied but destitute workers," he declared. "We must preserve not only the bodies of the unemployed from destitution but also their self-respect, their self-reliance and courage and determination."

The Emergency Relief Appropriation Act of 1935, passed at Roosevelt's recommendation, authorized a massive federal works program with an initial appropriation of nearly $5 billion. The Works Progress (after 1939 Projects) Administration, headed by Harry Hopkins, replaced the FERA as the key agency in the fight against unemployment. Over the next eight years the WPA received a total of $11.4 billion in appropriations and gave work and wages to 8.5 million people. WPA employment rolls varied from month to month and year to year in accordance with the availability of funds and the administration's not always accurate prediction of economic conditions. In September and October 1937, when a deep recession was commencing, the number of WPA workers fell below 1.5 million; during the latter half of 1938, when the recession was easing, there were more than 3 million WPA workers.

One of the WPA's tasks was to coordinate and report on the progress of the forty other federal agencies, including the CCC, the Public Works Administration, and the National Youth Administration (NYA), a subsidiary of the WPA, all of which participated in the works program. The NYA, for example, gave employment on work projects to 2.5 million out-of-school youth aged 16 to 25, and funded part-time work projects that allowed 2 million young people to remain in school. The WPA approved and supervised "small useful projects"—mainly in the fields of construction, reclamation, rehabilitation, and conservation—sponsored by state and local governments, which paid for most of the nonlabor costs. The 1935 Appropriation Act included "assistance for educational, professional, and clerical persons" among the projects authorized for support by the WPA. Drawing upon the experience of both the FERA and the CWA, Hopkins funded projects capable of using the labor or talent of people in fields as diverse as equipment operating, acting, dancing, painting, music, and historical research. WPA projects enhanced the quality of life in countless communities, not only in tangible, brick-and-mortar ways, but by supporting educational, cultural, and recreational opportunities and amenities. The projects promoted literacy programs, surveyed and preserved historical and architectural records, and fostered awareness and respect for the diversity and richness of American culture. In 1943, when Roosevelt awarded the WPA an "honorable discharge," he saluted its record in rendering "almost immeasurable kinds and quantities of service," and "reaching a creative hand into every county" of the nation. "It has added to the national wealth," he said, "has repaired the wastage of depression, and has strengthened the country to bear the burden of war."

The contributions of New Deal work projects to the morale of workers employed on them is harder to measure than the physical and social results of the programs. It is important to keep in mind that their purpose was not to rehabilitate the unemployed but to rescue them from idleness and to foster a sense of self-respect among people not deemed responsible for their misfortune. The distinction Roosevelt and the New Deal made between the unemployed and chronic dependents, and the special status accorded the "employables," made for a more favorable public attitude toward, and a better self-image among, the unemployed. But, as the years passed and the Depression dragged on, the difference between the "new poor" and the "old" became less apparent. The distinction between employables and unemployables, always sharper in principle than in application, became thoroughly blurred before the end of the 1930s.

A *Fortune* survey of unemployment and relief, made in 1937 under the mistaken impression that the Depression was over, concluded "the despised WPA" had worked, even if expensively. Most of the countless criticisms of the works program alleged waste, extravagance, and inefficiency on the part of project management and loafing on the part of employees. Hopkins, however, in a book appropriately entitled *Spending to Save* (1936), maintained that the most telling and truthful criticism was "We have never given adequate relief." In 1934–35 under FERA, the average *monthly* grant paid to an unemployed worker and his family (less than $30) was about the same as the average *weekly* wage of an industrial worker before the Depression. WPA workers received a "security wage," higher than direct relief under the FERA but less than the prevailing wage in the community for a comparable job in private industry. In 1941 WPA monthly earnings for the country as a whole averaged $60, somewhat less than the total benefits (cash allowance, clothing, shelter, subsistence, and medical care) received by CCC enrollees, which amounted to $67 a month.

Hopkins once acknowledged that the Roosevelt Administration, in its eagerness to win acceptance for the federal works program, "overemphasized the undesirability of relief." Roosevelt's 1935 State of the Union message denounced relief as "a narcotic, a subtle destroyer of the human spirit." Later in 1935, he admitted "a dole would be more economical than work relief," but added, "Most Americans want to give something for what they get. That something, in this case honest work, is the saving barrier between them and moral disintegration. We propose to build that barrier high." The WPA's official *Workers' Handbook* (1936), distributed to new employees, asked and answered a loaded question:

> What happens to us when we are on the dole? We lose our self-respect. We lose our skill. We have family rows. We loaf on street corners. Finally, we lose hope.

Such attacks on direct relief were unfortunate, as Hopkins conceded, "inasmuch as we have not been able to remove from hundreds of thousands of people the inescapability of accepting it." "Seeking" would have been a better word than "accepting" because New Deal work projects, despite their number, variety, and the large appropriations supporting them, were never adequate to care for all of the needy unemployed. There was always a pool of employable persons, certified to be in need and eligible for assignment to federal work projects or special youth programs, who were not added to the rolls because funds were not available for their employment. At various times after 1935, the number of these unfortunates ranged from 600,000 to 1.3 million a month.

After 1935, except for subsistence grants to poverty-stricken farmers, distribution of surplus commodities, and grants-in-aid for groups covered by the Social Security Act, the federal government left relief of the poor (often called general assistance) entirely to local communities, with such assistance as the states chose to provide. With federal aid withdrawn and with either no state funds or inadequate ones, local authorities faced, but seldom met, the need for helping both the unemployables and many of the employables. The federal relief administration no longer, as under the FERA, had any leverage for inducing or compelling states to bolster local efforts. Had Roosevelt and Hopkins chosen to do so, they might have diverted some funds from work relief to direct relief since all the emergency relief appropriation acts from 1935 through 1939 stated that the appropriated funds might be used for "relief" as well as "work relief." Their refusal to do so, despite clear need for such action, shows how strongly committed a supposedly pragmatic administration was to certain moral assumptions and to traditional assignments of responsibility for poor relief.

SOCIAL SECURITY

In 1928, while campaigning for the governorship of New York, Roosevelt endorsed his party's platform pledge for a study of old-age pensions, a subject then as radical and socialistic, he joked, as factory inspection and workmen's compensation had seemed twenty years earlier. After the election a commission jointly appointed by legislative leaders and Governor Roosevelt studied the problem, issued a report, and early in 1930 the chairman of the commission introduced an old-age pension bill in the legislature. Roosevelt was disappointed in the report and unenthusiastic about the bill which, instead of providing for a contributory system with uniform application throughout the state, made old-age pensions an extension of the poor laws and allowed local authorities wide discretion in administering them. "Our American aged do not want charity," Roosevelt asserted, "but rather old-age comforts to which they are rightfully entitled by their own thrift and foresight in the form of insurance." Despite his objections he accepted the measure as a stopgap and a possible beginning toward something better: "We can only hope that this will be a forerunner of a proper system of security against old-age want in the years to come."

In accepting the Democratic nomination in 1932, Roosevelt cited "work and security" as the goals toward which he and the party should strive. After a little more than a year in the presidency, he declared that the first objective of the administration was security for individuals and families and announced his intention of furthering the objective through social insurance. In June 1934, Roosevelt told Congress that he was looking "for a sound means which I can recommend to provide at once security against several of the great disturbing factors in life—especially those which related to unemployment and old age." Roosevelt made it clear that he believed the funds necessary to provide the insurance should be raised by contributions of workers and employers rather than by general taxation, and that the insurance system should be national in scope. To study the matter further and recommend a "sound means," he appointed a Committee on Economic Security, which he directed to report its findings and recommendations no later than December 1, 1934.

The committee consisted of the secretaries of the Departments of Labor (chairman), Treasury, and Agriculture, the Attorney General, the Federal Emergency Relief Administrator, an advisory council composed of representatives of industry, labor, and social welfare, a technical board made up of officials from interested federal agencies, and a staff directed by Edwin E. Witte, an expert on social legislation and chairman of the Department of Economics at the University of Wisconsin. The members and staff of the committee worked under the pressure of time; against the background of agitation for proposals such as the Townsend Plan and Huey Long's Share-Our-Wealth Plan,* which the President considered unsound and too radical to be considered; in receipt of contradictory testimony from expert witnesses; and amidst uncertainty whether the Supreme Court would recognize the constitutionality of any national system of social insurance. Committee members were divided in their opinions about the relative importance of

---

*The Townsend Plan proposed paying a pension of $200 per month to everyone over the age of sixty who promised to spend the sum within a month. Long's Share-Our-Wealth plan advocated the liquidation of private fortunes so that the government could distribute enough money for each family to buy a home, a car, and a radio.

unemployment and old-age insurance. Those who thought unemployment insurance was the most urgent issue were further divided between supporters of a national system under federal control and a federal-state system permitting the states greater freedom for experiment and innovation. The President's views, possible congressional reaction, and questions of administrative feasibility all had to be taken into consideration in weighing alternatives. As a result, a key member of the group, Arthur J. Altermeyer, recalled, "the committee did not arrive at its final recommendations without considerable travail." The legislative program recommended by the committee included:

1. a federal-state system of unemployment insurance;
2. a compulsory, federally administered old-age insurance system, financed by contributions from employees and employers, with benefits payable to insured workers at age 65; and
3. federal grants-in-aid to the states for old-age pensions (for people too old to benefit from the old-age insurance system), for the support of dependent children, for an expanded public health program, and to finance maternal and child health and welfare programs.

In January 1935, Roosevelt transmitted the committee's report to Congress with a message that strongly endorsed the proposed Economic Security Act and warned against discrediting "the sound and necessary policy of Federal legislation for economic security" by applying it, at the outset, on too ambitious a scale. He specifically noted that the measure he recommended for adoption did not include health insurance. During congressional consideration of the economic security bill, witnesses referred to it as the "social security bill" and it was the Social Security Act that finally received the approval of Congress and, on August 14, 1935, Roosevelt's signature. Social security, a more inclusive term than economic security, covered the three areas or kinds of programs provided for in the act: protection against some of the "hazards and vicissitudes of life" by social insurance; provision of public assistance for certain categories of the needy; and extension of public services to promote public health, child and maternal health and welfare, and rehabilitation of the handicapped. The act created a new federal agency, the Social Security Board, to keep the records and make payments to the millions of workers to be covered by the old-age insurance program, to exercise general responsibility for the federally subsidized (but state-administered) unemployment insurance plans, and to supervise the program of grants-in-aid to states for old-age assistance, aid to dependent children, and aid to the blind.

Roosevelt's statement on signing the Social Security Act sounded a note between pride in its enactment and modesty in recognition of its limitations. The measure, in his words, would give "at least some measure of protection" to an estimated 30 million persons who would benefit from unemployment compensation, the public assistance programs, and services for children and public health. It would give "some measure of protection to the average citizen and to his family against the loss of a job and against poverty-ridden old age." Most important, in the President's view, the law represented "a cornerstone in a structure which is being built but is by no means complete."

Knowledgeable contemporary observers mixed criticism of shortcomings of the act with recognition of its significance and optimism about possibilities of improving it. The economist Paul Douglas, a long-time advocate of social insurance, called it "a worthy effort to protect better the lives of wage-earners and salaried employees," but "full of weaknesses" and "merely a first step which must soon be followed by others." Edith Abbott, a noted social-work educator, criticized the act's failure to provide grants-in-aid for general relief, for low benefits, gaps in coverage, and absence of a health insurance program. On balance, however, she concluded: "We can also count great gains. In the first place, and of tremendous significance, the responsibility of government and industry to insure security will be recognized for the first time. The system can and will be improved in the light of experience."

In contrast to the CCC, the FERA, and the WPA, the Social Security Act was intended to launch a permanent, rather than a temporary, program. Appropriations to carry out its provisions were the first—with the exception of the Railroad Retirement Act of 1934, which was declared unconstitutional in 1935—in the area of relief and public welfare without the prefix "emergency." Adoption of the act inaugurated a lasting commitment, as well as a significant involvement, on the part of the federal government in social welfare. Supreme Court decisions in 1937 made possible continuance and further development of the federal government's activity in programs for protection against economic insecurity. In *Steward Machine Co. v. Davis*, a case involving the unemployment insurance titles of the act, Justice Benjamin Cardozo, noting the billions of dollars spent on unemployment relief between 1933 and 1936, declared "the parens patriae [the state as parent and protector] has many reasons—fiscal and economic as well as social and moral—for planning to mitigate disasters that bring these burdens in their train." In *Helvering et al. v. Davis*, Justice Cardozo, again speaking for the majority of the Supreme Court, unequivocally endorsed the constitutionality of the old-age insurance titles: "The problem [old-age poverty] is plainly national in area and dimensions. Moreover, laws of the separate states cannot deal with it effectively. . . . Only a power that is national can serve the interest of all."

On the same day the Supreme Court sustained the Social Security Act, the President sent a special message to Congress stating, "The time has arrived for us"—meaning the three branches of the federal government—"to extend the frontiers of social progress, by adopting a minimum wage law." Roosevelt presented the measure, which revived some of the wage, hours, and child-labor provisions of the NRA codes, overthrown by the

Supreme Court in 1935, as essential to economic recovery. Its objectives were "to reduce the lag in purchasing power of industrial workers and to strengthen and stabilize the markets for the farmers' products." In calling for a floor under wages and a ceiling over hours, he appealed to the nation's sense of fairness but not to pity: "A self-supporting and self-respecting democracy can plead no justification for the existence of child labor, no economic reason for chiseling workers' wages or stretching workers' hours."

In the year that elapsed, and during the three sessions of Congress that met while the wage-hour bill was under consideration, opponents offered numerous amendments and the House Rules Committee attempted to prevent a vote on the measure. Most of the seventy-two amendments sought to weaken the act by broadening the industries and occupations exempted and by narrowing the coverage of workers to whom it applied. Roosevelt vigorously supported the bill, always emphasizing economic rather than humanitarian arguments for its passage. In January 1938, referring to underpaid industrial workers, he said, "Aside from the undoubted fact that they thereby suffer great human hardship,"—and apparently of equal or greater import in Roosevelt's view—"they are unable to buy adequate food and shelter, to maintain health or to buy their share of manufactured goods." His approach may have been influenced by the sharp economic recession of 1937–38, but it was consistent with his general tendency to look at social problems from what he called "the practical, dollars-and-cents point of view" and to justify social legislation on the grounds of common sense and fair play.

As finally adopted in June 1938, the Fair Labor Standards Act provided, at the start—in those industries and occupations not exempted from its provisions—for a minimum wage of 25 cents an hour to go into effect at once and gradually to be increased to 40 cents; a maximum workweek of 44 hours (to be reduced within three years to 40 hours) with time-and-a-half pay for overtime work; a prohibition of the shipment in interstate commerce of goods produced by children under 16 years of age (18 in hazardous industries); and the establishment of a Wage and Hour Division in the Department of Labor to supervise application and enforcement of the Act.

Like the Social Security Act, the Fair Labor Standards Act represented only a modest beginning toward realization of its objectives. Roosevelt recognized that the rudimentary standards established by the Act fell far short of the ideal. "Backward labor conditions and relatively progressive labor conditions," he explained, "cannot be completely assimilated and made uniform at one fell swoop without creating economic dislocations." For constitutional reasons, the Act applied only to employees in manufacturing establishments that shipped their products in interstate commerce, and for political and/or expedient reasons it exempted agricultural workers, employees in intrastate retail and servicing establishments, seamen, fishermen, and employees in a number of other industries. Of the approximately

850,000 children under 16 years of age who were gainfully employed in 1938, only about 50,000 came within the purview of the act. Children in agriculture, the street trades (selling newspapers or other merchandise in the streets), messenger and delivery service, stores, hotels, restaurants, bowling alleys, filling stations, and similar intrastate enterprises were not subject to the law. As in the case of the Social Security Act, a favorable decision by the Supreme Court on the constitutionality of the Fair Labor Standards Act—*United States v. Darby Lumber Co.* (1941) in which the court endorsed a broad interpretation of the powers of Congress under the interstate commerce clause—permitted subsequent broadening of coverage and elevation of standards.

In 1939 Congress passed the first of a series of amendments to the Social Security Act, which extended its coverage to more workers and improved benefits to the insured and their dependents. The 1939 amendments incorporated recommendations developed over a period of two years by the President, the Advisory Council on Social Security, and the Social Security Board, which was given the task, in the 1935 Act, of conducting studies and making recommendations for legislation and policies to improve economic security through social insurance. The most important of the numerous changes made by the 1939 amendments converted old-age insurance into Old Age and Survivors' Insurance (OASI) by making wives and young children of insured workers eligible for monthly benefit payments in the event of the worker's death either before or after retirement. OASI thus became a system offering protection both to individual workers and their families. The amendments also improved benefits under the public assistance program for Aid to Dependent Children by increasing the federal matching ratio from one-third to one-half of the aid granted. The amendments also provided for larger federal contributions to federal-state programs in public health, maternal and child health, child welfare services, care of crippled children, and vocational rehabilitation.

Almost a decade earlier, disappointed in the New York State old-age pension law, Roosevelt admitted "progress comes slowly." He could point to the 1939 amendments with some pride as a further advance toward the "kind of old-age insurance . . . our most progressive thought demands" and as evidence that progress is possible, even if slow.

SOCIAL WELFARE

A year before Franklin Roosevelt was born and fifty-one years before his election to the presidency, William Graham Sumner, a Yale political economist, asserted that the task of dealing with social ills was not a new ideal but a continuation of humankind's age-old struggle with the problems of social welfare. Sumner, like Benjamin Franklin, regarded individualism and self-help as the only effective methods of securing improvement in human affairs. He was both pessimistic and cynical about the possibilities of social reform: "It would be hard to find a single instance of a direct assault by positive effort upon poverty, vice, and misery," he declared, "which has not either failed or, if it has not failed directly and entirely, has not entailed other evils greater than the one which it removed." In Sumner's opinion, "the only two things which really tell on the welfare of man on earth are hard work and self-denial . . . , and these tell most when they are brought to bear directly upon the effort to earn an honest living, to accumulate capital, and to bring up a family of children to be industrious and self-denying in their turn."

In 1883 the single-tax philosopher and reformer Henry George responded to Sumner in a series of magazine articles published in book form under the title *Social Problems*. (Sumner's articles in a rival periodical were also published in 1883 under the title *What Social Classes Owe to Each Other*.) George scoffed at Sumner's "Gospel of Selfishness," the teaching that "the saving word for society" was for each to mind his own business. Instead of individualism and self-help, George stressed the interdependence of individuals and classes imposed by modern technology and economic arrangements: "Social progess makes the well-being of all more and more the business of each. . . . He who observes the law and the proprieties, and cares for his family, yet takes no interest in the general weal, . . . is not a true Christian. Nor is he a good citizen."

Sumner and George differed not only on the methods of social progress but on the possibility of overcoming want. Sumner assumed that the pressure of population on scarce resources and the competitive struggle for existence circumscribed opportunities for wholesale improvement in economic conditions and restricted the enjoyment of wealth to the prudent, energetic, and lucky. George maintained that it was not the scarcity of resources but their waste, monopolization, and mismanagement that caused poverty. He believed that by adopting a comparatively simple reform—the single-tax on land values—society could unlock the bounty of nature and make it possible for all to live in comfort, decency, and security.

Sumner's and George's attitudes and approaches to social welfare represent the two sides of the American coin. In any period of American history each has its adherents; sometimes one view is dominant, sometimes the other. Although it is unlikely that Roosevelt consciously made a choice between them, his outlook in most respects was closer to George's than to Sumner's. Roosevelt was not a utopian. Unlike George, he had no panacea— except work—to cure social ills, and he did not expect social gains to be scored all at once and once and for all, but he did believe that American abundance in human and natural resources made hope and confidence more appropriate than despair. Roosevelt saw and always presented the nation's problems as man-made rather than imposed by providence; he not only accepted but welcomed the need for action to correct social ills; and he never doubted the possibility of achieving changes that would promote the common welfare. In his message to Congress proposing the minimum-wage, maximum-hours bill he cited cogent reasons why "exponents of the theory of private initiative as the cure for deep-seated national ills" were wrong:

> ... first, they see the problem from the point of view of their own business; second, they see the problem from the point of view of their own locality or region; third, they cannot act unanimously because they have no machinery for agreeing among themselves; and, finally, they have no power to bind the inevitable minority of chislers within their own ranks.

As Roosevelt saw it supporters of the private enterprise theory of reform had always resisted legislation to advance social progress. "In actual practice," he said, [social progress] "has been effectively advanced only by the passage of laws by state legislatures or the National Congress."

Sumner devoted two chapters of *What Social Classes Owe to Each Other* to "The Case of a Certain Man Who Is Never Thought Of" and made "The Forgotten Man" the subject and title of one of his most popular essays. The man (and woman) Sumner had in mind was the ordinary worker and taxpayer who, in Sumner's opinion, had been neglected by philanthropists and reformers; the latter seemed to think the only people worth attention were the poor and the weak, described by Sumner as "the nasty, criminal, whining, crawling and good-for-nothing people." Roosevelt, in a preconvention radio address in 1932, borrowed Sumner's phrase, "the forgotten man," and applied it to the same commonplace folk with whom Sumner had sympathized—homeowners, farmers, workers and would-be workers, "the infantry of our economic army"—but Roosevelt alleged they had not been forgotten by reformers, but by the Hoover Administration.

As President, Roosevelt used "the average man" or "the average citizen and his family" rather than "the forgotten man" to denote the segment of the population the New Deal meant to serve. After the policies of the Republican administrations of the 1920s, championship of the common man was novel enough to win Roosevelt the reputation of a radical among the groups he dubbed "economic royalists." New Deal programs were broad enough to bring a great many, varied people in different kinds of activities and representing different economic interest groups within the meaning of "the average man." Under the broader definition, the ordinary American came to seem a much more interesting and attractive figure than Sumner's prosaic "forgotten man," or the boobs and Babbitts who were thought by some to typify the population in the 1920s. Whether because of the New Deal or for other reasons, the 1930s was one of the few times in recent American history when intellectuals and artists treated the lives and experiences of everyday Americans with respect rather than contempt and derision.

Roosevelt's Second Inaugural Address, which contained the moving sentence, "I see one third of a nation ill-housed, ill-clad, ill-nourished," hinted that the New Deal might broaden its concern from the average to the less-than-average Americans, the people who were not so much forgotten as routinely overlooked and whose interests were seldom taken into consideration by shapers of public policy. Roosevelt declared, "We are determined to make every American citizen the subject of his country's interest and concern; and we will never regard any faithful, law-abiding group within our borders as superfluous."

Through various programs carried out under the FERA, the Resettlement Administration, and the Farm Security Administraion, the New Deal expressed at least intermittent concern for the plight of the desperately poor. Other New Deal decisions, such as the distinction drawn between employables and unemployables and the cessation of federal grants for direct relief, signified that the administration was willing to sacrifice the interest of marginal people to the welfare of people deemed more deserving of help from the federal government. Even being self-supporting was not enough to bring workers in low-status jobs under the coverage of the Social Security and Fair Labor Standards Acts, both of which, as originally adopted, excluded domestic and agricultural labor. Ten years after the passage of the Social Security Act, one-third of black male workers and two-thirds of black female workers were in jobs not covered by the act.

In the early years of Social Security, when contributions far exceeded disbursements, critics complained of the large reserves accumulating in the OASI trust fund. During World War II, against strenuous objections from Roosevelt, Congress postponed scheduled increases in contributions and limited taxes collected from employers and employees to 1 percent. The Revenue Act of 1944, which Roosevelt denounced as "a tax relief bill providing relief not for the needy but for the greedy," contained a provision (strongly backed by Republicans) authorizing appropriations to the trust fund of "such additional sums as may be required to finance the benefits and payments" provided under the OASI title of the Social Security Act. The provision was removed by the Social Security Amendments of 1950 which, for the first time, increased OASI contribution rates. Subsequent expansion of coverage and liberalization of benefits, like the original Act, were based on the assumption that the contributory method of financing old-age, survivors, and (after 1956) disability insurance was preferable to the so-called "charity method" of supporting the programs by appropriations from general revenue. In practice, payment to retirees, survivors, and the disabled depended on a steady flow of contributions from people still working. By the 1980s, demographic developments and projections, as well as widespread unemployment, made changes in financing the Social Security system imperative.

Fifty years after the start of the FERA, the federal governement was still deeply involved in the "business of relief." One of the main reasons was the program of grants-in-aid to states for Aid to Dependent Children inaugurated by the Social Security Act. Roosevelt never endorsed the view advanced in 1934 by a veteran social worker, Homer Folks, that receiving relief when it is needed and properly administered is less demoralizing for recipients and a sounder policy for society than allowing need to go unrelieved. Long before 1935, however, he supported the idea of public assistance for children "thrown on the mercy of the community by the death, the insanity, the desertion, or the incapacity of their fathers." Instead of institutionalizing the children, Roosevelt favored the mothers' pension method of helping mothers to raise the children at home. "Money used to give these children a mother's love and a mother's rearing can never be wasted," Roosevelt announced in a campaign address in 1928.

Aid to Dependent Children was included in the Social Security Act because the framers recognized that fatherless children would not benefit from other provisions of the act, from work projects, or even from economic recovery. It was believed, however, that need for the program would gradually decline as more and more families came under the protection of Social Security. Contrary to expectations, and largely because of the general increase in the child population in the 1950s, the survival of poverty, and high rates of illegitimacy and desertion, the number of children and adult caretakers served by Aid to Families with Dependent Children (AFDC) expanded rapidly during the 1960s and 1970s. In 1980 the program assisted nearly 4 million families and more than 11 million individuals, of whom 7.6 million were children. The federal share of the cost of the program was $7.8 billion in 1981, $7.7 billion in 1982.

Despite acknowledged shortcomings—low benefits, benefits that vary from state to state and from section to section, sometimes insensitive administration, and failure to provide for many poor families in which the father is present—AFDC continues as an important example of federal-state cooperation in the relief of need. It is an essential source of support for poor, female-headed households. The original justification for the program—"to make universally available throughout the United States certain minimum standards of public protection, without which any private effort or any purely local effort is bound to be uneven and most inadequate in the places and areas where children are in the greatest need"—is still valid and has not yet been fully realized. That the nation has not yet been able to agree upon any better way of providing for its most deprived and unfortunate children is a reminder both of the New Deal's lasting significance and limited achievement in social welfare.

The New Deal and Relief

Frances Fox Piven and
Richard A. Cloward

While the organizational shells of the various relief movements survived until late in the depression, they had really been destroyed much earlier by such measures as social security, by labor legislation, by the Wealth Tax Act, by massive work relief, and by partial economic recovery. Although it was not recognized at the time, the election of 1936 had sounded the death knell for those who believed that anything was possible in America. The signs were there to be read in the election returns: taken together, the extremist parties polled only 2.9 percent of the vote, down from 3.1 percent in 1932. Although the insurgent organizations persisted for a time, the underlying popular unrest upon which insurgency draws had been quelled. The little the poor had gotten was enough. Indeed, it was apparently more than enough, for with political stability restored by the great election victory in 1936, the Administration rapidly reduced concessions to the poor, not least by slashing emergency relief measures and by restoring the traditional practices by which relief systems help to maintain the marginal labor pool—all in the name of "reform."

THE "REFORM" OF RELIEF

Harry Hopkins, writing in 1936, had high hopes for the Works Progress Administration and what it signaled for the American future. The communities of America, he maintained, having experienced the benefits of new WPA parks, roads, schools, and hospitals, and WPA programs for hot school lunches, free theater, and public health services, would never again settle for the shabbiness of public life before WPA. And the American government, having once lifted millions of the poor out of destitution, would not allow them to sink back:

> Communities now find themselves in possession of improvements which even in 1929 they would have thought themselves presumptuous to dream of ... [but] everywhere there had been an overhauling of the word *presumptuous*. We are beginning to wonder if it is not presumptuous to take for granted that some people should have much, and some should have nothing; that some people are less important than others and should die earlier; that the children of the comfortable should be taller and fatter, as a matter of right, than the children of the poor.

SOURCE: Frances Fox Piven and Richard A. Cloward, in *Regulating the Poor* (New York: Random House, 1971), pp. 109–117.

Harry Hopkins was wrong. It was WPA that was presumptuous, for it ran against the grain, it violated the American way. Once Main Street began to feel that things were better, it wanted to return to that Way. The communities of America had never really accepted WPA, and they settled readily for its withdrawal. The poor settled as well.

By late 1936, WPA rolls were being reduced; early in 1937, it was announced that half of the remaining workers would be discharged. When the President's budget request of January 1937 allocated only 650 million dollars to WPA, there was considerable agitation across the country, but to little avail. During the peak month of March 1936, some 2.9 million workers had been employed; by September 1937 only 1.5 million persons were still on the WPA rolls. With the new recession of 1938, WPA appropriations were increased to 1.25 billion dollars, and for a brief period the rolls again rose to 3 million. But they were rapidly reduced the following year, when Congress stipulated that those who had been in the program for more than eighteen continuous months should be removed—a measure presumably intended to force project workers to seek private employment. Just how these workers fared is suggested in a report issued by the WPA in January 1940:

> In July and August more than 775,000 WPA project workers were dropped from their jobs in accordance with the 18-months' provision of the 1939 Relief Act. A survey covering more than 138,000 of these workers, in 23 large and representative cities, disclosed that 3 to 4 weeks after their lay-off 7.6 percent were employed in private jobs. In November, a second interview with the same group showed that 2 to 3 months after dismissal 12.7 percent, or fewer than 100,000 of the 775,000 workers, were employed in private industry. In industrial centers like Buffalo, Cleveland, Cincinnati, Detroit, and Birmingham, the proportion with jobs was about one in six; in eight of the 23 cities it was about one in ten.

With the onset of World War II, the work relief program was even more sharply reduced and then terminated altogether.

What programs then remained to sustain the poor of America? There were, to be sure, the new insurance plans for aged and unemployed workers passed under the Social Security Act. Both of these insurance provisions, however, covered only certain classes of workers in preferred occupations. Such low wage industries as agriculture and domestic service were exempted. Moreover, as noted earlier, the insurance benefits for the aged became payable only in 1942. As for unemployment insurance, the implementation was left to the states which were free to adopt any level of benefits they wished, to set any waiting periods, and to fix the maximum period of benefit. In any case, both insurance plans applied only to workers who established their eligibility by their sustained participation in the workforce, and then became eligible for aid only by virtue of age or job retrenchments.

The relief program that remained was the provision for the aged, the blind, and the orphaned also contained in the Social Security Act of 1935. Control over relief-giving was substantially returned to the states and localities, with the difference that federal grants-in-aid would be available to supplement their expenditures. And although these measures did not receive much public attention at the time, overshadowed as they were by the provisions of the Act providing unemployment insurance and old-age pensions, they laid the foundations for the contemporary public welfare system.

The new relief legislation did, however, receive considerable attention from some members of Congress, who eliminated various alternative proposals before settling on the final wording. That process suggests some of the concerns that shaped our contemporary public assistance program. For example, an Advisory Committee on Public Employment and Relief (appointed by Frances Perkins, the Secretary of Labor, and composed mainly of social workers) had strongly opposed "categorical" assistance—that is, assistance only to those categories of the poor who were aged, blind, or orphaned—and had called upon the federal government to retain substantial authority over state programs. Similarly, an early draft of the public assistance provisions prepared by the FERA staff had defined "dependent children" broadly, intending the legislation to cover all children who were in severe need, not just those who lacked a parent.

The measures enacted by the Congress were substantially different, however. The simple absence of money was not deemed sufficient to justify coverage, and so the absence of a parent was imposed as a condition for the aid of children, more or less duplicating the old Mothers Aid program; wording to the effect that the aged should receive a grant "compatible with decency and health" was eliminated; the federal administering agency was given little authority over the states, which reflected a growing concern with restoring local options in relief-giving, particularly the option to set grant levels.

Not surprisingly, the main push for narrow coverage and local autonomy in administering these narrow programs came from Southern Congressmen, who were already irritated by what they considered the high-handed practices of the Federal Emergency Relief program. Their concerns were twofold: that the grant levels, if set by the federal government, would undermine the low wage structure in the South; and that a federal supervisory agency, if vested with great authority, would curtail local prerogatives to say who should get relief, thus opening the rolls to blacks and undermining the caste economy of the South. The original wording of the bill reported to the House said that relief could not be denied to a citizen if qualifications regarding age and need were met; the final wording provided only that no citizenship requirement could be used to exclude applicants, thus allowing the state to discriminate against blacks. Finally, there was no provision at all for federal aid to those who had neither blindness nor age nor orphanhood to justify their poverty. The modified and amended provisions were submitted for a vote as part of the Social Security package, which, as noted earlier, passed overwhelmingly and was hailed widely as a major reform.

Between the years 1935 and 1939 most of the states enacted legislation to make use of the categorical grants-in-aid. In the main, the legislation enacted was modeled after the state mothers' aid programs and pension programs for the aged that had existed prior to the passage of the Social Security Act, since most of the traditional "poor relief" restrictions which had been the hallmark of these earlier relief programs were reintroduced. The states exercised their prerogative to establish grant levels by setting them very low. Some states set them much lower than others. In December 1939, for example, Arkansas gave an average of $8.10 a month to families with dependent children and Massachusetts gave such families $61.07. Nationally, levels of aid under categorical assistance averaged about half what employables were earning on federal work relief projects.

Most important, few got any aid at all. Just how few is vividly demonstrated by the future course of the categorical assistance program for dependent children (AFDC). For one thing, many states were slow to implement this program; some had not done so as late as 1940. By December 1940, as a consequence, only 360,000 families had been admitted to the nation's AFDC rolls. Nine states, five of them in the South, still had fewer than 1,000 families on their rolls; Texas, for example, had a caseload of 85 families, and Mississippi a caseload of 104.

The sluggish growth of the program was reversed by World War II; between December 1940 and December 1945, the rolls dropped by 25 percent. But with the end of the war, the upward trend resumed; between December 1945 and December 1950, the rolls rose 132 percent. Even so, only 635,000 families were obtaining AFDC payments in 1950. At this level, caseloads stabilized, rising only 17 percent between 1950 and 1960 (despite sharply mounting unemployment in both agriculture and in the cities).

The cycle was complete. Turbulence had produced a massive federal direct relief program; direct relief had been converted into work relief; then work relief was cut back and the unemployed were thrown upon state and local agencies, which reduced aid to the able-bodied in most places and eventually eliminated it in many. What remained were the categorical-assistance programs for the impotent poor—the old, the blind, and the orphaned. For the able-bodied poor who would not be able to find employment or secure local relief in the days, months, and years to come, the federal government had made no provision. Nor are there statistics that describe their fate.

Annual Message to the Congress
January 4, 1935

Mr. President, Mr. Speaker, Members of the Senate and of the House of Representatives:

I recall to your attention my message to the Congress last June in which I said: "among our objectives I place the security of the men, women, and children of the Nation first." That remains our first and continuing task; and in a very real sense every major legislative enactment of this Congress should be a component part of it.

In defining immediate factors which enter into our quest, I have spoken to the Congress and the people of three great divisions:

1. The security of a livelihood through the better use of the national resources of the land in which we live.

2. The security against the major hazards and vicissitudes of life.

3. The security of decent homes.

I am now ready to submit to the Congress a broad program designed ultimately to establish all three of these factors of security—a program which because of many lost years will take many future years to fulfill.

A study of our national resources, more comprehensive than any previously made, shows the vast amount of necessary and practicable work which needs to be done for the development and preservation of our natural wealth for the enjoyment and advantage of our people in generations to come. The sound use of land and water is far more comprehensive than the mere planting of trees, building of dams, distributing of electricity or retirement of sub-marginal land. It recognizes that stranded populations, either in the country or the city, cannot have security under the conditions that now surround them.

To this end we are ready to begin to meet this problem—the intelligent care of population throughout our Nation, in accordance with an intelligent distribution of the means of livelihood for that population. A definite program for putting people to work, of which I shall speak in a moment, is a component part of this greater program of security of livelihood through the better use of our national resources.

Closely related to the broad problem of livelihood is that of security against the major hazards of life. Here also, a comprehensive survey of what has been attempted or accomplished in many Nations and in many States proves to me that the time has come for action by the national Government.

SOURCE: Franklin D. Roosevelt, in *Public Papers and Addresses* 4 (New York: 1938), pp. 17–23.

I shall send to you, in a few days, definite recommendations based on these studies. These recommendations will cover the broad subjects of unemployment insurance and old-age insurance, of benefits for children, for mothers, for the handicapped, for maternity care and for other aspects of dependency and illness where a beginning can now be made.

The third factor—better homes for our people—has also been the subject of experimentation and study. Here, too, the first practical steps can be made through the proposals which I shall suggest in relation to giving work to the unemployed.

Whatever we plan and whatever we do should be in the light of these three clear objectives of security. We cannot afford to lose valuable time in haphazard public policies which cannot find a place in the broad outlines of these major purposes. In that spirit I come to an immediate issue made for us by hard and inescapable circumstance—the task of putting people to work. In the spring of 1933 the issue of destitution seemed to stand apart; today, in the light of our experience and our new national policy, we find we can put people to work in ways which conform to, initiate, and carry forward the broad principles of that policy.

The first objectives of emergency legislation of 1933 were to relieve destitution, to make it possible for industry to operate in a more rational and orderly fashion, and to put behind industrial recovery the impulse of large expenditures in Government undertakings. The purpose of the National Industrial Recovery Act to provide work for more people succeeded in a substantial manner within the first few months of its life, and the Act has continued to maintain employment gains and greatly improved working conditions in industry.

The program of public works provided for in the Recovery Act launched the Federal Government into a task for which there was little time to make preparation and little American experience to follow. Great employment has been given and is being given by these works.

More than two billion dollars have also been expended in direct relief to the destitute. Local agencies of necessity determined the recipients of this form of relief. With inevitable exceptions the funds were spent by them with reasonable efficiency and as a result actual want of food and clothing in the great majority of cases has been overcome.

But the stark fact before us is that great numbers still remain unemployed.

A large proportion of these unemployed and their dependents have been forced on the relief rolls. The burden on the Federal Government has grown with great rapidity. We have here a human as well as an economic problem. When humane considerations are concerned, Americans give them precedence. The lessons of history, confirmed by the evidence immediately before me, show conclusively that continued dependence upon relief induces a spiritual and moral disintegration fundamentally destructive to the national fibre. To dole out relief in this way is to administer a narcotic, a subtle destroyer of the human spirit. It is inimical to the dictates of sound policy. It is in violation of the traditions of America. Work must be found for able-bodied but destitute workers.

The Federal Government must and shall quit this business of relief.

I am not willing that the vitality of our people be further sapped by the giving of cash, of market baskets, of a few hours of weekly work cutting grass, raking leaves or picking up papers in the public parks. We must preserve not only the bodies of the unemployed from destitution but also their self-respect, their self-reliance and courage and determination. This decision brings me to the problem of what the Government should do with approximately five million unemployed now on the relief rolls.

About one million and a half of these belong to the group which in the past was dependent upon local welfare efforts. Most of them are unable for one reason or another to maintain themselves independently—for the most part, through no fault of their own. Such people, in the days before the great depression, were cared for by local efforts—by States, by counties, by towns, by cities, by churches and by private welfare agencies. It is my thought that in the future they must be cared for as they were before. I stand ready through my own personal efforts, and through the public influence of the office that I hold, to help these local agencies to get the means necessary to assume this burden.

The security legislation which I shall propose to the Congress will, I am confident, be of assistance to local effort in the care of this type of cases. Local responsibility can and will be resumed, for, after all, common sense tells us that the wealth necessary for this task existed and still exists in the local community, and the dictates of sound administration require that this responsibility be in the first instance a local one.

There are, however, an additional three and one-half million employable people who are on relief. With them the problem is different and the responsibility is different. This group was the victim of a nation-wide depression caused by conditions which were not local but national. The Federal Government is the only governmental agency with sufficient power and credit to meet this situation. We have assumed this task and we shall not shrink from it in the future. It is a duty dictated by every intelligent consideration of national policy to ask you to make it possible for the United States to give employment to all of these three and one-half million employable people now on relief, pending their absorption in a rising tide of private employment.

It is my thought that with the exception of certain of the normal public building operations of the Government, all emergency public works shall be united in a single new and greatly enlarged plan.

With the establishment of this new system we can supersede the Federal Emergency Relief Administration with a coordinated authority which will be charged with the orderly liquidation of our present relief activities and the substitution of a national chart for the giving of work.

This new program of emergency public employment should be governed by a number of practical principles.

1. All work undertaken should be useful—not just for a day, or a year, but useful in the sense that it affords permanent improvement in living conditions or that it creates future new wealth for the Nation.

2. Compensation on emergency public projects should be in the form of security payments which should be larger than the amount now received as a relief dole, but at the same time not so large as to encourage the rejection of opportunities for private employment or the leaving of private employment to engage in Government work.

3. Projects should be undertaken on which a large percentage of direct labor can be used.

4. Preference should be given to those projects which will be self-liquidating in the sense that there is a reasonable expectation that the Government will get its money back at some future time.

5. The projects undertaken should be selected and planned so as to compete as little as possible with private enterprises. This suggests that if it were not for the necessity of giving useful work to the unemployed now on relief, these projects in most instances would not now be undertaken.

6. The planning of projects would seek to assure work during the coming fiscal year to the individuals now on relief, or until such time as private employment is available. In order to make adjustment to increasing private employment, work should be planned with a view to tapering it off in proportion to the speed with which the emergency workers are offered positions with private employers.

7. Effort should be made to locate projects where they will serve the greatest unemployment needs as shown by present relief rolls, and the broad program of the National Resources Board should be freely used for guidance in selection. Our ultimate objective being the enrichment of human lives, the Government has the primary duty to use its emergency expenditures as much as possible to serve those who cannot secure the advantages of private capital.

Ever since the adjournment of the 73rd Congress, the Administration has been studying from every angle the possibilty and the practicability of new forms of employment. As a result of these studies I have arrived at certain very definite convictions as to the amount of money that will be necessary for the sort of public projects that I have described. I shall submit these figures in my budget message. I assure you now they will be within the sound credit of the Government.

The work itself will cover a wide field including clearance of slums, which for adequate reasons cannot be undertaken by private capital; in rural housing of several kinds, where, again, private capital is unable to function; in rural electrification; in the reforestation of the great watersheds of the Nation; in an intensified program to prevent soil erosion and to reclaim blighted areas; in improving existing road systems and in constructing national highways designed to handle modern traffic; in the elimination of grade crossings; in the extension and enlargement of the successful work of the Civilian Conservation Corps; in non-Federal works, mostly self-liquidating and highly useful to local divisions of Government; and on many other projects which the Nation needs and cannot afford to neglect.

This is the method which I propose to you in order that we may better meet this present-day problem of unemployment. Its greatest advantage is that it fits logically and usefully into the long-range permanent policy of providing the three types of security which constitute as a whole an American plan for the betterment of the future of the American people.

I Will Not Promise the Moon
Economic Security,
Administration Bill,
Republican Proposal

Alfred M. Landon
Milwaukee, September 26, 1936

I am going to talk tonight about economic security—economic security for the men and women obliged to earn their daily bread through their own daily labor.

There is no question that is of deeper concern to us all. Even in good times there is ever-present in the minds of workers the fear of unemployment. In periods of deep depression there is the fear of protracted idleness. And always, in prosperity and in depression, there is the ever-present dread of penniless old age.

From the standpoint of the individual, I know of no more intensely human problem than that of economic security. From the standpoint of the government there is no problem calling more for a sympathetic understanding and the best efforts of heart and mind.

But to solve the problem we must have more than a warm heart and a generous impulse. We must have the capacity and the determination to translate our feelings into a practical, workable program. Daydreams do not pay pensions.

Now in broad terms there are two ways to approach the development of a program of economic security. One is to assume that human beings are improvident—that it is necessary to have the stern management of a paternal government to force them to provide for themselves—that it is proper for the government to force them to save for their old age.

The other approach is to recognize that in an industrial nation some people are unable to provide for their old age—that it is a responsibility of society to take care of them.

The act passed by the present administration is based upon the first of these approaches. It assumes that Americans are irresponsible. It assumes that old-age pensions are necessary because Americans lack the foresight to provide for their old age. I refuse to accept any such judgment of my fellow-citizens.

I believe that, as a nation, we can afford old-age pensions—that in a highly industrialized country they are necessary. I believe in them as a matter of social justice.

SOURCE: Alfred M. Landon, *Vital Speeches* IV, no. 2 (November 1, 1937), pp. 26–29.

Because of my firm belief in the justice, necessity, and feasibility of old-age pensions, I am going to discuss the present act with the utmost frankness. It is a glaring example of the bungling and waste that have characterized this administration's attempts to fulfill its benevolent purposes. It endangers the whole cause of social security in this country.

In my own judgment—and I have examined it most carefully—this law is unjust, unworkable, stupidly drafted, and wastefully financed.

Broadly speaking, the act is divided into three main sections. One deals with compulsory old-age insurance. It applies to about one-half of our working population. It excludes, among others, farmers and farm laborers and domestic servants.

Another part of the act attempts to force States to adopt unemployment insurance systems.

The third part of the act provides old-age pensions for those in need who do not come under the compulsory plan.

Now let us look at the so-called old-age insurance plan in more detail, and on a dollars-and-cents basis. In other words, let us see just how much the old people of this country are going to get, when they are going to get it, and who is going to pay for it.

Here we are dealing not with opinions but with hard facts, with the provisons of the law.

Under the compulsory insurance plan of the present law, none of our old people will get any pension at all until 1942. If you happen to be one of those insured—and remember about half of our workers are not—you have to earn, on the average, $125 a month every single month for the next twenty years to get a monthly pension of $37.50. And you have to earn $125 a month for the next forty-five years to get a pension of $59.38 a month. Besides, these sums have to support both the worker and his wife.

But meanwhile, beginning January 1 of next year, 26,000,000 working people begin paying taxes to provide these pensions. Beginning next January employers must start deducting these taxes from the pay envelopes of their employees and turn them over to the government.

Beginning next January employers must, in addition, begin paying taxes on the payrolls out of which your wages are to come. This is the largest tax bill in history. And to call it "social security" is a fraud on the workingman.

These taxes start at the rate of $2 in taxes for every $100 of wages. They increase until it is $6 in taxes for every $100 in wages.

We are told that this $6 will be equally divided between the employer and the employee. But this is not so, and for a very simple reason. The actual fact will be, in almost every case, that the whole tax will be borne either by the employee or by the consumer through higher prices. That is the history of all such taxes. This is because the tax is imposed in such a way that, if the employer is to stay in business, he must shift the tax to someone else.

Do not forget this: such an excessive tax on payrolls is beyond question a tax on employment. In prosperous times it slows down the advance of wages and holds back re-employment. In bad times it increases unemployment, and unemployment breaks wage scales. The Republican party rejects any feature of any plan that hinders re-employment.

Yet is is solely by such a tax that the plan of this administration is financed. Its entire cost is to be raised by a 3 percent tax on wages and a 3 percent on payrolls. I do not see how anyone can believe that the average man making $100 a month should be compelled to save 3 percent of his wages. Certainly he is not in a position to save 6 percent of his wages.

One more sample of the injustice of this law is this: Some workers who come under this new Federal insurance plan are taxed more and get less than workers who come under the State laws already in force.

For instance, under the new law many workers now 50 years old must pay burdensome taxes for the next fifteen years in order to receive a pension when they are 65; whereas those of the same age who come under some State laws pay no taxes and yet actually get a larger pension when they reach the age of 65.

These are a few reasons why I called this law unjust and stupidly drafted.

There is a further important point in connection with the compulsory saving provided by the plan of the present administration. According to this plan, our workers are forced to save for a lifetime. What happens to their savings? The administration's theory is that they go into a reserve fund, that they will be invested at interest, and that in due time this interest will help pay the pensions. The people who drew this law understand nothing of government finance.

Let us trace the process step by step.

The worker's cash comes into the Treasury. What is done with it? The law requires the Treasury to buy government bonds. What happens when the Treasury buys government bonds? Well, at present, when there is a deficit, the Treasury gives some nice new bonds in exchange for the cash which the Treasury gives the Treasury. Now what happens to the cash that the Treasury gives the Treasury? The answer is painfully simple. We have good spenders at Washington, and they spend the cash that the Treasury gives the Treasury.

Now I know all this sounds silly, but it happens to be an accurate recital of what this administration has been foolish enough to enact into law.

Let me explain it in another way—in the simple terms of the family budget.

The father of the family is a kindly man, so kindly that he borrows all he can to add to the family's pleasure. At the same time he impresses upon his sons and daughters the necessity of saving for their old age.

Every month they bring 6 percent of their wages to him so that he may act as trustee and invest their savings for their old age. The father decides that the best investment is his own IOU. So every month he puts aside in a box his IOU carefully executed, and, moreover, bearing interest at 3 percent.

And every month he spends the money that his children bring him, partly in meeting his regular expenses and the rest in various experiments that fascinate him.

Years pass, the children grow old, the day comes when they have to open their father's box. What do they find? Roll after roll of neatly executed IOU's.

I am not exaggerating the folly of this legislation. The saving it forces on our workers is a cruel hoax.

There is every probability that the cash they pay in will be used for current deficits and new extravagances. We are going to have trouble enough to carry out an economy program without having the Treasury flush with money drawn from the workers.

Personally, I do not want the Treasury flush with trust funds—funds which the trustee can mingle with its own general funds. I want the Treasury to be in a position where it must consider every penny it spends. I want the Secretary of the Treasury to be obliged to say to committees of Congress every time a new appropriation is proposed, "Gentlemen, you will have to provide some new taxes if you do this."

With this social security money alone running into billions of dollars, all restraint on Congress will be off. Maybe some people want that, but I don't.

And even if the budget is balanced, the fact that there is a billion dollars and more of extra cash on hand each year that can be instantly available for any purpose by issuing special bonds to the trust fund is too great a temptation.

This temptation is further increased by another provision of the law— that provision relating to how much of the cash collected will be paid out in pensions. During the next ten years only 10 cents out of every dollar collected from the workers will be paid out as benefits. And from now until 1950 only 16 cents out of every dollar collected will be paid out as benefits.

The workers asked for a pension and all they have received is just another tax.

There is one more point that I want to mention about the compulsory old-age pension system. This is the question of keeping records.

The administration is preparing a plan, the exact nature of which we shall not know until after the election, for keeping the life records of 26,000,000 of our working people. These records are necessary because the amount of the pension anyone is to receive depends upon how much he has earned after the act goes into effect.

The record must show every job a man has and every dollar he earns so long as he is working at something that brings him under the plan. If he is working in a factory and changes to another factory, a government agent must keep track of him.

Imagine the vast army of clerks which will be necessary to keep these records. Another army of field investigators will be necessary to check up on the people whose records are not clear, or regarding whom current information is not coming in. And so bureaucracy will grow and grow, and Federal snooping flourish.

To get a workable old-age pension plan we must repeal the present compulsory insurance plan. The Republican party is pledged to do this. The Republican party will have nothing to do with any plan that involves prying into the personal working records of 26,000,000 people.

Before discussing the positive part of our program, however, I want to take up the second main feature of the present act, the part dealing with unemployment insurance.

The problem of unemployment insurance differs fundamentally from that of old-age pensions. Old-age pensions were reasonably well established in a number of States even prior to the passage of the Social Security Act. Federal grants to States to supplement State old-age pensions do not differ from the practice followed for years—the practice of making grants to States to supplement and encourage prospects for the general welfare.

Unemployment insurance is something new and of a different character. We have never had unemployment insurance in this country. With the exception of two States, and their laws are of recent origin, there were no unemployment insurance laws on the statute books of our States before the Social Security Law.

Under these circumstances for the Federal Government to step in and use its taxing power to compel all of the States immediately to enact unemployment insurance statutes is something unheard of. It is most unwise. There is no element of real help to the States in the present statute. There is merely compulsion. It completely ignores what has been of priceless value to us—the use of the States as experimental workshops in which new methods and policies may be tried out and gradually perfected.

The Republican platform proposes to encourage adoption by the States of honest and practical measures for meeting the problems of insurance against unemployment. It does so because we recognize that we live on a continent with a wide range of working conditions and standards of living. It does so because we have still nearly everything to learn in this field.

With State experiments, different States trying out different plans and watching the results, we shall work out a much better system than could possibly be imposed at this time from Washington. The impatient advocates of almost every social reform are disposed to seek the short cut of Federal action rather than to wait for slower, but more certain, progress achieved under State auspices. If a State makes a mistake, the effect is local and limited. With State action we avoid mistakes involving the whole country. As Woodrow Wilson said of State action, it "has given speed, facility, vigor, and certainty to the progress of our economic and political growth."

It is urged that competition among industrial States will prevent State action in this field. But forward-looking States like your own have been disproving this for twenty-five years.

This brings us to the third main feature of the present act—the section dealing with pensions for the needy aged not covered by the compulsory insurance plan. This part of the present law can be made to serve as the foundation of a real old-age pension plan. This, the Republican Party proposes to do. It proposes to overhaul this section and make of it a workable, common-sense plan—a plan to be administered by the States.

We propose through amendments to this section to provide for every American citizen over 65 the supplementary payment necessary to give a minimum income sufficient to protect him or her from want.

Frankly, I am not in a position to state with finality the total cost of this plan. One of the most serious criticisms to be made of the present Social Security Act is the haste with which it was constructed, and the inadequate knowledge on which it rests. I do not intend to repeat this error. I have been studying this problem closely for the past year and a half, and I have had the benefit of the opinions of many close students of these problems. Elaborate computations of the probable costs have been prepared for me. And while I am not willing to accept these computations as final, it is clear from them that the plan which we propose will be much less expensive than the plan of the present administration because we will not create a needless reserve fund of $47,000,000,000.

Our plan will be on a pay-as-you-go basis, with the result that we will know year by year just what our pensions are costing us. That is sound, common-sense financing.

There is one other point I want to impress upon you. This is the question of raising the money to pay the pensions. The precise method of taxation used will depend upon the decision of Congress working in cooperation with the Treasury. But there are three essential principles which should be complied with: the necessary funds should be raised by means of a special tax earmarked for this purpose, so that the already-difficult problem of budget-balancing may not be further complicated. The tax should be direct and visible. And the tax should be widely distributed. Only if every member of the great body of our citizens is conscious of his share of the cost can we hope to resist the constant pressure to increase pensions to the point where the burden will be unbearable; only if every one bears his just share can we hope to prevent the plan being used for political purposes.

If we will prevent such exploitation, and if we will put the plan on a sound financial basis, we can afford to be liberal to our old people. If the present compulsory insurance plan remains in force, our old people are only too apt to find the cupboard bare.

Let me repeat! I am a profound believer in the justice and necessity of old-age pensions. My criticism of the present act is not that its purpose is bad. It is that this act will involve a cruel disappointment for those of our people least able to bear the shock of disappointment.

To these—our old people, our workers struggling for better conditions, our infirm—I will not promise the moon. I promise only what I know can be performed: economy, a living pension, and such security as can be provided by a generous people.

CHAPTER 7

Beyond the New Deal

INTRODUCTION

Republicans in Congress never made absolute peace with the New Deal, even during World War II, and their hostility carried into the postwar period. Harry S Truman confronted this opposition as he sought to move the nation beyond the New Deal program. Truman proposed to extend the New Deal social policy through a legislative program calling for full employment, national health insurance, a permanent Fair Employment Practices Commission, and the extension of Social Security. With the exceptions of a federal housing act in 1949 and the extension of the Social Security system in 1950, Republicans defeated Truman's social program on each of these issues.

Conservatives attacked Truman's Fair Deal as "socialistic." Warnings about America's drift toward socialism found frequent expression in conservative rhetoric of the day. Conservative social thinkers warned in speeches, magazine articles, radio addresses, and books that Americans were being threatened with regimentation and the subversion of individual rights. As one opponent of the Fair Deal's social program warned, "there are certain individuals and families who lack incentive or sense of responsibility. Leisure and freedom from the discipline of a job were seemingly more important to these people than care of their families."

The clearest sign that Republicans had not accommodated themselves to the New Deal was evidenced in the fight over a Full Employment bill, introduced in 1945 by Senator James Murray and Senator Robert Wagner. The bill was an attempt to legislate liberal social policy into law by guaranteeing government's commitment to full employment through mandatory spending provisions in deflationary times and the creation of a Council of Economic Advisors. The act expressed liberal economists' fear that a post war depression was imminent. Early in 1946, Republicans forced Democrats to modify a bill that dropped "full employment" mandates for a more ambiguous commitment to full economic growth. A Council of Economic Advisors was established, but most Republicans saw the modified bill as a victory for their party.

The 1946 congressional elections gave Republicans control of Congress. Anti–New Deal rhetoric now rang through the halls of Congress. As one Republican declared, "The results of last November's election showed a strong protest against Federal bureaucracy and its dictatorial tactics. They indicate that our people are at last coming to realize the growing menace to our liberties under the New Deal regime."

The confrontation between the Democrats intent upon extending the liberal social agenda and the Republicans steadfast in their commitment to preventing the revolution from going any further came to a head over a proposal for a national health insurance system. Liberals, who had dreamed of national health insurance since the Progressive era, had proposed that a national insurance system be included in the original Social Security Act of 1935. The American Medical Association defeated their plans. Then, in 1943, Senators Robert Wagner and James Murray revived the issue when they sponsored a new national health insurance bill. Although a *Fortune* magazine poll in 1942 showed an impressive 74.3 percent of the American people favoring national health insurance, the Wagner-Murray-Dingell bill quickly stalled in Congress. Truman tried to aid the passage of the bill when he urged Congress to establish a comprehensive medical system prepaid through Social Security taxes. The bill quickly came under attack from the American Medical Association and by Republicans in Congress who warned of "socialized medicine." By 1948, national health insurance had been defeated.

One issue in which Truman enjoyed a measure of success proved to be in extending Social Security. In 1948, Truman recommended increasing Social Security benefits and extending coverage to include the farmers, widows and dependents of war veterans, and regular domestic and farm workers. Republicans, who initially had called Social Security a step toward totalitarianism, now accepted this extension of the system. A consensus concerning Social Security had been reached and would hold for the next 50 years.

Richard O. Davies traces the history of social welfare during the Truman administration. As Davies observes, Truman's social welfare policies reflected his loyalty to the New Deal, as well as his deep sympathy for the average American. Truman felt that Roosevelt had accomplished "a social revolution which swept out obsolete notions cluttering our economy and substituted a bold program of decisive action designed to improve the standard of living and the level of security of the common man." Truman's proposals for a full employment bill, national health insurance, civil rights, and other measures never captured the imagination of the American people as had FDR's program. Some of this, Davies observes, was due to Roosevelt's suave style, but he also points to the liberal community's distrust of Truman, the former machine politician from Kansas City, Missouri. Truman's break with Henry Wallace did little to instill trust on the part of liberals. More importantly, political conditions had changed in the postwar period. By 1946, the American people were indifferent to reform. Truman enjoyed some success in passing a federal housing bill in 1949 because of the postwar housing shortage. Middle-class pressure for better housing resulted in the Housing Act of 1949, which provided for a limited amount of public housing and slum clearance. Similar middle-class pressure was to be brought to bear on the extension of the Social Security system to new groups, small businessmen, war widows, and domestic servants in 1950. Once again, middle-class support proved to be decisive in enacting social legislation.

The debate over national health insurance was a different matter altogether. Middle-class support for the bill was not enough to overcome anxieties concerning "socialized medicine,"costs of the program, and overwhelming conservative opposition to the bill. The issues and perspectives of this debate are poignantly summarized in a radio debate held on June 3, 1947. Representing the affirmative position were J. Howard McGrath, Democratic Senator from Rhode Island, and Dr. Michael M. Davis, a leading proponent of national health in the United States. Opposition to the Wagner-Murray-Dingell bill was set forth by Senator Robert A. Taft of Ohio and Dr. H. H. Shoulder, president of the American Medical Association. The ensuing debate illustrates the profound differences that separated Republicans and Democrats, liberals and conservatives, in these years.

Further Readings

A number of good histories on national health insurance have been written, including Daniel S. Hirshfield, *The Lost Reform: The Campaign for Compulsory Health Insurance in the United States from 1932 to 1943* (Cambridge: Harvard University Press, 1970), and Monte M. Poen, *Harry S Truman versus the Medical Lobby* (Columbia: University of Missouri Press, 1979).

The best overview of the Truman administration remains Alonzo L. Hamby, *Beyond the New Deal: Harry S Truman and American Liberalism* (New York: Columbia University Press, 1973). Also of interest is Otis L. Graham, Jr., *Toward a Planned Society: From Roosevelt to Nixon* (New York: Oxford University Press, 1976).

The politics of social security is thoroughly analyzed in Martha Derthick, *Policymaking for Social Security* (Washington, D.C.: The Brookings Institution, 1979).

Social Welfare Policies

Richard O. Davies

Military and diplomatic decisions necessarily received Truman's first consideration, and he was not able to devote close attention to domestic problems until he boarded the U.S.S. *Augusta*, following the Potsdam Conference. As the *Augusta* plowed westward, Truman requested Samuel I. Rosenman to supervise the drafting of a detailed message that would outline his program in considerable detail. After Truman had presented his basic ideas to the former Roosevelt adviser, Rosenman reportedly erupted into enthusiastic praise for the reformist position Truman had sketched: "You know, Mr. President, this is the most exciting and pleasant surprise I have had in a long time," Rosenman is reported to have told Truman. Rosenman had undoubtedly been led by widely circulating rumors to believe that Truman would not seek to continue and expand the New Deal. The document went to Congress on September 6, 1945, just four days after General Douglas MacArthur accepted the formal Japanese surrender in Tokyo Bay.

This message provided the cornerstone of Truman's social welfare program. It was definitely a Truman-inspired message, but it also had a resonant Roosevelt ring. Although Rosenman directed the preparation of this lengthy document, his papers show that he drew upon all relevant government agencies for ideas and even drafts of entire sections of the message. Thus, the Message on Reconversion bore a definite New Deal imprint; the general authorship of Rosenman, in fact, symbolizes the close relationship between the Roosevelt and Truman programs.

The message was deeply rooted in the progressive tradition, but its immediate inspiration was the 1944 Economic Bill of Rights. In this message, Truman demonstrated beyond doubt his intention to make good on his predecessor's 1944 campaign promises. Most of the twenty-one points in the document were noncontroversial, such as increasing congressional salaries, selling excess ships, and stockpiling strategic materials, but his call for a comprehensive housing bill, a full employment bill, increases in unemployment benefits, a fair employment practices commission, and increase of the minimum wage gratified the uneasy liberal community and shocked—even angered—the conservatives. During Truman's first five months in office, while he was preoccupied with foreign policy, the conservatives had apparently deluded themselves with the notion that the new President would begin to roll back the New Deal. The message, they contend, was a terrible

SOURCE: Richard O. Davies, in *The Truman Period as a Research Field*, ed. Richard S. Kirkendall (Columbia: University of Missouri Press, 1967), pp. 149–86. Reprinted with permission of Richard S. Kirkendall and Richard O. Davies.

blow, and Joseph Martin summarized this feeling in his memoirs: It was, he says, an obvious case of "out-New Dealing the New Deal," because Truman was endorsing "the same old dreary circuit of paternalism, controls, spending, high taxes, and vague objectives."

The cry of betrayal from the aroused conservatives, however, seems to have expressed political viewpoint rather than actual surprise, because Truman's general position on social welfare had been clearly established. Although the exact circumstances of his nomination to the Vice-Presidency are unclear and probably will remain muddled forever, Truman definitely had been "cleared by Sidney," and this leader of organized labor would not have accepted anyone who was allied with the forces of reaction. In fact, in his maiden presidential speech in April, Truman had briefly mentioned social welfare: "Here in America we have labored long and hard to achieve a social order worthy of our great heritage. In our time tremendous progress has been made toward a really democratic way of life. Let me assure the forward-looking people of America that there will be no relaxation in our efforts to improve the lot of the common people." Even the barometer of liberalism, T. R. B. of the *New Republic*, had indicated a comfortable future to his apprehensive readers in June with the news that the new President was going to continue the New Deal: "His Administration is more homespun and less cosmopolitan than Roosevelt's, with a good deal more emphasis upon party regularity, but it is pretty evident in which direction it is going; it is going a little left of center."

Truman, of course, had always considered himself to be a strong "New Dealer," although his public career prior to 1934 fails to support this contention. Throughout his ten years in the Senate, however, Truman was solidly behind the Roosevelt program. By September 6, 1945, however, Truman had decided that the growing public speculation on his domestic program had gone far enough, and he determined that the time had arrived to "let the Hearsts and McCormicks know that they were not going to take me into camp."

The social welfare policies Truman pursued during his Presidency reflected not only his New Dealism as a senator but also his experiences as a farmer, unsuccessful businessman, and Jackson County politician of a Pendergast hue. All of these activities helped mold a deep sympathy for the average American. Truman's memoirs implicitly disclose the development of his liberalism. As a young man in Kansas City, he worked for a time with the Santa Fe Railroad as a paymaster. "I learned what it meant to work for ten hours for $1.50," he wrote. As a member of the Pendergast political organization, Truman learned the political importance of good works—as a Presiding Judge of the Jackson County Court during the early days of the depression he saw how social welfare neatly fused with political expediency. Hence, social welfare provided by government was an important dimension of Truman's political philosophy: "I was a New Dealer back in Jackson County, and there was no need for me to change," he recalls. "I believed in the program from the time it was first proposed." Thus, to Truman, his Message on Reconversion "symbolizes for me my assumption of the office of President in my own right. It was on that day and with this message that I first spelled out the details of the program of liberalism and progressivism which was to be the foundation of my administration." It was, Truman affirms, "my opportunity as President to advocate the political principles and economic philosophy which I had expressed in the Senate and which I had followed all my political life." And, he concludes, with a high degree of accuracy, it "set the tone and direction for the rest of my administration and the goals toward which I would try to lead the nation."

He never lost sight of the objectives he established on September 6, 1945. His published Presidential Papers document beyond any doubt his commitment: "The basic objective," he told Congress in his first State of the Union Message, "is to improve the welfare of the American People." On the first anniversary of the death of Roosevelt, Truman observed, "The domestic principles and policies which were laid down and put into practice by President Roosevelt have come almost to be accepted as commonplace today. Yet, they constitute a program of social reform and progress unequalled in the history of the United States." Roosevelt, Truman said, accomplished "a social revolution which swept out obsolete notions cluttering our economy and substituted a bold program of decisive action designed to improve the standard of living and the level of security of the common man."

Truman's social welfare policies, therefore, were based upon the New Deal and, indirectly, upon the progressive tradition, but unlike other reform Presidents, he faced new problems—conserving and improving what had already been accomplished. From the perspective of 1945, the specter of the repeal of the New Deal had become a vivid possibilty; the fate of the progressive reforms following the First World War had not been forgotten. Truman was determined to prevent a repeat performance. At the same time, he sought to move on to new areas that he believed required attention.

The first order of business was to end the fear of widespread unemployment. The memory of depression hung over the nation as the war ended, and many fully expected another economic crisis. Stephen Bailey has demonstrated the slipshod manner in which the Employment Act of 1946 was enacted. This significant legislation had been in the congressional mill since 1943, and Truman merely accepted it as part of his program. The affirmation of employment opportunities for all neatly meshed with his hope that the American workingman might be spared another severe depression.

Truman's aspirations for the achievement of new vistas of social legislation, however, never captured the public imagination; where Roosevelt's eloquence thrilled the depression-ridden nation, Truman's flat Missouri twang and modest physique produced only widespread indifference. Truman lacked a certain special something—charisma—that could evoke enthusiasm for his program. No matter how he tried—and try he did—Truman could not produce a ground swell of public support for his reforms. "During his first two years in office," J. Joseph Huthmacher cogently summarizes, "Truman appeared to be not only new at his job, but inept and indecisive. Liberals, with whom Truman sought to identify himself early in his administration, were dismayed by his seeming lack of forcefulness in pushing his program before Congress. On the other hand, conservatives took the President's professions of New Dealism at face value, and transferred to the new Administration all the venom that Roosevelt had engendered among them earlier."

The crucial factor of leadership is perhaps best understood by examining Truman's relationship with American liberalism. If one simply compares the written records of Truman and Roosevelt, the liberal community should have loved the Missourian; on almost all issues, Truman was far in advance of FDR. As James MacGregor Burns and William E. Leuchtenburg have demonstrated, throughout the New Deal years Roosevelt frequently dragged his feet on social reform, labor, public works, relief, and housing legislation. Roosevelt never stormed any barricades for such reforms as a minimum wage or social security, and only the determined efforts of congressional liberals, such as Robert F. Wagner, carried the day for liberalism. Even at the time of his death, the "broker state" concept still pervaded Roosevelt's Administration, and FDR had yet to formulate a well-defined plan for postwar reform.

Truman, however, never demonstrated Roosevelt's tepidity toward social reform, but he also never enjoyed the luxury of a friendly Congress—indeed, even of a united party receptive to his social welfare policies. Truman lacked Roosevelt's charm, sophistication, and facility with the language. Unlike Roosevelt, Truman never appreciated ideas and intellectuals for their own sake, and he replaced the Rooseveltian rhetorical liberalism with a brand of hardheaded political activism that somehow struck the liberals as too cold, too coarse, and too matter-of-fact. Truman's bluntness did not compare favorably with Roosevelt's eloquence, nor could he excite the American people as had Theodore Roosevelt or infuse in them the moral fervor and resolution as had Wilson. "Alas for Truman," T. R. B. complained, "there is no bugle note in his voice; little evidence that he has shown of being able to lift and inspire the masses."

Whereas Roosevelt's suave style camouflaged his essential conservatism, Truman's pragmatic liberalism only re-emphasized his middle-class and middle-western origins. The replacement of ardent New Dealers by the "Missouri Gang" completed the alienation of the liberal community. As the mediocre likes of John W. Synder, Harry Vaughan, John Steelman, Robert Hannegan, and George Allen entered the inner circles of the White House and such liberal favorites as Harold Ickes, Henry Wallace, and Wilson Wyatt departed, liberals felt unappreciated and unwanted. T. R. B. complained that the new group of advisers was "too humdrum and prosaic" and lamented that the "gay, audacious, erratic New Deal days ended with the war."

Truman's personal commitment to furthering social welfare is beyond question, but his selection of key advisers raises several important questions. None of his White House advisers had held important positions in the New Deal, and few can accurately be described as enthusiastic liberals. Truman's close relationship with John W. Snyder, who had considerable influence upon economic policy, cannot be explained except on the basis of personal friendship, because Snyder's conservatism was notorious among liberals. The entire Truman Cabinet reflected an inexplicable aversion to liberals, and the exodus of New Dealers in 1945 and 1946 quickly resulted in a lackluster Cabinet. Frequently, the administration of important social welfare programs fell to persons not recognized for reformist zeal. Because presidential decisions are made upon the advice and information received, Truman's Cabinet and White House staff needs considerable study before we can resolve the inner contradiction of a reformist President choosing a group of advisers and Cabinet officers that was, at best, lukewarm to the extension of the New Deal.

The suspicious liberals, however, were always ready to believe the worst of the man who had replaced Henry Wallace on the Democratic ticket in 1944. Within two weeks after Truman took office, the *New Republic* expressed its fears about Truman's devotion to reform: especially, it fretted about the new President's political skills: "Has Mr. Truman the imagination, the daring, the sensitiveness to new currents of popular need and pressure, to continue the advance as President Roosevelt would presumably have continued it?" Following the imbroglio over price controls in the autumn of 1945, T. R. B. decided that Truman did not. "The trouble here is that the Administration has merely taken off the brakes, and the nation is coasting down the steep hill to 'normalcy' under its own huge dead weight," he lamented. Truman was proving to be, at best, "a well meaning man who does as well as he knows how," and this certainly was not sufficient.

The liberals' dissatisfaction with Truman, despite his strong advocacy of social reform, suggests that liberalism itself was beginning to undergo a significant transformation. The so-called "bread and butter" reforms that had distinguished the New Deal evoked far less response from American liberals in the postwar era, because they were now turning toward the fight for civil rights for the American Negro and to the preservation of civil liberties. Perhaps even more important is the decline of the antibusiness theme in American liberalism as the "mixed economy" of the postwar era quickly ended the threat of massive unemployment.

In their criticism of Truman's domestic record, the liberals failed to recognize that the ability to secure new legislative welfare programs lay beyond any President's normal powers. Tremendous obstacles blocked Truman. The times simply were not propitious for new reform measures.

The war years had numbed the catalytic effect of the depression, and the economic boom that began in 1940 continued throughout the Truman years with but a minor interruption in 1949; consequently, few individuals could be convinced of the need for starting new departures in social reform. A postwar reaction against reform precluded the enactment of most new programs. Truman's urgent appeals to the public met with an indifferent yawn because the American people were more concerned with the price of hamburger and the scarcity of houses and automobiles than with social welfare legislation. The New Deal had already effected tremendous changes in the individual's relationship with the government, and no new departures seemed necessary. Full employment, abetted by considerable overtime pay, proved to be a soothing tranquilizer. Later in the Administration, the influence of Senator Joseph R. McCarthy succeeded in associating many reforms with subversion; if this were not a sufficient brake, after June 25, 1950, military expenditures forced an abandonment of any serious intentions of establishing new and costly programs.

If the mood of the nation provided a depleted soil upon which to sow the seeds of the Fair Deal, the composition of Congress only compounded Truman's problems. Ever since the congressional elections of 1938, Congress had been firmly controlled by a coalition of Southern Democrats and conservative Republicans. Although one cannot be too precise in analyzing the structure of this conservative coalition, since its composition fluctuated on any given issue, its hard core reflected the attitudes of rural America. Although the agricultural regions benefited from the social welfare programs, the bulk of the programs were oriented toward urban American. Because the ethos of a rural society normally tends to oppose change, the natural result was concerted opposition to the Truman social welfare policies. Despite its minority status in a now predominantly urban nation, rural America effectively controlled the congressional committee system. This coalition was most powerful in the House of Representatives; here the legislative gates were rendered inaccessible by the labyrinth of committees that had fallen to the conservatives through the workings of the seniority system. Truman's comprehensive housing bill, for example, passed the Senate in 1946 and 1948 (and would have passed in 1947 had it been brought to a vote), but the lower house never had the opportunity of voting on it. The Banking committee killed it in 1946, the Rules committee in 1948. Had the bill ever reached the House floor, a speedy passage was assured. Stuck on dead center, Congress did not respond to Truman's program, but conversely, it could not retreat to the days of Calvin Coolidge either. As Samuel Lubell points out, Truman was forced to mark time. In a time of congressional deadlock, Truman's Administration made two significant contributions to the American reform tradition: (1) the prevention of repeal of New Deal reforms, and (2) the strengthening of existing programs via vigorous executive action.

Students of American politics could profitably devote considerable attention to the four Congresses with which Truman had to work. The new research tools of the political scientists should be utilized, as well as the traditional research methods of the historian. David Truman provides us with some useful quantitative information about the Eighty-first Congress, but he leaves too many questions unanswered, primarily because he does not ask the questions of the political historian. We need not only the institutional studies of Congress but also biographies of such congressional leaders as Robert A. Taft, Alben Barkley, Sam Rayburn, and Joseph Martin. The composition of the so-called "conservative coalition" needs detailed study as does the ineffectual liberal bloc.

Directly related to Truman's relationship with Congress are the structural changes occurring within the Presidency itself. Truman was the first President who was forced to conduct a "dual presidency." Due to the development of Russian intransigence in the postwar period and the resulting Cold War, Truman had to conduct, simultaneously, fully developed domestic and foreign policies. While he worked to extract from Congress new departures in social welfare, he also had to rely upon it for financial support for his new concept of America's role in world politics. The impact of his absorption with foreign policy undoubtedly affected adversely his domestic reform program, but no research has been conducted to support this hypothesis. In this regard, one speculative question stands out: Did Truman compromise on domestic policy in order to get congressional support for his dramatic new departures in foreign policy?

There was, however, one area in which Truman definitely did not compromise. This was housing reform, which provided an outstanding exception to the dull pattern of legislative stalemate and executive caretaking. This singular success of a highly controversial program demonstrates that the congressional blockade was vulnerable to a reform that attracted widespread public support. The Fair Deal enjoyed a fleeting moment of legislative triumph when the Housing Act of 1949 was signed by a jubilant President. This act created the present slum clearance and urban redevelopment program and markedly expanded the existing public housing program. Truman's activity in housing reform illustrates his deep commitment to improved social conditions for the nation's poor. Beyond any doubt he desired to provide every American family with an opportunity of enjoying "decent" housing. Truman was deeply disturbed by the appalling discrepancy between the nation's affluence and the condition of the millions forced to live in slum housing. "A decent standard of housing for all is one of the irreducible obligations of modern civilization," he told Congress in 1945. "The people of the United States, so far ahead in wealth and productive capacity, deserve to be the best housed in the world. We must begin to meet the challenge at once."

Truman used every available presidential power to force Congress into facing this challenge; finally, after four years of intense political infighting, Congress passed the comprehensive housing bill, cosponsored by three unusual political bedfellows: Robert F. Wagner, Robert A. Taft, and Allen J. Ellender. The Truman Papers show the President's strong position on housing reform; this is corroborated by the public record. "For some reason," David D. Lloyd, a White House staff member, recalled in 1961, "Mr. Truman was hot on housing." This presidential interest and action, while important, alone would not have jarred the housing bill loose from the tenacious clutches of the House leadership. Ultimately, a public demand for housing legislation, prompted by the postwar housing shortage, proved decisive. On most issues, Truman could arouse little public interest, but middle-class America, thoroughly irritated by the shortage of apartments and houses, created such a demand for congressional action that the bill finally was passed. Ironically, however, the Housing Act of 1949 was concerned with the slum dweller and not with the middle-class family seeking a nice place in which to live. Truman and his associates neatly transferred the middle-class pressure created by the shortage into an effective tool with which to secure public housing and slum clearance from a reluctant Congress.

Truman apparently fought equally hard for other major domestic reforms, but he did not receive sufficient public support. Quite possibly, he might have compromised to get crucial appropriations for his foreign policy. He fervently desired, it is quite obvious, to create a national compulsory health program that would ensure every American of adequate medical care, but he could not convince the Congress—or the American Medical Association—of the need for such a program. "I have never been able to understand all the fuss some people make about government wanting to do something to improve and protect the health of the people," he comments in his memoirs. "I have had some bitter disappointments as President, but the one that has troubled me most, in a personal way, has been the failure to defeat the organized opposition to a national compulsory health insurance program."

Although Truman never enjoyed the pleasure of public support for most of his social welfare policies, he nonetheless plodded doggedly ahead. Setback was compounded by failure. His record with the Democratic Seventy-ninth Congress was dismal; only the watered-down Employment Act and the Veterans' Emergency Housing Act (which became a bureaucratic nightmare and failed miserably) interrupted a succession of rebuffs from Congress. Many observers expected him to soften his reform requests when the first Republican-controlled Congress in seventeen years convened in 1947, but Truman merely intensified his efforts and bombarded the Congress with special messages urging enactment of a wide assortment of social welfare programs.

Inevitably, as the presidential election approached, altruism fused with political expediency. The important connection between Truman's social welfare policies and political strategy is basic to the proper understanding of his re-election. Many individuals consider Truman's victory over Thomas

E. Dewey the greatest upset in American presidential elections. Certainly, the external appearances create such an impression; two secessions—Henry Wallace to the left, J. Strom Thurmond to the right—wracked the Democratic party and ultimately deprived Truman of at least eighty-six electoral votes. Even within the remnant of the Democracy, a "dump Truman" movement fizzled, at least partially because an attractive candidate, such as Justice William O. Douglas or General Dwight D. Eisenhower, could not be secured. In Washington, Democrats arranged to sell their houses or allowed leases to expire as they faced the inevitable. Most ominous, however, was the rejuvenated Republican party that had selected an impressive ticket of Dewey and Earl Warren. Even Walter Lippmann publicly wondered if the nation could survive until January 20; smug Republicans could find precious little Truman money, even at three to one.

But, somehow, Harry S Truman won. For the popular radio newscaster, H. V. Kaltenborn, the shock was simply too much. His dumbfounded commentary on election night perhaps best expressed the astonishment of the American people, who had been convinced by the press and pollsters that a Dewey victory was certain. Then there was, of course, that priceless headline of Colonel McCormick's overanxious *Chicago Tribune*, which announced, a bit too soon the restoration of legitimacy.

Samuel Lubell has demonstrated, however, that a Dewey victory would have been the real upset. Throughout the campaign a fundamental factor had been concealed: There were more Democrats than Republicans. Probably better than any other American, Truman realized the significance of this simple demographic fact. "I want to say to you at this time that during the next four years there will be a Democrat in the White House," he told a group of Young Democrats in May. "And you are looking at him."

The rising crest of Republican confidence concealed Truman's shrewdly prepared plan for victory. The grand strategy was ingenious in its simplicity: Truman merely sought to maintain intact the Roosevelt coalition that had worked so effectively in 1940 and 1944. Beyond any doubt, Truman established himself in the voters' minds as the inheritor of the Roosevelt mantle, and he did so by shaping his entire campaign around social welfare policies. In fact, he presented the major issue as a referendum on the New Deal. Because his opposition lolled in the languid atmosphere of overconfidence, he was never effectively challenged as he accused *all* Republicans of being completely opposed to the New Deal. "The Republicans don't like the New Deal," he told an audience in Akron. "They never liked the New Deal, and they would like to get rid of it." The Republicans, he said, were hiding behind Dewey's "soothing syrup" and were "waiting eagerly for the time when they can go ahead with a Republican Congress and a Republican President and do a real hatchet job on the New Deal without interference."

Truman actually began his campaign on January 7, 1948, when he informed the Eightieth Congress of the state of the Union. In this politically inspired message, he called for a wide assortment of social reforms, the scope of which prompted the *Philadelphia Inquirer* to observe, "Truman leaves out practically nothing but the beatitudes and the Ten Commandments." From this time forward, Truman cleverly coupled social welfare with the practical consideration of getting himself re-elected. Scarcely a week passed that he did not dispatch a special message to Congress on some reform program. Special messages on civil rights, housing, rent controls, medical care, price controls, social security, and education descended upon the Republican Congress, and he made frequent reference to these reforms during his press conferences.

Truman clearly perceived the political importance of these reforms. If the Republican Congress should have passed any of his programs, then he would have been able to tell the voters about his legislative triumphs; but if it turned down his suggestions, as seemed most likely, then he could blame the Republican leadership in the Congress. No matter what Congress did, therefore, Truman stood to reap the political harvest. When the Senate, under the whip of presidential aspirant Robert A. Taft, passed the comprehensive housing bill, Truman fired off a memorandum to the Administrator of the Housing and Home Finance Agency: "We must make every effort now to see that the House passes an equally good bill." Cogently pointing up the political implications of this legislation, he wrote, "I know that we face strong opposition; but if this legislation should fail, we must at least be sure that the responsibility for its failure is placed where it belongs."

To dramatize the issues he had been creating since January, Truman embarked on a two-week train trip to the Far West in early June. Ostensibly, he undertook the journey to receive an honorary degree from the University of California at Berkeley, but the political motives of what he called "this nonpartisan, bipartisan trip" soon became apparent. For the first time, he attacked the Eightieth Congress in a concerted manner, as he unveiled his new, folksy, off-the-cuff speaking technique. In Gary, Indiana, he flailed the Congress for refusing to admit war refugees; at Grand Island, Nebraska, he promised to use a pair of spurs, just received from a local welcoming committee, on the Republican congressional leaders. And so it went. As the trip progressed, the "new" Truman emerged—a confident, articulate, and highly effective speaker.

As his audiences increased in size and enthusiasm, he undoubtedly realized that his strategy of focusing his campaign upon social welfare policies was sound. By the time he reached the Coast, he was now hearing his audiences respond to his criticism of Congress with "Pour it on, Harry!" and "Give 'em hell, Harry!" to which he grinned and replied, "I'm going to, I'm going to." He told his track-side listeners, "This Congress is interested in the welfare of the better classes. They are not interested in the welfare of the common everyday man." Repeatedly, the phrases "special interest Congress" and "do-nothing Congress" were sprinkled in his short speeches. On his return trip, he significantly pointed out that the basic issue of the ensuing campaign would be "special privilege against the interests of the people as a whole." By the time the trip ended on June 18 in Baltimore, Truman had succeeded in directing the nation's attention to the conservative congressional wing of the Republican party. Thus, when the Republican Convention adopted a platform that endorsed the basic social welfare policies he had been urging upon Congress, the GOP leadership had exposed itself at its weakest point—the liberal-conservative split over domestic issues.

The Democratic faithful, however, had failed to recognize Truman's strategy; dissension riddled the party. Wallace had already abandoned ship, and what would become the Dixiecrat party stomped out of the national convention in Philadelphia in protest over a strong civil rights plank in the platform. The apathetic center that remained perfunctorily renominated Truman.

The President realized the precarious position of his party and attempted to instill new life into it with his acceptance speech. This exciting address proved to be one of the most significant and probably the most effective of his entire political career. Speaking before a benumbed convention at 2 A.M., he accepted the nomination few Democrats really wanted him to have and ridiculed the obvious disparity between the Republican platform and the record of "the worst" Eightieth Congress. On each of his social welfare policies, he pointed out, the Congress had refused to act, and yet, the GOP platform endorsed essentially the same program. "There is a long list of these promises in that Republican platform," he told a suddenly enthusiastic convention. "I have discussed a number of these failures of the Republican Eightieth Congress. Every one of them is important." Because the Republican Convention had essentially endorsed the Truman social welfare program, he excited his audience with the announcement that he was going to give the Republican-controlled Congress the opportunity to enact its party's platform so that the voters could be certain that the Republican platform was a sincere pledge. "On the 26th day of July, which out in Missouri we call 'Turnip Day,' I am going to call Congress back and ask them to pass laws to halt rising prices, to meet the housing crisis—which they say they are for in their platform," Truman said. At the same time, he announced, Congress would have the opportunity of enacting his entire social reform program, which had been adopted by the Republican Convention. Truman then hammered home his major point: "Now my friends, if there is any reality behind this Republican platform, we ought to get some action from a short session of the Eightieth Congress. They can do the job in fifteen days, if they want to. . . . Now what that worst Eightieth Congress does in the special session will be the test."

The Turnip Day strategy proved more than successful; the Republicans stormed and sputtered, spent most of the two weeks bickering among themselves in the heat and humidity of a typical Washington summer, and adjourned without passing any significant legislation. Truman's dramatic call for a special session had exposed a deep division within his opposition's ranks and, most important, had forcefully demonstrated that the Republican congressional delegation was not disposed to honor most of its party's campaign pledges.

The actual campaign was anticlimactic. By Labor Day Truman had shaped the issues to his own advantage, and Governor Dewey, aware of the embarrassing split within his own party and probably mesmerized by the predictions of his inevitable victory, failed to respond to Truman's charges, let alone take the offensive himself. Instead, Dewey contented himself by taking the "high road" and, consequently, never attacked Truman's vulnerable flanks.

Truman devoted almost every one of his 354 campaign speeches to social welfare policies; significantly, he concentrated his attention upon the Republican congressional leadership and not on his opponent. In making fallacious but politically useful connections between Dewey and the Republican right wing, Truman affirmed that the Eightieth Congress was "merely a symbol and instrument of Republican Party policy." When he was not busy attacking the "Tafts and Tabers" and the "do-nothing Congress," he was reinforcing his own image as that of the inheritor of the New Deal tradition. Truman gave few speeches in which he failed to mention the magic name of Franklin D. Roosevelt. He repeatedly emphasized that the underlying issue of the election was "to preserve the gains made since 1933 when President Roosevelt took office." Time and again he returned to this central theme: "The Democratic Party gave the country a New Deal. And that New Deal paid off too. It was good for the country. It was good for labor. It was good for the farmer. It was good for every citizen in the United States." He warned, "These Republicans would like to turn back the clock" and restore the "boom and bust" policies of Harding, Coolidge, and Hoover. The Eightieth Congress, he charged, "repeatedly flouted the will of the people," and he warned that a Dewey victory would "deliver this country into the hands of the special interests and big business." In short, "The record of the Republican Party is a story of obstruction, objection, and reaction from the days of the Hoover depression to the end of the Eightieth Congress." In contrast to this dismal situation, Truman pictured in Roosevelt and the New Deal the essential spirit of the American Way of Life: "The Democractic Party represents the people. It is pledged to work for agriculture. It is pledged to work for labor. It is pledged to work for the small businessman and the white collar worker." Getting to the crux of the matter, "The Democratic Party puts human rights and human welfare first."

Truman's ten-month campaign, therefore, was exceedingly liberal in content, but equally conservative in purpose—liberal in the vast assortment of social welfare policies advocated, but conservative in that Truman sought primarily to hold intact the social service state erected by the New Deal and also to preserve for his own political advantage the support of the Roosevelt coalition.

A scholarly assessment of the election of 1948, however, has not been written. While we know a great deal from the published sources and from Jules Abels's popular study, significant questions are yet to be answered. Why, for example, was the total vote in 1949 relatively small in relationship to eligible voters? Did the Wallace movement really serve as a "lightning rod" and prevent a "soft on communism" charge from being made against Truman? Similarly, did the Thurmond candidacy remove the stigma of racism from the Democratic party and thus help it in the northern states? What was the actual composition of the Dixiecrat party, and how did this dissident movement affect the final result of the election? Why did Dewey refuse to attack the Truman record? Finally, did the voters re-elect Truman because of a conservative motivation to preserve the New Deal from possible Republican repeal, or did foreign policy, which was scarcely mentioned throughout the campaign, play a hidden but crucial role in determining voter preference? One thing is quite evident, however. This was the last presidential election to be based primarily upon the rhetoric of domestic reform; by 1952 foreign policy clearly became the vital concern of most voters.

The election, however, did not diminish the power of the conservative coalition in the Congress. When the Democratic Eighty-first Congress met, Truman proved unable to transfer his popularity with the voters into success with his legislative program. Except for the Housing Act of 1949, Congress rejected outright his other controversial proposals. This same congressional bloc was to remain intact and later was to stifle the New Frontier. Not until the combination of *Baker v. Carr* (1962) and the 1964 Republican debacle would the congressional log jam be broken and a new flood of social welfare legislation stream off Capitol Hill.

This essay has focused primary attention upon the activities of the Truman Administration, but two significant developments in the realm of social welfare occurred during the Truman period that are only indirectly connected to the action of the Administration. They require, however, some consideration in an essay of this nature. The first of these is the general acceptance by the American people of the permanency of the social service state. Most liberals expected a concerted effort by conservatives in the immediate postwar period to eradicate the New Deal—but this movement never gained sufficient momentum. The near-complete acceptance of the social service state needs examination, especially on the local and state level. The factors contributing to this fundamental change in the American mind have never been studied in any systematic manner.

Another important development was the professionalization of social welfare. During the progressive era and the 1920's, social reforms originated primarily from within private reform organizations. Even during the New Deal, the impetus for many reforms came from outside of government. As the New Deal established new social welfare agencies, however, the reformers frequently assumed positions administering the various programs. Thus, by the time Truman took office, the demand for reform came, not from private reform groups, but increasingly from within various federal agencies. The growth of the professionalization of social welfare and the institutionalization of reform seemingly culminated with the establishment of the Department of Health, Education and Welfare in 1953 and the Department of Housing and Urban Development in 1965. These important changes in social service and social reform need careful research.

Harry S Truman left office, as he had entered, during a period of political deadlock. He had, however, preserved the social welfare programs of the New Deal and, through strong executive action and some enabling legislation, strengthened considerably many existing programs. His determined action would prove to be decisive in preserving the New Deal and in providing the critical bridge to the remarkably successful Great Society legislative program of Lyndon B. Johnson. Circumstances prevented Truman from establishing many new, exciting reform programs, but in a time of public indifference and political stalemate, he labored to provide the American people with his conception of a Fair Deal. The significance of these efforts should not be allowed to go unnoticed, or unappreciated, by the historians of the Truman Administration.

What Should Congress Do About Health Insurance

Senator Robert A. Taft
Dr. H. H. Shoulders
Senator J. Howard McGrath
Dr. Michael M. Davis

Announcer:

Is national health insurance essential? Compulsory or voluntary—which is the best system? What should Congress Do About Health Insurance? Once again, the vital issue of the week discussed on your American Forum of the Air. [Applause.]

Good evening, ladies and gentlemen. From the Shoreham Hotel in your nation's capital, Mutual proudly presents America's pioneer public service radio program, the American Forum of the Air, founded nineteen years ago by Theodore Granik, attorney and moderator.

The Forum presents every week at this time the vital issue of the week, both sides of that issue, and the men who affect the decisions. Tonight our four authorities are Senator Robert A. Taft, Republican of Ohio; Dr. H. H. Shoulders, President, American Medical Association; Senator J. Howard McGrath, Democrat of Rhode Island, and Dr. Michael M. Davis, Chairman of the Executive Committee of the Committee for the Nation's Health.

And now here is your Chairman, Theodore Granik.

Chairman Granik:

Good evening. What Should Congress Do About Health Insurance? Two weeks ago President Truman renewed his plea that Congress adopt a National Health Insurance Act at this session. His plea was embodied in a bill submitted to the Congress by six Democratic senators and by Representative Dingell of Michigan in the House.

One of the Senate sponsors is Senator J. Howard McGrath of Rhode Island, a member of our panel of authorities this evening.

This year with the Republican Party in the majority on Capitol Hill, the National Health Insurance Plan meets opposition in the form of a National Health Act, sponsored by Senator Taft of Ohio and other Republican senators. Senator Taft is also a member of our panel this evening.

Perhaps the basic difference between these two plans lies in the fact that national health insurance carries with it a compulsory feature. The opposition contends that voluntary health insurance is far superior and in keeping with our concept of democracy.

Another basic difference is on the operational level; the health insurance supporters champion national operation through national collection of funds and national standards.

SOURCE: Senator Robert A. Taft, H. H. Shoulders, Senator J. Howard McGrath, and Michael M. Davis, *The American Forum of the Air* 9, No. 22 (June 3, 1947).

The opposition maintains that only by working through the various states and through the local medical associations in those states can the full benefits of health care be given to the people.

The third major difference is in the method of financing. The national health insurance people propose a form of payroll tax deduction according to earnings. The opposition charges that no honest estimate of the ultimate cost can be determined by this method.

There are other differences between the two schools of thought. Our panel of four authorities this evening will debate the pros and cons. Now let's hear from the first of our speakers, one of the leading Republicans of the nation, Chairman of the Republican Steering Committee of the Senate, Senator Robert A. Taft of Ohio. Senator Taft!

SENATOR TAFT:

Congress should pass the law introduced by Senators Smith, Ball, Donnell and myself providing Federal financial aid to every state which undertakes to make all-inclusive a plan for providing medical care for those unable to pay for it, and to encourage voluntary health insurance funds in every state. All the cities and states have recognized their obligation to do this, and most cities and states have carried out the obligation, but there are gaps, particularly in the poorer districts and the rural districts, resulting largely from the lack of state and local funds. The Federal Government should assist in expanding our present excellent system of medical care along the lines which have made this country the best-cared-for people in the world from a medical standpoint and given us the most progressive and brilliant medical profession. It should not deprive the states and local governments of the power to administer their own health programs. It should not throw this system into the ash can and turn all medical care over to the Federal Government.

The so-called compulsory health insurance plan is not insurance. It is the levying of a tax on all the people to bring four or five billion dollars into Washington to be used by the Federal Government to pay all the doctors of the United States to render free medical care to all the people of the United States. It is not only the socialization of medicine; it is the nationalization of medicine.

Chairman Granik:

Thank you, Senator Taft.

And now one of the Sponsors of the National Health Insurance Act, Senator J. Howard McGrath, Democrat of Rhode Island. Senator McGrath!

SENATOR McGRATH:

I am very glad that at long last the American Medical Association and the Republican Party have reluctantly conceded what the American people have known for years, namely, that we cannot individually buy good medical care, that health insurance is essential. That makes the answer to tonight's question obvious: The Congress should do what the American people will most certainly demand, once they know the facts; it should reject as no less than an attempted fraud on public expectation the bill now advanced by the Republican leadership, a bill which pretends to solve your medical care problems but which actually doles out help only if you are willing publicly to ask for charity.

The Congress should promptly pass a real bill—Senate Bill 1320—the National Health Insurance Bill, a measure advocated by President Truman and which I have had the honor of sponsoring along with Democratic Senators Wagner, Murray, Pepper, Chavez, and Senator Taylor—a bill which follows the American tradition, the insurance way, not the charity way, complete medical care as a right for which we have paid rather than limited charity care which we are forced to beg for.

Chairman Granik:

Thank you, Senator McGrath.

Next, the distinguished President of the American Medical Association, Dr. H. H. Shoulders, of Nashville, Tennessee. Dr. Shoulders!

DR. SHOULDERS:

The medical profession is opposed to the enactment of a compulsory health insurance law by the Congress because our present system of medical care is in complete harmony with our ideas of freedom. It has demonstrated its effectiveness in service to the people over a long period of years, first by great progress in medicine, by a reduction in the death rate to a very low level, by a remarkable increase in the health and longevity of the people. The life expectancy of the people of the United States has been increased to the high level of over 65 years, and life expectancy at birth is the most reliable index of social progress and well-being.

The enactment of the health insurance law would to a large extent destroy this proved system and erect in its place a political system of medical care administered by a Federal bureaucracy of gigantic proportions, which would impair the freedom of the people and the medical profession. It would impair the quality of the medical care the people would receive. It would increase the over-all cost of medical care, and it is not necessary to accomplish a solution of the economic problems involved in the financing of medical care.

Chairman Granik:

Thank you, Dr. Shoulders.

And now the Chairman of the Executive Committee of the Committee for the Nation's health, Dr. Michael M. Davis. Dr. Davis!

DR. DAVIS:

Congress should turn down the Taft-Smith-Ball-Donnell medical charity bill. Congress should pass the National Health Insurance Bill. How would national health insurance work? Here is Mr. Thomas Brown. He is a neighbor of mine in White Plains, New York. He has a wife and three children, and he earns $45 a week. He would pay 67½ cents a week into the National Health Insurance Fund, and his employer would put in an equal amount. When Mr. Brown or any one of his family was sick, he would call in or go to see a doctor, any doctor he chose, the same as he does today, only he would pay nothing to the doctor. So also with the hospital if he needed hospital care.

The National Health Insurance Fund would be divided up among the states, and the states in turn would allocate money to each locality. The

Health Insurance Fund would pay the doctors and hospitals through a local committee in which both doctors and the people would be represented.

If Mr. Brown belonged to a voluntary health insurance plan which furnished adequate services, he could keep on being a member and the Health Insurance Fund would pay the plan for serving him. Mr. Brown and all other self-supporting families would be able to get medical care as a right, not a charity. The very poor who cannot pay insurance would be paid for out of local and state tax funds, with Federal aid.

The doctors would not be government employees; they would be in practice as they are now, only they would not have to worry about uncollected bills.

Congress should not wait to pass National Health Insurance, because while we wait, millions of Americans are suffering, sometimes dying, because they do not get the medical care they need, and other millions are going into debt because they did get it.

Chairman Granik:

Thank you, gentlemen. There we have the issues and the sides are clearly drawn.

And now to start our spontaneous discussion, Senator Taft, Senator McGrath and Dr. Davis have both charged that your bill means charity and not health insurance. What would you say to that?

SENATOR TAFT:

We recognize that the Government has an obligation to give free service only to those people who are unable to pay for it themselves in full, directly or through voluntary health insurance. State medicine proposes that the Government tax everybody to the tune of about four or five billion dollars a year, and then give medical aid free to over one hundred million people. That is what socialism is. If free medical care for all at the expense of taxation, why not free food, clothing, housing for all at the expense of taxation?

SENATOR McGRATH:

I believe that Senator Taft misconstrues the issue entirely. We are talking about health for the American people, not health for only those who are unable to pay for it.

SENATOR TAFT:

Those who are able to pay for it can pay for it. My only insistence is that they do pay for it, not that the Government pay for it.

SENATOR McGRATH:

The fact of the matter is that they are dying by the hundreds—

SENATOR TAFT:

[Interposing]: Nonsense, Senator McGrath!

SENATOR McGRATH:

More deaths are occurring in the wealthy classes—that is, when I say the wealthy classes, I refer to the middle classes—than in the poorer classes.

SENATOR TAFT:

And our death rate is steadily declining, owing to the excellent service given by a free medical profession in the United States.

SENATOR McGRATH:

Our plan proposes that the doctors be paid for that service so that they don't have to give it free.

Chairman Granik:

Let's hear from the doctors. Dr. Shoulders?

DR. SHOULDERS:

Dr. Davis made the assertion that the $45-a-week employee in New York would pay 60 cents a week for his medical care and that he would go to his doctor and obtain all the care he wants and needs, and without the disturbance of the doctor-patient relationship. That is beautiful in theory, but in fact it isn't so. The fact is he would apply to the doctor of his choice provided that doctor has agreed to serve under the terms and conditions provided, and under regulations that are yet to be prescribed.

Chairman Granik:

Dr. Davis, would you care to answer that?

DR. DAVIS:

Certainly. The doctors of the United States are going to keep on serving the patients whom they now serve and who know them, and when this law is passed, the great majority of the doctors are going to keep on giving service to their patients as they have been doing under this law and people will be able to choose their doctors and go to them more freely than they do now, because they won't be held back by the financial limitation.

DR. SHOULDERS:

I would like to ask Dr. Davis this question: If that patient just developed the notion that he might have a cancer someplace, in the stomach we will say, and he wanted consultation or wanted a lot of other investigations, x-rays, and whatnot, because they are free, what would result if the doctor didn't think he needed it? If the doctor declines to recommend it, what happens?

DR. DAVIS:

Under the law, if the doctor refuses to recommend a consultation with a specialist or a laboratory—which is very unusual for the doctor to do, because the patient would choose another doctor—

DR. SHOULDERS:

Very promptly!

DR. DAVIS:

If the doctor did that, the patient could go to the medical administrative officer and ask to be referred to another doctor by that officer as a referee.

DR. SHOULDERS:

All right, if the doctor recommended that service, which he didn't think was necessary, what is his position?

DR. DAVIS:

Which doctor?

DR. SHOULDERS:

The doctor the patient went to first.

DR. DAVIS:

If the doctor didn't think it would be necessary, it would be just as it is today; if I go to a doctor and he doesn't think something is necessary and I do, I go to another doctor.

DR. SHOULDERS:

The point is this: If he fails to recommend, he is fired by the patient; if he agrees to recommend what he does not believe to be necessary, in good service, and honestly believes it and is perfectly correct—A lot of people, I am sure, people who do not engage in practice, develop a notion that they may have an organic illness when they really haven't, and it takes a great deal of examination to prove they haven't rather than to cure them.

DR. DAVIS:

Isn't it true it is estimated that some 40,000 people die every year from cancer because they do not get to a doctor early enough?

DR. SHOULDERS:

I do not think that is true, Dr. Davis, at all.

SENATOR TAFT:

May I say this: Isn't it perfectly obvious that if you have state medicine, you have to have regulations? The Federal bureau issues those regulations, tells you when you can go to a doctor, how often you can visit him on your insurance, whether the doctors can come to your home or can't come to your home for this disease or that disease, when he can prescribe x-ray, when he cannot prescribe x-ray. In England the public health people have a book of something like 350 pages of regulations for every doctor, because this is state medicine. This is a condition where a bureaucrat in Washington dictates to every doctor and every patient exactly what is covered by his insurance. They have to. They have to protect the Government. They can't give a man all the medical service he might like, and so state medicine, particularly national state medicine, means that every family in the United States is interfered within their own personal wishes and desires, and every doctor, of course, by some regulation issued from the capital here in Washington.

SENATOR McGRATH:

You are entirely wrong, Senator Taft. This is no more state medicine that the operation of the Workmen's Compensation Law can be called state medicine because no man can receive his benefits under the Workmen's Compensation Law unless some medico certifies that he was injured and his injury incapacitated him for a certain length of time. There is nothing in the law that is now proposed that prevents any man from going to the doctor of his choice, and having the doctor of his choice receive the fee of his choice, so long as that fee comes within the ethics of the profession as set up by a committee of his own profession within his own community. I cannot see how you can hope to blind the American people for long by calling this plan out of name, that is, socialized medicine. It is nothing of the kind.

SENATOR TAFT:

Of course it is; that is just a camouflage to say it isn't.

Listen to what the International Labor Office says (and they were for this). They say, "The fact is that once the whole population is brought within the scope of compulsory sickness insurance, the great majority of doctors, dentists, nurses, and hospitals find themselves engaged in the insurance medical service, which squeezes out most of the private practice on the one hand, and most of the medical care hitherto given by the public assistance authorities on the other. The next step to a single national medical service is a short one."

And that is what this means—a single national medical service directed by a Federal bureau in Washington.

SENATOR McGRATH:

Senator Taft, what is your alternative to provide health to the people who cannot afford or who neglect their health because of the cost and the obstructions that are placed in their way?

SENATOR TAFT:

You have two classes, Senator. You have the indigent class, and our bill provides adequately for the extension of state and city service to that class, a service recognized today. In the case of the intermediate class, our bill provides voluntary health insurance plans so that they can go and buy health insurance—which, incidentally, is going to be cheaper than this insurance— and those people, of course, if they don't choose to take it, don't choose to take it. This is American freedom. Incidentally, if they do run up against a heavy year, they will have no trouble today borrowing the money and spreading it out over three or four years on the insurance principle.

SENATOR McGRATH:

Do you believe in having people borrow money in adversity or preparing for it in advance?

SENATOR TAFT:

I believe people have the right to get medical service if they want to get it, and not to get it if they don't want to get it. A lot of people don't want to go to doctors, I am sorry to say. Those people ought to have the freedom to spend their own money.

This is no 60-cent proposition. That is a 4 percent pay roll tax provided in this bill itself. That means that a man getting $2500, about what Dr. Davis prescribes, has to pay $100 a year in taxes. That is more than any income tax he would have to pay.

SENATOR McGRATH:

I beg your pardon, it is nothing of the kind. It is a 1½ percent tax.

SENATOR TAFT:

This bill provides for a 4 percent pay roll tax.

SENATOR McGRATH:

It doesn't say whether the employer is going to pay it.

SENATOR TAFT:

But the labor organizations' plans in the past recent years have been that the employee pay it all. If he doesn't pay it, if the employer pays it, it is still a tax on the employee, because a pay roll tax is always a tax on the employee. If the employer pays it, it simply means that the cost of everything that is made by that employer increases, and so the employee pays it either in a reduction in his own pay or in increased cost of the things he has to buy.

DR. DAVIS:

What the Senator, I am afraid, forgets is this: The people of the United States are spending now out of their current income about 4 percent of their income; out of the average family budget, except the very poor and the very rich, about 4 percent is spent now for medical care.

SENATOR TAFT:

Why shouldn't they go on spending it? They are spending about 6 percent on cosmetics?

SENATOR McGRATH:

That sounds like Republican philosophy.

DR. DAVIS:

All that the National Health Insurance Bill proposes is that we should use in an organized way the money that people are spending now so that they can get a doctor and hospital when they need it without, on the average, its costing them any more than it does today.

SENATOR TAFT:

What I think we need less of in the United States is an organized way. It is the organization of every individual which is contrary to the whole concept of Anglo-Saxon philosophy and free government in the United States.

DR. DAVIS:

I do not think this organizes people; it organizes payment. It gives opportunity to people and to the doctor, both, to make the best use of medical science which the scientists and some of the medical practitioners have developed in this country.

DR. SHOULDERS:

I should like to ask Senator McGrath to explain an apparent inconsistency to me. I noticed in the paper this morning that 48,000,000 people in the United States paid income tax last year, and he says those same people cannot pay for medical care. Now, that is an inconsistency that I cannot quite understand, that these heads of families are required to pay income tax and yet cannot pay medical care, which is a small part of it.

SENATOR McGRATH:

The philosophy of your partner on this program is that they cannot afford to pay their income tax, let alone pay for their health insurance.

SENATOR TAFT:

I am in favor of reducing the income tax and giving them more money for the things they want to spend it on, including medical care.

Chairman Granik:

Let's get back to the question of the voluntary plans. Dr. Shoulders, here is a question we have received directed to you: If the American Medical Association believes that voluntary health insurance plans are the answer, why do your state medical societies get laws passed, as they have in 20 states, which prevent anyone but the doctors from starting such plans?

DR. SHOULDERS:

The medical societies of the several states have not sponsored that kind of law limited only to doctors. In the first place, the experiments that have been conducted on this voluntary prepayment health insurance have been underwritten by doctors for the purpose of conducting a logical experiment to determine whether or not the insurance principle is applicable to the financing of medical care. The doctors underwrite it, and the doctors have sponsored and promoted it. In my own state it is a mixed board of doctors and laymen.

SENATOR McGRATH:

Do you know, Doctor, of any state where there is a health program sponsored by anybody but the medical profession; or do you know of any state where it would be safe and sane for any group to sponsor a health program?

SENATOR TAFT:

What about the Blue Cross plan?

SENATOR McGRATH:

The Blue Cross Plan is a hospital care plan.

SENATOR TAFT:

That is hospital insurance, yes.

DR. SHOULDERS:

That is included in medical care, under the broad definition.

SENATOR McGRATH:

If you approve the principle of Blue Cross, I cannot see why you do not approve the principle of health insurance. It is only an extension of a system that has been proved to be very sound.

SENATOR TAFT:

Oh, Senator, I think voluntary health insurance ought to be available to everyone who wants it, and this bill proposes to promote that idea. It is rapidly spreading throughout the United States. It is experimental. It is difficult to know what the costs are. Nobody knows what the costs are. Nobody knows what the cost of our compulsory health insurance is. Most people think it will go far beyond the 4 percent suggested in your bill.

SENATOR McGRATH:

Senator Bob, let me say this to you: Our bill does not outlaw the plan of any local community or state which would set up a health plan. The difficulty is that with all the controversies that have been going on through all these years in the United States, no community yet has an adequate health plan.

SENATOR TAFT:

It doesn't outlaw it; it just taxes you 4 percent for the Federal Government, and then you can pay 4 more if you want to for a voluntary health insurance plan. That would be nice!

SENATOR McGRATH:

No, it does not. Any voluntary plan could be adopted that is satisfactorily meeting the requirements of this law; is that not correct, Dr. Davis?

DR. DAVIS:

Yes, the voluntary plan providing adequate medical service can continue to operate under this law.

SENATOR TAFT:

And relieve the people from this general Federal tax we are going to enact?

DR. DAVIS:

No, they wouldn't pay any money into the voluntary plan. The Health Insurance Fund would pay for the voluntary plan.

SENATOR TAFT:

Then it isn't a voluntary plan because people have to pay the tax. That takes the whole voluntary feature out of it.

DR. DAVIS:

The Blue Cross plans and the medical societies are asking that they be subsidized by government tax funds to get the low income people into their plans.

SENATOR TAFT:

That is satisfactory; yes, I am for that. I am for that, but that is for the people who cannot pay themselves. They are not asking for any subsidies for the people who can pay for themselves. They sell the insurance because it is good insurance, or they don't sell it if people don't want to buy it.

DR. DAVIS:

The people who cannot pay for voluntary insurance plans, in my opinion, constitute more than half the population.

Chairman Granik:

Let's get back to the question of the patient-doctor relationship. Dr. Davis, here is a question we have received directed to you: The medical profession holds to the view that the confidence of a patient in his doctor and the interest of a doctor in his patient are factors of importance in determining the quality of medical care. How would you preserve this factor or policy in a compulsory system?

DR. DAVIS:

A compulsory system is only compulsion on payment and not a compulsion on service. If you remove the financial barrier between doctor and patient, instead of making the personal relation more difficult, you make it more free and full, because you remove the financial barrier which is now a detriment to their personal relations.

DR. SHOULDERS:

I should say that the freedom of choice and the individual responsiblity are two factors that are inseparable in this matter of medical care, that is, the freedom of the individual and the responsibility of the individual, and when one goes, the other will go with it. Attempting to secure a service without cost will be equivalent to the sacrifice of freedom in the hope of obtaining a benefit. I should say under that system the only thing that the beneficiary is assured of is a political promise that a contract will be made for his care. That is the only promise he has. It is not insurance, because he has no contract indicating to him that he has a definite right, and he cannot sue on it.

The Veterans Administration issues insurance, but the beneficiary has a contract indicating what that benefit will be.

DR. DAVIS:

Dr. Shoulders, you have not answered the question Mr. Granik raised: Why have the state medical societies, 20 of them, enacted laws which are preventing the people from organizing their own health insurance plans? That is a fact.

DR. SHOULDERS:

I know of no such prevention.

DR. DAVIS:

I have the list of the states here—there isn't time to read them. There are 20 such states; Tennessee is one of them. The farmers' plans in Tennessee were put out of business since that law was passed in 1945.

DR. SHOULDERS:

That was a regulation by the Commissioner of Insurance and not by the Medical Society. I remember that.

DR. DAVIS:

The Commissioner of Insurance was given the right to do that by the law that was passed and sponsored by your State Medical Society.

SENATOR TAFT:

One thing that is absolutely necessary if you have one of these plans is that it must be sound. Otherwise, people are fooled and defrauded; so they all must be subjected to a strict insurance control.

DR. DAVIS:

I quite agree with that, but what I am getting at is this: I want to see the people able to organize their own health insurance plans, as well as the doctors.

SENATOR TAFT:

So do I, Dr. Davis; there is no dispute about that.

SENATOR McGRATH:

When the question of fraud arises, it seems to me that when the Congress of the United States attempts to write a national health law which at the maximum can only apply to 8 to 10 percent of the people, then we certainly are committing a mental fraud on the whole people of the United States.

SENATOR TAFT:

What we are doing is simply saying this: This is simply a state and local administration matter. We propose that the Federal Government help every state so that they can do a complete job. In general, health in these states has come along later than schools and so forth, and they have been short of funds. We propose to supplement those funds so every state can do the job, but on the present system, on a free medical service, on freedom of the people to pay for their own medical service and get the kind of medical service they want.

DR. DAVIS:

I wonder whether the Senator has read this new bill and seen how this places the responsibility for administration on the states, and particularly on every locality, with a responsible local committee in each locality of doctors and people who share the responsibility.

SENATOR TAFT:

Dr. Davis, I would say that was a complete fraud. Yes, I have read it. It is a provision that each state can administer this law. How? As agents of a Federal bureau under the regulations issued by the chief of the bureau here in Washington, with no power whatever to do anything or set in any kind of system they want to set in. The whole thing is directed from here. It is supposed to be decentralized. There is no such a thing as a decentralized Federal system. We have seen it in every bureau in the Federal Goverment; once the power is given, the power is centralized in Washington.

DR. DAVIS:

Under this law, the Federal Government has got to allocate money to the states, and the states to the localities.

SENATOR TAFT:

Oh, no, the states just administer the law and the Federal Government tells them exactly how they administer it, just exactly the way they would tell a Federal official located down in those states.

DR. SHOULDERS:

Isn't it true that the money would be allocated to the state when it has devised a plan, by the legislature or otherwise, that is approved by the Federal administration; isn't that a fact?

DR. DAVIS:

The Federal board has to approve the plan if it complies with the general requirements stated in the law itself.

SENATOR TAFT:

They can change the regulations every day; they can go in and fire anybody who doesn't do it. If they don't run it just the way they want them to, the administrator can throw the state out and step in and administer it under this bill. This is just to give it a state appearance, this new provision in the Wagner-Murray-Dingell bill, but it is the same old Wagner-Murray-Dingell plan in the bill introduced last year.

SENATOR McGRATH:

It seems to me we can place plenty of safeguards against the thing you fear, Senator Taft, in this bill. What we are contending for here is a national health insurance law as against your proposal which is a proposal to give health benefits to the pauper class who absolutely cannot afford to pay for it themselves.

SENATOR TAFT:

Compulsory insurance is not insurance at all; it is taxation. Insurance is the payment of something in return for taking care of a certain risk.

SENATOR McGRATH:

For an anticipated risk.

SENATOR TAFT:

This tax has no relation to that risk at all. A man with a $3600 income is going to have to pay $144, even though he has only himself and his wife. A fellow with a $1000 income pays $40 a year though he has a wife and six children. It is a principle of taxation.

SENATOR McGRATH:

Senator, you are still using percentage figures that are beyond anything in the bill.

SENATOR TAFT:

No, no, this will be a 4 percent tax.

SENATOR McGRATH:

But he is not paying the 4 percent.

SENATOR TAFT:

If that were so, why didn't you introduce a tax bill. It is easy to introduce a bill about spending money like this, but you have not introduced a tax bill providing the money.

SENATOR McGRATH:

Your bill is a spending bill. Your bill proposed to appropriate $200,000,000, and we do not appropriate one cent from the treasury.

SENATOR TAFT:

Your bill will cost $5,000,000,000, and you don't dare tell where you are going to get it. You don't dare introduce a tax bill that will take care of it.

SENATOR McGRATH:

We are going to get it from the people of America who are begging for this kind of program, and dying for lack of it.

SENATOR TAFT:

You are going to get it through a pay roll tax, I presume, but you don't introduce the pay roll tax bill; you don't bring that in and tell us about it.

Presumably it is going to be a pay roll tax bill so that a man with $2500 income is going to have to pay $100 a year for medical service. He can go and get voluntary medical insurance for about $87 for a family of five in Michigan today.

DR. DAVIS:

He can only get partial medical service. All he can get is hospital service and care while in a hospital. That is about half of the total medical bill. That is all he can get in Michigan today. He cannot get complete medical service.

SENATOR McGRATH:

He cannot get it in Ohio and he cannot get it in Rhode Island, in spite of what you say, Senator.

Chairman Granik:

Senator McGrath, here is a question we have received directed to you: Is there proof that the establishment of a compulsory health insurance has improved the quality and decreased the costs of medical care in the countries in which it has been adopted?

SENATOR McGRATH:

The answer is yes. In fact, the people of most democratic countries that have adopted these systems—and I refer to the Scandinavian countries, New Zealand, and so on—have had many plebiscites on this question, and in all of these plebiscites which have come along year after year, not once has any one of these countries which have adopted a national health insurance program, based upon insurance, ever rejected it, but rather in every plebiscite the plurality has been increased.

SENATOR TAFT:

Let me read what the *New York Times* said last year about the New Zealand system: "This governmental admission [made by the Minister of Health who thought they would have to abolish the system] of widespread racketeering which followed the institution of a system under which any New Zealander may consult any physician as frequently as he likes and the doctor can collect a fee for each visit follows efforts by the National Health Council to have the Health Ministry act to control what it holds to be an unwarranted drain on the social security fund.

"It has been revealed that, though many doctors are still in the armed forces, payments to doctors have been 50 per cent higher than the $5,000,000 a year that the government calculated."

DR. DAVIS:

May I comment on that? That report in the *New York Times* was written by the Associated Press correspondent in Wellington, New Zealand. Shortly after it was written, the Minister of Health of New Zealand wrote a letter, a copy of which I have here. It is too long to read, but in substance it says this: What the Minister of Health said about the New Zealand system was not that the abuses were such that they were going to stop the system, but that they were going to take action to stop the abuses and extend the system.

SENATOR TAFT:

The truth is, there isn't the slightest evidence that national health insurance where it has been tried has provided anything like as good a system as we have in the United States today. There is no such evidence.

DR. DAVIS:

In the last three years since the war, take the seven countries in Western Europe that are democratic countries, England, the three Scandinavian countries, France, Holland, Belgium; every one of those countries, despite the devastation which some of them have been through, has since the war extended their health insurance system, and mark you, with the cooperation of their organized medical profession in those countries.

SENATOR TAFT:

Surely; most of them have gone socialist, and we do not want to go socialist. We do not want to follow Europe with socialization and reduction of the freedom of the people.

DR. SHOULDERS:

You attempt to compare the whole people of the United States, consisting of 48 states and all the varieties of climates that exist, and the varieties of population that exist, with the small Scandinavian countries of uniform population, uniformity of climate, uniformity of every condition, and uniformity of race included. There is no possitility of comparing the two on any basis, and notwithstanding that fact, taking the conditions of the United States and all the wide variety of conditions that exist, we have a death rate close to theirs, if not below. And we must mention one other fact, that in New Zealand they do not include the colored population in their mortality records, so their statistics are deceptive.

SENATOR McGRATH:

It would seem to me their uniformity would make it less necessary for them to have a national health insurance policy than for ourselves here where we have this great diversification and the great many elements of physiology which we have to contend with.

DR. SHOULDERS:

The opposite is true.

SENATOR McGRATH:

Why is it true?

SENATOR TAFT:

It is true because socialism is a much easier thing to run—

SENATOR McGRATH:

[Interposing]: I am not talking about socialism.

SENATOR TAFT:

This is socialism. It is a question as to whether a socialistic plan will work. It will work better in a small, integrated community than in a country like the United States.

SENATOR McGRATH:

It isn't socialism when we are trying to save the lives of human beings which our country may someday be sadly in need of.

DR. SHOULDERS:

I would like to ask this question. If this is insurance, what objection do you have to providing for the issuance of a contract to the beneficiary, the individual citizen who pays the tax, stipulating the benefits he is entitled to, so that he has constant evidence of the fact that he is entitled to it?

DR. DAVIS:

Doctor, the law does exactly that. The law states who is eligible, and it states what he is entitled to, and that is a contract written by the Congress of the United States.

DR. SHOULDERS:

In line 6 of the law, it states the director has the power to determine eligibility, even. He has the power to limit the benefit arbitrarily, on his own decision.

DR. DAVIS:

Doctor, you are not saying what is in the law.

DR. SHOULDERS:

Yes, I will give you the line. It says that the board will establish standards, and each agreement—Section 217 contains "an undertaking to comply with this title and with the regulations prescribed thereunder." The word "regulation" occurs 22 times in Title II, and no one knows what those regulations will be.

Chairman Granik:

Gentlemen, we pause now for a summation of the arguments advanced this evening. Dr. Shoulders, will you sum up for your side?

DR. SHOULDERS:

Title II of this bill does not provide for insurance but, to the contrary, is a violation of insurance principles. First, there is no contract between the insured and the insuror. The beneficiaries pay the tax and get in return a promise—a political promise, if you please—of service, with the power vested in a board to alter the benefits and by regulation to alter the contract, if such exists. It is a power to tax, to spend, to regulate, to dominate both the people and the medical profession. It is tyranny parading as welfare.

We who oppose the enactment of this law recognize the importance of individual freedom and individual responsiblity in this matter of medical care. We want freedom of decision and freedom of action with the individual patients and the doctor. Freedom and responsibility will either stand or go together.

For aid to those who need and desire aid, administered on such a basis as not to impair the freedom of those people involved, we stand for progress but progress with prudence, prudence requiring that the new be tested and proved before it is used, regardless of whether it is a drug, an operation, a procedure, or a governmental plan—and we want those plans tested and proved.

Finally, I must say that the issue is this: Shall patients and doctors retain their freedom of judgment in this matter of medical care or shall these freedoms be surrendered to a Federal bureaucracy? This is the basic issue involved in this proposition.

Chairman Granik:

I am sorry, Dr. Shoulders, your time has expired. Dr. Davis, will you sum up for your side?

DR. DAVIS:

This bill has been incorrectly presented again and again and again with labels of socialism and tyranny, and so forth, that arouse emotions without evoking intelligence. This bill gives the American people the opportunity to spend the money which they are now spending in a definite way through which they can get medical care from their own doctors and their hospitals as a right and not a charity.

Health insurance is a way of using the people's money democratically to furnish the medical service. It underwrites the low income paying power of the poorer sections and the poorer rural areas and will draw doctors to those areas.

On the other side, the Taft-Smith-Ball-Donnell bill applies the principle of compulsion on me and on other taxpayers to pay for the medical care of somebody else, whereas the Health Insurance Bill requires me to pay what I am spending now to assure me medical care for myself and my family.

The American Medical Association presents a program, if you can call it a program, which wants to have voluntary health insurance plans run by doctors, which bans in a growing number of states health insurance plans run by anybody else, plans which give only partial service as mentioned before. They have been restricting their service as they have grown in number, instead of expanding their service, and the program which they present, and which this bill of Senator Taft and his colleagues propose to offer, would help voluntary plans only as private organizations.

Chairman Granik:

I am sorry, gentlemen, our time is up [Applause.]

You have been listening to the American Forum of the Air Discussion, "What Should Congress Do About Health Insurance?" Our speakers have been: Senator Robert A. Taft, Republican of Ohio; Dr. H. H. Shoulders, President, American Medical Association; Senator J. Howard McGrath, Democrat of Rhode Island; and Dr. Michael M. Davis, Chairman of the Executive Committee of the Committee for the Nation's Health.

Your letters and comments are welcome.

CHAPTER 8

The Eisenhower Era

INTRODUCTION

Attacks on the welfare state found a receptive audience in the decade of the 1950s, and such rhetoric placed limits on the Eisenhower administration and its ability to develop a Republican social program. The Eisenhower administration no longer questioned whether the federal government had a role to play in social policy, but it believed the New Deal had weakened traditional work values and self-reliance in American society. Moreover, federal welfare programs were perceived by Republicans as having undergone an irresponsible expansion from 1933 through 1953.

In the immediate postwar years, poverty declined significantly in a vibrant economy. The percentage of those below the poverty line fell from 33 percent in 1947 to 23 percent in 1956. In the following five years, poverty continued to decline, dropping another 2 percent. As overall poverty rates fell, there was an important shift in the AFDC recipient population from white widows to black women with children. In 1931 the government estimated that 96 percent of the beneficiaries of Aid to Dependent Children were white widows. By 1948, the percentage of black families receiving AFDC had risen to 29 percent, and by 1961 the percentage had grown to 44 percent. In 1940, 42 percent of the fathers of dependent children were dead; by 1963, 94 percent were living.

These changes in the welfare population went unnoticed by the Eisenhower administration. Critical of the welfare state, Eisenhower and administration officials sought to rehabilitate traditional social values, while leaving primary social responsibilities to state and local governments and to private corporations. Still Eisenhower wanted his administration to prove that the Democrats did not have "a monopoly on the goals of a good society." Eisenhower therefore favored limited expansion of federal activity in housing, medical care, and education. Moreover, in 1950, he approved the biggest single expansion of Social Security coverage when he brought self-employed people into the system. In this way, Eisenhower accepted and expanded the welfare state.

Early in his administration, Eisenhower called upon Nelson Rockefeller, then serving in the newly created Department of Health, Education and Welfare, to review existing federal welfare programs so that his administration might be able to contribute something worthwhile to the welfare of the nation. At the same time, Eisenhower saw Social Security as a "humane, forward looking, yet not New Dealish" program founded on conservative principles of self-reliance. Given this sentiment, Eisenhower took readily to Rockefeller's proposal that the Social Security system be expanded to include the self-employed and to enable disabled workers to receive full benefits. The expansion of Social Security under the Eisenhower administration further marked the incremental growth of the system under both Democratic and Republican administrations. Yet it should be noted that the system expanded in ways unforeseen by Eisenhower.

Edward D. Berkowitz and Kim McQuaid examine welfare reform in the 1950s with particular emphasis on the expansion of disability insurance. Berkowitz and McQuaid maintain that the main responsibility for expanding the system came from a group of New Deal bureaucrats, including Wilbur Cohen and Robert Ball, who had remained in the Social Security Administration under Eisenhower. These men proposed that Eisenhower tackle the issue of disability and vocational rehabilitation.

Specifically, Cohen and Ball proposed a "disability" freeze, which would allow a disabled worker to gain full Social Security benefits once he reached the age of 65. Moreover, once a worker became permanently disabled, he became eligible for rehabilitation. Cohen saw that the next step in the program was to offer direct benefits to all disabled workers, but his intentions remained unknown to Eisenhower, who accepted the moderate "disability freeze." The proposal was approved by Congress in 1954. Within two years, the bureaucrats at HEW, along with Democrats in Congress, extended permanent disability insurance to all over 50 years of age. In 1960, the program was further changed to cover other age groups. In this way the 1954 amendments, supported by Eisenhower, opened the door for broadening the program in 1956. Eisenhower, now aware of the game plan, nevertheless failed in his fight to defeat further changes in disability insurance.

It should be noted that political differences separated Democrats and Republicans concerning which responsibilities they were willing to give the federal government. But both liberals and conservatives, politicians and HEW bureaucrats, Republicans and Democrats initially promoted rehabilitation as a means of removing people from the welfare rolls and lowering program costs. In this way, work values continued to be emphasized even as the federal government's role in welfare grew.

Eisenhower's special message to Congress on the health needs of the American people, delivered on January 18, 1954, framed his proposals for a state-federal program of vocational rehabilitation in terms of putting people back to work. Eisenhower considered rehabilitation to be a matter of both "humanity and national self-interest. . . . [I]t is a program that builds a stronger America."

In this message, Eisenhower also discussed the issue of the nation's health care system. The thrust of the Eisenhower administration's involvement in health had been to avoid any direct subsidy of services, while providing funds for long-term investment in hospital construction, biomedical research, and the funding of health manpower programs. The enactment of the Hill-Burton Act of 1946 provided a major impetus for hospital construction by offering federal matching grants up to one third of costs for construction of nonprofit hospitals. In his message to Congress, Eisenhower proposed that the Hill-Burton Act (Hospital Survey and Construction Act) be extended to provide funds for construction of nursing and convalescent homes, and of nonprofit rehabilitation facilities. Between 1946 and 1968, nearly $3.2 billion in federal funds were to be channeled through the program.

The Eisenhower administration also developed a plan to subsidize private health insurance programs, but this proposal died in Congress under attacks from both the American Medical Association, which viewed the plan as socialized medicine, and liberal Democrats, who criticized the proposal as wholly inadequate. As a consequence, the United States remained the only major Western nation without a national health insurance system.

Further Readings

The history of welfare policy in the 1950s remains a relatively unexplored area. An excellent overview of the Eisenhower administration may be found in Charles C. Alexander, *Holding the Line: The Eisenhower Era, 1952–1961* (Bloomington: Indiana University Press, 1964).

A good start for understanding welfare in this period can be found in James L. Sundquist, *Politics and Policy: The Eisenhower, Kennedy, and Johnson Years* (Washington, D.C.: The Brookings Institution, 1968), relevant chapters in James T. Patterson, *America's Struggle Against Poverty, 1900–1980* (Cambridge: Harvard University Press, 1981), and Edward Berkowitz and Kim McQuaid, *Creating the Welfare State* (New York: Praeger Books, 1980).

Welfare Reform in the 1950s

Edward Berkowitz
Kim McQuaid

Conventional historical wisdom holds that domestic reform languished during the Eisenhower era. With the single exception of civil rights, the domestic politics of the 1950s have tended to become isolated from those of the political eras that preceded and followed them. Even historical admirers of the period concentrate their attention on the Eisenhower administration's leadership in foreign affairs. As for domestic affairs, historians content themselves with the estimate that Eisenhower "held the line." His administration countenanced the reform programs of the New and Fair Deals but introduced no new initiatives of its own. The Eisenhower era, then, is of little or no importance to students of twentieth-century reform.

Such well-established viewpoints, however, obscure as much as they clarify the history of reform in modern America. Interpretations based on the personal qualities of political leaders need to be revised by analyses of the activities of the public institutions over which these political leaders presided. In what follows, we analyze the Eisenhower administration's activities in social welfare legislation—paying particular attention to programs aimed at dealing with the problem of disability. The result of this analysis is to change our picture of reform during the Eisenhower era from an image characterized by isolation and inactivity to an image of concerted activity with direct links to both the New Deal and the New Frontier.

The federal government inherited by Dwight D. Eisenhower and the Republican party in 1953 was a greatly changed organization from what it had been only a decade and a half before. On the eve of the Second World War, paid civilian employees of the federal government numbered about 1 million. Forty percent of these civil servants occupied positions that had been created during the New Deal era. By 1945, however, almost 4 million civilians labored on federal payrolls. Demobilization pared these numbers briefly, but the Korean War helped boost federal officeholders to 2.5 million by 1953. Throughout Eisenhower's entire tenure as president, federal employees never totaled less than 2.4 million men and women.

These numerous federal officials spent a vastly increased number of federal dollars. In 1940 it cost about $10 billion to run the government. Thirteen years later this total had risen to almost $80 billion a year. By the time Eisenhower left Washington, federal outlays approached $100 billion annually.

SOURCE: Edward Berkowitz and Kim McQuaid, *Social Service Review* 54, no. 1 (March 1980), pp. 45–58. ©1980 by the University of Chicago. All rights reserved. Reprinted by permission.

These statistics illustrated fundamental and important differences between the conservatism of the 1950s and that of preceding political eras. Postwar conservatives did not wish a return to predepression-style minimal government, nor did they want to revoke key pieces of New Deal social welfare legislation such as the Social Security Act. Instead, twenty years of depression, war, and cold war had impressed mainstream conservatives with the central government's role as a "necessary agent for change in a hostile world." Conservatives remained more enthusiastic as supporters of "big government" in foreign—as opposed to domestic—affairs. Even in domestic affairs, however, they increasingly perceived the major differences between themselves and liberals in relative terms. The fundamental question was no longer whether the government should serve. It was, rather, whom the government should serve—and how it should go about serving them.

For President-elect Eisenhower and his major advisers, the time had clearly come for the federal government to "serve business." The ultimate paradox of the Eisenhower era, however, was that such service was of an activist variety in which Washington authorities found themselves in the anomalous position of doing more and more things in order to "preserve free enterprise." In the perceived conservative wisdom of the 1950s, debate no longer hinged on whether the federal government should spend money. The question, instead, was how the money should be spent.

Washington, mainstream conservatives concluded, should finance, but it should not seek to control. Instead of being a direct provider of welfare and other services to the populace, the federal government must cooperate with lower levels of government and with private corporations. Accordingly, a federal government which had become big in reaction to the failures of states, localities, and large corporations would remain big in cooperation with these same institutions.

How, then, did Eisenhower and his advisers believe that they could accomplish this difficult rapprochement between more federal power and less federal power? At the heart of their efforts lay the notion of efficient management. In the nation's military affairs, for example, Democratic mismanagement of nonnuclear conflicts like the Korean War would be replaced with a "new look," a defense program based on air power, nuclear weaponry, and a doctrine of "massive retaliation." That is well known. Less understood, however, is the important fact that the "new look" in military and foreign policy had a domestic counterpart: the "rehabilitation" approach to the solution of the nation's social welfare problems. Rehabilitation programs, cast in the same cost-efficient rhetoric that was applied to bombers, rockets, and foreign aid, became the cornerstone of the Eisenhower administration's social welfare policy.

The administration's "rehabilitation" concept originated in July of 1953 when the president asked his chief aides for proposals which would demonstrate that the Roosevelt and Truman administrations "did not have a monopoly on the goals of a good society." One of the people confronted with this call to action was Nelson Rockefeller, then serving as the under-secretary of the newly created Department of Health, Education, and Welfare (HEW). In the autumn of 1953, Rockefeller and an aide began to review existing federal welfare programs. They soon came upon one whose structure and concept met their needs precisely.

The program was vocational rehabilitation. Begun in the wake of World War I, the civilian vocational rehabilitation program evolved during the twenties into a system of federal grants-in-aid to the states which helped state and local authorities to finance job training for the physically handicapped. Thirty years later, the Eisenhower administration seized upon this program as a model on which to base its domestic social welfare policy. Three characteristics of the program made it particularly attractive to postwar conservatives. First, the rehabilitation program relied upon local, as opposed to federal, administrative initiative. Second, it provided services, rather than cash grants, to welfare recipients. And, last, the program's clear purpose was to make people less dependent upon long-term public assistance by enabling disabled individuals to recover their earnings potentials in private labor markets.

For all these reasons, then, the vocational rehabilitation concept fit into the emerging Republic synthesis of the postwar era. It enabled the Eisenhower administration to meet social welfare problems and, simultaneously, to encourage individual self-reliance. The vocational rehabilitation program was a form of positive federal action which sought to end America's dependence on the federal government. As such, it became the peg upon which the administration hung the social welfare program that it presented to Congress in 1954.

The administration's legislative program contained four specific social welfare provisions. One involved an expansion of the vocational rehabilitation program, including money for rehabilitation research and training. The second provision would aid the states in constructing rehabilitation centers under an expanded program of federal assistance for hospital construction. The third provision proposed amending the Social Security Act to allow a disabled person to receive retirement benefits at age sixty-five. The fourth and final provision was a complicated "reinsurance" plan under which the federal government was to help private companies finance a voluntary program of health insurance.

This last provision died quickly in Congress—opposed by both the America Medical Association and liberal congressmen interested in compulsory national health insurance. President Eisenhower pressed for the passage of the other three elements of his administration's social welfare program in a series of special messages to Congress. The messages all centered around a central theme: rehabilitation as the proper approach to solving welfare problems. Rehabilitation forwarded "freedom and individual responsibility," "usefulness, independence, and self-respect." Two million Americans could and should be rehabilitated; but only 60,000 of these individuals were currently being treated. "Conditions of both humanity and national self-interest," Ike declaimed, demanded that this situation be changed.

Congress endorsed the Eisenhower rehabilitation program enthusiastically. It was, for the moment, a Republican-controlled institution. For the Eighty-third Congress, at least, the Republicans held a bare one vote majority in the Senate and a ten vote majority in the House. In the next Congress, the Democrats gained similarly small margins. These small margins to the contrary, "rehabilitation" proved compatible with either a liberal or a conservative political style. Liberals noted that the administration's agenda meant more money for social welfare programs in the short run, while conservatives contented themselves with the expectation of saving government money in the long run. For some, rehabilitation meant a vital and humane form of social service. For others, rehabilitation was the "new look" in federal social welfare strategy which would wean people away from the government and into the labor force. Rehabilitation, in short, was an ambiguous term which everyone could translate in a personally congenial way—just the sort of ambiguity which lies at the heart of successful political compromise.

Eisenhower himself managed to capture the essence of rehabilitation's almost mystical political appeal when he spoke at the White House bill-signing ceremony for the new vocational rehabilitation legislation. Vocational rehabilitation, the former general said, was "a humanitarian investment of great importance, yet it saves substantial sums of money."

THE BUREAUCRATIC COUNTERATTACK

If Eisenhower thought that his administration had provided for the country's welfare in a triumphant, middle-of-the-road manner, he was mistaken. Liberal forces agreed with the vocational rehabilitation legislation and the other paraphernalia of Eisenhower's 1954 program. But they saw it as only the first step toward a truly adequate social welfare program, one which included the key elements of a compulsory national health insurance statute and a national disability insurance law. For the remainder of his presidential tenure, Eisenhower was required to defend his administration's domestic welfare policies from repeated liberal attacks. The aging general ended up losing as many battles as he won.

In their fight to keep the New Deal alive, liberals had the support of an important group of people—and one much neglected by historians. These were the bureaucrats, the career employees of the Department of Health, Education, and Welfare. Eisenhower's rehabilitation approach might satisfy welfare bureaucrats in the federal government's Office of Vocational Rehabilitation, but it did nothing to mollify other HEW officials anxious to broaden the scope of direct federal controls over the administation of social welfare services to the populace. Emphases on rehabilitation programs could—and did—imply that bureaucrats operating other types of federal social welfare programs would become less and less important over time. To expect these same bureaucrats to preside over a "new look" in welfare policy which threatened their own disappearance reflected a flaw in the administration's analysis of the political import of its rehabilitation program.

This flaw resulted largely from the fact that the administrative models commonly held by the president and his advisers were ones in which the bureaucracy's role was essentially passive. Eisenhower, a career army officer, believed that the executive branch of the federal government should function along the orderly, "nonpartisan," lines customary in the military. Eisenhower's cabinet officers, most of whom were the executives of large corporations, saw themselves as systems managers, captains of functionally specialized teams. Such administrative perspectives led to an assumption that an identity of interest existed between the presidentially appointed heads of federal departments and the career civil servants that staffed those same departments. In corporations, after all, workers produced what management ordered them to produce. What applied to the employees of the armed forces or private companies, however, failed to apply to the federal civil service. Government was not big business carried on by other means. Since the Eisenhower rehabilitation approach implied that the federal welfare bureaucracy might well have to eliminate itself, there was every reason for a growing political disjunction between the career welfare bureaucracy and the executive branch.

This separation of the bureaucracy from the leadership of the executive branch was not a new phenomenon. As early as 1939, bureaucrats grouped around the Social Security Administration had formulated an agenda for expansion of federal social welfare programs which included the passage of a nationwide disability insurance program and a compulsory national health insurance program. Although Roosevelt had refused to support such moves on a mixture of tactical and philosophic grounds, the agenda remained firmly in place, awaiting only the right political circumstances. The Truman administration failed to provide those circumstances; national health insurance was hotly debated and resoundingly defeated in Congress.

Defeats like these taught the bureaucracy political lessons. By the time of Eisenhower's arrival in Washington, the subcabinet officials in HEW had begun to practice a more sophisticated, if less heroic, form of politics. Instead of presenting the Congress with legislative proposals which the bureaucracy regarded as the correct solution to problems such as health care or income maintenance, bureaucrats began to formulate new, less ambitious proposals designed for congressional consumption. No longer would federal welfare bureaucrats push for an all-inclusive program of disability and health insurance as they had throughout the 1940s. In the 1950s the bureaucrats separated health insurance proposals from their disability insurance proposals. Remembering the political clout that the nation's elderly had exercised in the Townsend Movement of the 1930s, the bureaucrats went further: health insurance for the entire population was transformed into health insurance for the elderly alone. The bureaucrats now tailored their proposals to specific interest groups and lobbied for their proposals' passage. In the process, they acquired a new degree of independence from the executive branch.

Despite this new independence, the advent of Eisenhower posed serious problems. Many upper-level bureaucrats, such as those working for the Social Security Administration, owed their existence to Democratic legislation and Democratic administrations. The transition to Eisenhower and the Republicans provided a crucial test of whether there would be continuity of principle and personnel within the leadership of Washington's welfare bureaucracy. Republican administrators were pressured to replace these high-level bureaucrats with loyal party members, some of whom had been waiting for twenty years for a Washington post. Even Mary Switzer, the director of a pre-New Deal program like vocational rehabilitation, a woman who had once worked as a special assistant to Herbert Hoover's Secretary of the Treasury Andrew Mellon, faced the threat of termination. She was slated to be replaced by the chairperson of the California Republicans for Nixon and kept her job only after her friends in the medical profession and the pharmaceutical industry talked to Sherman Adams and the president's personal physician on her behalf. But others, like Arthur Altmeyer, head of the Social Security Administration, symbolized the New Deal with too much clarity to survive the transition. Altmeyer left. Jane Hoey, the head of the "public assistance" program, left. I. S. Falk, the Social Security Administration's research director and the nation's leading health insurance advocate, left.

The principles of the federal welfare bureaucracy, however, survived. So did the intent to increase the number of direct federal welfare services. This survival of New Deal agenda and approach was made possible by a combination of presidential weakness and internal bureaucratic strength. During the course of his presidency, Eisenhower very nearly abdicated domestic legislative responsibilities to his cabinet officers and the Republican leadership in Congress. He assumed that his job was to "propose needed [domestic] measures on the advice of his cabinet and other high-level officials, but not to lead, pressure, or persuade congressmen into voting as he wished." Leaving domestic affairs to subordinates, Eisenhower devoted his presidential instincts to resolving international crises. As he pondered what he should do about Guatemala, Hungary, Lebanon, Quemoy, and Matsu, he left little time for consideration of the intricacies of domestic social welfare legislation.

With Eisenhower distracted, the bureaucracy utilized its organizational advantages to maximum effect. When Eisenhower became president, the bureaucrats had had almost twenty years to build internal cohesion and alliances with congressmen, to translate social welfare concepts into a special rhetoric of which they were the masters, and to accumulate an institutional memory which made them the social welfare experts on whom any new administration must depend. If Arthur Altmeyer paid the price of visible leadership by losing his job, other social welfare bureaucrats, equally knowledgeable and equally partisan, remained to advise the new Republican administration.

Wilbur Cohen was among the New Deal graduates who matriculated in the Eisenhower administration. Cohen, who had once worked as a special assistant to Arthur Altmeyer, was almost Altmeyer's alter ego. When Altmeyer left Washington in 1953, his friend Cohen managed to stay on by transferring to the research department of the Social Security Administration. The transfer involved a demotion in rank, but not a lessening of Cohen's influence in social welfare policymaking councils. Within months of his arrival, Eisenhower's appointee who headed the Social Security Administration told his boss, the secretary of health, education, and welfare, that he "couldn't get along" without the assistance tendered to him by Cohen and Robert Ball, a Social Security Administration actuary and another Democratic holdover.

Nor were the Republican-appointed social security commissioners opposed to social security's expansion. The job required expertise in the field and led to the appointment of such professionals as John Tramberg and Charles Schottland, who operated from within a broad professional consensus. This consensus held that social security was a desirable social welfare institution.

The appointment of Schottland, who served as commissioner of social security from 1954 to 1959, was typical of the general process. He was educated at the New York University School of Social Work and the University of Southern California Law School. A social work professional, he had worked over the years for the California Relief Administration, the Children's Bureau of the Department of Labor, and the California Department of Social Welfare. As a prominent state administrator and a friend of Earl Warren, Schottland appeared to be a safe appointee. For all of his safety, however, he remained deeply committed to social security and to the passage of disability insurance.

THE CASE OF DISABILITY

Bureaucrats like these worked to keep the Eisenhower administration's welfare proposals consistent with the long-range social welfare agenda formulated by the federal bureaucracy itself. Their efforts to educate and influence the Eisenhower administration tested all of their new-found political skill. In 1954 Cohen complained privately to Arthur Altmeyer that "we do not know what the guidelines and policies [of the executive branch] are—so we work in the dark—we are holding

the fort, it is true. But the expenditures of energy are tremendous."
Although Cohen complained, his unheroic efforts had their programmatic
rewards. Amendments to the Social Security Act passed by Congress in
1954 and afterward amounted to a victory for the forces of continuity in
federal welfare procedure. The sections of these amendments which deal
with the problem of disability illustrated the more general phenomenon.

Permanent disability insurance was one of the domestic reform programs which federal welfare bureaucrats had been suppporting since the
eve of the Second World War. The idea behind this reform was relatively
simple. The social security program passed into law by the Roosevelt
administration in 1935 contained an old-age pension program. Bureaucrats
like Cohen wanted to extend social security to cover disability as well. In
this way, workers who became disabled would receive a pension similar to
the ones that retired workers already received.

Over the years, the bureaucrats had built up an impressive legislative
record on disability insurance—a record which included numerous congressional hearings and the passage of a disability measure by the House of
Representatives. The Senate, however, posed a continuing and apparently
insurmountable obstacle. To ease around the obstacle, bureaucrats abandoned their existing diability program early in the 1950s in favor of a more
limited program, known in HEW as a "disability freeze." The dynamics
of this plan were relatively simple. A worker who became permanently
disabled would receive an enhanced retirement pension when he reached
age sixty-five. Even though he had not paid into the social security trust
fund since the time that he had become disabled his retirement benefits
would be calculated and paid out to him as if he had never become disabled
and had paid into his old-age retirement fund during his entire working
lifetime. Passage of the "disability freeze" plan would mean, in short, that
the federal government subsidized the disabled worker.

Wilbur Cohen's proposal for a "disability freeze" blended in nicely
with the efficiency-oriented rhetoric of key Eisenhower advisers like Nelson
Rockefeller. One of Rockefeller's assistants remarked of Cohen's plan that
"it seemed fair. It seemed humane. It didn't cost much." It also had the
advantage of resembling a provision of private insurance contracts, the so-
called waiver-of-premium clause. In addition, the disability-freeze proposal
appeared consistent with the Eisenhower administration's emphasis on
rehabilitation as a social welfare strategy. Once a worker was declared
"permanently" disabled (i.e., disabled for a lengthy period), he became a
candidate for rehabilitation. In this manner, the disability-freeze program
proposed by Cohen served, in Republican eyes, "as a great, huge recruiting
system for rehabilitation."

The Eisenhower administration might see the disability freeze as a
logical component of its "new look" social welfare arsenal. To the bureaucrats at HEW the freeze represented something very different. Cohen, for
one, realized that the disability freeze marked a crucial first step toward

a disability insurance program, long an item on the New Deal welfare agenda. To participate in the program, Cohen realized, a worker had first to be declared permanently disabled. The program that Cohen constructed, therefore, put federal officials in the business of making disability declarations.

Cohen also realized the virtues of programmatic gradualism. He moved slowly, in the hope that incremental movement would accomplish what the grand programmatic leaps of the past had failed to accomplish. From federal subsidies for social security retirement accounts to even more direct federal subsidy in the form of disability benefits paid to people at the onset of their disability was a relatively short step, once the principle of allowing federal officials to define an individual as disabled was conceded. Considered in this light, then, Cohen's successful attempt to get the Eisenhower administration first to sponsor, and then pass into law, the disability-freeze program was an act of consummate political skill, one which advanced the scope of direct federal welfare controls by playing upon the ambiguities of the rehabilitation approach to social welfare problems.

Back home in Madison, Wisconsin, Altmeyer listened to President Eisenhower announce his support for the disability freeze and other 1954 amendments to the Social Security Act with a sense of relief. Dismissing Eisenhower and his top aides as secondary, Altmeyer credited Cohen with the real victory. The administation's acceptance of the beginnings of the federal welfare bureaucracy's disability insurance agenda was a personal triumph for Cohen. "Not only have you translated the technical material into understandable form," Altmeyer told his protégée, "but you have enabled the administration to understand and take into account the attitude of interested groups and public relations generally. I shudder to think of what might have happened if you had not been there to facilitate the thinking and bridge the transition."

The bureaucrats managed to hold the fort when the Republicans returned to executive control in Washington. Democratic victory in the congressional elections of 1954 made them even bolder. In the following years, they made a final push for the enactment of a disability insurance program administered by the federal government. A strong prodisability insurance lobby aided them in their efforts. The lobby had two leaders: Wilbur Cohen, who left the federal government in 1956 to take a job at the University of Michigan, and Nelson Cruikshank, who directed the newly merged AFL-CIO's Department of Social Security. From outside the government, Cohen maintained his close advisory relationships with key federal welfare bureaucrats and with influential Democratic congressmen such as Wilbur Mills and Lyndon Baines Johnson. The only difference that Cohen's departure from the government made was that he acquired more freedom to engage in partisan politics. As for Cruikshank, the significance of his position lay in the fact that he lobbied for an organized labor movement that had put aside many internal jurisdictional squabbles and thereby strengthened its political clout.

Between June of 1955 and July of 1956 the bureaucrats, assisted by their allies in the House and Senate, engaged in a complex process of legislative infighting aimed at adding disability insurance provisions to the Social Security Act. To maximize the program's political impact, bureaucrats proposed a program of disability insurance restricted to the nation's elderly (defined as those over fifty years old). Despite the fact that the Eisenhower administration opposed the bill, the Senate voted in favor of permanent disability insurance for all Americans over fifty by a one-vote margin. The Senate's position prevailed in conference committee and withstood the threat of a presidential veto. The federal welfare bureaucracy had enacted a major piece of the reform agenda that they had formulated almost twenty years before. They had done so, moreover, in unpromising political circumstances.

Victory remained partial for only a short time. Writing a report several months after the passage of disability insurance for the elderly, Cruikshank decided to delete a section in which he prophesied that Congress would soon extend protection against disability to all age groups. To have included the thought would have been indiscreet, but it would have reflected an underlying truth. As Cruikshank and other unheroic bureaucratic reformers of the 1950s understood, the existence of a law was an invitation to its liberalization. The trick within the American social welfare system was to get a law passed creating a new federal welfare program. The expansion of that program would follow. The passage of disability insurance, then, acted as a guarantee that the program would someday be extended and liberalized. In fact, "someday" arrived soon. By 1960 disability insurance coverage had been extended to all age groups. The "efficiency management" welfare ideology of the 1950s had been made to serve New Deal welfare ends.

CONCLUSION

In this essay we have described the 1950s in uncustomary ways. Mainstream accounts of the domestic politics of the Eisenhower era generally concentrate on civil rights as the only "new" social welfare issue that emerged during the 1950s. This selection is not accidental. As we have tried to show, liberal historians of the postwar United States have searched for the hero as an antidote to the ambiguities, the unromantic qualities, of American power. Civil rights struggles have provided historians with the heroes, the profiles in individual courage, which they have sought.

By comparison, social welfare activities like the passage of a disability insurance program appear distinctly unheroic. Bureaucrats like Wilbur

Cohen enunciated no glowing charismatic visions of the American future to the masses of the populace. They engaged the political order of which they were a part in no fundamental philosophic arguments as to the human values of the Good Society. Actuarial tables, congressional committee reports, and prints of draft legislation are not of much interest to romantic historians. By means of these instruments, however, a group of bureaucrats, buried deep within the federal government, succeeded in enacting key elements of the New Deal social reform agenda. Heroism was not an essential component of this process.

One of the ironies of this process, moreover, was that the Eisenhower administration played a key role in its development. Offering a distinctive, rehabilitation-oriented social welfare program in 1954, the administration played into the bureaucrats' hands by paving the way for a more liberal program passed into law shortly thereafter. Rehabilitation, intended as an end in itself, served the bureaucrats as a justification for increased government activity in the social welfare field. Such ironies underscore our thesis: heroism is not essential to the progress of reform.

Special Message to the Congress on the Health Needs of the American People January 18, 1954

Dwight D. Eisenhower

To the Congress of the United States:
I submit herewith for the consideration of the Congress recommendations to improve the health of the American people.

Among the concerns of our government for the human problems of our citizens, the subject of health ranks high. For only as our citizens enjoy good physical and mental health can they win for themselves the satisfactions of a fully productive, useful life.

THE HEALTH PROBLEM

The progress of our people toward better health has been rapid. Fifty years ago their average life span was 49 years; today it is 68 years. In 1900 there were 676 deaths from infectious diseases for every 100,000 of our people; now there are 66. Between 1916 and 1950, maternal deaths per 100,000 live births dropped from 622 to 83. In 1916, ten percent of the babies born in this country died before their first birthday; today, less than 3 percent die in their first year.

This rapid progress toward better health has been the result of many particular efforts, and of one general effort. The general effort is the partnership and teamwork of private physicians and dentists and of those engaged in public health, with research scientists, sanitary engineers, the nursing profession and the many auxiliary professions related to health protection and care in illness. To all these dedicated people, America owes most of its recent progress toward better health.

Yet, much remains to be done. Approximately 224,000 of our people died of cancer last year. This means that cancer will claim the lives of 25,000,000 of our 160,000,000 people unless the present cancer mortality rate is lowered. Diseases of the heart and blood vessels alone now take over 817,000 lives annually. Over seven million Americans are estimated to suffer from arthritis and rheumatic diseases. Twenty-two thousand lose their sight each year. Diabetes annually adds 100,000 to its roll of sufferers.

SOURCE: *Public Papers of the President: Dwight D. Eisenhower* (1954) #11, pp. 69–77.

Two million of our fellow citizens now handicapped by physical disabilities could be, but are not, rehabilitated to lead full and productive lives. Ten million among our people will at some time in their lives be hospitalized with mental illness.

There exist in our Nation the knowledge and skill to reduce these figures, to give us all still greater health protection and still longer life. But this knowledge and skill are not always available to all our people where and when they are needed. Two of the key problems in the field of health today are the *distribution* of medical facilities and the *costs* of medical care.

Not all Americans can enjoy the best in medical care—because not always are the requisite facilities and professional personnel so distributed as to be available to them, particularly in our poorer communities and rural sections. There are, for example, 159 practicing physicians for every 100,000 of the civilian population in the Northeast United States. This is to be contrasted with 126 physicians in the West, 116 in the North central area, and 92 in the South. There are, for another example, only 4 or 5 hospital beds for each 1,000 people in some States, as compared with 10 or 11 in others.

Even where the best in medical care is available, its costs are often a serious burden. Major, long-term illness can become a financial catastrophe for a normal American family. Ten percent of American families are spending today more than $500 a year for medical care. Of our people reporting incomes under $3000, about 6 percent spend almost a fifth of their gross income for medical and dental care. The total private medical bill of the nation now exceeds nine billion dollars a year—an average of nearly $200 a family—and it is rising. This illustrates the seriousness of the problem of medical costs.

We must, therefore, take further action on the problems of distribution of medical facilities and the costs of medical care, but we must be careful and farsighted in the action that we take. Freedom, consent, and individual responsibility are fundamental to our system. In the field of medical care, this means that the traditional relationship of the physician and his patient, and the right of the individual to elect freely the manner of his care in illness, must be preserved.

In adhering to this principle, and rejecting the socialization of medicine, we can still confidently commit ourselves to certain national health goals.

One such goal is that the means for achieving good health should be accessible to all. A person's location, occupation, age, race, creed, or financial status should not bar him from enjoying this access.

Second, the results of our vast scientific research, which is constantly advancing our knowledge of better health protection and better care in illness, should be broadly applied for the benefit of every citizen.

There must be the fullest cooperation among the individual citizen, his personal physician, the research scientists, the schools of professional education, and our private and public institutions and services—local, State, and Federal.

The specific recommendations which follow are designed to bring us closer to these goals.

CONTINUATION OF PRESENT FEDERAL PROGRAMS

In my Budget Message appropriations will be requested to carry on during the coming fiscal year the health and related programs of the newly-established Department of Health, Education, and Welfare.

These programs should be continued because of their past success and their present and future usefulness. The Public Health Service, for example, has had a conspicuous share in the prevention of disease through its efforts to control health hazards on the farm, in industry and in the home. Thirty years ago, the Public Health Service first recommended a standard milk sanitation ordinance; by last year this ordinance had been voluntarily adopted by 1558 municipalities with a total population of 70 million people. Almost twenty years ago the Public Health Service first recommended restaurant sanitation ordinances; today 685 municipalities and 347 counties, with a total population of 90 million people, have such ordinances. The purification of drinking water and the pasteurization of milk have prevented countless epidemics and saved thousands of lives. These and similar field projects of the Public Health Service, such as technical assistance to the States, and industrial hygiene work, have great public value and should be maintained.

In addition, the Public Health Service should be strengthened in its research activities. Through its National Institutes of Health, it maintains a steady attack against cancer, mental illness, heart diseases, dental problems, arthritis and metabolic diseases, blindness, and problems in microbiology and neurology. The new sanitary engineering laboratory at Cincinnati, to be dedicated in April, will make possible a vigorous attack on health problems associated with the rapid technological advances in industry and agriculture. In such direct research programs and in Public Health Service research grants to State and local governments and to private research institutions lies the hope of solving many of today's perplexing health problems.

The activities of the Children's Bureau and its assistance to the States for maternal and child health services are also of vital importance. The programs for children with such crippling diseases as epilepsy, cerebral palsy, congenital heart disease, and rheumatic fever should receive continued support.

MEETING THE COST OF MEDICAL CARE

The best way for most of our people to provide themselves the resources to obtain good medical care is to participate in voluntary health insurance plans. During the past decade, private and non-profit health insurance organizations have made striking progress in offering such plans. The most widely purchased type of health insurance, which is hospitalization insurance, already meets approximately 40 percent of all private expenditures for hospital care. This progress indicates that these voluntary organizations can reach many more people and provide better and broader benefits. They should be encouraged and helped to do so.

Better health insurance protection for more people can be provided.

The Government need not and should not go into the insurance business to furnish the protection which private and non-profit organizations do not now provide. But the Government can and should work with them to study and devise better insurance protection to meet the public need.

I recommend the establishment of a limited Federal reinsurance service to encourage private and non-profit health insurance organizations to offer broader health protection to more families. This service would reinsure the special additional risks involved in such broader protection. It can be launched with a capital fund of twenty-five million dollars provided by the Government, to be retired from reinsurance fees.

NEW GRANT-IN-AID APPROACH

My message on the State of the Union and my special message of January fourteenth pointed out that Federal grants-in-aid have hitherto observed no uniform pattern. Response has been made first to one and then to another broad national need. In each of the grant-in-aid programs, including those dealing with health, child welfare and rehabilitation of the disabled, a wide variety of complicated matching formulas have been used. Categorical grants have restricted funds to specified purposes so that States often have too much money for some programs and not enough for others.

This patchwork of complex formulas and categorical grants should be simplified and improved. I propose a simplified formula for all of these basic grant-in-aid programs which applies a new concept of Federal participation in State programs. This formula permits the States to use greater initiative and take more responsibility in the administration of the programs. It makes Federal assistance more responsible to the needs of the States and their citizens. Under it, Federal support of these grant-in-aid programs is based on three general criteria:

First, the States are aided in inverse proportion to their financial capacity. By relating Federal financial support to the degree of need, we are applying the proven and sound formula adopted by the Congress in the Hospital Survey and Construction Act.

Second, the States are also helped, in proportion to their population, to extend and improve the health and welfare services provided by the grant-in-aid programs.

Third, a portion of the Federal assistance is set aside for the support of unique projects of regional or national significance which give promise of new and better ways of serving the human needs of our citizens.

Two of these grant-in-aid programs warrant the following further recommendations.

REHABILITATION OF THE DISABLED

Working with only a small portion of the disabled among our people, Federal and State governments and voluntary organizations and institutions have proved the advantage to our nation of restoring handicapped persons to full and productive lives.

When our State-Federal program of vocational rehabilitation began in 1920, the services rendered were limited largely to vocational counseling, training and job placement. Since then advancing techniques in the medical and social aspects of rehabilitation have been incorporated into that program.

There are now 2,000,000 disabled persons who could be rehabilitated and thus returned to productive work. Under the present rehabilitation program only 60,000 of these disabled individuals are returned each year to full and productive lives. Meanwhile, 250,000 of our people are annually disabled. Therefore, we are losing ground at a distressing rate. The number of disabled who enter productive employment each year can be increased if the facilities, personnel and financial support for their rehabilitation are made adequate to the need.

Considerations of both humanity and national self-interest demand that steps be taken now to improve this situation. Today, for example, we are spending three times as much in public assistance to care for non-productive disabled people as it would cost to make them self-sufficient and taxpaying members of their communities. Rehabilitated persons as a group pay back in Federal income taxes many times the cost of their rehabilitation.

There are no statistics to portray the full depth and meaning in human terms of the rehabilitation program, but clearly it is a program that builds a stronger America.

We should provide for a progressive expansion of our rehabilitation resources, and we should act now so that a sound foundation may be established in 1955. My forthcoming Budget Message will reflect this objective. Our goal in 1955 is to restore 70,000 disabled persons to productive lives. This is an increase of 10,000 over the number rehabilitated in 1953. Our goal for 1956 should be 100,000 rehabilitated persons, or 40,000 persons more than those restored in 1953. In 1956, also, the States should begin to contribute from their own funds to the cost of rehabilitating these additional persons. By 1959, with gradually increasing State participation to the point of equal sharing with the Federal government, we should reach the goal of 200,000 rehabilitated persons each year.

In order to achieve this goal we must extend greater assistance to the States. We should do so, however, in a way which will equitably and gradually transfer increasing responsibility to the States. A program of grants should be undertaken to provide, under State auspices, specialized training for the professional personnel necessary to carry out the expanded program and to foster that research which will advance our knowledge of the ways of overcoming handicapping conditions. We should also provide, under State auspices, clinical facilities for rehabilitative services in hospitals and other appropriate treatment centers. In addition, we should encourage State and local initiative in the development of community rehabilitation centers and special workshops for the disabled.

With such a program the Nation could during the next five years return a total of 660,000 of our disabled people to places of full responsibility as actively working citizens.

CONSTRUCTION OF MEDICAL CARE FACILITIES

The modern hospital—in caring for the sick, in research, and in professional educational programs—is indispensable to good medical care. New hospital construction continues to lag behind the need. The total number of acceptable beds in this nation in all categories of non-Federal hospital services is now about 1,060,000. Based on studies conducted by State hospital authorities, the need for additional hospital beds of all types—chronic disease, mental, tuberculosis, as well as general—is conservatively estimated at more than 500,000.

A program of matching State and local tax funds and private funds in the construction of both public and voluntary non-profit hospitals where these are most needed is therefore essential.

Since 1946, nearly $600 million in Federal funds have been allocated to almost 2,200 hospital projects in the States and Territories. This sum has been matched by over one and a quarter billion dollars of State and local funds. Projects already completed or under construction on December 31, 1953, will add to our national resources 106,000 hospital beds and 464 public health centers. The largest proportion of Federal funds has been and is being spent in low-income and rural areas where the need for hospital beds is greatest and where the local means for providing them are smallest. This Federally stimulated accomplishment has by no means retarded the building of hospitals without Federal aid. Construction costing in excess of one billion dollars has been completed in the last six years without such aid. Hospital construction, however, meets only part of the urgent need for medical facilities.

Not all illness need be treated in elaborate general hospital facilities, costly to construct and costly to operate. Certain non-acute illness conditions, including those of our hospitalized aged people, requiring institutional bed care can be handled in facilities more economical to build and operate than a general hospital, with its diagnostic, surgical and treatment equipment and its full staff of professional personnel. Today beds in our hospitals for the chronically ill take care of only one out of every six persons suffering from such long-term illnesses as cancer, arthritis, and heart disease. The inadequacy of facilities and services to cope with such illnesses is disturbing. Moreover, if there were more nursing and convalescent home facilities, beds in general hospitals would be released for the care of the acutely ill. This would also help to relieve some of the serious problems created by the present short supply of trained nurses.

Physical rehabilitation services for our disabled people can best be given in hospitals or other facilities especially equipped for the purpose. Many thousands of people remain disabled today because of the lack of such facilities and services.

Many illnesses, to be sure, can be cared for outside of any institution. For such illnesses a far less costly approach to good medical care than hospitalization would be to provide diagnostic and treatment facilities for the ambulatory patient. The provision of such facilities, particularly in rural areas and small isolated communities, will attract physicians to the sparsely settled sections where they are urgently needed.

I recommend, therefore, that the Hospital Survey and Construction Act be amended as necessary to authorize the several types of urgently needed medical care facilities which I have described. They will be less costly to build than general hospitals and will lessen the burden on them.

I present four proposals to expand or extend the present program:

1. Added assistance in the construction of non-profit hospitals for the care of the chronically ill. These would be of a type more economical to build and operate than general hospitals.

2. Assistance in the construction of non-profit medically supervised nursing and convalescent homes.

3. Assistance in the construction of non-profit rehabilitation facilities for the disabled.

4. Assistance in the construction of non-profit diagnostic or treatment centers for ambulatory patients.

Finally, I recommend that in order to provide a sound basis for Federal assistance in such an expanded program, special funds be made available to the States to help pay for surveys of their needs. This is the procedure that the Congress wisely required in connection with Federal assistance in the construction of hospitals under the original Act. We should also continue to observe the principle of State and local determination of their needs without Federal interference.

These recommendations are needed forward steps in the development of a sound program for improving the health of our people. No nation and no administration can ever afford to be complacent about the health of its citizens. While continuing to reject government regimentation of medicine, we shall with vigor and imagination continuously search out by appropriate means, recommend, and put into effect new methods of achieving better health for all of our people. We shall not relax in the struggle against disease. The health of our people is the very essence of our vitality, our strength and our progress as a nation.

I urge that the Congress give early and favorable consideration to the recommendations I have herein submitted.

DWIGHT D. EISENHOWER

CHAPTER 9

The New Frontier
and the
Great Society

INTRODUCTION

In the decade of the 1960s the federal government, under the presidential leadership of John F. Kennedy and Lyndon B. Johnson, launched an attack designed to eliminate poverty within a generation. The campaign called for innovative strategies, fresh approaches, and, indeed, a new definition of poverty in America. Poverty became a way of life, a culture.

Throughout the fifties poverty had remained principally a Democratic issue. Democrats had linked poverty to problems of unemployment and economic productivity. This view of poverty was carried into the Kennedy administration, which continued to view antipoverty remedies in terms of area redevelopment, training legislation, and vocational rehabilitation.

In 1962 and 1963, a series of books and magazine articles portrayed poverty as a social and cultural problem of poor rural whites in the South and poor blacks who had migrated to northern cities in the postwar period. Michael Harrington's *The Other America*, and Dwight Macdonald's essay, "Our Invisible Poor" in *The New Yorker* caught President Kennedy's attention. Moved by his reading, Kennedy directed the Council of Economic Advisers to re-examine the issue of poverty in America.

The Council of Economic Advisers concluded in 1964 that income transfers of $11 billion would, in fact, eliminate poverty but that this would leave the roots of poverty untouched. Putting the poor to work, providing the skills and the opportunity for jobs, was far better. They proposed to Kennedy that an antipoverty program be sold to the American people as practical, and they urged the president to appeal to the idealism of the people as well.

After he assumed the presidency, Johnson saw the poverty issue as a cause he could make his own as he sought to create the Great Society. In his State of the Union address to Congress on January 8, 1964, Johnson declared "a war on poverty." "As disease can be conquered, as space can be mastered, so too can poverty yield to our determined efforts to bring it to an end." Shortly after his address, LBJ chose R. Sargent Shriver, director

219

of the Peace Corps and Kennedy's brother-in-law, to draft antipoverty legislation. In August, Congress voted to establish the Office of Economic Opportunity (OEO). Shriver and his staff were to draft an omnibus bill that called for job training, work relief, remedial and adult education, rural assistance, small business loans, a domestic Peace Corps, and a community action program that would enlist the poor in the war against poverty.

The Community Action Program became the most visible agency, although the Office of Economic Opportunity included an array of programs. The Community Action Program attempted to organize the poor within their communities, and in so doing became a lightning rod for attacks from both the right and the left. In these circumstances Johnson began to distance himself from the OEO. In 1966 and 1967 he ordered that the OEO's budget be directed more to job creation and job training programs. Reallocation of resources allowed the administration to continue to defend the Great Society as a program intended to cut welfare costs by putting people to work.

Under the Johnson administration, Social Security, welfare, and veterans benefits were liberalized, increasing total social welfare expenditures from $67 billion to $127 billion. Increases in social insurance jumped from $25.6 billion to $40.8 billion, while public assistance more than doubled from $5 billion to $11.9 billion. Particularly bothersome to the middle class was the growth of Aid to Families with Dependent Children. AFDC grew from $1.5 billion to $3.6 billion as the number of families and children in the program more than doubled.

Johnson's growing commitment to war in southeast Asia in 1965 doomed the domestic war on poverty. In the end Johnson's War on Poverty was perceived by contemporaries (and later by some scholars) as having failed to address the "welfare mess," although the number of persons classified as poor in the period from 1959 to 1968 decreased by 36 percent. Wilbur Cohen expressed the disappointment of those who had sympathized with the goals of the Great Society when he declared, "It got out of hand. . . . We tried to do too much in too many places in too short of a time."

Johnson's greatest accomplishments were establishing Medicare and Medicaid and further extending Social Security. Federal expenditures for health care rose from $8.5 billion to over $24 billion, and they continued to rise. Within a three-year period alone, payments to physicians climbed from $665 million in 1966 to $1.6 billion in 1969. Yet even as federal health care expanded, the focus of the program remained on the elderly, while less attention was given to the health of those on public assistance.

By expanding the Social Security system to include medical care for the elderly and the poor, Johnson fulfilled the promise of the New Deal. For this he should be given credit. Despite his good intentions, however, he failed to bring innovative solutions to the problems of those persons categorically dependent upon public assistance. In 1962 the Social Security

Act was amended to make funds available to the states to provide intensive social casework services aimed at preventing and reducing economic
dependency. These amendments concentrated on correcting the personal
defects of the poor, mainly by offering provisions for psychological analysis
and restoration.

The 1962 amendments proved to be a disappointment. Although the
federal government paid 75 percent of the cost of rehabilitative and preven-
tative services, welfare rolls continued to swell. As a consequence, in 1967
Congress instituted a new program, the Work Incentive Program (WIN),
which offered able-bodied adults the opportunity to acquire vocational skills
and work epxerience. Estimates made in 1975 showed that the WIN program helped only 51,627 recipients to relinquish welfare benefits. These
welfare reform programs only further reinforced the perception of poverty
as a personal disorder.

Explaining the failure of the Great Society has proven to be an easier
task for historians and social scientists than explaining the genesis of the
War on Poverty. Brauer examines a number of explanations why the War
on Poverty was launched under the Kennedy and Johnson administrations.
He credits the Kennedy administration with laying the foundation for Johnson's subsequent antipoverty program. Brauer also finds that Johnson's
interest in poverty stemmed from his own experience with poverty as a
young man, as well as from a shrewd political understanding that poverty
was an issue that could distinguish Johnson's administration. Also, as a
Southerner Johnson believed that if blacks were able to secure good jobs
and decent incomes, much of the racial problem in the nation could be
alleviated.

Johnson's views of the social and economic problems of blacks in
America are found in his address at Howard University on June 4, 1965.
President Johnson's speech called attention to what became known as the
Moynihan Report, issued three months earlier by the Office of Policy Planning and Research, Department of Labor. The Moynihan Report traced
the historic poverty of blacks to the breakdown of the black family structure, which had resulted after years of degradation and discrimination. The
address and the report soon came under attack from civil rights activists
and black leaders, who accused the administration of being racist and
insensitive. The furor caused by the address and the report revealed the
problems the Johnson administration would have in convincing blacks and
political activists that its antipoverty program was sincere.

As noted earlier, President Johnson found his greatest success in the
passage of the Medicare Bill in July 1965. The final readings in this chapter
follow the course of the Medicare Bill from its first proposal by JFK through
its enactment. Kennedy's speech summarizes the plight of the elderly in
these years of rising health care costs and inadequate health insurance.
Kennedy's proposals for extending health insurance to the elderly and the
poor through the Social Security system bogged down in Congress, as did

many of Kennedy's proposals. The later signing of the Medicare Bill by Lyndon Johnson marked a high point of his career and fulfilled the early promise of the New Deal and Fair Deal to enact a health insurance program for the elderly. LBJ arranged to have the bill signed in Independence, Missouri, at the home of Harry S Truman. President Johnson's remarks summarize the Medicare and Medicaid program, while conveying the optimism of his administration in 1965. The great tragedy of the Johnson administration was that the decade was to end in disillusionment rather than fulfilled dreams.

Further Readings

There is a rich and still growing literature on the Great Society. Michael Harrington's *The Other America* (New York: Penguin, 1972) is required reading. General overviews of the period may be found in Jim F. Heath, *Decade of Disillusionment: The Kennedy-Johnson Years* (Bloomington: Indiana University Press, 1975); and Allen J. Matusow, *The Unraveling of America: A History of Liberalism in the 1960s* (New York: Harper & Row, 1984).

For more detailed studies of welfare policy, see Sar A. Levitan and Robert Taggart, *The Promise of Greatness* (Cambridge: Harvard University Press, 1976); Robert D. Plotnick and Felicity Skidmore, *Progress Against Poverty: A Review of the 1964–1974 Decade* (New York: Academic Press, 1975); and Robert H. Haveman, ed., *A Decade of Federal Antipoverty Programs: Achievements, Failures and Lessons* (New York: Academic Press, 1977).

A useful study of the role of rhetoric in the Great Society is found in David Zarefsky, *President Johnson's War on Poverty* (University: University of Alabama Press, 1986).

The origins and implementation of OEO are discussed in Stephen Goodell and Bennet Shiff, *The Office of Economic Opportunity During the Administration of President Lyndon B. Johnson, 1963–1969* (Washington, D.C.: The Brookings Institution, 1973). The Moynihan controversy is recorded in Lee Rainwater and William L. Yancey, eds., *The Moynihan Report and the Politics of Controversy* (Cambridge: MIT Press, 1967).

Kennedy, Johnson
and the War on Poverty

Carl M. Brauer

When President Lyndon B. Johnson declared metaphorical war on poverty in 1964, he set in motion an important, complex, and controversial phase in the history of reform in the United States, whose shockwaves were still being felt in the early 1980s, a time of counterreformation. Although poverty reform in the 1960s influenced the historical profession no less than some others—in the rise of social history, for example—historians concentrated their research efforts on the more distant past. Analysis of the history, workings, consequences, and lessons of the War on Poverty remained largely the business of social scientists, who turned it into a sizable industry. The passage of time and the growing availability of primary sources now invite historical investigation, which has no more apposite starting point than the War on Poverty's genesis.

Social scientists explain the War on Poverty's creation in essentially three different ways. Daniel P. Moynihan in his *Maximum Feasible Misunderstanding* does not treat motive systematically or explicitly, but he builds a powerful implicit argument that the War on Poverty grew out of the rising influence of social science itself. In particular, Moynihan attributes the Community Action Program, which became central to the War on Poverty, to reform-minded, though unscientific, sociologists. A second school of thought emphasizes interest groups and political calculation. Among those who take this approach, Frances Fox Piven and Richard Cloward have probably been most widely read. President John F. Kennedy and President Johnson, they argue, launched the War on Poverty in order to attract a high percentage of black votes in the 1964 election. Third, the War on Poverty's birth has been explained through the cyclical theory of reform. After a period of dormancy, James Sundquist maintains, the reform impulse once again swept through the American political system, bringing with it a national effort to eradicate poverty.

These treatments have value, particularly in describing the intellectual and institutional backgrounds of specific programs associated with the War on Poverty and in providing eyewitness accounts. Separately from his analytical chapters, it should be noted, Sundquist presents an accurate, though incomplete, narrative of events. In light of documentary and oral evidence now available, however, none of these treatments provides a satis-

SOURCE: Carl M. Brauer, *Journal of American History* 69, no. 1 (June 1982), pp. 95–119. ©Organization of American Historians, 1982.

factory explanation of the War on Poverty's beginnings. Historical research leads to a different picture of them than social scientists have thus far painted.

The War on Poverty most definitely had politically motives, but not the particular ones that Piven and Cloward claim. It also had intellectual motives and did reflect the rising influence of social science, yet Moynihan emphasizes sociology when economics figured far more significantly. Political and intellectual motives were intertwined, though in flux, throughout the War on Poverty's gestation. At some moments, political calculation was narrow; at others, broad. Likewise the ideas involved varied widely in terms of complexity, implication, and ideology. The very slogan "War on Poverty" represented the marriage of political self-interest to political culture. Although a cycle of reform may be observed in American politics, its existence alone fails to explain why poverty was singled out for attention.

Most accounts of the War on Poverty's birth make it seem inevitable, but historical research highlights the roles of chance—the assassination of President Kennedy—and of circumstance—the succession of President Johnson. Indeed, discussions of its birth sometimes pay too little attention to an obvious, but critical, fact: the War on Poverty was called into being by a president. Government policies sought to reduce poverty long before then; they continued to do so well after the rallying cry, War on Poverty, faded into memory. An examination of why President Kennedy considered making the elimination of poverty a centerpiece of his program in 1964 and why President Johnson did so proves instructive about the problem of origins while simultaneously illuminating the role of the presidency in recent American history.

From its rediscovery in the 1950s, poverty was a partisan issue, pushed by Democrats, usually liberal Democrats, and resisted by Republicans. Campaigning for reelection in 1954, Senator Paul H. Douglas of Illinois, a liberal and a professional economist, made the economic depression that gripped the southern part of his state an effective issue. When he was returned to office, he sponsored legislation to aid depressed areas, through which the fedeal government would underwrite public works projects, job retraining, and business expansion in high unemployment areas. President Dwight D. Eisenhower and a majority of Republicans would only go along with a much smaller program than Douglas and a majority of Democrats sought; so the legislation stalled.

While some liberals and Democrats were rediscovering poverty and questioning the extent and moral worth of affluence, many conservatives and Republicans were celebrating prosperity and the wondrous benefits of the free enterprise system. The Advertising Council, for example, hailed the arrival of "people's capitalism" for creating prosperity and making workers stockholders. The Eisenhower administration expanded some of the broad-based social programs of the New Deal, such as Social Security, but resisted special assistance to the poor. Campaigning for president in West Virginia in 1960, the Republican nominee, Richard M. Nixon, castigated his Democratic opponent's assertion that seventeen million people went to bed hungry every night. That only provided "grist for the Communist propaganda mill," Nixon charged. He recounted Eisenhower's response: "Now look, I go to bed hungry every night, but that's because I'm on a diet. The doctor won't let me eat any more."

Although international threats in the 1940s and early 1950s had served to discourage critical examination of America's internal shortcomings, the growing perception of renewed dangers from abroad in the late 1950s had the opposite effect. The Soviet Union's successful launching of Sputnik, the first artificial earth satellite, galvanized American fears of Soviet technical, educational, and military prowess and precipitated a wide-ranging questioning of America's ability and resolve to meet the communist challenge. Democratic politicians both led and exploited this questioning process. The theme of Kennedy's presidential campaign in 1960, as set out for his speechwriters, was "to summon every segment of our society . . . to restore America's relative strength as a free nation . . . to regain our security and leadership in a fast changing world menaced by communism."

Kennedy called attention to weaknesses in the American economy, in particular its sluggish rate of economic growth. Too many of America's workers were unemployed, he insisted, too much of its industrial capacity idle. He criticized Republicans for opposing legislation to aid the nation's economically depressed areas. In the important West Virginia primary election, he made the poverty, unemployment, and hunger he witnessed in that state major themes of his winning effort. During the general election campaign, he occasionally singled out poverty. Commemorating the anniversary of the Social Security Act, he called that legislation an "opening battle" while declaring that the "war against poverty and degradation is not yet over."

In his eloquent inaugural address, Kennedy several times mentioned the fight against poverty; but characteristic both of the speech and his early administration, he referred to poverty as a foreign or international problem, not a domestic one. American poverty did not become a focal point of debate or policy during his first two years in office. Kennedy signed area redevelopment and manpower development and training legislation. He created a Committee on Juvenile Delinquency and Youth Crime, which he placed under the direction of his brother, Robert, the attorney general. At his behest, Congress emphasized the rehabilitation of welfare clients. Each repesented a discrete response to discrete social or economic problems, which were not collectively identified as poverty.

Sluggish economic growth, slack demand, and unacceptably high rates of unemployment, not poverty, captured Kennedy's attention in his first two years as president. After his first approaches to these interrelated problems failed to stimulate the economic expansion he desired or, in the case of expenditures, were ruled out by congressional opposition, he gradually, in 1962, came to adopt the solution put forth by professional economists on the Council of Economic Advisers (CEA), across-the-board tax reduction for individuals and corporations. Although a significant part of the economics profession and some influential businessmen welcomed this proposal, it encountered opposition from those who believed in balanced budgets, from those who worried greatly about inflation, and from certain liberals who preferred tax reform to tax reduction and increases in social expenditures to a potential diminution of government's capacity to spend on worthy causes. Hence the tax cut made slow progress through Congress.

The tax cut left President Kennedy open to criticism that he was indifferent to poverty. Prior to appearing on a year-end interview show in 1962, Kennedy asked Walter Heller, chairman of the CEA, for an analysis of assertions by Harrington and Leon Keyserling that poverty was much more widespread than commonly assumed. Harrington, a journalist, socialist, and social activist, estimated that 50 million Americans were poor. Keyserling, once chairman of Harry S. Truman's CEA and an acerbic critic of the tax cut, put the number at thirty-eight million and said an additional 39 million lived above the poverty line though still in deprivation. In responding to President Kennedy's request, Heller noted that "there was controversy about past and future progress against the scourge of poverty" but insisted that under "any *absolute* poverty line, we have reduced the share of the population in poverty during all periods of prosperity." "Contemporary poverty," he observed, though, "to the extent it is peculiarly associated with nonwhite color, widowhood, old age, etc.—may be harder to overcome than the more generalized poverty of earlier generations."

No one, in fact, asked Kennedy about poverty on the show, but in February a television documentary narrated by Howard K. Smith stimulated about one hundred letters to the president, most of them, it appeared, from Democrats who were neither poor nor southern. The writers wanted the president "to adopt a mood either of sympathy for the poor (like Eleanor Roosevelt) or of vigorous demands for action (like FDR)," according to a summary prepared for the White House. Frequently the letters referred to phrases from Kennedy's own campaign or from his inaugural address. Many proposed public works projects, training programs, and increased social services, but few mentioned "the tax cut as a way to alleviate or prevent poverty." Indeed, more correspondents singled it out for opposition than any other policy.

Although poverty was not producing a groundswell of public interest or an outbreak of public protest, it was attracting more attention in 1962 and early 1963 than at any time since the 1930s. Dwight MacDonald's long review essay in *The New Yorker* in January 1963 undoubtedly was more widely read than the books it discussed, including Harrington's *The Other America*, which, it should be noted, did not become a best seller until after the War on Poverty was declared the following year. President

Kennedy read MacDonald's essay and Harrington's book. Born to wealth and privilege himself, Kennedy had been brought up with a firm sense of noblesse oblige. He believed in government's duty and ability to solve social and economic problems. In addition, he was sensitive to the intellectual currents of his times and to any suggestion that he was not meeting the country's problems. So it is not surprising that he asked Heller to look into the poverty issue in greater depth.

Heller welcomed the assignment. Although he had been instrumental in selling Kennedy on the tax cut, stressing growth and efficiency objectives, he had been trained in the economics department of the University of Wisconsin, which, since the days of John R. Commons, had been concerned with distributional objectives, with social justice and economic equity. Heller thus combined the techniques of modern post-Keynesian economics with the moral ideals of Wisconsin progressivism. In Heller's view, the elimination of poverty was not only to be sought on moral grounds but on efficiency ones, for poverty bred disease, ignorance, and crime and therefore reduced productivity. Like his mentor, Harold Groves, and other Wisconsin economists, such as Edwin Witte or Commons himself, Heller operated comfortably in the world of politics, which meant living with small, incremental steps on the road to the ideal.

Heller turned to Robert J. Lampman for assistance. Lampman, a fellow student of Groves and a leading expert on wealth and income distribution, had come to the CEA as a consultant in 1961 and as a full-time staff member in 1962. He now updated an earlier study he had done for the Joint Economic Committee of Congress. He found that the impressive rate of reduction in income-poverty, which he had previously documented for the ten years, 1947 to 1956, had slowed down. Between 1947 and 1956, the percentage of families with less than $3,000 of total money income (in 1961) declined from 33 percent to 23 percent; in the five years since 1956, though, it dropped only 2 percent more. The findings distressed Heller. "They offer one more demonstration of the costs of economic slack," he wrote President Kennedy, "and they, therefore, also provide another dimension of what's at stake in the proposed tax cut."

In Heller's view, economic growth historically held the key to reducing poverty, and the tax cut held the key to economic growth. Yet several things in the spring of 1963 caused Heller to focus on the poverty problem itself. The new data from Lampman indicated a worse picture than one might have expected from his earlier study. Sensitive to politics, Heller worried about the tax cut's liabilities, for its greatest immediate benefits would go to those with middle or upper incomes. It might simply be politically prudent, he reasoned, for the president to have something specifically aimed at helping the poor. Heller was impressed when Kenneth O'Donnell, a political aide to the pesident whose judgment Heller respected, told him to "stop worrying about the tax cut." "It will pass and pass big," O'Donnell optimistically forecast; "worry about something else." Heller has also recalled learning from a newspaper story that a Republican presidential aspirant was considering an antipoverty program of his own. It was folly, Heller believed, to allow a Republican to steal a march on a naturally Democratic issue. A search of Heller's papers and clippings files at the Kennedy Library failed to turn up the particular story; so it is possible that Heller's memory was faulty. Accurate or not, however, the recollection reveals that Heller viewed poverty not only as an economic or moral problem but also as a political one.

Heller assigned William M. Capron, the CEA's senior staff man, to work with Lampman. Capron had played an important role in the CEA's successful campaign to win the president over to the tax cut. Although he was familiar with the field, he was not an expert in income distribution. He had been trained in public administration, not economics, specializing in the application of economic tools to policy issues. He knew the ins and outs of Washington bureaucracy and had the advantage of enjoying good relationships with Theodore C. Sorenson, a top presidential aide, and with the Bureau of the Budget, where he had once worked. Under President Kennedy, it should be noted, the Budget Bureau had become unusually involved in policy making. Over the summer, Capron and Lampman convened an informal group of staff members, largely fellow economists, from several departments and agencies to discuss ideas and proposals. In the fall, Lampman returned to the University of Wisconsin and the burden of developing a program fell largely to Capron, working closely with Budget officials Charles L. Schultze, William Cannon, and Michael March.

These planners were generally unimpressed with the recommendations they received. From the departments came numerous program suggestions which had been languishing on Capitol Hill. Each department watered its own field; the Labor Department wanted a massive jobs program; the Department of Health, Education, and Welfare, educational and health programs; and so on. This confirmed the planners' skepticism toward the departments, a skepticism that permeated the upper reaches of the Kennedy administration. The departments and agencies, it was believed, were bureaucracies with their own internal agendas whose programs were often ineffectual. Experts they consulted from social work and the social sciences, meanwhile, made divergent recommendations, based on sharply differing diagnoses of the poverty problem.

The planners did like the idea of local demonstration or community action projects, which they heard about from people who have been involved in such projects—David Hackett and Richard Boone of the President's Committee on Juvenile Delinquency and Youth Crime, Paul Ylvisaker of the Ford Foundation, Mitchell Sviridoff in New Haven, and George Esser in North Carolina. In a "community action project," "demonstration project," or "development corporation," as the idea was variously called, the federal government would directly fund service-oriented, coordinated efforts in localities where poor people resided in significant numbers, such as Appalachia and the nation's largest black ghettoes.

The planners were attracted to this idea because it seemed to hold out the promise of having a dramatic impact. "Rather than developing a 'program' which simply adds funds to existing across-the-board programs, or creates new programs in which a large part of the funds are spent on those whose need is marginal," one of the planners argued, "we ought to make a concentrated effort to assist those whose needs are substantial." They liked the emphasis on experimentation, for total funding was expected to be small and social welfare experts were divided about what should be done. Because of the expectations of low funding as well, they wanted to prevent the money from being spread around so thin as to negate its effects, which is what had happened to the Area Redevelopment Administration (ARA). When ARA was first considered by the Senate in 1956, it was estimated that 69 areas would qualify for assistance; in 1963, however, 780 areas qualified. Congress had sliced a small pie exceedingly thin. Each member had wanted to have a piece for himself, so everyone had received a diet portion.

A coordinated and concentrated federal effort at the local, level also appealed to the planners precisely because of their skepticism of federal bureaucracies. It offered a way of bypassing them or at least shaking them up. They perceived in a localized approach advantages that were partly ideological and partly political. "The program ought to be presented quite frankly in terms of the obligations which a prosperous majority owes to a submerged and desperately poor minority," one of them, probably Schultze, observed at the time. Although he wanted to highlight the practical aspects of the program, such as its impact on economic growth or on reducing welfare costs, he believed that "poverty-in-the-midst of plenty" should be the main theme. He explained:

> There are two ideas which go hand-in-hand in this approach: First, the concept of equity—initial opportunities for all as close to equal as possible (Remember, even Bob Taft was strong for this); and second, the concept of the social obligation of the "rich" to the "poor." Both of these are powerful themes in American history, and, after all the political cynicism is taken into account, may well form a more realistic approach than the alleged realism of narrow self-interest Congressional District by Congressional District. Moreover, a party division along these lines would be "duck-soup" for Democratic candidates.

Finally, this approach promised the mobilization of people at the local level, of getting previously uninvolved people to work for their communities. It therefore accorded with Kennedy's call to patriotic sacrifice in his inaugural address, his challenge to Americans to ask what they could do for their country, something the tax cut had obviously not required.

Although the planners paid considerable attention to political considerations, particularly to how an antipoverty program might be framed to win united Democratic support in Congress, there is no evidence to support the Piven-Cloward thesis that community action was intended to shore up black support in the 1964 election. At a conference in 1973, antipoverty planners, though acknowledging certain political motives, challenged Piven and Cloward fare to face. "We would have run it completely different if we had followed your thesis," argued Hackett. "If it had been a political program and if the administration wanted to cater to the black votes, we would have done it completely different. We didn't do it that way. We were going initially with the mayors and the establishment."

Like community action, the National Service Corps, a domestic version of the Peace Corps, appealed to the planners for summoning the nation's idealism. Legislation to create such a corps was stalled on Capitol Hill, but the planners hoped they might pry it loose by including it in the president's antipoverty program. In addition, they looked forward to incorporating the recommendations of a special interagency task force the president had appointed to look into the problem of selective service rejectees. In the spring of 1964, Secretary of Defense Robert S. McNamara observed that President Kennedy himself frequently expressed his concern that "poverty was becoming an inherited trait," as evidenced by the failure of a third of the young men examined each year for the military draft to pass either mental or physical examinations. Kennedy's elusive logic reflected acceptance of culture-of-poverty assumptions.

As discussion proceeded on an antipoverty program in the fall, members and friends of the Kennedy administration raised questions about the whole enterprise. Wilbur Cohen, an influential assistant secretary of Health, Education, and Welfare, and others with backgrounds in Social Security observed that programs benefiting the poor alone were bound to be impoverished ones—that is, inadequately funded. Myer Feldman, a White House counsel, pointed out to Lampman that his ideas would make good ammunition for Republicans in that they implied the failure of social welfare programs long identified with the Democrats. At a general strategy meeting on the 1964 election in November, Richard Scammon, director of the Census Bureau, in answer to a question from the president about the pending poverty program, noted that most people did not consider themselves poor. At an informal seminar in Robert F. Kennedy's home, George F. Kennan, the diplomat, departed from his topic to reflect that nothing could be done about poverty since, as the Bible said, the poor would be with us always. Heller strenuously objected and was joined in the ensuing debate by Robert F. Kennedy and Harriman against Kennan, Supreme Court Justice Potter Stewart, and Randolph Churchill, son of the former British prime minister.

Criticisms like these made those planning the poverty program acutely aware of its packaging, and so they considered such titles as "Human Conservation and Development," "Access to Opportunity," and "Widening Participation in Prosperity," in order to broaden its appeal. They thought of billing it as a "domestic aid program" in order to "capitalize on some of the anti-foreign aid sentiment—especially on the part of those who continually chide us for 'sending money overseas when there is so much to do at home.'" On the other hand, they worried that whatever was gained for the domestic aid programs might be lost to foreign aid, and they were concerned about giving the Soviet Union "a well-documented stick to beat us over the head with—although this will be true of any case we make that there are important segments of the U.S. population living a submarginal existence."

In considering possible constituencies for this program, some political operatives in the White House looked to the upper middle class; "suburban women" was the catchphrase. The poor themselves were assumed to be politically passive, and an antipoverty effort was therefore most likely to impress those who were among the most affluent and presumably most conscience-stricken. John F. Kennedy himself was puzzled that the poor in this country were not angrier and more demanding. "In England," he commented to Arthur M. Schlesinger, Jr., in the spring of 1963, "the unemployment rate goes to two per cent, and they march on Parliament. Here it moves up toward six, and no one seems to mind." Although there had been more agitation among the poor in the 1930s than was usually recalled in the 1950s and 1960s, it was also true that by international standards the American poor in this century were relatively quiescent. Civil rights demonstrations in the early 1960s repeatedly focused on access to the political and economic systems, not on economic inequality or poverty. Labor unions, whom socialists like Harrington thought of as allies of the poor, generally failed to beat the drum for an antipoverty program. When Heller gave a speech about poverty to the Communication Workers of America, his audience responded indifferently. It made Lampman recall a lesson that Selig Perlman, the labor economist, had taught him as a graduate student at the University of Wisconsin: that unionists regard the poor as competitive menaces.

Given all the doubts expressed, the planners were sometimes uncertain whether the president would even decide to adopt an antipoverty program. A timely piece of reporting helped their cause. In October Homer Bigart wrote grippingly in the *New York Times* about the plight of impoverished miners in Kentucky. The report prompted President Kennedy to observe to Heller "that there was a tremendous problem to be met." According to Heller's notes, Kennedy indicated that "if he could get sufficient *substance* in a program to deal with poverty, he would like to make a two- or three-day trip to some of the key poverty-stricken areas to focus the spotlight and arouse the American conscience on this problem from which we are so often shielded." To Heller it seemed "perfectly clear" that Kennedy was "aroused about this and if we would really produce a program to fill the bill, he would be inclined to run with it." Soon thereafter, Heller wrote the heads of several departments and agencies to tell them that the president had "tentatively decided that a major focus in the domestic legislative program in 1964 will be on a group of programs variously described as 'Human Conservation and Development,' 'Access to Opportunity' and 'Attack on Poverty' " and to ask their help formally in devising a general framework as well as specifics.

After November's election strategy meeting, the president remained interested, though circumspect. "I'm still very much in favor of doing something on the poverty scheme if we can get a good program," is how Heller summed up Kennedy's attitude on November 19, "but I also think it's important to make clear that we're doing something for the middle-income man in the suburbs, etc. But the two are not at all inconsistent with one another. So go right ahead with your work on it." At the time of Kennedy's assassination on November 22, 1963, antipoverty plans emphasized youth, human services rather than income transfers, experimentation, selectivity, coordination, and local administation. They included a domestic Peace Corps and a remedial effort aimed at Selective Service rejectees. There is no telling, of course, what would have happened to these plans had the president not been shot.

The day after the assassination Heller met with Johnson. He informed the new president, among other things, of the CEA's work in developing the "attack on poverty," as his notes of the conversation termed it. He told Johnson there was enthusiasm within the government for the idea, but it was uncertain whether an attractive program could be constructed. He also reported President Kennedy's last words to him on the subject. According to Heller's notes, Johnson "expressed his interest" in the poverty program, and "his sympathy for it, and in answer to a point-blank question, said we should push ahead full-tilt on this project." As Heller was about to depart, Johnson drew him back in and said:

> Now I wanted to say something about all this talk that I'm a conservative who is likely to go back to the Eisenhower ways or give in to the economy bloc in Congress. It's not so, and I want you to tell your friends—Arthur Schlesinger, Galbraith and other liberals—that it is not so. I'm no budget slasher. I understand that expenditures have to keep on rising to keep pace with the population and help the economy. If you looked at my record, you would know that I am a Roosevelt New Dealer. As a matter of fact, to tell the truth, John F. Kennedy was a little too conservative to suit my taste.

Through his service as senator from Texas and Democratic leader in the Senate, Johnson had indeed developed a rather conservative reputation, but a combination of influences—personal, political, and cultural—led him to adopt the poverty issue and make it his own. In his postpresidential memoir, Johnson noted he was always an activist, taking pleasure in getting things done. Profoundly impressed by the New Deal, Johnson believed in government, in its responsibility, and in its capacity to solve problems. For social change to occur, he reflected, three conditions had to be met: a recognition of need, a willingness to act, and someone to lead the effort. Johnson recalled that in 1963 America had the needs, the launching of Sputnik and the shock of President Kennedy's assassination had produced a popular readiness for change, and he was personally disposed to lead. . . .

The particular tragic circumstances of Johnson's assumption of office also help explain his adoption of the poverty issue. During his early weeks as president, Johnson strove to show members of the Kennedy administration, the nation, and the world that there would be continuity in policy, yet at the same time to establish his own authority, identity, and constituency. The poverty issue afforded him a way of doing both. By giving Heller the go-ahead, Johnson signaled the Kennedy team that he planned to carry on as President Kennedy would have, but because Kennedy had not publicly announced the drive against poverty, Johnson could present it as his own to the nation. Since he was assuming so many of Kennedy's policy commitments, including civil rights, the tax cut, medical insurance for the aged, and federal aid to education, Johnson welcomed the chance to promote his very own cause.

Finally, the poverty issue appealed to Johnson because, like many southerners, he believed that the nation's racial problems were essentially economic in nature. If blacks only had good jobs and decent incomes, whites would, in his view, respect them and let them exercise their civil rights. President Kennedy would not have disagreed, though he had felt it necessary to address racial discrimination directly. When Kennedy was contemplating his request for major civil rights legislation in the spring of 1963, Johnson had privately expressed reservations about its timing to the president's aides. He was not opposed to the legislation, he told Sorensen— indeed, he wanted President Kennedy to take a strong moral stand in favor of civil rights—but he feared that "we run the risk of touching off about a three- or four-month debate that will kill his program and inflame the country and wind up with a mouse." To Assistant Attorney General for Civil Rights Burke Marshall, Johnson recommended that the administration concentrate on solving underlying economic problems, specifically black unemployment, and harked back to his own experience with the NYA.

When Johnson suddenly became president, he could not have reversed his predecessor's commitment to civil rights legislation, even if he had wanted to, for that would have violated the whole spirit of continuity that he was trying to engender and would have cast Johnson as a parochial, sectional leader, not up to national responsibilities or national office. It would have alienated the significant pro–civil rights constituency in the Democratic party. Given the political situation, his desire for continuity, and his own genuine sympathy for the civil rights cause, Johnson, in one of his first public statements as president, committed himself unequivocally to passage of President Kennedy's civil rights legislation. That legislation would be Kennedy's, a memorial to him, but the poverty issue, with its economic instead of racial thrust, would be quintessentially Johnson's. Perhaps his fellow white southerners would even forgive him his transgressions on civil rights as matters of personal loyalty to the slain president and political necessity, especially when they saw he was addressing the underlying problem on his own.

Johnson worried, though, about how to identify the problem. Walt Rostow, an economist and foreign-policy aide, recounted Johnson's views at a meeting in late December on the State of the Union message: "In domestic affairs, civil rights was at the top of the list. Then the tax bill. He would move ahead with the poverty program, but he wanted it to be a positive effort to fulfill human needs and widen opportunity. Poverty was too negative a concept. (General discussion yielded no satisfactory alternative phrase.) We had to fulfill Kennedy's programs and move beyond. He wanted to see military resources shifted to education, human needs, and manpower development."

In his State of the Union address to Congress on January 8, Johnson did not find a substitute for the term *poverty* when he announced his emphatic opposition to the condition it described. "This administration today, here and now, declares unconditional war on poverty," asserted the president. The analogue of war, a legacy of progressivism and World War I, had been popular during the depression and the New Deal when Johnson was young and had entered public life. The idea of invoking it once again in 1964, if not Johnson's originally—its exact paternity is uncertain—appealed to him viscerally. "It will not be a short or easy struggle, no single weapon or strategy will suffice," Johnson said, "but we shall not rest until that war is won." Alluding to the country's prosperity, he observed that "the richest nation on earth can afford to win it." But he also immediately set forth a practical, efficiency argument to justify the effort: "We cannot aford to lose it. One thousand dollars invested in salvaging an unemployable youth can return $40,000 or more in his lifetime."

Lacking specific antipoverty plans, Johnson emphasized the general recommendations of the economists and budget officials who had begun to work under President Kennedy: improved coordination of existing federal programs, new efforts organized and carried out locally. "For the war against poverty will not be won here in Washington," Johnson explained. "It must be won in the field, in every private home, in every public office, from the court house to the White House." "The program I shall propose," he said, "will emphasize this cooperative approach to help that one-fifth of all American families with incomes too small to even meet their basic needs."

Beyond his new antipoverty program, Johnson called for "better schools, and better health, and better homes, and better training, and better job opportunities to help more Americans, especially young Americans, escape from squalor and misery and unemployment rolls where other citizens help to carry them." Thus Johnson went beyond mere efficiency justifications for fighting poverty to a frankly antiwelfare position. Give the poor the tools to lift themselves out of poverty, he told Congress, and working Americans would no longer have to support them on relief. Lack of money or employment, he asserted, were often symptoms of poverty, not its cause, which he speculated lay deeper, perhaps in society's failure to give everyone a fair chance. "But whatever the cause," he said, "our joint Federal-local effort must pursue poverty, pursue it wherever it exists." He requested legislative action in a wide variety of areas, including special aid to Appalachia and expansion of ARA, youth employment, a broader food stamp program, a national service corps, and a higher minimum wage. Although Johnson had essentially argued that poverty be taken out of people, his inclusion of food stamps and minimum wages implied acceptance of the opposite idea as well, that people would also have to be taken out of poverty through income transfers and entitlements. The importance of the latter idea had been recognized from the beginning by experts like Lampman, but it had been downplayed largely for political and budgetary reasons.

The president's speech was interrupted frequently by applause, more than any State of the Union message for which such interruptions had been recorded, according to a newspaper search that was done for Johnson. "There was scarcely a sentence in the speech that was not applauded," James Reston reported in the *New York Times*, "but most of the 80 demonstrations from the floor of the House came from the Democratic side, and it was obvious that there was strong opposition on the Republican side, precisely because his poverty program was so reminiscent of the New Deal programs the G.O.P. fought for so many years." "'War on Poverty' is the President's new and disarming name for a whole bundle of old programs leavened with a few new wrinkles," one skeptical Republican reported to his constituents after the specifics were provided. Republican members of the Joint Economic Committee likewise cast a wary eye: "A war on poverty will not be won by slogans, nor by shopworn programs dressed up in new packaging; nor by the defeatist relief concept of the thirties; nor by the cynical use of poverty for partisan political ends; nor by overstating the problem and thereby inexcusably lowering America's prestige in the eyes of the world." Poverty had long been a partisan issue; the Republican reaction suggested that it would remain so.

Several weeks after his State of the Union address, Johnson asked R. Sargent Shriver, director of the Peace Corps and brother-in-law of the late president Kennedy, to assemble his antipoverty program and guide it through Congress. Shriver adopted community action but added to it a variety of other ideas. His overall thrust was the creation of new programs and services rather than improved operation or coordination of existing ones, and he downplayed income transfers. Shriver became identified as field marshal in Johnson's domestic war, and the Office of Economic Opportunity (OEO), which Congress established in August in a heavily partisan vote and which Shriver ran in its early years, was widely thought of as its headquarters. OEO, of course, proved to be highly controversial, with far-reaching ramifications which cannot be examined here.

A review of the key steps taken on the road to the War on Poverty requires substantial revision of current explanations. First, although social scientists did play a significant role in launching the war, they were economists, not the sociologists that Moynihan and others feature. These economists were in part guided by ideals of social justice, but their approach to poverty also reflected efficiency ideals, faith in human-capital theory, and culture-of-poverty assumptions. Equally important, they acted politically. Heller was concerned about protecting the Kennedy administration's left flank on the tax cut. He and his colleagues abandoned discussion of income transfers, redistribution, and inequality largely because of their perceived political liabilities. They were prepared to accept a modest antipoverty program aimed at the nation's youth even though it would do nothing for many of the poor. Thus it would be wrong to think of these economists simply as technocrats; they had technical knowledge and skills, it is true, but they were consciously and explicitly political as well. They loyally served the presidents they worked for, and they operated comfortably in the world of political compromise.

Just as the economists were not purely technocratic in their motives or behavior, Presidents Kennedy and Johnson were not solely political. Both believed that poverty amidst plenty was intolerable and that government had the responsibility and capacity to reduce or even eliminate it. Expert opinion and information impressed them, and they wanted programs with substance, ones that would work. Not surprisingly, of course, political self-interest also motivated them and political realities shaped their responses. Contrary to Piven and Cloward's view, neither John F. Kennedy nor Johnson was drawn to the poverty issue because of black votes; in fact, they each hoped that poverty might transcend the politically nettlesome racial issue in their party. Both men also hoped poverty would be a popular issue, one that would appeal to the nation's conscience, though each worried about the opposite possibility. Thus, when Johnson declared war on poverty, he said the cause was not only just and winnable but practical and economical, able to prevent dependency and welfare, thereby saving public expenditures and expanding government revenues. That kind of rhetoric and the impulses behind it stand in sharp contrast to the popular reputation that the War on Poverty eventually acquired for largesse, egalitarianism, and humanitarianism.

Politics and ideas were entwined at every turn on the road to the War on Poverty, but fortune also played a role. There is no certainty that President Kennedy would have made poverty a leading issue had he lived. His assassination, however, created fortuitous circumstances, including most importantly Johnson's succession. Poverty was the right issue for the right man at the right time. Although poverty was receiving considerable attention from intellectuals, social critics, and journalists in the period immediately preceding Johnson's declaration, it differed from the civil rights issue. Masses of people were not demonstrating about it; that would only come after Johnson used his office to legitimize and publicize the issue. Like America's involvement in the undeclared war in Vietnam that was already in progress, its declared War on Poverty came on presidential initiative, another powerful example of the presidency's pivotal role in recent American history.

Special Message to the Congress on the Needs of the Nation's Senior Citizens February 21, 1963

John F. Kennedy

To the Congress of the United States:

On the basis of his study of the world's great civilizations, the historian Toynbee concluded that a society's quality and durability can best be measured "by the respect and care given its elderly citizens." Never before in our history have we ever had so many "senior citizens." There are present today in our population 17½ million people aged 65 years or over, nearly one-tenth of our population—and their number increases by 1,000 every day. By 1980, they will number nearly 25 million. Today there are already 25 million people aged 60 and over—nearly 6 million aged 75 and over— and more than 10 thousand over the age of 100.

These figures reflect a profound change in the composition of our population. In 1900, average life expectancy at birth was 49 years. Today more than 7 out of 10 new-born babies can expect to reach age 65. Life expectancy at birth now averages 70 years. Women 65 years old can now expect to live 16 more years, and men 65 years old can expect to live 13 additional years. While our population has increased 2½ times since 1900, the number of those aged 65 and over has increased almost sixfold.

This increase in the lifespan and in the number of our senior citizens presents this Nation with increased opportunities: the opportunity to draw upon their skill and sagacity—and the opportunity to provide the respect and recognition they have earned. It is not enough for a great nation merely to have added new years to life—our objective must also be to add new life to those years.

In the last three decades, this Nation has made considerable progress in assuring our older citizens the security and dignity a lifetime of labor deserves. But "the last of life, for which the first was made ... " is still not a "golden age" for all our citizens. Too often, these years are filled with anxiety, illness, and even want. The basic statistics on income, housing and health are both revealing and disturbing:

The average annual income received by aged couples is half that of younger two-person families. Almost half of those over 65 living alone receive $1000 or less a year, and three-fourths receive less than $2000 a year. About half the spending units headed by persons over 65 have liquid

SOURCE: John F. Kennedy, *Public Papers of the Presidents: John F. Kennedy*, no.74 (Washington, D.C.: U.S. Government Printing Office, 1963), pp. 188–201.

assets of less than $1000. Two-fifths have a total net worth, including their home, of less than $5000. The main source of income for the great majority of those above 65 is one or more public benefit programs. Seven out of 10—12.5 million persons—now receive social security insurance payments, averaging about $76 a month for a retired worker, $66 for a widow, and $129 for an aged worker and wife. One out of 8—2¼ million people—are on public assistance, averaging about $60 per month per person, supplemented by medical care payments averaging about $15 a month.

A far greater proportion of senior citizens live in inferior housing than is true of the houses occupied by younger citizens. According to the 1960 census, one-fourth of those aged 60 and over did not have households of their own but lived in the houses of relatives, in lodging houses, or in institutions. Of the remainder, over 30 percent lived in substandard housing which lacked a private bath, toilet, or running hot water or was otherwise dilapidated or deficient, and many others lived in housing unsuitable or unsafe for elderly people.

For roughly four-fifths of those older citizens not living on the farm, housing is a major expense, taking more than one-third of their income. About two-thirds of all those 65 and over own their own homes but, while such homes are generally free from mortgage, their value is generally less than $10,000.

Our senior citizens are sick more frequently and for more prolonged periods than the rest of the population. Of every 100 persons age 65 or over, 80 suffer some kind of chronic ailment; 28 have heart disease or high blood pressure; 27 have arthritis or rheumatism; 10 have impaired vision; and 17 have hearing impairments. Sixteen are hospitalized one or more times annually. They require three times as many days of hospital care every year as persons under the age of 65. Yet only half of those age 65 and over have any kind of health insurance; only one-third of those with incomes under $2000 a year have such insurance; only one-third of those age 75 and over had such insurance; and it has been estimated that 10 to 15 percent of the health costs of older people are reimbursed by insurance.

These and other sobering statistics make us realize that our remarkable scientific achievements prolonging the life-span have not yet been translated into effective human achievements. Our urbanized and industrialized way of life has destroyed the useful and satisfying roles which the aged played in the rural and small-town family society of an earlier era. The skills and talents of our older people are now all too often discarded.

Place and participation, health and honor, cannot, of course, be legislated. But legislation and sensible, coordinated action can enhance the opportunities for the aged. Isolation and misery can be prevented or reduced. We can provide the opportunity and the means for proper food, clothing, and housing—for productive employment or voluntary service—for protection against the devastating financial blows of sudden and catastrophic illness. Society, in short, can and must catch up with science.

All levels of government have the responsibility, in cooperation with private organizations and individuals, to act vigorously to improve the lot of our aged. Public efforts will have to be undertaken primarily by the local communities and by the States. But because these problems are nationwide, they call for Federal action as well.

RECENT FEDERAL ACTION

In approaching this task, it is important to recognize that we are not starting anew but building on a foundation already well laid over the last 30 years. Indeed, in the last two years alone, major strides have been made in improving Federal benefits and services for the aged:

1. The Social Security Amendments of 1961, which increased benefits by $900 million a year, substantially strengthened social insurance for retired and disabled workers and to widows, and enabled men to retire on Social Security at age 62. Legislation in 1961 also increased Federal support for old-age assistance, including medical vendor payments.

2. The Community Health Services and Facilities Act of 1961 authorized new programs for out-of-hospital community services for the chronically ill and the aged, and increased Federal grants for nursing home construction, health research facilities, and experimental hospital and medical care facilities. Such programs are now underway in 48 states.

3. The Public Welfare Amendments of 1962 authorized a substantial increase in Federal funds for old-age assistance, reemphasized restorative services to return individuals to self-support and self-care, and provided encouragement for employment by permitting States to allow old-age assistance recipients to keep up to $30 of his first $50 of monthly earnings without corresponding reductions in his public assistance payments.

4. The Housing Act of 1961 included provisions for the rapid expansion of housing for our elderly through public housing, direct loans, and FHA mortgage insurance. Commitments in 1961 and 1962 were made for more than 1½ times the number of housing units for older citizens aided in the preceding five years.

5. The Senior Citizens Housing Act of 1962 provided low-interest long-term loans and loan insurance to enable rural residents over 62, on farms and in small towns, to obtain or rent new homes or modernize old ones.

6. The new Institute of Child Health and Human Development, which was authorized last year, is expanding programs of research on health problems of the aging.

7. Other new legislation added safeguards on the purchase of drugs which are so essential to older citizens—boosted railroad retirement and veterans benefits—helped protect private pension funds against abuse—and increased recreational opportunities for all.

8. By administrative action we have (a) increased the quality and quantity of food available to those on welfare and other low-income aged persons and (b) established new organizational entities to meet the needs and coordinate the services affecting older people:

   - a new Gerontology Branch in the Chronic Disease Division of the Public Health Service, the first operating program geared exclusively to meeting health needs of the aging and giving particular emphasis to the application of medical rehabilitation to reduce or eliminate the disabling effects of chronic illness (such as stroke, arthritis, and many forms of cancer and heart disease) which cannot yet be presented; and

   - a new President's Council on Aging, whose members are the Secretaries and heads of eight cabinet departments and independent agencies administering in 1964 some $18 billion worth of benefits to people over 65. These and other actions have accelerated the flow of Federal assistance to the aged; and made a major start toward eliminating the gripping fear of economic insecurity. But their numbers are large and their needs are great and much more remains to be done.

HEALTH

Hospital Insurance

Medical science has done much to ease the pain and suffering of serious illness; and it has helped to add more than 20 years to the average length of life since 1900. The wonders worked in a modern American hospital hold out new hopes for our senior citizens. But, unfortunately, the cost of hospital care—now averaging more than $35 a day, nearly 4 times as high as in 1946—has risen much faster than the retired worker's ability to pay for that care.

Illness strikes most often and with its greatest severity at the time in life when incomes are most limited; and millions of our older citizens cannot afford $35 a day in hospital costs. Half of the retired have almost no income other than their Social Security payments—averaging $70 a month per person—and they have little in the way of savings. One-third of the aged family units have less than $100 in liquid assets. One short hospital stay may be manageable for many older persons with the help of family and savings; but the second—and the average person can expect two or three hospital stays after age 65—may well mean destitution, public or private charity, or the alternative of suffering in silence. For these citizens, the miracles of medical science mean little.

A proud and resourceful nation can no longer ask its older people to live in constant fear of a serious illness for which adequate funds are not available. We owe them the right of dignity in sickness as well as in health.

We can achieve this by adding health insurance—primarily hospitalization insurance—to our successful Social Security system.

Hospital insurance for our older citizens on Social Security offers a reasonable and practical solution to a critical problem. It is the logical extension of a principle established 28 years ago in the Social Security system and confirmed many times since by both Congress and the American voters. It is based on the fundamental premise that contributions during the working years, matched by employers' contributions, should enable people to prepay and build earned rights and benefits to safeguard them in their old age.

There are some who say the problem can best be solved through private health insurance. But this is not the answer for most, for it overlooks the high cost of adequate health insurance and the low incomes of our aged. The average retired couple lives on $50 a week, and the average aged single person lives on $20 a week. These are far below the amounts needed for a modest but adequate standard of living, according to all measures. The cost of broad health insurance coverage for an aged couple, when such coverage is available, is more than $400 a year—about one-sixth of the total income of an average older couple.

As a result, of the total aged population discharged from hospitals, 49 percent have no hospital insurance at all and only 30 percent have as much as three-fourths of their bills paid by insurance plans. (Comparable data for those under 65 showed that only 30 percent lacked hospital insurance, and that 54 percent had three-fourths or more of their bills paid by insurance.) Prepayment of hospital costs for old-age by contributions during the working years is obviously necessary.

Others say that the children of aged parents should be willing to pay their bills, and I have no doubts that most children are willing to sacrifice to aid their parents. But aged parents often choose to suffer from severe illness rather than see their children and grandchildren undergo financial hardship. Hospital insurance under Social Security would make it unnecessary for families to face such choices—just as old-age benefits under Social Security have relieved large numbers of families of the need to choose between the welfare of their parents and the best interests of their children.

Others may say that public assistance or welfare medical assistance for the aged will meet the problem. The welfare medical assistance program adopted in 1960 now operates in 25 states and will provide benefits in 1964 to about 525,000 persons. But this is only a small percentage of those aged individuals who need medical care. Of the 111,700 persons who received medical assistance for the aged in November, more than 70,000 were in only three States: California, Massachusetts, and New York.

Moreover, 25 States have not adopted such a program, which is dependent upon the availability each year of State appropriations, upon the financial condition of the States, and upon competition with many other calls on State resources. As a result, coverage and quality vary from State to State.

Surely it would be far better and fairer to provide a universal approach, through social insurance, instead of a needs test program which does not prevent indigency, but operates only after indigency is created. In other words, welfare medical assistance helps older people get health care only if they first accept poverty and then accept charity.

Let me make clear my belief that public assistance grants for medical care would still be necessary to supplement the proposed basic hospitalization program under social security—just as old-age assistance has supplemented old-age and survivors insurance. But it should be regarded as a second line of defense. Our major reliance must be to provide funds for hospital care of our aged through social insurance, supplemented to the extent possible by private insurance.

The hospital insurance program achieves two basic objectives. First, it protects against the principal component of the cost of a serious illness. Second, it furnishes a foundation upon which supplementary private programs can and will be built. Together with retirement, disability, and survivors insurance benefits, it will help eliminate privation and insecurity in this country.

For these reasons, I recommend a hospital insurance program for senior citizens under the Social Security system which would pay:

1. all costs of in-patient hospital services for up to 90 days, with the patient paying $10 a day for the first 9 days and at least $20, or, for those individuals who so elect, all such costs for up to 180 days with the patient paying the first 2½ days of average costs, or all such costs for up to 45 days;

2. all costs of care in skilled nursing home facilities affiliated with hospitals for up to at least 180 days after transfer of the patient from a hospital;

3. all costs above the first $20 for hospital out-patient diagnostic services, and;

4. all costs of up to 240 home health-care visits in any one calendar year by community visiting nurses and physical therapists.

Under this plan, the individual will have the option of selecting the kind of insurance protection that will be most consistent with his economic resources and his prospective health needs—45 days with no deductible, 90 days with a maximum $90 deductible, or 180 days paying a "deductible" equal to 2½ days of average hospital costs. This new element of freedom of choice is a major improvement over bills previously submitted.

These benefits would be available to all aged Social Security and railroad retirement beneficiaries, with the costs paid from new social insurance funds provided by adding one-quarter of one percent to the payroll contributions made by both employers and employees and by increasing the annual earnings base from $4,800 to $5,200.

Hospitals, skilled nursing facilities, and community health-service organizations would be paid for the reasonable costs of the services they furnished. There would be little difference between the procedures under the proposed program and those already set up and accepted by hospitals in connection with Blue Cross programs.

Procedures would be developed, utilizing professional organizations and State agencies, for accrediting hospitals and for assisting nonaccredited hospitals and nursing facilities to become eligible to participate.

I also recommend a transition provision under which the benefits would be given to those over 65 today who have not had an opportunity to participate in the Social Security program. The cost of providing these benefits would be paid from general tax revenues. This provision would be transitional inasmuch as 9 out of 10 persons reaching the age of 65 today have Social Security coverage.

The program I propose would pay the costs of hospital and related services but it would not interfere with the way treatment is provided. It would not hinder in any way the freeedom of choice of doctor, hospital, or nurse. It would not specify in any way the kind of medical or health care or treatment to be provided by the doctor.

Health insurance for our senior citizens is the most important health proposal pending before the Congress. We urgently need this legislation— and we need it now. This is our number one objective for our senior citizens.

Commencement Address at Howard University: *"To Fulfill These Rights"* June 4, 1965

Lyndon B. Johnson

Dr. Nabrit, my fellow Americans:

I am delighted at the chance to speak at this important and this historic institution. Howard has long been an outstanding center for the education of Negro Americans. Its students are of every race and color and they come from many countries of the world. It is truly a working example of democratic excellence.

Our earth is the home of revolution. In every corner of every continent men charged with hope contend with ancient ways in the pursuit of justice. They reach for the newest of weapons to realize the oldest of dreams, that each may walk in freedom and pride, stretching his talents, enjoying the fruits of the earth.

Our enemies may occasionally seize the day of change, but it is the banner of our revolution they take. And our own future is linked to this process of swift and turbulent change in many lands in the world. But nothing in any country touches us more profoundly, and nothing is more freighted with meaning for our own destiny than the revolution of the Negro American.

In far too many ways American Negroes have been another nation: deprived of freedom, crippled by hatred, the doors of opportunity closed to hope.

In our time change has come to this nation, too. The American Negro, acting with impressive restraint, has peacefully protested and marched, entered the courtrooms and the seats of government, demanding a justice that has long been denied. The voice of the Negro was the call to action. But it is a tribute to America that, once aroused, the courts and the Congress, the President and most of the people, have been the allies of progress.

LEGAL PROTECTION OF HUMAN RIGHTS

Thus we have seen the high court of the country declare that discrimination based on race was repugnant to the Constitution, and therefore void.

SOURCE: Lyndon Baines Johnson, *Public Papers of the Presidents: Lyndon Baines Johnson*, II, no. 301 (Washington, D.C.: U.S. Government Printing Office, 1966), pp. 635–40.

We have seen in 1957, and 1960, and again in 1964, the first civil rights legislation in this Nation in almost an entire century.

As majority leader of the United States Senate, I helped to guide two of these bills through the Senate. And, as your President, I was proud to sign the third. And now very soon we will have the fourth—a new law guaranteeing every American the right to vote.

No act of my entire administration will give me greater satisfaction than the day when my signature makes this bill, too, the law of this land.

The voting rights bill will be the latest, and among the most important, in a long series of victories. But this victory—as Winston Churchill said of another triumph for freedom—"is not the end. It is not even the beginning of the end. But it is, perhaps, the end of the beginning."

That beginning is freedom, and the barriers to that freedom are tumbling down. Freedom is the right to share, share fully and equally, in American society—to vote, to hold a job, to enter a public place, to go to school. It is the right to be treated in every part of our national life as a person equal in dignity and promise to all others.

FREEDOM IS NOT ENOUGH

But freedom is not enough. You do not wipe away the scars of centuries by saying: "Now you are free to go where you want, and do as you desire, and choose the leaders you please."

You do not take a person who, for years, has been hobbled by chains and liberate him, bring him up to the starting line of a race and then say, "you are free to compete with all the others," and still justly believe that you have been completely fair.

Thus it is not enough to just open the gates of opportunity. All our citizens must have the ability to walk through those gates.

This is the next and the more profound stage of the battle for civil rights. We seek not just freedom but opportunity. We seek not just legal equity but human ability, not just equality as a right and a theory but equality as a fact and equality as a result.

For the task is to give 20 million Negroes the same chance as every other American to learn and grow, to work and share in society, to develop their abilities—physical, mental and spiritual—and to pursue their individual happiness.

To this end equal opportunity is essential, but not enough, not enough. Men and women of all races are born with the same range of abilities. But ability is not just the product of birth. Ability is stretched or stunted by the family that you live with, and the neighborhood you live in—by the school you go to and the poverty or the richness of your surroundings. It is the product of a hundred unseen forces playing upon the little infant, the child, and finally the man.

PROGRESS FOR SOME

This graduating class at Howard University is witness to the indomitable determination of the Negro American to win his way in American life.

The number of Negroes in schools of higher learning has almost doubled in 15 years. The number of nonwhite professional workers has more than doubled in 10 years. The median income of Negro college women tonight exceeds that of white college women. And there are also the enormous accomplishments of distinguished individual Negroes—many of them graduates of this institution, and one of them the first lady ambassador in the history of the United States.

These are proud and impressive achievements. But they tell only the story of a growing middle class minority, steadily narrowing the gap between them and their white counterparts.

A WIDENING GULF

But for the great majority of Negro Americans—the poor, the unemployed, the uprooted, and the dispossessed—there is a much grimmer story. They still, as we meet here tonight, are another nation. Despite the court orders and the laws, despite the legislative victories and the speeches, for them the walls are rising and the gulf is widening.

Here are some of the facts of this American failure.

Thirty-five years ago the rate of unemployment for Negroes and whites was about the same. Tonight the Negro rate is twice as high.

In 1948 the 8 percent unemployment rate for Negro teenage boys was actually less than that of whites. By last year that rate had grown to 23 percent, as against 13 percent for whites unemployed.

Between 1949 and 1959, the income of Negro men relative to white men declined in every section of this country. From 1952 to 1963 the median income of Negro families compared to white actually dropped from 57 percent to 53 percent.

In the years 1955 through 1957, 22 percent of experienced Negro workers were out of work at some time during the year. In 1961 through 1963 that proportion had soared to 29 percent.

Since 1947 the number of white families living in poverty has decreased 27 percent while the number of poorer nonwhite families decreased only 3 percent.

The infant mortality of nonwhites in 1940 was 70 percent greater than whites. Twenty-two years later it was 90 percent greater.

Moreover, the isolation of Negro from white communities is increasing, rather than decreasing as Negroes crowd into the central cities and become a city within a city.

Of course, Negro Americans as well as white Americans have shared in our rising national abundance. But the harsh fact of the matter is that in the battle for true equality too many—far too many—are losing ground every day.

THE CAUSES OF INEQUALITY

We are not completely sure why this is. We know the causes are complex and subtle. But we do know the two broad basic reasons. And we do know that we have to act.

First, Negroes are trapped—as many whites are trapped—in inherited, gateless poverty. They lack training and skills. They are shut in, in slums, without decent medical care. Private and public poverty combine to cripple their capacities.

We are trying to attack these evils through our poverty program, through our medical care and our other health programs, and a dozen more of the Great Society programs that are aimed at the root causes of this poverty.

We will increase, and we will accelerate, and we will broaden this attack in years to come until this most enduring of foes finally yields to our unyielding will.

But there is a second cause—much more difficult to explain, more deeply grounded, more desperate in force. It is the devastating heritage of long years of slavery and a century of oppression, hatred, and injustice.

SPECIAL NATURE OF NEGRO POVERTY

For Negro poverty is not white poverty. Many of its causes and many of its cures are the same. But there are differences—deep, corrosive, obstinate differences—radiating painful roots into the community, and into the family, and the nature of the individual.

These differences are not racial differences. They are solely and simply the consequence of ancient brutality, past injustices, and present prejudice. They are anguishing to observe. For the Negro they are a constant reminder of oppression. For the white they are a constant reminder of guilt. But they must be faced and they must be dealt with and they must be overcome, if we are ever to reach the time when the only difference between Negroes and whites is the color of their skin.

Nor can we find a complete answer in the experience of other American minorities. They made a valiant and a largely successful effort to emerge from poverty and prejudice.

The Negro, like these others, will have to rely mostly upon his own efforts. But he just can not do it alone. For they did not have the heritage of centuries to overcome, and they did not have a cultural tradition which had been twisted and battered by endless years of hatred and hopelessness, nor were they excluded—these others—because of race or color—a feeling whose dark intensity is matched by no other prejudice in our society.

Nor can these differences be understood as isolated infirmities. They are a seamless web. They cause each other. They result from each other. They reinforce each other. Much of the Negro community is buried under a blanket of history and circumstance. It is not a lasting solution to lift just one corner of that blanket. We must stand on all sides and we must raise the entire cover if we are to liberate our fellow citizens.

THE ROOTS OF INJUSTICE

One of the differences is the increased concentration of Negroes in our cities. More than 73 percent of all Negroes live in urban areas compared with less than 70 percent of the whites. Most of these Negroes live in slums. Most of these Negroes live together—a separated people.

Men are shaped by their world. When it is a world of decay, ringed by an invisible wall, when escape is arduous and uncertain, and the saving pressures of a more hopeful society are unknown, it can cripple the youth and it can desolate the men.

There is also the burden that a dark skin can add to the search for a productive place in our society. Unemployment strikes most swiftly and broadly at the Negro, and this burden erodes hope. Blighted hope breeds despair. Despair brings indifferences to the learning which offers a way out. And despair, coupled with indifferences, is often the source of destructive rebellion against the fabric of society.

There is also the lacerating hurt of early collision with white hatred or prejudice, distaste or condescension. Other groups have felt similar intolerance. But success and achievement could wipe it away. They do not change the color of a man's skin. I have seen this uncomprehending pain in the eyes of the little, young Mexican-American schoolchildren that I taught many years ago. But it can be overcome. But, for many, the wounds are always open.

FAMILY BREAKDOWN

Perhaps most important—its influence radiating to every part of life— is the breakdown of the Negro family structure. For this, most of all, white America must accept responsibility. It flows from centuries of oppression and persecution of the Negro man. It flows from the long years of degradation and discrimination, which have attacked his dignity and assaulted his ability to produce for his family.

This, too, is not pleasant to look upon. But it must be faced by those whose serious intent is to improve the life of all Americans.

Only a minority—less than half—of all Negro children reach the age of 18 having lived all their lives with both of their parents. At this moment, tonight, little less than two-thirds are at home with both of their parents. Probably a majority of all Negro children receive federally-aided public assistance sometime during their childhood.

The family is the cornerstone of our society. More than any other force it shapes the attitude, the hopes, the ambitions, and the values of the child. And when the family collapses it is the children that are usually damaged. When it happens on a massive scale the community itself is crippled.

So, unless we work to strengthen the family, to create conditions under which most parents will stay together—all the rest: schools, and playgrounds, and public assistance, and private concern, will never be enough to cut completely the circle of despair and deprivation.

TO FULFILL THESE RIGHTS

There is no single easy answer to all of these problems.

Jobs are part of the answer. They bring the income which permits a man to provide for his family.

Decent homes in decent surroundings and a chance to learn—an equal chance to learn—are part of the answer.

Welfare and social programs better designed to hold families together are part of the answer.

Care for the sick is part of the answer.

An understanding heart by all Americans is another big part of the answer.

And to all of these fronts—and a dozen more—I will dedicate the expanding efforts of the Johnson administration.

But there are other answers that are still to be found. Nor do we fully understand even all of the problems. Therefore, I want to announce tonight that this fall I intend to call a White House conference of scholars, and experts, and outstanding Negro leaders—men of both races—and officials of Government at every level.

This White House conference's theme and title will be "To Fulfill These Rights."

Its object will be to help the American Negro fulfill the rights which, after the long time of injustice, he is finally about to secure.

To move beyond opportunity to achievement.

To shatter forever not only the barriers of law and public practice, but the walls which bound the condition of many by the color of his skin.

To dissolve, as best we can, the antique enmities of the heart which diminish the holder, divide the great democracy, and do wrong—great wrong—to the children of God.

And I pledge to you tonight that this will be a chief goal of my administration, and of my program next year, and in the years to come. And I hope, and I pray, and I believe, it will be a part of the program of all America.

WHAT IS JUSTICE

For what is justice?

It is to fulfill the fair expectations of man.

Thus, American justice is a very special thing. For, from the first, this has been a land of towering expectations. It was to be a nation where each man could be ruled by the common consent of all—enshrined in law, given life by institutions, guided by men themselves subject to its rule. And all—all of every station and origin—would be touched equally in obligation and in liberty.

Beyond the law lay the land. It was a rich land, glowing with more abundant promise than man had ever seen. Here, unlike any place yet known, all were to share the harvest.

And beyond this was the dignity of man. Each could become whatever his qualities of mind and spirit would permit—to strive, to seek, and, if he could, to find his happiness.

This is American justice. We have pursued it faithfully to the edge of our imperfections, and we have failed to find it for the American Negro.

So, it is the glorious opportunity of this generation to end the one huge wrong of the American Nation and, in so doing, to find America for ourselves, with the same immense thrill of discovery which gripped those who first began to realize that here, at last, was a home for freedom.

All it will take is for all of us to understand what this country is and what this country must become.

The Scripture promises: "I shall light a candle of understanding in thine heart, which shall not be put out."

Together, and with millions more, we can light that candle of understanding in the heart of all America.

And once lit, it will never again go out.

NOTE: The President spoke at 6:35 p.m. on the Main Quadrangle in front of the library at Howard University in Washington, after being awarded an honorary degree of doctor of laws. His opening words referred to Dr. James M. Nabrit, Jr., President of the University. During his remarks he referred to Mrs. Patricia Harris, U.S. Ambassador to Luxembourg and former associate professor of law at Howard University.

The Voting Rights Act of 1965 was approved by the President on August 6, 1965.

Remarks with President Truman at the Signing in Independence of the Medicare Bill
July 30, 1965

President Truman:

Thank you very much. I am glad you like the President. I like him too. He is one of the finest men I ever ran across.

Mr. President, Mrs. Johnson, distinguished guests:

You have done me a great honor in coming here today, and you have made me a very, very happy man.

This is an important hour for the Nation, for those of our citizens who have completed their tour of duty and have moved to the sidelines. These are the days that we are trying to celebrate for them. These people are our prideful responsibility and they are entitled, among other benefits, to the best medical protection available.

Not one of these, our citizens, should ever be abandoned to the indignity of charity. Charity is indignity when you have to have it. But we don't want these people to have anything to do with charity and we don't want them to have any idea of hopeless despair.

Mr. President, I am glad to have lived this long and to witness today the signing of the Medicare bill which puts this Nation right where it needs to be, to be right. Your inspired leadership and a responsive forward-looking Congress have made it historically possible for this day to come about.

Thank all of you most highly for coming here. It is an honor I haven't had for, well, quite awhile, I'll say that to you, but here it is:

Ladies and gentlemen, the President of the United States.

The President:

President and Mrs. Truman, Secretary Celebrezze, Senator Mansfield, Senator Symington, Senator Long, Governor Hearnes, Senator Anderson and Congressman King of the Anderson-King team, Congressman Mills and Senator Long of the Mills-Long team, our beloved Vice President who worked in the vineyard many years to see this day come to pass, and all of my dear friends in the Congress—both Democrats and Republicans:

The people of the United States love and voted for Harry Truman, not because he gave them hell—but because he gave them hope.

SOURCE: Lyndon Baines Johnson, *Public Papers of the Presidents: Lyndon Baines Johnson*, II, no. 394 (Washington, D.C.: 1966), pp. 811–28.

I believe today that all America shares my joy that he is present now when the hope that he offered becomes a reality for millions of our fellow citizens.

I am so proud that this has come to pass in the Johnson administration. But it was really Harry Truman of Missouri who planted the seeds of compassion and duty which have today flowered into care for the sick and serenity for the fearful.

Many men can make many proposals. Many men can draft many laws. But few have the piercing and humane eye which can see beyond the words to the people that they touch. Few can see past the speeches and the political battles to the doctor over there that is tending the infirm, and to the hospital that is receiving those in anguish, or feel in their heart painful wrath at the injustice which denies the miracle of healing to the old and to the poor. And fewer still have the courage to stake reputation, and position, and the effort of a lifetime upon such a cause when there are so few that share it.

But it is just such men who illuminate the life and the history of a nation. And so, President Harry Truman, it is in tribute not to you, but to the America that you represent, that we have come here to pay our love and our respects to you today. For a country can be known by the quality of the men it honors. By praising you, and by carrying forward your dreams, we really reaffirm the greatness of America.

It was a generation ago that Harry Truman said, and I quote him: "Millions of our citizens do not now have a full measure of opportunity to achieve and to enjoy good health. Millions do not now have protection or security against the economic effects of sickness. And the time has now arrived for action to help them attain that opportunity and to help them get that protection."

Well, today, Mr. President, and my fellow Americans, we are taking such action—20 years later. And we are doing that under the great leadership of men like John McCormack, our Speaker; Carl Albert, our majority leader; our very able and beloved majority leader of the Senate, Mike Mansfield; and distinguished Members of the Ways and Means and Finance Committees of the House and Senate—of both parties, Democratic and Republican.

Because the need for this action is plain; and it is so clear indeed that we marvel not simply at the passage of this bill, but what we marvel at is that it took so many years to pass it. And I am so glad that Aime Forand is here to see it finally passed and signed—one of the first authors.

There are more than 18 million Americans over the age of 65. Most of them have low incomes. Most of them are threatened by illness and medical expenses that they cannot afford.

And through this new law, Mr. President, every citizen will be able in his productive years when he is earning, to insure himself against the ravages of illness in his old age.

This insurance will help pay for care in hospitals, in skilled nursing homes, or in the home. And under a separate plan it will help meet the fees of the doctors.

Now here is how the plan will affect you.

During your working years, the people of America—you—will contribute through the social security program a small amount each payday for hospital insurance protection. For example, the average worker in 1966 will contribute about $1.50 per month. The empoyer will contribute a similar amount. And this will provide the funds to pay up to 90 days of hospital care for each illness, plus diagnostic care, and up to 100 home health visits after you are 65. And beginning in 1967, you will also be covered for up to 100 days of care in a skilled nursing home after a period of hospital care.

And under a separate plan, when you are 65—that the Congress originated itself, in its own good judgment—you may be covered for medical and surgical fees whether you are in or out of the hospital. You will pay $3 per month after you are 65 and your Government will contribute an equal amount.

The benefits under the law are as varied and broad as the marvelous modern medicine itself. If it has a few defects—such as the method of payment of certain specialists—then I am confident those can be quickly remedied and I hope they will be.

No longer will older Americans be denied the healing miracle of modern medicine. No longer will illness crush and destroy the savings that they have so carefully put away over a lifetime so that they might enjoy dignity in their later years. No longer will young families see their own incomes, and their own hopes, eaten away simply because they are carrying out their deep moral obligations to their parents, and to their uncles, and their aunts.

And no longer will this Nation refuse the hand of justice to those who have given a lifetime of service and wisdom and labor to the progress of this progressive country.

And this bill, Mr. President, is even broader than that. It will increase social security benefits for all of our older Americans. It will improve a wide range of health and medical services for Americans of all ages.

In 1935 when the man that both of us loved so much, Franklin Delano Roosevelt, signed the Social Security Act, he said it was, and I quote him, "a cornerstone in a structure which is being built but it is by no means complete."

Well, perhaps no single act in the entire administration of the beloved Franklin D. Roosevelt really did more to win him the illustrious place in history that he has as did the laying of that cornerstone. And I am so happy that his oldest son Jimmy could be here to share with us the joy that is ours today. And those who share this day will also be remembered for making the most important addition to that structure, and you are making it in this bill, the most important addition that has been made in three decades.

History shapes men, but it is a necessary faith of leadership that men can help shape history. There are many who led us to this historic day. Not out of courtesy or deterence, but from the gratitude and remembrance which is our country's debt, if I may be pardoned for taking a moment, I want to call a part of the honor roll: it is the able leadership in both Houses of the Congress.

Congressman Celler, Chairman of the Judiciary Committee, introduced the hospital insurance in 1952. Aime Forand from Rhode Island, then Congressman, introduced it in the House. Senator Clinton Anderson from New Mexico fought for Medicare through the years in the Senate. Congressman Cecil King of California carried on the battle in the House. The legislative genius of the Chairman of the Ways and Means Committee, Congressman Wilbur Mills, and the effective and able work of Senator Russell Long, together transformed this desire into victory.

And those devoted public servants, former Secretary, Senator Ribicoff; present Secretary, Tony Celebrezze; Under Secretary Wilbur Cohen; the Democratic whip of the House, Hale Boggs of the Ways and Means Committee; and really the White House's best legislator, Larry O'Brien, gave not just endless days and months and, yes, years of patience—but they gave their hearts—to passing this bill.

Let us also remember those who sadly cannot share this time for triumph. For it is their triumph, too. It is the victory of great Members of Congress that are not with us, like John Dingell, Sr., and Robert Wagner, late a Member of the Senate, and James Murray of Montana.

And there is also John Fitzgerald Kennedy, who fought in the Senate and took his case to the people, and never yielded in pursuit, but was not spared to see the final concourse of the forces that he had helped to loose.

But it all started really with the man from Independence. And so, as it is fitting that we should, we have come back here to his home to complete what he began.

President Harry Truman, as any President must, made many decisions of great moment, although he always made them frankly and with a courage and a clarity that few men have ever shared. The immense and the intricate questions of freedom and survival were caught up many times in the web of Harry Truman's judgment. And this is the tradition of leadership.

But there is another tradition that we share today. It calls upon us never to be indifferent toward despair. It commands us never to turn away from helplessness. It directs us never to ignore or to spurn those who suffer untended in a land that is bursting with abundance.

I said to Senator Smathers, the whip of the Democrats in the Senate, who worked with us in the Finance Committee on this legislation—I said, the highest traditions of the medical profession are really directed to the ends that we are trying to serve. And it was only yesterday, at the request of some of my friends, I met with the leaders of the American Medical Association to seek their assistance in advancing the cause of one of the greatest professions of all—the medical profession—in helping us to maintain and to improve the health of all Americans.

And this is not just our tradition—or the tradition of the Democratic Party—or even the tradition of the Nation. It is as old as the day it was first commanded: "Thou shalt open thine hand wide unto thy brother, to thy poor, to thy needy, in thy land."

And just think, Mr. President, because of this document—and the long years of struggle which so many have put into creating it—in this town, and a thousand other towns like it, there are men and women in pain who will now find ease. There are those, alone in suffering, who will now hear the sound of some approaching footsteps coming to help. There are those fearing the terrible darkness of despairing poverty—despite their long years of labor and expectation—who will now look up to see the light of hope and realization.

There just can be no satisfaction, or any act of leadership, that gives greater satisfaction than this.

And perhaps you alone, President Truman, perhaps you alone can fully know just how grateful I am for this day.

CHAPTER 10

Critics of the
Welfare State

INTRODUCTION

By 1967 the white middle class, as well as poor whites, had turned against the Great Society as the War on Poverty became increasingly identified with black militants and race riots. Harris polls showed that poor whites held particularly negative feelings toward the War on Poverty. Harris reported that whites believed that Johnson's program was designed only for blacks and "does not deal with their [whites] needs. . . . " As much as the White House and the Office of Economic Opportunity publicists tried to sell the *poverty of culture* notion, the majority of Americans continued to believe that poverty was caused by an individual's "lack of effort." One survey concluded at the end of the decade that "America's vast middle class views the poor as culpable rather than a victimized group."

The Community Action Program's attempt to organize the poor within their communities drew attacks from both the right and the left. Racial riots in the summer of 1965 further heightened conservative fears that CAP had become a tool of black nationalists intent upon revolution. CAP workers were accused of organizing the riots that summer. In turn, militant blacks, including Charles Hale of the Brooklyn chapter of the Congress of Racial Equality, charged OEO with being dominated by "fascist thinking" and using "Uncle Toms" to "corral niggers." Such accusations were extreme, but it remains clear that significant groups at both ends of the political spectrum continued to distrust LBJ and his Great Society.

Frank Annunziata examines "The Revolt Against the Welfare State: Goldwater Conservatism and the Election of 1964." The Goldwater movement in the Republican party, which brought the presidential nomination to this conservative Arizona senator in 1964, showed that many conservatives were distressed by the direction of federal welfare policy since the New Deal. In his essay, Annunziata argues that these conservatives had not accepted the liberal consensus that had taken shape concerning the welfare state. Barry Goldwater's *Conscience of a Conservative* (1960), which sold over 3,500,000 copies, exhorted conservatives to regain control of the Republican party from the liberal eastern establishment of Nelson Rockefeller, Henry Cabot Lodge, Jr., and Milton Eisenhower. Goldwater and conservative party activists sought to "accentuate its differences with the New Deal and its legacy." In his unsuccessful campaign, Goldwater criticized the Social Security system, the income tax, the Tennessee Valley Authority, and the War on Poverty. If the New Deal had been so successful, he asked, why were liberals still claiming in the 1960s that one third of the nation still lived in poverty. He felt that liberal efforts to reduce poverty had failed because they had stilted free enterprise and economic incentives in America. Goldwater was resoundingly defeated by Lyndon Johnson in 1964. He received 7,500,000 votes fewer than Richard Nixon had received in 1960, but Goldwater's campaign, as Annunziata astutely observes, "illuminates the festering resentment toward past liberal social reforms," at least among a small group of conservatives.

Those on the radical left were no less discontented with the War on Poverty program. Elinor Graham, then a student at Antioch College, offered a radical critique of the Great Society in her essay, published in 1965. Graham argued that the War on Poverty, for all of its rhetoric, continued to place the burden of being poor on the poor through its means test. In this way, she concludes, most of the War on Poverty programs place "a stigma of failure and dependency upon aid recipients." Moreover, Graham developed a theme common among leftists: The War on Poverty "reasserts and stabilizes the power of the political elite, whose positions have been threatened by enfranchisement of the Negro." She concludes, "For reasons of a less than morally commendable nature, white America has responded to the Negroes' demands for an integrated society with an antipoverty movement. . . . Those who are within the socio-economic structure will not give up their positions to Negroes seeking entrance."

Writing at the same time as Graham, conservatives also roundly criticised Great Society liberalism. Murray A. Rothbard, a well-known libertarian, offered a free-market, laissez-faire critique of the War on Poverty. Rothbard maintains that the development of the liberal state is a result of economic elites trying to maintain their well-being through political means. The liberal political state as a consequence, he suggests, "discourages and drains off production and output in society." In creating this liberal state, Rothbard maintains, social scientists and the liberal intelligentsia have played key roles in rationalizing economic self-interest with their rhetoric of "humanity" and the "common good." Yet behind the Great Society is the cruel "myth" that only deceives the poor that their lives will improve. In the end, "the poor are the major victims of the welfare state. The poor are the ones to be conscripted to fight and die at literally slave wages in the Great Society's imperial wars."

These critiques of the Great Society later found expression in the 1980s.

Further Readings

The liberal consensus and its critics are discussed by Godfrey Hodgson, *America In Our Time* (Garden City, N.Y.: Doubleday, 1976).

For analysis of the radical left as a political movement, a clear chronicle is found in Irwin Unger, *The Movement: A History of the American New Left, 1959–1972* (New York: Harper & Row, 1974).

Other studies of the period are offered by Guida West, *The National Welfare Rights Movement: The Social Protest of Poor Women* (New York: Praeger Books, 1981), and Frances Fox Piven and Richard A. Cloward, *Poor People's Movements: Why They Succeed, How They Fail* (New York: Random House, 1979).

The New left perspective of the War on Poverty is captured in Marvin E. Gettleman and David Mermelstein, eds., *The Great Society Reader: The Failure of American Liberalism* (New York: Random House, 1967).

The Revolt Against
the Welfare State:
Goldwater Conservatism and the
Election of 1964

Frank Annunziata

In the 1964 presidential election the animating axioms of many historians and political scientists were shattered. Senator Barry Goldwater's nomination by the Republican Party contravened the proposition that neither of America's major parties could abandon electoral pragmatism for an intense ideological campaign. The presumptive realities of pragmatic "brokerage" parties, an electorate unreceptive to an "issues" appeal, and the acceptance of the welfare state's egalitarian politics were important elements in establishing "the end of ideology" theme in American social thought. America's welfare state, developed during the New Deal and subsequently extended and refined in Fair Deal, Modern Republican, New Frontier and Great Society programs, appeared as a permanent and revered institution. Its acceptance was attested to, submitted Walter Rostow, by "a consensus among a substantial majority of the population that government should continue to perform a wide range of economic functions." Historians concluded that Americans no longer thought that government was best which governed least: laissez-faire economics "survives more as a tradition than actuality." The "searing ordeal" of our Great Depression "purged the American people of their belief in the limited powers of the federal government and convinced them of the necessity of the guarantor state." The New Deal symbolized "the crossing of a divide from which, it would seem, there could be no turning back." It has become so significant a part of "the American Way, that no political party which aspires to high office dares now to repudiate it."

It is true that the Republican Party from 1936 through 1964 refrained from directly challenging the New Deal's social welfare reforms. When in the Congressional elections of 1934, Republicans castigated Roosevelt's programs as "socialistic" and "un-American," they became the first party since 1866 which failed to augment its Congressional strength after losing the presidential election. Having absorbed this punishment, Republicans pragmatically began emphasizing their progressive policies and leaders. In 1936 they chose a progressive Midwestern governor, Alfred Landon of

SOURCE: Frank Annunziata, *Presidential Studies Quarterly* 80, no. 2 (Spring 1980), pp. 254–65. Reprinted with permission of the Center for the Study of the Presidency, publisher of *Presidential Studies Quarterly*.

Kansas, to battle Franklin Roosevelt on an unusual Republican platform. Landon, unlike Herbert Hoover, dismissed antistatist appeals. "As civilization becomes more complex," said Landon, "government must increase." The 1936 Republican platform affirmed the principle of old age and unemployment payments. It pledged to protect the rights of labor to organize and bargain collectively, through representatives of its own choosing "without interference from any source." It endorsed state minimum wage and hours laws for women and children despite the Supreme Court's rulings. Denouncing the New Deal only in the "generalities of campaign oratory," the Republicans concealed the "abandonment of traditional principles behind a smokescreen of rhetoric." The United States experienced its first election in which no major political party espoused the philosophy of limited government. The surging popular acceptance of the New Deal compelled Republican adjustments to new political realities. The election of 1936 became a great watershed in American political history because the philosophy of the "abortive Bull Moose movement of 1912 had finally captured both major parties."

Other examples which illuminate the Republicans' acquiescence to the New Deal's ideological *coup* came in 1940 when they nominated Wendell Willkie, a former Democrat, for President. They repeated this strategy in 1944 and 1948 by selecting Thomas Dewey, a progressive governor of New York state. And by 1952 they were vying with Democrats regarding which party had really been responsible for particular social reforms. Finally, neither Dwight Eisenhower's presidency nor Richard Nixon's candidacy threatened to repeal New Deal policies.

Senator Goldwater's presidential nomination in 1964, however, constituted a direct assault upon the welfare state and an attempt to govern the United States on a pre–New Deal basis. Goldwater's role in the American political tradition has been to question the legitimacy of the New Deal. His political language functioned not to reinforce in people's minds the reassuring primal symbol of government as protector. Instead he served as an anatomist of social malaise—an incorruptible, audacious advocate of the politics of redemption. By invoking polar imagery and contrasting a deracinated, inchoate "welfare state America" with the idyll of a productive, content, self-adjusting society, he tried to reorient the contours of our national political consciousness. He intended his candidacy to serve as a national referendum on the federal government's proper role in American life. That this became obscured during the campaign should not distract us from its permanent significance. Thirty-two years after Herbert Hoover had solemnly warned that his struggle against Franklin Roosevelt was "more than a contest between two men and more than a contest between two parties," but rather "a contest between two philosophies of government," Barry Goldwater came to ask whether America truly desired to continue this perhaps imperceptible but destructive course "down the road to socialism." By presenting "a choice, not an echo" he resolved to show that the New Deal hardly symbolized "a divide from which . . . there could be no turning back," only a temporary aberration in American history. What distinguished Goldwater from his Republican predecessors was not his ideology, rhetoric or even political philosophy, but what Hans Morgenthau called his "willingness to put that philosophy into practice."

Dwight Eisenhower's electoral sweep in 1952 helped Goldwater defeat the Democrats' Senate Majority Leader, Ernest W. McFarland of Arizona. When questioned, after his victory, about what "kind" of Republican he was, Goldwater replied: "Well, I am not a me-too Republican . . . I am a Republican opposed to the superstate and to gigantic, bureaucratic, centralized authority." He respected Eisenhower and believed their political attitudes were congruent. When the administration's specific proposals, however, belied its rhetoric, Goldwater complained that concessions to "the New Deal philosophy of government" were being made. Eisenhower's "Modern Republicanism" advocated a shift in party strategy away from denunciations of a "dead Roosevelt" to positive policy alternatives. Such Republicans as Arthur Larson, Henry Cabot Lodge, Jr., Malcolm Moos and Milton Eisenhower, advised Eisenhower that old-age security, medical care, unemployment compensation, public housing projects and federal aid to education were essential government responsibilities in an industrial society. Goldwater regretted that Eisenhower was not reversing the New Deal trend. Only a modified approach, not a substantive difference, distinguished Progressive Republicans from the Democrats. This ideological affinity with New Deal collectivism would mean disaster for the party and the nation.

Goldwater's ideas on political decentralization and economic individualism placed him in the "Old Guard" wing of the Republican Party. He served on the Senate Labor Committee on Public Welfare and its subcommittees on Labor (1955), Veteran's Affairs (1955), Aging (1959), Education (1960), Migratory Labor (1960–62), and Railroad Retirement (1963). Along with Senators William Knowland and John Bricker, he fought to halt welfare state incursions. In a Senate speech of April 8, 1957, he protested President Eisenhower's budget request, charging that while twenty years of New Deal–Fair Deal experiments in socialism had made many Americans susceptible to the doctrine of federal paternalism, Republicans had to repudiate that approach and unshackle the free enterprise system.

> It is equally disillusioning to see the Republican Party plunging headlong into the dismal state experienced by the traditional Democratic principles of Jefferson and Jackson during the days of the New Deal and Fair Deal. As a result of those economical and political misadventures, that great party has now lost its soul of freedom; its spokesmen are peddlers of the philosophy that the Constitution is outmoded, that states' rights are void, and that the only

hope for the future of the United States is for our people to be federally born, federally housed, federally clothed, federally supported in their occupations and to be buried in a federal box in a federal cemetery.

Goldwater's degree of support for the Eisenhower administration's programs ranged from a high of 63% to a low of 52%. Invariably, he voted against legislation that initiated or continued federal social welfare responsibilities. Representing an arid state dependent for its prosperity on the federal reclamation system did prevent him, however, from opposing such federal works projects as the Colorado River Storage Program. He favored returning the tidelands to the states, exempting independent natural gas producers from federal control, and the Bricker amendment. When the Senate voted on December 2, 1954, to censure Senator Joseph McCarthy, Goldwater prophesied that in another era, when they understood the meaning of his implacable hostility to Communists, Americans would revere McCarthy. Several years later, he repeated that "because Joe McCarthy lived, we are a safer, freer, more vigilant nation. . . . " Goldwater's advocacy of national "right-to-work" legislation and mandatory secret union votes before strikes could begin alarmed labor organizations.

> I strongly favor enactment of State right-to-work laws which forbid contracts that make union membership a condition of employment. These laws are aimed at removing a great blight on the contemporary American scene, and I am at a loss to understand why so many people who so often profess concern for civil rights and civil liberties are vehemently opposed to them.

The American Federation of Labor and the Congress of Industrial Organizations tried in 1958 to prevent his re-election. When the Senate approved the 1959 Kennedy-Ervin labor bill (90 to 1), Goldwater cast the sole dissenting vote because this labor reform bill did not eliminate "black-mail picketing" and secondary boycotts. John Kennedy believed his Senate colleague "would be satisfied with no bill that did not destroy the organized trade union movement in the United States."

Goldwater's voting record exemplified his conviction that the Republican party should present an unequivocal choice to the American voter. "Let the Republican Party quit copying the New Deal seeking only for votes," he told a Republican National Committee meeting in 1959, "and remember that a two party system needs two philosophies, not just one." The 1960 Republican platform, however, exhibited no "Old Guard" skepticism regarding the federal government's role in American life. An Eisenhower administration sponsored study of 1959, *Decisions for a Better America*, provided the Republican conspectus. The party promised to extend federal aid to education, double the rate of immigration, submit a medical care program and extensive civil rights legislation, and help labor win "closed shop" agreements. Eisenhower's "New Republicanism" was to be sustained by the successor Nixon-Lodge administration.

Republicans believe in a central government vigilantly alert to the needs of the people and strong enough to defend the people, to help keep the economy in balance, and to make certain that a life of dignity is within the reach of every American. . . . The Republican Party stands for a strong responsive Federal Government opening and advancing economic opportunity for the American people . . . raising its strength to ward off inflation and depression . . . restraining and disciplining any who use their power against the common welfare regulating wisely when the national interest demands it.

Goldwater refused to challenge Nixon at the 1960 convention. He exhorted Republicans to unite and ignore any heretical platform principles because, despite "individual points of difference, the Republican Party Platform deserves the support of every American over the blueprint for socialism presented by the Democrats."

Conservative Republicans attributed the party's narrow defeat in 1960 to the party's derivative and imitative liberalism. Millions of conservatives, they claimed, refused to vote because no real choice existed. Nixon and Lodge had devoted unnecessary effort to win Northern votes when the South and Midwest provided a natural and congenial constituency. "We who are conservatives," Goldwater commented, "will stoutly maintain that 1960 was a repeat performance of 1944 and 1948, when we offered the voters insufficient choices. . . . " The Republican right wing, in the aftermath of the 1960 defeat, succeeded in securing many strategic party positions. Goldwater withstood the liberal Republican stratagem of Governor Rockefeller and New York Senators Javits and Keating to eliminate him from the post (to which the party had elected him three times) as Chairman of the Republican Senatorial Campaign Committee. He used this position to preach conservatism and captivate important party leaders. "I am watching with growing hope and enthusiasm your political strategy," General Douglas MacArthur wrote to him in 1961. "A great vacuum exists that you can fill. Never let up and never flinch. Dramatic and startling events lie just ahead."

With his syndicated column "How Do You Stand, Sir?" and his book, *The Conscience of a Conservative* (1960), Goldwater attracted a burgeoning following to his crusade against the federal government. From 1960 through 1964, *Conscience of a Conservative* sold over three and a half million copies. Goldwater's entire political philosophy, as expressed in this apologia, could be reduced to Calvin Coolidge's maxim that "where the people are the government, they do not get rid of their burdens by attempting to unload them on the government" and Grover Cleveland's admonition that "though the people supported the government, the government should not support the people." Moreover, in no respect did Goldwater acquiesce to the social welfare developments of American history since 1930. That there existed a special ideological selectivity in Goldwater's attacks on the "superstate" and on "gigantic, bureaucratic centralized authority" is best demonstrated in remembering that he was extremely favorable toward a large military establishment and toward the expansion of federal police powers, especially those of the Federal Bureau of Investigation. Pre–New Deal, rather than anti–New Deal, is the more apposite characterization of his principles.

Conscience of a Conservative castigated domestic policies of Franklin Roosevelt, Harry Truman, and Dwight Eisenhower.

> The farmer is told how much wheat he can grow. The wage earner is at the mercy of national union leaders whose great power is a direct consequence of federal labor legislation. The businessman is hampered by a maze of government regulations, and often by direct government competition. The government takes six per cent of most payrolls in Social Security taxes and thus compels millions of individuals to postpone until later years the enjoyment of wealth they might otherwise enjoy today.

Federal aid to education was unconstitutional and unnecessary. All incomes should be taxed at the same rate. The graduated tax was a confiscatory tax. A free market should be restored to agriculture because price supports dissipated the farmer's freedom and were economically misconceived. Franklin Roosevelt should have made the Social Security Act of 1936 voluntary. The pernicious aspect of the social welfare programs inspired by the New Deal was that they debased "the individual from a dignified, industrious self-reliant *spiritual* being into a dependent animal creature without his knowing it. There is no avoiding this damage to character under the Welfare State."

Goldwater implored Americans to return to authentic entrepreneurial capitalism, individualism, and the Constitution "as it was written one hundred and eighty years ago, not as it is being interpreted today." The nation had to understand that government regulation and supervision only aggravated social problems. Indeed, the federal government should disengage itself from reform programs begun during the New Deal.

> The government must begin to *withdraw* from a whole series of programs that are outside its constitutional mandate—from social welfare programs, education, public power, agriculture, public housing, urban renewal, and all the other activities that can be better performed by lower levels of government or by private institutions or by individuals. I do not suggest that the federal government drop all of these programs overnight. But I do suggest that we establish, by law, a rigid timetable for a staged withdrawal.

Both *Conscience of a Conservative* and his presidential campaign demonstrated Goldwater's politics of nostalgia or the quest for the *status quo ante-* America before the New Deal. "My aim is not to pass laws," Goldwater wrote, "but to repeal them. It is not to inaugurate new programs, but to cancel old ones that do violence to the Constitution, or that have failed in their purpose, or that have imposed on the people an unwarranted financial burden. I will not attempt to discover whether legislation is 'needed' before I have first determined whether it is constitutionally permissible."

As chairman of the Senatorial Campaign Committee, best-selling author of *Conscience of a Conservative* and vigorous guardian of the "Old Guard" faction's principles, Barry Goldwater became the New Frontier's nemesis in the United States Senate. He became an aggressive leader of the right-wing Republican and Southern Democrat forces that resisted major Kennedy administration proposals. Civil rights legislation, medical care for the aged, tax reform and aid to education were defeated by Congress. In 1962 Goldwater boasted of how congressional conservatives had preserved the national equilibrium from the New Frontier's insouciance:

> Congress has rejected plans for marked change in our political and economic structure. It has refused to open the way to federal management and control of the education system, except through the limited provisions of the National Defense Education Act. It has compelled both Republican and Democratic presidents to reduce ambitious and ill-defined foreign aid programs. It has declined to approve any large-scale expansion of the Social Security Act. It has kept a jealous eye on labor union power. It has refused to sanction federal intervention in local municipal affairs by rejecting a Department of Urban Affairs proposed by the President.

On January 11, 1961, he spoke on "Proposed Republican Principles" to the Senate. This manifesto differed sharply from the 1960 Republican platform and presaged the platform Goldwater Republicans would frame in 1964. He revived a phrase first used by William Graham Sumner and later suggested to Franklin Roosevelt by Raymond Moley—"the forgotten man." Goldwater meant exactly what Sumner did almost a century before. Diligent, dutiful, religious middle-class Americans were being penalized by paternalists in Washington who redistributed their incomes to deprived Americans and, more importantly, to citizens speaking through powerful interests. "The Republican Party in this era in which so many pressure groups are seeking to dominate the 'total man,'" intoned Goldwater, "should be the voice of the ignored individual, 'the forgotten American.'" With the publication in 1962 of "Declaration of Republican Principle and Policy" by the Joint Congressional Committee on Republican Principles, a salient shift in the party's ideology became apparent. The progressive Republicanism suffusing the 1960 platform was absent. This report criticized the Democrats' repudiation of the free enterprise system, its use of governmental coercion in the steel crisis and condemned the federal government's inordinate power. It was a remarkable adumbration of the 1964 platform.

"If you want to make American politics logical and clear and get a final clear-cut decision," Walter Lippmann argued in 1963, "the Republicans ought to nominate Goldwater and at least get a Republican who is a Republican." While Lippmann's statement was not a personal endorsement of Goldwater, it did capture the attitudes of many different people. President Kennedy, for example, "fervently hoped" that Goldwater would oppose him. Kennedy anticipated the easy routing of "right wing radicalism." On January 3, 1964, Barry Goldwater declared his candidacy for the Republican presidential nomination promising to offer the American voter "a choice, not an echo." This pronouncement implied the strategic decision to redefine Republicanism and "to accentuate its differences with the New Deal and its legacy."

Barry Goldwater succeeded in becoming the first Republican "Congressional conservative" to be nominated for the presidency since Warren Harding by embodying the "policy preferences of many party activists and leaders" whose dominance at the convention did not represent the "ascendancy of an ideological faction alien to the party." Goldwater's Republicanism evoked frenetic support from those party members frustrated with adjustments and acquiescence to New Deal policies. What excited his devotees was his scorn for the politics of compromise. Nelson Polsby and Aaron Wildavsky have isolated the distinguishing characteristics of Goldwater convention delegates as "their emphasis on internal criteria for decision, on what they believe 'deep down inside': their rejection of compromise; their lack of orientation toward winning; their stress on the style and purity of decision—integrity, consistency, adherence to internal norms." This "fundamentalist conservatism" was strong in the Middle and Rocky Mountain West among Republicans who believed they were "the heart and soul of the Republican Party, uncorrupted by the liberalism that . . . softened the eastern wing, and [who wanted] to recapture the conservative spirit of the 1920's and earlier times." They were part of what Seymour Martin Lipset once described as the "radical right"—individuals trying "to eliminate from American political life those persons which threaten its values or its economic interests." "For twenty years, the controversy on the conservative position has hovered over our party like a menacing specter," cried Everett Dirksen placing Goldwater's name in nomination at the 1964 convention. In Dirksen's opinion, enough concessions had been made. At last the party had a Republican capable of extricating America from the morass. "Why is it that this man who so certainly has sounded the call to conservatism," asked Dirksen, "should be subjected to the abuse which has been heaped upon him? Is it because he offers a choice, a clear-cut choice, that the Democrat Party, as now constituted, does not dare face?"

Barry Goldwater achieved the nomination because he persuaded convention delegates that he could obliterate the welfare state. He expressed one facet of a very persistent theme in American political thought that of "anti-governmentalism." For Richard Hofstadter, Goldwater personified the "revolt against the whole modern condition as the old-fashioned American sees it—against the world of organization and bureaucracy, the welfare state, our urban disorders, secularism, the decline of American entrepreneurial bravura, the apparent disappearance of individualism and individuality and the emergence of unwelcome international burdens." If Henry Commager was right in contending that Goldwater's views did not even "rise to the dignity of clichés" and were "declarations of intellectual bankruptcy," they were sufficient enough, in any case, to thrust a new function upon the Republican party. They dared to test whether it was possible to reverse and repeal American political history. And they pursued that goal passionately even though so much past social welfare legislation represented genuinely bipartisan measures which would never have occurred without a national consensus operative in the ranks of both parties.

The ideological purism possessing conservative Republicans became manifest when they rejected amendments to the 1964 platform (on civil rights, the John Birch Society, and tactical control of nuclear weapons) offered by the party's liberal wing. The fragility and diversity of American political parties and the presumptive necessity to embrace the political center for electoral victory has traditionally precluded extreme doctrinaire behavior. Yet both the 1964 Republican platform and the refusal to placate the losing faction by proffering it the vice-presidential nomination prevented party reconciliation. The Goldwater Republicans' intransigence [Paul Tillet noted] exhibited a "churlish and paranoid desire for vengeance rather than for accommodation and a closing of ranks against the Democrats." "I know we probably won't win in November," remarked one Goldwater assistant after the nomination. "Winning control of one of the two major parties is victory enough for me." Karl Hess, Goldwater's chief speech writer, explained that the Senator knew the nature of his movement was not organizational, but ideological. The salvific message would be brought to his "true believers." Not since William Jennings Bryan had there been a presidential aspirant so determined to propagate a holy cause. After carefully studying him during the 1964 campaign, Theodore H. White could only conclude that Barry Goldwater wanted "believers" more than he wanted the presidency. Precisely because he was an evangelist reinforcing the original beliefs of sympathetic audiences, Goldwater was unwilling rather than unprepared to forge his dissent into a political program with national appeal. Programs never replaced the polemics which had catapulated him to party prominence.

The Politics of Poverty

Elinor Graham

In January 1964, a man familiar to congressional surroundings delivered his first address to a joint session of Congress in his new role as President of the United States. As he presented his presidential program to Congress, Lyndon Johnson called for an "unconditional war on poverty," a government commitment "not only to relieve the symptoms of poverty, but to cure it; and above all, to prevent it."

The complex of ideological themes and political programs officially recognized and initiated by this address—all under the slogan of a War on Poverty—is the topic of this paper. The analysis developed here views this "war" as a key ingredient in the social and political ideology embraced by President Johnson, his administrative officials, and his advisers. As part of an ideology, it is designed to motivate elements in the society to political action. The language of the War on Poverty and the form of its accompanying social-welfare programs are set within the boundaries of traditional social beliefs, arise from the pressure of political needs, and are molded by the nature of those groups seeking action, as well as by the official bodies from which they must receive approval.

Poverty, consequently, is now a major preoccupation of hundreds of public officials, statisticians and social planners across the nation. In less than a year it has been thrust dramatically into the center of governmental programming on local, regional, and national levels. President Johnson has called for "total victory" in a national War on Poverty—"a total commitment by the President, and this Congress, and this Nation, to pursue victory over the most ancient of mankind's enemies." Joining the administration forces and local and state governments, private social-welfare organizations and institutions normally engaged in nonwelfare activities have increasingly indicated an awareness of possibilities, and a willingness, to engage their organizational resources in "extrainstitutional" activities aimed at the alleviation of poverty. Colleges, churches, and corporations have plunged into a potpourri of activities designed to provide "opportunities" for deserving members of low-income groups in forms, and to an extent, that welfare workers could previously conceive only in their wildest dreams.

Given an "understanding of the enemy" which emphasizes the special characteristics of certain low-income groups that cannot easily be integrated into the market economy, what "strategy of attack" is advocated by the national policy-makers? The "war on poverty" proposed in 1964

SOURCE: Elinor Graham, in *Poverty as a Public Issue*, ed. Ben B. Seligman (New York: Free Press, 1965), pp. 231–50.

consisted of a ten-point attack which strikingly resembled the President's entire domestic program: income tax cuts, a civil rights bill, Appalachian regional development, urban and rural community rehabilitation, youth programs, teenage and adult vocational training and basic educational programs, and hospital insurance for the aged. A special "antipoverty package" was introduced—the Economic Opportunity Act of 1964. The Office of Economic Opportunity created by this legislation was to be the headquarters for the new "war."

Administration of the Economic Opportunity Act and supporting programs, as well as plans for future expansion, indicate that the War on Poverty seeks to mobilize the social services of the nation along three major lines: youth education and employment programs, planned regional and community redevelopment, and vocational training and retraining under the beginnings of a national manpower policy.

Under this "strategy of attack," aid to the poor is, in theory, provided in the nature of a new and expanded "opportunity environment." Such aid is primarily directed toward the youth and employable heads of poor families; it will not reach the really critical poverty categories—the aged, female heads of families, and poor farm families—except in the form of improvements in the surrounding physical and economic environments or the administration of welfare and health services. As the Council of Economic Advisers noted in their 1964 report, the proposed programs are designed "to equip and to permit the poor of the Nation to produce and to earn . . . the American standard of living by their own efforts and contributions." Those Americans who are not in a physical or family position which allows them to earn their way out of poverty will not be immediately aided by the programs under the War on Poverty. This situation simply illustrates the difference between social needs defined in a statistical manner and a political designation of poverty. It does not indicate that the War on Poverty is a political hoax or a hollow slogan to attract votes; on the contrary, its ideology and programs respond to social and political needs of a very real, although very different, nature, than those of poverty per se.

THE SOCIOLOGY OF POVERTY PROGRAMS

It is useful to locate welfare-state programs on two scales, vertically and horizontally, in order to visualize the range and nature of programs open to government planners in formulating the War on Poverty and to understand the implications of the particular path chosen. The vertical scale of our imaginary axes indicates at one end whether the poverty-stricken are singled out of the total society as objects for special aid or, at the opposite pole, social services and income payments are provided to all as a right of citizenship. The latter method is followed in most of the Swedish welfare programs. Family payments, old-age pensions, and health services are provided for all members of the society regardless of their financial position. Most United States welfare programs, including those proposed under the War on Poverty, are located at the opposite pole: programs are focused at a particular low-income category and need must be proven in order to receive aid. The second (and horizontal) scale indicates at one end that aid may be provided in the form of direct income payments and at the other extreme through social services. The major portion of the welfare activities in the United States, and particularly those connected with the War on Poverty, are found in the service category, even though, as was argued above, the nature of American poverty in the sixties indicates an urgent need for consideration of direct income payments to critical poverty-stricken groups.

Certain important implications follow from the need-based and service-oriented nature of the War on Poverty programs. First, separation of the poor from the rest of the society by means of need requirements, increases the visibility of the low-income earners. This is a "war" *on poverty*—the very nature of such a proposal requires an exposure of "the enemy" in its human form. In addition, separation of the poor creates a donor-donee relationship whether it exists between the income-tax-paying middle and upper classes and the low-income earners, or the social worker and his client. In the context of American social philosophy, such a situation enhances the self-image of the well-to-do and places a stigma of failure and dependency upon aid recipients. Above all, it is "the American way" to approach social-welfare issues, for it places the burden of responsibility upon the individual and not upon the socioeconomic system. Social services are preferred to income payments in an ideological atmosphere which abhors "handouts."

Second, a focus upon *poverty* allows for a redefinition of the racial clash into the politically understandable and useful terms of a conflict between the "haves" and the "have-nots." The donor-donee relationship, sharply cast into relief by the poverty label, reasserts and stabilizes the power of the political elite, whose positions have been threatened by enfranchisement of the Negro.

Third, the social-service orientation, particularly the stress upon the "reorganization" and "total mobilization" of existing programs, is strongly supported by the nature of the experimental programs started during the Kennedy years. These programs and, of more importance, the ideas and "method of attack" which they initiated, are vigorously advocated by a well-organized and sophisticated lobby within the administrative branch.

Fourth, the social-service orientation of the War on Poverty is *activity-* and *job*-creating for the middle and upper classes. Provision of social services, as opposed to income payments, requires the formation of new organizations and institutions which in turn are the source of activities and income-paying roles for the nation's expanding number of college-educated individuals. The War on Poverty, its programs and ideology, are a response to the demands of an educated "new class": it provides a legitimate outlet for the energies of a group that poses a greater threat to the political system and moral fabric of the society than the inadequately educated poor who are the official objects of aid.

IDEOLOGY AND POVERTY

A nation which confidently points to its unparalleled level of wealth, the "magnificent abundance" of the American way of life, has been suddenly and surprisingly engaged in the public unveiling of the impoverished degradation of one-fifth of its population. Affluence and poverty confront each other, and the shock of the encounter is reflected in the phrase that acknowledges the "stranger's" presence: a "paradox"—the "paradox of poverty in the midst of plenty." This mysterious stranger is apparently inconsistent with the nation's vision of itself and particularly with its moral notions of equality.

One supposes that there is an element of honest surprise and, with many, disbelief, for they *know* that if you work hard and take advantage of all of the opportunities available, you *can* climb out of poverty and reach the top—well, perhaps not *the* top, but certainly a comfortable level of living. It is axiomatic. Numerous individuals will tediously cite their own life experiences as examples of this general law of dynamics of American society. The following account was provided by a retired educator who sought to establish his qualification to talk about poverty in the sixties:

> I was born in a homestead on the lowland swamps of Louisiana. There were no schools. We lived off the land. And, since I have viewed the very sections of the underprivileged and poor people in the Appalachian highland, I decided I must have been very poor, because those children there have much more now than I had. We lived from game, and we had no electric lights. We got food if there were plenty of ducks and geese and rabbits. . . . I was a drop-in at school when they finally got a little one- or two-room school. I mean, I dropped in when there were no potatoes to plant or corn to pull, or something of that sort. I have three college degrees from standard universities, and I never spent a day on a college campus during regular session. I belong to the old school. I took correspondence; I did some summer terms, and I did extension work, traveling sometimes a hundred miles each weekend to take it. So I think I know what it means to get an education the hard way. . . . I understand the phrase in our help to the underprivileged.

Everyone who is over thirty will say that they know what it is like to be poor because they lived during the Great Depression; that is taken as automatic qualification. When attacked by his Democratic "brethren" for a lack of understanding of the complexities of the problem, Representative Griffin (R.-Mich.) responded with, "my father worked most of his life in a plant; and I worked my way through school, and I believe I do know a little bit about poverty." Without denying the achievements of the poor boy from the swamps of Louisiana who is now a distinguished educator, or the son of a worker holding the office of U.S. congressman, such accounts and their implications for the "struggling young men" from present-day poor families reflect a general confusion of the income and social-class mobility of an individual with a rising national standard of living. The American dream is substituted for the American reality and evidence drawn from the second is said to be proof of the first.

President Johnson intertwined the two concepts when he declared in his 1964 War on Poverty message that:

> With the growth of our country has come opportunity for our people— opportunity to educate our children, to use our energies in productive work, to incease our leisure—opportunity for almost every American to hope that through work and talent he could create a better life for himself and his family.

Traditional themes of the bright boy attaining entrance to the world of wealth through "work and talent" are intermingled with the profit figures of economic growth. In suggesting that the benefits of a rising standard of living include increased opportunity for bettering income and even social-class position, two distinct and different concepts are equated for ideological purposes.

Fusion of dream and actuality in the national vision has been strongly influenced by the American business creed and its image of the relationship between the economic system and the individual. Benefits derived from the economic growth of the nation are not conceived as social products. The idealized "free-enterprise" system produces the national wealth through the efforts of atomized individuals operating within a "free competitive market system with individual freedom." A guarantee of the rights of the individual to insure his freedom and free opportunity are thus essential. Since mythology need not correspond to reality (particularly if believed in strongly enough), equality of opportunity is assumed and is "proved" through the individual success stories which abound in the popular literature. Such "proof" is, however, subject to a great deal of doubt. Citing several sociological studies, the authors of *The American Business Creed** observe that a survey of the overall statistical situation "might well lead to more tempered conclusions about American freedom of opportunity."

With an image of itself that denies the possibility of widespread poverty, a nation bent on "recognizing realities" must squeeze the poor in through the basement window. We are told that we are not faced with extensive conditions of poverty (as are other less fortunate nations). Poverty in the United States is "grinding poverty," found only in "pockets of poverty" and has defied all laws of genetics to acquire an hereditary quality exhibited in the "ruthless pattern" and "cycle of poverty." This is not a

---

*Francis X. Sutton et al. (Cambridge: Harvard University Press, 1956).

case of good old-fashioned poverty; it is a special and uniquely American 1964 brand.

A particularly vivid exposition of this version of poverty can be found in the explanation of the Economic Opportunity Act prepared by Sargent Shriver's office for the first congressional hearings. Much of the credit for the modern version of poverty expounded within its covers must go to the influence of John Kenneth Galbraith's writings. He broke the poor into two groups—those afflicted with *case* poverty and those who are victims of *insular* poverty. Characteristics of the individual afflicted with case poverty prevent him from mastering his environment, while the environment proves to be the handicapping factor for those living in "islands of poverty." In both situations an hereditary factor is introduced either in fact (as a physical tendency toward poor health or mental deficiency) or in effect through the deficiencies of the social environment (as with poor schools, lack of job opportunities, lack of motivation, and direction from parents). Whether or not such a view corresponds to reality, it should be recognized that when one maintains that the society is affluent, poverty can hardly be tolerated as a widespread phenomenon and must be of a very special and individual variety. With such a thesis, one is not likely to observe that an average American family with an income of $5665—the median for all families in 1960—may not feel particularly affluent at this "modest but adequate" level.

Where, then, are the roots of poverty in an affluent society? Few combatants in the war of ideologies argue that the fault underlies the American landscape and may be lodged in the economic system. The principle according to which the wealth of the society is divided is left unscathed. On official levels, voices do not openly suggest that a system which distributes economic goods solely upon the basis of the individual's present or past functional role within the economy may be at the source of American poverty now and increasingly so in the future. Although not reflecting official opinion, the statement of the Ad Hoc Committee on the Triple Revolution was a notable exception. This group of distinguished educators, labor leaders, economists, and critics suggested in part that:

> The economy of abundance can sustain all citizens in comfort and economic security whether or not they engage in what is commonly reckoned as work. . . . We urge, therefore, that society through its appropriate legal and governmental institutions undertake an unqualified commitment to provide every individual in every family with an adequate income as a matter of right.

Right-wing reaction is clear and quite predictable when the legitimacy of the American economic system is questioned in any context. There was no doubt in the mind of Representative Martin (R.-Neb.) that the suggestions of the committee were of "the same kind of plan worked out in Communist nations." Such a reaction hardly leaves room for political debate.

Where questions regarding "the system" are taboo, those focusing upon the individual are welcome and quite comprehensible to the political protagonists. In acceptable political circles, the causes of poverty are sought in the process through which individuals acquire qualities enabling them to succeed and share in the national wealth. Conservatives argue that the fault lies with the poor for being lazy or stupid, and not taking advantage of opportunities to obtain education, good health, a marketable skill, and a stable family life. "The fact is that most people who have no skill, have had no education for the same reason—low intelligence or low ambition!" says Barry Goldwater. On the other hand, liberals maintain that something is wrong with the present means provided for individuals to obtain these desirable attributes—in short, the society is at fault: the poor are the "have-not people of America. They are denied, deprived, disadvantaged, and they are discriminated against," argues Walter Reuther of the United Auto Workers. President Johnson and Sargent Shriver, commander of the poverty forces, bow to both groups. They maintain that it is first necessary to change the attitudes of the poor—to give them achievement motivations by changing "indifference to interest, ignorance to awareness, resignation to ambition, and an attitude of withdrawal to one of participation." At the same time, present education, social-welfare, and job-training programs sponsored at all levels of government and in both the public and private sectors of society, must be coordinated, consolidated and expanded to provide a new "opportunity environment" for the poor.

The emphasis is upon the process by which Americans attain the attributes necessary to achieve economic success rather than the legitimacy of the system to distribute the national wealth. This view is enhanced by the assumption that Americans, and poor Americans in particular, must earn and "want to earn" any social or economic benefits they receive. In our society, states former Senator Goldwater, one receives rewards by "merit and not by fiat"—essentially, you earn your keep or you get out (or stay out):

> I strongly believe that all people are entitled to an opportunity . . . to get an education and to earn a living *in keeping with the value of their work* [emphasis supplied]. . . . But I do not believe that the mere fact of having little money entitles everybody, regardless of circumstance, to be permanently maintained by the taxpayers at an average or comfortable standard of living.

Conservatives make no effort to conceal their reliance on this basic assumption; they quite frankly do not want to change the present distribution of wealth, or potential advantages they may have in gaining a greater future share. They are successful because they deserve to be successful, while others are poor because they are innately incapable of doing any better. This assumption about human nature is an integral part of the business creed, for the idealized economic system is dependent upon the "achievement motivations" of the individual. These crucial motivations could easily be destroyed if people became dependent upon goverment doles. If this happened, the greatest welfare system of all, the "free-enterprise system," would be destroyed. As the witness from the Chamber of Commerce explained to Representative Edith Green during the House antipoverty hearings, the Chamber does not support "programs for people" because:

> ... economic measures to improve the efficiency of production and thus to get a larger output for our people from the same input of materials and manpower and capital goods is one of the greatest contributions to wealth that has ever been discovered in the history of mankind and the United States excels among all nations of the world in providing this kind of welfare.

Despite conservative denunciations, President Johnson eagerly reserves a benevolent role for the federal government, and particularly on an ideological level. He counters conservative views by adding a second act to the drama of the poor, struggling young man working his way to the top in the "free-enterprise system." A magnanimous millionaire, glowing with compassion and wisdom, stretches out a benevolent helping hand to enable "Ragged Dick" to make good in the final panel of the American dream. Evoking an image of a goddess of peace and plenty rather than lanky Uncle Sam, Johnson declares that both at home and abroad, "We will extend the helping hand of a just nation to the poor and helpless and the oppressed." In the American reality, however, "we" take care to see that the "helping hand" doesn't contain money or tangible goods—just opportunities to earn a better way of life and opportunities to *learn* to "want to earn" in the American way.

Such a sense of *noblesse oblige* is not inherent in the actual programs and techniques proposed in the War on Poverty, but it plays a part in the language which is inevitably used to describe them (and which is perhaps latent within our "progressive" attitudes toward social welfare). It is also the result of the effective control and administration of the government by the affluent and educated classes. In short, the official government attitude toward poverty should be expected to reflect the views arising from the life-situations of those who have formulated it. In speaking of poverty, no one bothers to deny or hide the fact that the federal government is an instrumentality of the successful classes. This is assumed. The poor are recognized as not having a significant political voice. The entire War on Poverty was created, inspired, and will be carried out by the affluent. Action by the upper classes and all superior groups is urged on moral grounds, because it is right, because, as Senator Robert Kennedy stated simply, "those of us who are better off, who do not have that problem, have a responsibility to our fellow citizens who do."

Without an economic crisis which affects the upper-income groups as well as the poor, the social philosophy of the federal antipoverty programs will necessarily contain this strong moral emphasis. Caught between the language of American social mythology and the attitudes generated by the existing social and political realities of a wealthy nation ruled by a distinct class of successful men, the public debate generated by the proposed "war" can only reveal our poverty of ideology. Conservatives balk at action because the poor are "getting what they deserve," and liberals cannot seem to act without assuming the "white man's burden." The militants of the new "war" look for the enemy and find him all too often in the personal attributes of the poor. The remedy offered for poverty amounts to a middle-class success formula (and, perhaps it *is* the route to success in American society): education, a stable family life, and above all, the proper attitudes. In short, there appears to be justification for the charge that the War on Poverty can be more accurately characterized as a "war on the poor."

THE POLITICS OF POVERTY AND RACE

Confronted with a social ideology which easily obscures the existence of poverty, and lacking a thunderous economic crisis that directly threatens the middle and upper classes, the public concern with poverty of a traditionally reactive government is most remarkable. Why did poverty become a politically important issue in 1964?

When asked the reasons for a War on Poverty, President Johnson and Sargent Shriver presented themselves as puppets of the American people who "are interested in the Government and in themselves making a focused or concentrated effort to attack poverty." A public demand for the elimination of poverty did not, however, exist before it was deliberately made into an issue by the Johnson Administration in 1964. Government programs were not a response to public protests against conditions of poverty for one-fifth of a nation. (An exception to this was perhaps the March on Washington in the summer of 1963, which came close to protesting poverty directly with demands for more jobs; but the publicity impact of this event was channeled into exclusive concern with civil rights.)

After President Johnson announced his War on Poverty in his State of the Union address on January 8, 1964, the nation was deluged with vivid descriptions of the life of the poor, statistical accounts of their number and characteristics, and details of their geographic location. Poverty became such a "problem" that, by the time Shriver testified at the congressional hearings, there was a degree of truth to his statement. The power of the presidency to stimulate the news media into undertaking a massive effort to increase public awareness, if not to generate actual demands for government action, was dramatically demonstrated. This achievement should not, however, obscure the fact that demands for action directly focused upon poverty did not exist prior to the time that the administration began to produce its new policy line.

Political power-needs, rather than an articulated public demand, were at the source of the sudden resolution to recognize poverty in 1964. Briefly, the most plausible occasion for the urgency and publicity devoted to poverty by the Executive Office can be found in the political and emotionally disrupting effects of the civil-rights movement, especially in regard to white morality and the white power structure. Emotionally, the nation needed to redefine the racial conflict as a conflict between the "haves" and the "have-nots." Politically, a transmutation of the civil-rights movement secured the threatened power position of whites as whites, and further eased the agonies of the slow political death of the south. The latter, with its implications for the composition of the national political parties, has held special meaning for Johnson in his struggle to unify the Democratic Party and attain congressional compliance with presidential programs. In practical terms, the War on Poverty and its implications for opening a new field of jobs and social status, is the means by which American society will expand to accommodate the Negroes' demands for integration.

For over four years, white America has been forced into a state of acute consciousness of its prejudices and unexamined beliefs. In a white man's world, however, Negroes from the time of their early years live with a racial awareness. They must know and understand this world in a very practical sense in order to survive. But whites "experience race" at a more mature age—they are not "born" with it—and in the past they gained their experience somewhat at their own convenience. Suddenly in the sixties, the Negro has become a political power; he has become a "new" Negro who won't fit into the old images. This forced racial confrontation has caught the white off-guard. He does not possess a cultural reservoir that would allow him to interact—or avoid interaction—easily and unemotionally. Political protests, in short, have resulted in a social dislocation of the Negro and have created a necessity for both races to become aware of themselves and their inter-projective images. Politically, this awareness and the knowledge it can bring, is both necessary and beneficial. But this is an inconvenience for the white, an inconvenience requiring extra effort that may result in heightened tension as well as awareness.

The task of knowing is greatly simplified for the white American if he substitutes "poverty" for "race." He can more easily understand the frustrations of job hunting or unemployment than what it means to possess a black skin. "Poverty" has a comfortable sound to it, it makes "sense" and is not emotionally upsetting. Politically speaking, to *redefine* race and civil-rights as a manifestation of conditions of poverty, opens a path for action. Where race and nationalism are vivid, emotion-based issues, not easily resolved through reason and logic, conflict between the "haves" and the "have-nots" is well understood. The Western world has a supply of practical tools and intellectual theories with which this persistent enemy can be explained and controlled. Marxian ideology, liberal benevolence, or a religious morality all allow for practical political action that is denied when confronted by race in and of itself. Whether or not the civil-rights movement dramatized existing conditions of poverty, white Americans had to raise the poverty issue to relieve the emotional tension and political impasse created by the racial confrontation. The dollar costs of a War on Poverty are exchanged for the high emotional price-tag attached to race.

Aside from this exchange of emotion for practicality, poverty redefines civil rights in a manner that secures the power positions of white public leaders and places them in control of a movement which frequently has attempted to exclude them, on racial grounds, from exercising a directing influence. Three groups are the principal beneficiaries of this effect: the white liberal "sympathetic" to the Negro cause, public officials in the large urban centers, and the southern politician.

The white liberal has found himself increasingly excluded from policy-making positions in the civil-rights movement. He has been told that he could contribute his warm body and little else in a revolution which was felt to express legitimately only the suffering of the American Negro. However, when the "movement" is placed in the context of a battle between the wealthy and the poor, between the "power-lords" and the "exploited underdog," it is possible to carve out a legitimate place for whites within a dynamic and powerful social movement. Such a recasting of the Negro struggle cuts across racial boundaries to transform it into a fight for "all humanity." A new struggle is created which has a great potential for rallying sustained activities within accepted political channels. But, also, it may push the Negro to the background once again, for he does not have the same priority for a leading role in the new antipoverty struggle. Professional and respectable, social revolutionaries assume directing positions in a poverty war whereas indigenous leadership was beginning to develop out of the civil-rights struggle.

Public officials in the large urban centers have also found their authority threatened and severely shaken by a groundswell which they had to appease in order to survive. Something had to be offered the angry Negro segment of the populace. They couldn't offer to make a Negro white, or at least they couldn't overtly approach the racial question in this manner, although such an objective may underlie the antipoverty programs offered the Negro, with their emphasis upon instilling white middle-class motivations and values. They could, however, offer to train him, to educate him, and perhaps give him a little more *hope* of obtaining solid employment. In other words, the Negro must be viewed as "poor," as deprived of services which the government apparatus can provide, in order to engage him in political bargaining. The demonstrators are taken off the streets and placed in the hands of the welfare bureaucracies and the new "antipoverty" programs which can placate demands more quickly than the courts. (And, hopefully, in a more substantial and lasting manner.) This need exists on the national level, but in its War on Poverty the federal government has left the distribution of public goods and services to the local political leaders, whose positions are most immediately threatened by the volatile protest and developing political power of the Negro.

Reaction to the race riots of previous summers provides ample illustration of the ideological function of an antipoverty slogan and the practical role of its accompanying programs. Immediately after the 1964 riots in New York City, Wagner made a special trip to Washington to see if more antipoverty projects and other federal money could be directed toward the slum areas of the city. As *The New York Times* interpreted the visit:

> It would be highly surprising if Mr. Wagner—Mayor of the city where the present epidemic of racial disturbances began—did not mean, as part of his mission, to remind members of the House of the intimate connection between the battle against poverty and the battle against riots. . . . The antipoverty bill, in the new perspective given by the disturbances of this long, hot summer, is also an anti-riot bill. The members of the House of Representatives will do well to bear that in mind when the time comes for a vote.

The fact that Wagner's trip produced few promises for programs and less cash was not as important as the public assurance that something could and would be done. Fortunately, the city had initiated its own antipoverty planning in the spring and could point to several programs already underway. Both large federal juvenile-delinquency programs, Mobilization for Youth and Haryou-Act, as well as the city's own program, Job Opportunities in Neighborhoods, were paraded before public view. In addition, the city signed a contract providing a $223,225 grant for Youth in Action, Inc., to develop an antipoverty program for youth in Brooklyn's Bedford-Stuyvesant area. A job-finding project for semiskilled and unskilled youngsters was accelerated. Programs of training and basic education conducted under MDTA received personal inspections from the mayor with attendant publicity.

Not only has the President's War on Poverty provided evidence of sincere efforts to alleviate some of the needs of the low-income Negro ghettos, but it also provided white society with a defense against charges of overt racism. Poverty and racism have joined hands to create the Negro's hell—the effects of one cannot be separated easily from the other. When given the choice, however, white society prefers to attribute the source of Negro resentment and protests to poverty. *The New York Times* employed this defense when it maintained that the race riots were "as much demonstrations against Negro poverty as against discrimination and what some call 'policy brutality'." In this respect, we should note the extent to which right-wing politicians ignore the racial aspect of the Negro protest and refer to it almost exclusively as a conflict between the "haves" and the "have-nots." They simply make it clear that they are on the side of the "haves." Morally there may be something wrong with denying privileges on the basis of race, but within the right-wing ideology, there is "nothing wrong" with defending your own property and privileges from someone who is not as successful.

For reasons of a less than morally commendable nature, white America has responded to the Negroes' demands for an integrated society with an antipoverty movement: a response slow in coming and pitifully inadequate at first, but still a response. In terms of realistic social dynamics, integration is not, and will not be, an interpenetration of the old by the new, but will be a process of *expansion* and then assimilation. Societies expand and contract; they do not bend except with passing of generations, and that cannot even be predicted with assurance. Those who are within the socioeconomic structure will not give up their positions to Negroes seeking entrance. New roles must be added to the job structure and new status rungs created in the social ladder.

Such is the function of the War on Poverty. As was pointed out, it is a service-oriented welfare measure. The activity- and job-creating nature of its programs are presently opening and shaping new fields in the social services, a process that is certain to increase its range in the future. New professional positions in community organization and social planning, as well as the clerical and blue-collar jobs created to staff the research institutions and service organizations of the "antipoverty" projects, are particularly accessible to the Negro. This is true, above all, for the now small but increasing ranks of the college educated and professionally trained Negro. The politically dangerous energies of the Negro elite can be molded into socially legitimate channels through the creation of roles in an entirely new area of the nation's job structure.

The Negro asks for integration and receives a War on Poverty: it is perhaps not exactly what he ordered nor in the form he imagined, but it is the first step American society is capable of providing. And it is a step that can lead potentially through jobs and social status toward the dignity and justice he desires.

The Great Society:
A Libertarian Critique

Murray N. Rothbard

The Great Society is the lineal descendant and the intensification of those other pretentiously named polities of twentieth-century America: the Square Deal, the New Freedom, the New Era, the New Deal, the Fair Deal, and the New Frontier. All of these assorted Deals constituted a basic and fundamental shift in American life—a shift from a relatively *laissez-faire* economy and minimal state to a society in which the state is unquestionably king. In the previous century, the government could safely have been ignored by almost everyone; now we have become a country in which the government is the great and unending source of power and privilege. Once a country in which each man could by and large make the decisions for his own life, we have become a land where the state holds and exercises life-and-death power over every person, group, and institution. The great Moloch government, once confined and cabined, has burst its feeble bonds to dominate us all.

The basic reason for this development is not difficult to fathom. It was best summed up by the great German sociologist Franz Oppenheimer; Oppenheimer wrote that there were fundamentally two, and only two, paths to the acquisition of wealth. One route is the production of a good or service and its voluntary exchange for the goods or services produced by others. This method—the method of the free market—Oppenheimer termed "the economic means" to wealth. The other path, which avoids the necessity for production and exchange, is for one or more persons to seize other people's products by the use of physical force. This method of robbing the fruits of another man's production was shrewdly named by Oppenheimer the "political means." Throughout history, men have been tempted to employ the "political means" of seizing wealth rather than expend effort in production and exchange. It should be clear that while the market process multiples production, the political, exploitative means is parasitic and, as with all parasitic action, discourages and drains off production and output in society. To regularize and order a permanent system of predatory exploitation, men have created the state, which Oppenheimer brilliantly defined as "the organization of the political means."

Every act of the state is necessarily an occasion for inflicting burdens and assigning subsidies and privileges. By seizing revenue by means of coercion and assigning rewards as it disburses the funds, the state *creates*

SOURCE: Murray N. Rothbard, in *The Great Society Reader: The Failure of American Liberalism*, eds. Marvin E. Gettleman and David Mermelstein (New York: Random House, 1967), pp. 503–11.

ruling and ruled "classes" or "castes"; for one example, classes of what Calhoun discerned as net "taxpayers" and "tax-consumers," those who live off taxation. And since by its nature, predation can only be supported out of the surplus of production above subsistence, the ruling class must constitute a minority of the citizenry.

Since the state, nakedly observed, is a mighty engine of organized predation, state rule, throughout its many millennia of recorded history, could be preserved only by persuading the bulk of the public that its rule has not really been exploitative: that, on the contrary, it has been necessary, beneficent, even, as in the Oriental despotisms, divine. Promoting this ideology among the masses has ever been a prime function of intellectuals, a function that has created the basis for co-opting a corps of intellectuals into a secure and permanent berth in the state apparatus. In former centuries, these intellectuals formed a priestly caste that was able to wrap a cloak of mystery and quasi divinity about the actions of the state for a credulous public; nowadays, the apologia for the state takes on more subtle and seemingly scientific forms. The process remains essentially the same.

In the United States, a strong libertarian and antistatist tradition prevented the process of statization from taking hold at a very rapid pace. The major force in its propulsion has been that favorite theater of state expansionism, brilliantly identified by Randolph Bourne as "the health of the state": namely, war. For although in wartime various states find themselves in danger, from one another, every state has found war a fertile field for spreading the myth among its subjects that *they* are the ones in deadly danger from which their state is protecting them. In this way states have been able to dragoon their subjects into fighting and dying to save them under the pretext that the *subjects* were being saved from the dread Foreign Enemy. In the United States, the process of statization began in earnest under cover of the Civil War (conscription, military rule, income tax, excise taxes, high tariffs, national banking and credit expansion for favored businesses, paper money, land grants to railroads), and reached full flower as a result of World Wars I and II, to finally culminate in the Great Society.

The recently emerging group of "libertarian conservatives" in the United States have grasped a part of the recent picture of accelerated statism, but their analysis suffers from several fatal blind spots. One is their complete failure to realize that war, culminating in the present garrison state and military-industrial economy, has been the royal road to aggravated statism in America. On the contrary, the surge of reverent patriotism that war always brings to conservative hearts, coupled with their eagerness to don buckler and armor against the "international Communist conspiracy," has made the conservatives the most eager and enthusiastic partisans of the Cold War. Hence their inability to see the enormous distortions and interventions imposed upon the economy by the enormous system of war contracts.

Another conservative blind spot is their failure to identify *which groups* have been responsible for the burgeoning of statism in the United States. In the conservative demonology, the responsibility belongs only to liberal intellectuals, aided and abetted by trade unions and farmers. Big businessmen, on the other hand, are curiously exempt from blame (farmers are small enough businessmen, apparently, to be fair game for censure.) How, then, do conservatives deal with the glaringly evident onrush of big businessmen to embrace Lyndon Johnson and the Great Society? Either by mass stupidity (failure to read the works of free-market economists), subversion by liberal intellectuals (e.g., the education of the Rockefeller brothers at Lincoln School), or craven cowardice (the failure to stand foursquare for free-market principles in the face of governmental power). Almost never is *interest* pinpointed as an overriding reason for statism among businessmen. This failure is all the more curious in the light of the fact that the *laissez-faire* liberals of the eighteenth and nineteenth centuries (e.g., the Philosophical Radicals in England, the Jacksonians in the United States) were never bashful about identifying and attacking the web of special privileges granted to businessmen in the mercantilism of their day.

In fact, one of the main driving forces of the statist dynamic of twentieth century America has been big businessmen, and this long before the Great Society. Gabriel Kolko, in his path-breaking *Triumph of Conservatism*, has shown that the shift toward statism in the Progressive period was impelled by the very big business groups who were supposed, in the liberal mythology, to be defeated and regulated by the Progressive and New Freedom measures. Rather than a "people's movement" to check big business, the drive for regulatory measures, Kolko shows, stemmed from big businessmen whose attempts at monopoly had been defeated by the competitive market, and who then turned to the federal government as a device for compulsory cartellization. This drive for cartellization through government accelerated during the New Era of the 1920s and reached its apex in Franklin Roosevelt's NRA. Significantly, this exercise in cartellizing collectivism was put over by organized big business; after Herbert Hoover, who had done much to organize and cartellize the economy, had balked at an NRA as going too far toward an outright fascist economy, the US Chamber of Commerce won a promise from FDR that he would adopt such a system. The original inspiration was the corporate state of Mussolini's Italy.

The formal corporatism of the NRA is long gone, but the Great Society retains much of its essence. The locus of social power has been emphatically assumed by the state apparatus. Furthermore, that apparatus is permanently governed by a coalition of big business and big labor groupings, groups that use the state to operate and manage the national economy. The usual tripartite *rapprochement* of big business, big unions, and big government symbolizes the organization of society by blocs, syndicates, and corporations, regulated and privileged by the federal, state, and local governments. What this all amounts to in essence is the "corporate state," which during the 1920s served as a beacon light for big businessmen, big unions, and many liberal intellectuals as the economic system proper to a twentieth century industrial society.

The indispensable intellectual role of engineering popular consent for state rule is played, for the Great Society, by the liberal intelligentsia, who provide the rationale of "general welfare," "humanity," and the "common good" (just as the conservative intellectuals work the other side of the Great Society street by offering the rationale of "national security" and "national interest"). The liberals, in short, push the "welfare" part of our omnipresent welfare–warfare state, while the conservatives stress the warfare side of the pie. This analysis of the role of the liberal intellectuals puts into more sophisticated perspective the seeming "sellout" of these intellectuals as compared to their role during the 1930s. Thus, among numerous other examples, there is the seeming anomaly of A. A. Berle and David Lilienthal, cheered and damned as flaming progressives in the thirties, now writing tomes hailing the new reign of big business. Actually, their basic views have not changed in the least. In the thirties, these theoreticians of the New Deal were concerned with condemning as "reactionaries" those big businessmen who clung to older individualist ideals and failed to understand or adhere to the new monopoly system of the corporate state. But now, in the 1950s and 1960s, this battle has been won, big businessmen are all eager to be privileged monopolists in the new dispensation, and hence they can now be welcomed by such theorists as Berle and Lilienthal as "responsible" and "enlightened," their "selfish" individualism a relic of the past.

The cruellest myth fostered by the liberals is that the Great Society functions as a great boon and benefit to the poor; in reality, when we cut through the frothy appearances to the cold reality underneath, the poor are the major victims of the welfare state. The poor are the ones to be conscripted to fight and die at literally slave wages in the Great Society's imperial wars. The poor are the ones to lose their homes to the bulldozer of urban renewal, that bulldozer that operates for the benefit of real estate and construction interests to pulverize available low-cost housing. All this, of course, in the name of "clearing the slums" and helping the aesthetics of housing. The poor are the welfare clientele whose homes are unconstitutionally but regularly invaded by government agents to ferret out sin in the middle of the night. The poor (e.g., Negroes in the south) are the ones disemployed by rising minimum wage floors, put in for the benefit of employers and unions in higher-wage areas (e.g., the North) to prevent industry from moving to the low-wage areas. The poor are cruelly victimized by an income tax that left and right alike misconstrue as an egalitarian program to soak the rich; actually, various tricks and exemptions insure that it is the poor and the middle classes who are hit the hardest. The poor are victimized, too, by a welfare state of which the cardinal macro-economic tenet is perpetual if controlled inflation. The inflation and the heavy government spending favor the businesses of the military–industrial complex, while the poor and the retired, those on fixed pensions or Social Security, are hit the hardest. (Liberals have often scoffed at the anti-inflationists' stress on the "widows and orphans" as major victims of inflation, but these remain major victims nevertheless.) And the burgeoning of compulsory mass public education forces millions of unwilling youth off the labor market for many years, and into schools that serve more as houses of detention than as genuine centers of education. Farm programs that supposedly aid poor farmers actually serve the large wealthy farmers at the expense of sharecropper and consumer alike; and commissions that regulate industry serve to cartellize it. The mass of workers is forced by governmental measures into trade unions that tame and integrate the labor force into the toils of the accelerating corporate state, there to be subjected to arbitrary wage "guidelines" and ultimate compulsory arbitration.

CHAPTER 11

Nixon to Reagan

INTRODUCTION

By the end of the 1960s, policymakers felt the welfare system was out of control and accomplishing little. Increased expenditures for welfare seemed to bear little relationship to bettering the lives of the poor or getting recipients off the welfare rolls. Each administration, from Nixon through Reagan, promised to correct the "welfare mess." Each spoke a similar language: offer incentives to leave welfare, cut the rolls, put people to work and the system would succeed. And in each case it would be found that putting people to work was expensive, that incentives cost money, and that the system was not so easily reformed. Moreover, each administration refused to touch the middle-class entitlements that had been achieved through the expansion of the Social Security system.

Stagflation and early signs of economic instability, beginning in the late 1960s and continuing into the 1970s, put pressure on policymakers to call for welfare reform. By 1975 social services financed by the federal government were on their way to having universalistic coverage, not only for the poor but for the middle classes as well. By 1975 government social expenditures totaled approximately $388.7 billion, which covered an estimated 72.7 percent of all social welfare expenditures in the nation. Per capita social welfare expenditures had climbed from 38 percent of the poverty index for an urban family of four in 1960 to 107 percent by 1978. Neil Gilbert observed in *Capitalism and the Welfare State* (1978): "If these public expenditures were directly distributed to the entire population in the form of cash grants, nobody would have fallen below the established poverty line of $6,000 in 1978."

Having campaigned on the promise to address the "welfare mess," Richard Nixon came into the White House in 1968 with a political mandate to undertake welfare reform. In August 1969, Nixon unveiled his Family Assistance Plan (FAP), a proposal which promised to profoundly alter the structure of welfare in modern America. With Daniel Moynihan playing a key role in the drafting of the proposal, FAP called for the consolidation of current welfare programs into a guaranteed annual income. First proposed as early as 1962 by conservative economist Milton Friedman in his book *Capitalism and Freedom*, the guaranteed national income caught the attention of the Nixon administration as an imaginative solution to the "welfare mess," while at the same time offering to bring efficiency and economy to social services. The Family Assistance Plan called for AFDC to be replaced by a single cash program that provided a minimum cash payment to all families with dependent children. The proponents of FAP insisted that by providing a minimum income, set low enough to discourage dependency, welfare recipients would be induced to find work.

When first revealed, Nixon's proposal won enthusiastic support from Congress, the public, and the press. Soon, however, the program came under attack from welfare rights groups, liberals, and civil rights activists who attacked the proposal for lowering benefits and limiting coverage for those already receiving AFDC benefits. Differences soon arose over the amount the government should pay to families with dependent children. Finally, many began to wonder about the large costs of the program and its promises to reduce welfare rolls by putting people to work. By 1971 the proposal was all but dead in Congress. To save face, the Nixon administration pushed through two other programs: the Supplemental Security Income program, which provided additional income benefits to the elderly, blind, and disabled; and a food stamp program, which also represented direct cash-in-form payments to the poor.

As an approach to solving the welfare problem, however, the guaranteed income program was far from dead. In 1977, Jimmy Carter revived the issue when he placed welfare reform once again on the policy agenda. Carter enjoyed even less success than Nixon in presenting his plan to Congress. Within his own administration, an acrimonious fight broke out between experts in Health, Education, and Welfare and members of the Department of Labor over a better jobs program or an income program.

It was evident that something needed to be done. National statistics revealed dramatic changes taking place in the American family, workforce, and population. By 1976, the majority of mothers with school-age children were working in jobs outside the home. In that same year, the nation's bicentennial, the number of divorces in the nation exceeded one million. Moreover, the black family showed signs of further deterioration from traditional patterns. Only 44 percent of black children under the age of 18 lived with both parents.

Ronald Reagan attracted renewed attention to the problems of welfare as he attempted to control federal spending. Reagan's domestic advisers, Robert Carleson and Martin Anderson, abandoned the guaranteed annual income as an illusionary scheme that was impractical, economically and politically. Instead, the Reagan administration moved to cut excess social expenditures from the federal budget. In addition, Reagan felt that responsibility for financing and setting social policy should be shifted from the federal government to state and local levels. The Omnibus Budget and Reconciliation Act of 1981 proved to be a milestone in welfare policy as greater responsibility was given to state and local government and to the private sector in maintaining social programs. Between fiscal years 1981 and 1984, federal outlays for youth training, child nutrition programs, food stamps, preventive health service block grants, and AFDC decreased as a result of budget cuts.

The shift to state and local government and to private sector involvement did little to improve the welfare picture. Twenty percent of the nation's children continued to live in poverty. Among black children the proportion in poverty was nearly 50 percent. Black children were three times more likely than whites to be poor. Moreover, there was a feeling on the part of many policymakers and analysts that the problems were getting worse. It was clear that a robust, unfettered economy was simply not enough to ensure the general welfare of the nation's poor.

This chapter examines welfare policy in the Nixon and Reagan administrations. Both Richard Nixon and Ronald Reagan came into office promising to reform the federal welfare system. Each, in his own way, offered new approaches to welfare reform. David A. Rochefort examines the politics of the Family Assistance Plan of 1969 from its first appearance on the national policy-making agenda to its ultimate defeat in Congress. He shows how an array of forces converged in 1969 to give welfare reform a prominent place in the Nixon administration. Two key presidential advisors who played a key role in placing FAP on the agenda were Richard P. Nathan, an economist assigned to head a welfare task force, and Daniel Patrick Moynihan, head of the Urban Affairs Council in the White House. These men soon were joined by HEW secretary Robert Finch. Although the proposal was opposed by equally influential policy advisers, including Arthur Burns and Vice President Spiro Agnew, the president was attracted to the proposal in part because it suggested that social workers would play only a small role in the program. Nixon abhorred social workers.

FAP easily worked its way onto the House floor under the able direction of Wilbur Mills (D.-Ark.), who wanted fundamental reforms made in the system. The House passed FAP in April 1970, but in the Senate a different story was to be told. The powerful chairman of the Senate Finance Committee, Russell Long (D.-La.), opposed the plan. He was joined in his opposition by Senator Herman Talmadge (D.-Ga.). In the end, an odd coalition of conservative southern Democrats, liberal northern Democrats, and conservative Republicans united to defeat the bill.

The second reading in this chapter offers a defense of Ronald Reagan's social welfare program. Martin Anderson, a key adviser on domestic policy to the administration, defended the Reagan social program at a conference sponsored by the Urban Institute on "An Assessment of Reagan's Social Welfare Policy." At this conference, Anderson argued that President Reagan's program was not aimed at cutting expenditures on social welfare but only limiting their growth. In doing this, Anderson maintained, the Reagan administration sought to reduce welfare dependency, provide a "safety net" for the neediest, eliminate ineffective programs, and shift welfare responsibility to the states. The Reagan policy, he suggested, was to put people to work, both by providing incentives to those on welfare to find employment and by encouraging economic growth. Anderson also captured the administration's belief that the private sector should play a greater role in caring for the nation's dependents.

A brief comment by Stuart E. Eizenstat, also speaking at the conference, challenged Anderson's thesis that President Reagan has not believed in cutting spending on social welfare programs. A domestic adviser to President Carter in his administration, Eizenstat answered Anderson, "In program after program, real reductions have been the order of the day, particularly in discretionary social programs upon which many low-income citizens are dependent."

The final reading in this chapter allows the reader to hear Ronald Reagan at his best. Although he admitted that some cuts had been made, he conveyed to his audience a faith that "We must recapture the spirit of brotherhood . . . of family and community that once was the hallmark of this country." In appealing to the religious sensibility of his audience, he added, "Today I'm convinced that with God's help the American people are capable of great things and that we'll be blessed beyond all expectation if we only try."

Further Readings

There is no shortage of books on this period from Nixon to Reagan. A number of excellent studies of Nixon's proposals have been published, including Vincent J. Burke and Vee Burke, *Nixon's Good Deed: Welfare Reform* (New York: Columbia University Press, 1974); Kenneth M. Bowler, *The Nixon Guaranteed Income Proposal: Substance and Process in Policy Change* (Cambridge: Harvard University Press, 1974); and Daniel P. Moynihan, *The Politics of a Guaranteed Income: The Nixon Administration and the Family Assistance Plan* (New York: Random House, 1973).

Laurence E. Lynn, Jr., and David deF. Whitman describe welfare reform under Carter in *The President as Policymaker: Jimmy Carter and Welfare Reform* (Philadelphia: Temple University Press, 1981).

Conservative perspectives on welfare policy can be found in Martin Anderson, *Welfare: The Political Economy of Welfare Reform in the United States* (Palo Alto: Hoover Institution Press, 1981); Charles Murray, *Losing Ground: American Social Policy, 1950–1980* (New York: Basic Books, 1984), Lawrence M. Mead, *Beyond Entitlement: The Social Obligations of Citizenship* (New York: Free Press, 1985), and Stuart Butler and Anna Kondratas, *Out of the Poverty Trap: A Conservative Strategy for Welfare Reform* (New York: Free Press, 1988).

Critiques of the Reagan administration are found in Fred Block, Richard A. Cloward, Barbara Ehrenreich, and Frances Fox Piven, *The Mean Season: The Attack on the Welfare State* (New York: Pantheon, 1987), and Madeleine H. Kimmich, *America's Children: Who Cares? Growing Needs and Declining Assistance in the Reagan Era* (Washington, D.C.: Urban Institute Press, 1985).

Responding to the New Dependency: The Family Assistance Plan of 1969

David A. Rochefort

On August 8, 1969, President Richard Nixon went before a national television audience to outline and gather public support for a welfare reform package that he was soon to submit to Congress. The chief element of the president's proposal was a Family Assistance Plan (FAP) that would establish new nationwide minimum benefit levels for recipients of the Aid to Families with Dependent Children (AFDC) program and make eligible for income subsidies about 10 million of America's low-income working poor. At a time when the nation was up in arms over the growing size and expense of the welfare system, Nixon proposed doubling the rolls and adding $4.4 billion to total current costs.

Then as now, most observers have judged FAP to be a striking innovation in social welfare policy. Directly following the speech, *Newsweek* declared that Nixon had left his own Republican cabinet officers "gasping for conservative breath," and the *Economist* of London described FAP as perhaps "rank[ing] in importance with President Roosevelt's first proposals for a Social Security system in the mid-1930s." Daniel Moynihan, one of Nixon's key policy advisers at the time who later published the first book-length analysis of the FAP episode, has exclaimed with characteristic fervor that Nixon's envisioned reforms amounted to "an extraordinary, discontinuous, forward movement in social policy" that took place "in the very least promising of circumstances." And even more dispassionate analysts generally echo the view of historian James T. Patterson, writing with the perspective lent by the passage of more than a decade since FAP was first announced, that this was "the most ambitious effort for welfare reform in the forty years since creation of the welfare state in 1935."

*****

EMERGENCE OF FAP

Many forces converged to give welfare reform a prominent place on the national policy-making agenda by the time of Richard Nixon's election to the presidency. Rising costs and caseloads over the past decade had caught the attention of journalists who brought the message to a quickly incensed public. Analysts within the federal bureaucracy had also been laboring on

---

SOURCE: Reprinted by permission of Westview Press from *American Social Welfare Policy: Dynamics of Formulation and Change*, by David A. Rochefort, pp. 99–130. Copyright Westview Press, 1986, Boulder, Colorado.

family allowance and negative income tax plans since the early 1960s and quietly pressed the need for new legislation of this scope on national political leaders. And state and local officials who struggled with the ballooning costs of current programs were actively lobbying federal policymakers for a resolution of the "welfare crisis." Add to these pressures the passage of the 1967 Welfare Amendments to the Social Security Act and President Johnson's creation of a Special Commission on Income Maintenance in 1968, and it is clear that a certain inevitability determined that Richard Nixon would face the challenge of welfare reform as he assumed the presidency.

A brief chronology outlines the process by which FAP, rather than some other program, surfaced as Nixon's specific proposal for welfare reform. Shortly after the 1968 election, Nixon's headquarters created a welfare task force headed by economist Richard P. Nathan. Nathan identified gross variation in welfare benefits from state to state as the major problem of the AFDC program and proposed that the president ask Congress to legislate a nationwide minimum federal payment level. Deeply worried about spreading dependency and aware of the general concern it had caused, his third day in office President Nixon established a Council on Urban Affairs with a special subcommittee on welfare. The council discussed the Nathan plan at a meeting in February of 1969 and then referred it to a subcabinet task force for further work.

At this time, the task force formed a working group including some long-time bureaucratic advocates of a negative income tax (NIT). Almost in the manner of a conspiracy, these NIT advocates seized the opportunity to devise a more comprehensive reform of the AFDC program centering on an income support strategy. While other staff members refined the Nathan plan, they worked up a Family Security System, which subsequently gained the backing of the parent task force.

In essence, the Family Security System (FSS) was a negative income tax that would pay an annual federal minimum of $1,500 to a family of four having no income; larger families would get more money, smaller families less. Those receiving a FSS payment would also be eligible for Food Stamps—an amount equal in worth to $500 for those receiving a $1,500 payment. The basic guarantee level was thus equivalent to $2,000 for a family of four with zero income. Under FSS, payment levels would gradually decrease with a family's income until support would be cut off for recipients earning more than $3,000 in a year. Unlike AFDC, FSS would not be restricted to female-headed families. These last two provisions meant that FSS would extend aid to millions of the low-income poor not already on relief. To ensure that current welfare recipients would not be hurt by these changes, FSS also required states that already paid more than the proposed federal minimum to continue these higher benefit levels by supplementing the federal payment.

Once FSS emerged from the task force, a period of intense debate of its merits ensued within the White House. A deep split developed between advisers who supported FSS, like Urban Affairs Council head Moynihan and HEW secretary Robert Finch, and other, equally influential advisers who stood opposed, like Counselor to the President Arthur Burns and Vice President Spiro Agnew. During these months when Nixon weighed arguments pro and con FSS, important issues began to crystallize that both highlighted the nature of this welfare reform plan and foreshadowed some of the resistance it was to meet in Congress.

For example, it is significant in view of the contemporary professional debate stimulated by welfare that Nixon so appreciated the envisioned effects of FSS on social workers. Following an Easter weekend meeting with the president in April of 1969, Moynihan exclaimed jubilantly to a colleague that he had had "a good meeting, a very good meeting with Nixon. The president asked me, 'Will FSS get rid of social workers? ' and I promised him it would wipe them out!" Nixon later confirmed this report of his attitudes toward social workers when he wrote in his memoirs of how he "abhorred snoopy, patronizing surveillance by social workers which made children and adults on welfare feel stigmatized and separate. The basic premise of the Family Assistance Plan was simple: what the poor need to help them rise out of poverty is money."

To further sway the president to their side, proponents of FSS explained that monetary transfers could do more than merely replace social workers or alleviate poverty. If disbursed within a properly devised payment structure, they could also counter habitual dependency as the welfare poor reacted to financial incentives to alter their immoral or unproductive life-styles. The stimulation of rational economic interest would, in effect, act as a rehabilitative influence. Even granting the capability of dependent persons to function as rational economic actors, it seems strange that Nixon did not take pause when this assessment was contradicted by his own hardnosed economists Burns and Burns's aide, Martin Anderson. There was no proof that FSS would keep families together and it did not seem to contain adequate work incentives, they maintained. It was just these kinds of objections, and their relationship to contemporary views of dependent citizens, that would mire FAP within the Senate in just a short while.

The internal White House debate resulted in Nixon's acceptance of FSS with a few alterations in design. Levels of support were raised to a basic payment of $1,600 (with Food Stamps valued at $720). Secretary of Labor George Schultz persuaded the president that the plan should permit recipients to keep a portion of their yearly earnings—later fixed at $720—without reducing the size of their welfare payment. "While the system may appear complicated in Washington we can be sure that the individual will be able to figure it out in actual operation," he had argued. "He must, and can, make rational decisions affecting his economic interests." But should such an incentive for work not prove sufficient, a requirement for compulsory work or training was added for any family head who was not the mother of a preschool child—this provision chiefly resulted from Burns's criticism of FSS. Last there was a cosmetic change. The Family Security System, which to some sounded too much like a New Deal measure, was changed in name to the Family Assistance Plan. Even considering these modifications, those officials who favored a dramatic new approach to the welfare problem had won a big victory.

President Nixon went on television on August 8, 1969, to announce FAP. His speech presented a capsule summary of by now familiar themes concerning the problems of public relief policy, much as Kennedy's special messages on mental illness and retardation and the aging had done earlier concerning the problems in these two policy areas. Nixon described the great growth in the AFDC rolls and noted the disturbing paradox that it had occurred in a period of low employment. He explained further that this growth was exerting considerable fiscal pressure on city and state treasuries. Nixon went on to denounce the current welfare system: "Whether measured by the anguish of the poor themselves, or by the drastically mounting burden on the taxpayers, the present welfare system has to be judged a colossal failure." The president cited three major inequities under AFDC: variation in benefit levels from one state to the next; an incentive for family breakup in states without an AFDC-U program (more than half of all states at the time); and an incentive not to work because recipients could take in more money on relief than by working at low-paying jobs. This theme of work surfaced repeatedly throughout the message, and especially when the president outlined the mechanisms of FAP. The journalists Vincent and Vee Burke note that "work," "jobs," and other work-related words appeared sixty times in the thirty-five-minute speech.

REACTIONS TO FAP

Most early responses to FAP were positive. This reaction probably reflected not so much a reasoned appraisal of FAP as intense disenchantment with AFDC, the popularity of the president's "workfare" theme, and the customary initial backing given to decisive presidential action. Administration analysts estimated that 95 percent of editorial comment in the country was favorable with many newspapers and magazines declaring FAP to be a revolution in American social policy. "It is hardly possible to overemphasize the importance of President Nixon's new program for dealing with poverty in the United States," opined the *Christian Science Monitor*. "It is a major watershed—socially, economically, and politically."

A nationwide poll conducted one week following the address revealed that 65 percent of Americans with knowledge of the proposal were also favorable to FAP (20 percent were unfavorable and 15 percent were not sure). What the public liked best about FAP was its emphasis on work; that it would also greatly expand the welfare system pleased them much less. Citizens interviewed in the month of October, for example, favored inclusion of the working poor in FAP by a margin of 5 to 1; by virtually as great a margin they also approved FAP's work incentives. But when asked to consider the statement that "the trouble is that too much money will still be spent on welfare in this country," respondents were equally divided, with 25 percent uncertain about their feelings. From the start, then, FAP's inclusion of the welfare and working poor in a single program demonstrated the capacity to produce confusion and ambivalence, even among persons greatly enamored with other elements of the FAP proposal.

Although it was clearly a minority sentiment at this time, when first announced FAP did elicit some lukewarm and negative reactions. Business was sorely split concerning this sizable expansion of the welfare state. Labor, too, offered not much more than weak support. Its traditional interests lie with the fight for higher wages, *not* welfare, and certainly not an income program like FAP that could perpetuate low wage levels by subsidizing them. Just as understandable in its own way was the negative reaction of social workers and other welfare professionals, who recognized that FAP threatened their role in public assistance. Moynihan summarizes their response:

> From the first announcement of FAP . . . the *de facto* strategy of social welfare groups was to seek to kill the program, first, by insisting on benefit levels that no Congress would pass and no president would approve, and, second, by raising issues about deails of the legislation which allowed the entire initiative to be labeled oppressive, repressive, regressive, and worse.

However different their underlying motivations might have been, the substance of social workers' objections closely paralleled those of NWRO, which also complained that FAP's payments were too low—NWRO demanded a basic $5,500 for a family of four without income—and its work requirement punitive.

FAP IN CONGRESS

FAP was first introduced into Congress in the House of Representatives in October 1969 and referred to the Ways and Means Committee. All in all, at this stage of its life FAP underwent a comparatively gentle review that tended to center on consensual themes like the growing problem of chronic welfare dependency and the faults of the existing AFDC system. As chairman of Ways and Means at this time, Wilbur Mills (D.-Ark.) was a powerful leader who felt frustrated with past attempts in Congress to improve the welfare system by tinkering. He stood ready for more fundamental reform even in view of serious doubts about the workability of many of FAP's constituent elements. Only the following kinds of comments during committee hearings, from Mills and committee member Martha Griffiths (D.-Mich.), respectively, suggested the nature of the vehement resistance that FAP was to meet in the other chamber:

> There is nothing in welfare that I see, just welfare alone, that does anything except barely keep an individual alive. It doesn't motivate a person to change his circumstances. There is nothing within welfare itself that gives him any

> opportunity or motivation for improvement or self-reliance. . . . But I don't see anything in the program before us any more than in existing law that will motivate these people or give them the opportunity to be motivated.

and

> My viewpoint is that all you have added to this program is money and I believe that money is never going to do it. You are going to have to do something far different if you are ever going to cure the problem of welfare.

Put simply, despite their willingness to give support, both Mills and Griffiths doubted FAP's capacity to rehabilitate welfare dependents and get them off the rolls.

By a vote of 21 to 3 taken on March 5, 1970, Ways and Means reported the Family Assistance Act of 1970 to the House floor without significant changes in the administration-proposed bill. On the floor Mills sponsored and defended the bill, which the House considered under a closed rule allowing no amendments. The House passed FAP in mid-April with 243 for, 155 against, and 32 not voting. The two parties provided roughly comparable majorities in support. More than anything else, this vote perhaps symbolized the simultaneous hope that FAP would aid the cause of welfare reform and grudging acceptance of a guaranteed income as the price that such reform would exact.

The Senate Finance Committee began its review of FAP in late April. It was at this point that the FAP episode began a rapid denouement as several paradoxes inherent in the proposal became evident. The following list is illustrative: FAP sought to shrink welfare costs but, in the immediate, it would increase them greatly; most aid under FAP would go to the South even though it was northern states that were enduring the most severe welfare problem; FAP covered both the working and the nonworking poor under the same policy, but different causes were thought to account for the poverty of these two groups—low wages in the first instance, multifaceted and chronic dependency in the second; and finally, FAP was a welfare reform that would do more to help the working poor than welfare recipients, and what it would do to resolve the problem of dependency was unproven and, to many, unconvincing.

The much touted subject of work served as a kind of intense focal point for the airing of many of these issues and the image of dependent citizens that underlaid them. Did FAP provide an adequate incentive for the welfare poor to go to work? If so, then it truly was "welfare reform" and held out the possibility of resolving the "welfare mess." FAP would be the new approach to rehabilitation consistent with the Work Incentive Program (WIN) Amendments of 1967. But if the work incentive was not adequate, then FAP was simply a guaranteed income that subsidized the lazy and immoral life-style of dependent groups. This question of work, as much as any other element of the proposal, accounted for the outcome of FAP.

Excerpts from the Senate Finance Committee hearings demonstrate the centrality and broad implications of the work question. For instance, committee members hammered away at administration witnesses with abstract examples of how it would be a disadvantage for persons on FAP to go to work. The following exchange between Chairman Russell Long (D.-La.), an ardent welfare antagonist, and HEW secretary Finch captures the spirit of this line of questioning:

The Chairman:

You say that the present AFDC program "makes it possible for many welfare families to receive more money from welfare (or a combination of welfare and work) than other equally needy families who must rely solely on a low-paying job." Is it not true that this situation would still be largely true under the bill before us?

Secretary Finch:

It would not be true with regard to women. It would be less true than it is now with regard to men.

Moynihan comments in his review of these hearings that to many senators on the committee Finch's reply was unsatisfactory. In a related vein, Senator Herman Talmadge (D.-Ga.), a long-time foe of "immoral" welfare behavior since his tenure as governor of Georgia in the early 1950s, disputed whether the penalty of $300 under FAP constituted much of a disincentive for an adult male's refusal to go to work. In speculation that spoke reams about his own image of the problem of dependency, Talmadge imagined that such an individual "could do a little casual labor on somebody's yard from time to time and maybe sell a little heroin or do a little burglary and he would be in pretty good shape, wouldn't he?"

Much time during Senate hearings went to a discussion of how the "notch" might keep welfare recipients from taking employment. The "notch" refers to the effect of going to work when public housing, Food Stamps, government-provided health insurance, and other in-kind benefits in addition to direct payments are calculated in the loss of welfare income. To illustrate the severity of the notch, Senator John J. Williams (R.-Del.) directed HEW personnel to analyze how a "fully supported" four-person female-headed family living in various American cities, and subject to federal and state taxes, would fare as the mother's earnings increased. The results generally showed that FAP's discounting of the first $720 in earnings and 50 percent of the rest failed to make it profitable or, by the same token, "rational" for such an individual to seek full-time work.

Having witnessed the exposure of these notches, Chairman Long recessed the Senate hearing and instructed HEW staff to redesign FAP by removing the work disincentives that were posed by loss of all potential forms of aid for which welfare recipients might qualify. This HEW analysts did in a new version of FAP that was ready by June. Among other changes, FAP as revised included a federally subsidized health insurance plan for the working poor to lessen the notch created by loss of Medicaid benefits; it raised from $300 to $500 the amount forfeited by eligible persons who refused training or employment; and it did away with the AFDC-U program.

Major difficulties related to these changes in FAP design surfaced when Senate hearings reconvened in late July. Committee members criticized the termination of the AFDC-U program. After all, Nixon had already promised that FAP would not reduce the benefits of any current welfare recipient. Even more serious, it came to the attention of the committee that HEW analysts had raised the marginal tax rate on lower incomes under FAP. A mathematical necessity of doing away with notches at the higher earnings level, this meant that some welfare recipients who went to work would get to keep a smaller proportion of each additional dollar earned than under the prior proposal. In short, while maximizing the incentive of some FAP recipients to go to work, the revision had lessened the incentive facing others.

The Senate Finance Committee voted on FAP on November 20, 1970, and rejected the measure 10 to 6. In December, committee members Abraham Ribicoff (D.-Conn.) and Wallace Bennet (R.-Utah) attempted to bring still another, slightly altered version of FAP to the Senate floor as an amendment to the larger Social Security bill that the Senate Finance Committee had been working on. This effort also met with defeat.

An assortment of reasons helps explain why the Senate rejected FAP. Some southerners feared the effect of FAP in undermining the low wage base of their part of the country. Other senators, who for the first time were discovering the complex problems of public relief, voted against FAP because of its various technical imperfections; they did not seem to appreciate the real improvements over AFDC that the proposal represented— mainly, the standardization of benefits and extension of aid to the working poor. A few liberals sided with groups like NWRO who wanted more generous benefit levels without strict work requirements, but, over all, liberal and conservative ideologies helped little in explaining the treatment of the proposal. FAP was just too disorienting an issue for this traditional split to matter much. As Burke and Burke summarize, "The long fight over the Family Assistance Plan set conservative against conservative and liberal against liberal in an alignment both unusual and unstable."

The single most important factor accounting for the demise of FAP was the "impact of policy design." Leman explains that "the Nixon welfare reform package suffered politically because its outwardly unitary design gave identical federal benefits and work incentives to groups that the public thought should be treated differently." In other words, FAP failed because it combined the welfare and working poor in the same policy, thereby failing to take a specialized approach to either group that was consistent with dominant contemporary images. True, there had been evidence of public support for FAP when Nixon first announced his proposal, but this support was owed largely to the president's heavy emphasis on work incentives. Later, when the Senate exposed the probability that these same incentives were invalid, FAP lost much of its claim to being meaningful welfare reform. Moynihan himself makes this point well in discussing the course of the Senate Finance Committee hearings: "FAP, having first benefited from the near unanimous judgment that *something* had to be done about welfare, now began to suffer as it was revealed that it appeared to do little."

Anticlimactic though it was, the epilogue to the FAP episode was as instructive as the main drama. The administration resubmitted FAP to the Ninety-second Congress, where the House Ways and Means Committee undertook a careful and lengthy reexamination of its provisions. When the full House approved it in late June, 1971, H.R.1, as FAP was now designated, embodied a more restrictive work requirement, a higher penalty for refusal to work, a higher basic payment level ($2,400, but with no eligibility for Food Stamps), and a revised schedule for taxing earnings. Despite these changes, FAP once more foundered in the Senate largely because of the belief that it too greatly expanded welfare and lacked sufficient work incentives. The possibility did develop in mid-1972 that a compromise of the administration's proposal and one backed by Senate liberals led by Ribicoff might yet yield a viable welfare reform bill. But Nixon himself pulled out from the deal, at least partly in reaction to the political controversy that was then growing around the now-infamous $1,000 "demogrant" proposal of Democratic presidential aspirant George McGovern. Clearly, welfare reform was not seen as a suitable cause for a Republican president to be pushing in an election year.

POLICY AFTERMATH, 1972–1980

For all intents and purposes, the death of H.R.1 in 1972 marked the fading of the last real chance for the enactment of comprehensive welfare reform for the remainder of the decade. A number of other plans were formulated in this period, and some of these did receive careful consideration within the Congress. None, however, came very close to overcoming the political stalemate on the issue that first crystallized into characteristic form in the FAP policy-making episode. Meanwhile, within these subsequent proposals as well as other significant policy initiatives of the decade, an almost irresistible pull was manifested toward the increasing use of employment as a substitute for cash aid or as part of the basic requirements for receipt of income and in-kind assistance. This trend, combined with certain restrictive developments in public assistance funding and administration on the state level, gave the measure of the continuing welfare backlash in the United States.

Neither Nixon in the tumultuous two years that were left in his presidency after 1972, nor President Gerald Ford in the succeeding two years that he held the executive office, proposed new welfare reform plans to the Congress. Although the issue thus temporarily lost its high-priority agenda status, it did not completely disappear from the national policy-making scene in this period. Both HEW and the Congress gave some consideration to the design of income support programs that might replace the existing welfare system and extend assistance to large numbers of Americans who were the working poor. One of these actually was part of an ambitious plan to reorganize HEW. The so-called Mega-Proposal included an income security element that would have dispensed aid to unemployable household members while providing a job to those persons deemed employable. One scholar on the topic notes that "this proposal was the first major HEW proposal that incorporated different guarantee levels for employable and unemployable people," a method of discrimination that was to become prevalent in post-FAP reform schemes. Under President Ford, HEW analysts produced a negative income tax-type of proposal called the Income Supplement Program (ISP), which would have paid a basic benefit of $3,600 to a four-person family with a 50 percent reduction in each dollar of benefits for each dollar earned up to a total income level of $7,200; ISP would have covered couples without children and single individuals in addition to families, and states were to be responsible for putting in place a work registration program. A roughly similar plan was put forward in late 1974 by the Subcommittee on Fiscal Policy of the Joint Economic Committee after its conclusion of an in-depth two-year examination of the subject of welfare reform.

Congress did enact a significant piece of related tax reform legislation in 1975 with the establishment of the Earned Income Tax Credit (EITC). This measure provided families with dependent children a refundable tax credit of up to $400 (this maximum would be for yearly earnings of $4,000) to be administered through the Internal Revenue Service as part of the annual tax collection process. (In 1978, the EITC was expanded to supply a maximum of $500 on yearly earnings of $5,000.) By restricting support only to families that had some earnings, the program managed to avoid some of the most difficult issues that were implicit in a more inclusive guaranteed income proposal. Significantly, the bill's strongest advocates included Senator Long, who had first put forward the tax change in 1972 when his Senate Finance Committee was reworking the House-approved version of Nixon's welfare reform plan.

After Nixon's FAP, the major welfare reform proposal of the decade was Jimmy Carter's Program for Better Jobs and Income (PBJI). Carter had been the only southern governor to back FAP, and he made welfare reform a top priority of his administration, promising within his first week in office that a comprehensive plan would be forthcoming shortly. When PBJI finally emerged in August of 1977, it was a complex program that incorporated a mix of income and employment assistance with benefit structures that varied depending on what tier of the program the recipient was placed into.

In the first place, PBJI combined AFDC, SSI, and Food Stamps into a single income support plan with a uniform federal benefit. The basic payment for a family of four with no employable member was $4,200, with a tax rate on earnings that would allow the household to keep 50 cents of each $1 earned up to an annual maximum of $8,400, at which point aid ended. A household headed by a person judged eligible for full-time employment (the head of a two-parent family, mothers with no children below fourteen, and able-bodied childless individuals) was to be given an income supplement to a maximum of $2,300, with the same 50 percent tax rate after the first $3,800 in earnings; a public service job was to be provided to the employable member who tried and failed to find nonsubsidized employment. (For mothers with no child younger than seven years part-time work was judged suitable.) PBJI also proposed an expansion of the Earned Income Tax Credit for any earnings not derived from the specially created public jobs, and it would have offered a measure of fiscal relief to states and localities with their share of welfare costs.

Within Congress the first stop for Carter's bill was a special House Welfare Reform Subcommittee, which revised and approved the administration's proposal. Things soon ground to a halt at the next legislative stage, however, when the bill was referred to the subcommittee's three parent committees—Ways and Means, Education and Labor, and Agriculture. Major items of concern were PBJI's expense—Congressional Budget Office estimates put the federal costs of the revised bill at around $20 billion—and the feasibility of the public service jobs component. By mid-1978 after a number of rival plans had surfaced, energies became focused on an attempt to negotiate some compromise acceptable to both the administration and House leaders. This effort eventually fell through, its demise greatly facilitated by the approval on June 6 of Proposition 13, an amendment to the California state constitution that slashed property taxes and dramatically symbolized a brewing nationwide tax revolt against expensive social programs and other forms of government expenditure.

In the following session of Congress Carter proposed a more modest welfare reform bill that, among other provisions, specified a national minimum benefit level for AFDC recipients and required all states to operate an AFDC-U program. Carter again proposed the creation of new public service jobs, but on a less sweeping scale than under PBJI, and he recommended the stimulation of new employment opportunities in the private sector. All told, the administration's 1979 offering would have amounted to some $5.7 billion in new federal expenditures. The House had approved the cash portion of the bill when, under the press of persistent malaise in the nation's economy, problems in foreign relations (chiefly Iran and Afghanistan), and primary campaign politics, the president himself seemed to lose heart in the cause and asked for the funding of his jobs bill to be delayed a year. The House obliged by ending altogether its active consideration of the president's job plan. Meanwhile, the cash benefits bill came to a standstill in the Senate, which did not even hold hearings on the measure in 1980.

In the end, disjunction, contradiction, and disorientation emerge as the principal themes of this interim period of the 1970s in welfare policy-making. Major new policy-making efforts, as we have seen, were stymied. At the same time, there was actually striking growth in selected federal welfare programs that happened to have special sources of political backing and were acceptable in programmatic form. A good example is Food Stamps. Supported both by urban members of Congress, whose districts enclosed some of poverty's worst extremes, and by rural members of Congress, who wanted price supports and markets for their constituents' farm products, the program came by 1980 to include in excess of 16 million participants at a total cost of about $8 billion. Federal outlays for employment and training programs—including, among others, the Work Incentive Program (WIN) and the Comprehensive Employment and Training Act (CETA)— also expanded greatly in this period, going from about $5 billion in 1972 to roughly $14 billion in 1980. Yet on some other fronts, the unmistakable thrust was retrenchment and restriction. California and other states acted to tighten eligibility for AFDC benefits and to crack down on welfare fraud. At the federal level, a work requirement was added to the Food Stamp program during the early 1970s, and existing work requirements under AFDC were made more encompassing and more stringent. Never had the variable meanings associated with the concept of welfare reform been more clearly in evidence as the decade of the 1980s arrived and a Republican administration made ready to assume the powers of the presidency.

CONCLUSION

President Nixon attempted to advance FAP as a program that would modify the behavior of dependent citizens by removing incentives under the current welfare program thought to contribute to problems like desertion, illegitimacy, and mass migration. But, much like the community mental health movement of the early 1960s, FAP grew out of a composite of prox-imate guesses about desirable policy, not definitive knowledge. Moynihan, who was deeply involved in the process of formulating FAP and then sell-ing it to Congress, afterward was quite open about this lack of knowledge. In *The Politics of a Guaranteed Income* he admitted that *"no one could anticipate what would be the consequences of FAP"* (emphasis in original). Moynihan wrote further that "there was no guarantee that FAP would suc-ceed where other efforts had failed. . . . In particular, it was not clear how FAP would have any but the most indirect effects on the problem of welfare dependency as it had developed in cities such as New York." At the time Nixon himself reportedly told senators, House members, governors, and other interested parties privately that he was "not absolutely sure FAP would work" or "that it would take us down the right road." The public rhetoric of the period aside, then, FAP represented another instance of a bold innovation in social welfare policy that was based less on tried-and-true solutions than some reasonable-seeming responses to a social problem perceived in a certain way.

The Objectives of the Reagan Administration's Social Welfare Policy

Martin Anderson

*****

THE REAGAN ADMINISTRATION'S SOCIAL WELFARE PHILOSOPHY

Five important elements of the Reagan administration's social welfare philosophy seem to me to define and explain its basic thrust:

1. A sound and growing economy is vital to reducing poverty and ensuring the opportunity for prosperity for everyone.

2. Eligibility standards for social welfare programs should be fair, setting reasonable limits as to who qualifies for aid.

3. Fraud, waste, and extravagance in social welfare programs should be substantially reduced.

4. In order to improve effectiveness and to lower costs, the responsibility for certain social welfare programs, together with the tax resources necessary to fund them, should be returned to the states and localities (the New Federalism).

5. A guaranteed income is unconscionable and impractical. To the extent that people are able to take care of themselves, they should do so.

A SOUND AND GROWING ECONOMY

The general level of economic prosperity largely determines the personal prosperity of those in the society who are relatively poor.

First, the level of government support and the extent of that support is largely determined by the size of government tax revenues and that, in turn, is largely determined by the size and health of the economy. There is no way that a country like India, with its weak and relatively stagnant economy, could provide—even if it wished to do so—anywhere near the extent of social welfare benefits that exist in the United States.

Second, how well the economy is functioning can have a powerful effect on low-income people. How much money they have is important, but what

SOURCE: Martin Anderson, in *The Social Contract Revisited: Aims and Outlines of President Reagan's Welfare Policy* (conference volume), ed. D. Lee Bawden (Washington, D.C.: Urban Institute Press, 1984), pp. 15–32:

they can buy with the money is equally important. The devastating effect of inflation on poor people is often overlooked. One would expect that low-income people would be less able to adapt quickly to a rapidly escalating cost of living than their more financially agile brothers and sisters with higher incomes. The differences in well-being that result from not being able to adjust one's income to inflation can be very large.

For example, if sound economic policies kept the rate of inflation at zero instead of, say, 10 percent, it would mean that after just two years someone with a low, fixed income would have real purchasing power that would be roughly one fifth higher than it would have been under the higher rate of inflation. There are few social welfare programs that could expect to enjoy growth of this magnitude.

High interest rates are another manifestation of high inflation. The higher cost of borrowing money can be especially painful to those without substantial liquid assets who must borrow if they want to use and enjoy something while they pay for it, rather than wait until they have saved enough to buy it outright.

High tax rates, especially high marginal tax rates, can have a severely inhibiting effect on people's work effort. And they can be particularly discouraging to someone who is considering entering the work force at low- to moderate-income levels. Our tax system, if we look just at federal taxes, or state taxes, or Social Security taxes, is fairly reasonable. But if we look at it from the perspective of a low- or moderate-income taxpayer who must pay all these taxes simultaneously, it becomes quite irrational. The effect of federal, state, and Social Security taxes acting together often produces effective marginal tax rates of almost 30 percent for incomes only slightly above the poverty level.

A high unemployment rate, especially if it is sustained and unemployment benefits run out, can make a lot of people poor very quickly.

In sum, all the characteristics of a poorly functioning economy—high inflation and high interest rates, rising unemployment, and high marginal tax rates—produce a powerful economic effect that constitutes a double whammy on the poor. It hurts them directly by reducing the purchasing power of their money, throwing them out of work, and eroding their incentives to work if they can find work. At the same time, a poorly functioning economy reduces the tax revenues that must pay for the social welfare programs that provide aid to them.

For anyone concerned about the long-term well-being of the poor in the United States, the achievement and maintenance of a healthy, growing economy should be of paramount importance.

ELIGIBILITY STANDARDS

Another important aspect of the Reagan administration's social welfare philosophy is the determination of who should receive social welfare benefits. Over the years, as the size and scope of our social welfare programs have grown, there has been a gradual increase in income eligibility levels.

The purpose of welfare, as understood by most Americans, is to provide help and support to poor people, to those who cannot care for themselves. One of the primary reasons we developed poverty statistics was to determine what kinds and what degree of help should be provided by government social welfare programs. Unfortunately, two developments in recent years have combined to blur our understanding of poverty in the United States and to compromise the validity of those programs in the eyes of the public.

The official poverty statistics published each year by the Bureau of the Census consistently and deliberately overstate the incidence of poverty in the United States. Many years ago, when this series was first put together, it was decided to focus on cash income only, disregarding the value of in-kind services received by the poor, such as medical care or housing assistance. At the time, this was a reasonable decision because in-kind benefits were then only a small fraction of total welfare benefits received, and the loss of completeness in the statistics was more than made up by the savings in the effort of compiling those statistics.

But as the years rolled by, the value of in-kind benefits grew and grew and grew. As the relative amount of in-kind benefits increased, the validity of the poverty statistics decreased. This problem is further compounded by the consistent underreporting of income to the Bureau of the Census. The extent of this underreporting is known, but the poverty series is not adjusted to take it into account.

The benign neglect of in-kind benefits and the disregarding of underreporting of income have gradually eroded the validity of the official poverty statistics to the point where they are not only unreliable but are very misleading. The census statistics, according to estimates by the Congressional Budget Office and independent scholars, indicate that poverty is at least twice as great as it really is.

The truly regrettable part of this whole affair is that social welfare experts who have been aware of the problem for many years continue to use discredited data while efforts to correct the data proceed with "all deliberate speed." The Bureau of the Census now has a significant effort underway to correct these statistics, but for at least five or more years the numbers have been badly misleading to those who are unfamiliar with their deficiencies.

An interesting question arises as to why otherwise reputable scholars would continue to use the discredited official poverty numbers. It may be that they do not know any better or that it is too much trouble to change. But these are unlikely explanations.

As time goes on one has to give more and more credence to the suspicion that the discredited numbers continue to be used because of, not in spite of, the fact that they grossly overstate the incidence of poverty and thus buttress the ideological view shared by most scholars in the field. To the extent that this is perceived to be true, it causes injury to the professional reputation of the entire field. The time appears long overdue for a little intellectual self-policing.

As we have gradually lost track of the true nature and extent of poverty in the United States, we have also begun to slide away from a clear idea of who should be eligible for social welfare benefits. Most Americans probably share the rather uncomplicated view that by and large only poor people should be eligible for benefits. One problem with this view is that as soon as you draw a clear line between the *poor* and *nonpoor* you create an insoluble problem, namely that those a few dollars over the line are very, very close in the nature of their financial circumstances to those just below the line. Yet those above the line are not eligible, while their neighbors just below the line are eligible for many social welfare benefits.

Partly in response to this, the eligibility levels of many programs have been increased far above the poverty level, so that many individuals and families who are not classified as officially poor receive social welfare benefits. For example, a family is eligible for Food Stamps if its income is less than 130 percent of the poverty level, and for child health care if family income is less than 185 percent of the poverty level. To qualify for certain rent subsidies, income must be less than 50 percent of the area median income (it used to be 80 percent but was recently changed). Families asking for student financial aid at one time had no income restrictions at all, and the spectacle of wealthy students investing their subsidized loans in the financial markets finally resulted in a rather generous ceiling of $30,000 being placed on "countable" family income.

These and other expansions of eligibility standards have greatly blurred our common understanding of who is poor and who should be eligible to receive government aid. As the eligibility levels are raised, the number of people at the margin who qualify for social welfare programs increases rapidly and this, in turn, sharply boosts the cost of these programs. At the same time, the public sees more and more people receiving aid whose justification for receiving that aid becomes increasingly questionable as the income eligibility levels rise.

There is no easy way to draw the line on eligibility. What the Reagan administration has done as one of the main thrusts of its social welfare policy has been to restore more of a sense of balance and fairness in federal programs designed to aid the poor. In proposing slower rates of spending growth—and, in some cases, reductions—for certain social welfare programs, the guiding principle has been that the adjustments be made primarily at the expense of those people at the upper end of the eligibility scale. To use one of the most glaring examples, it was felt to be somewhat unseemly for people with six-figure incomes to be bellying up to the federal bar for their share of the guaranteed student loan money for their precocious offspring, especially when many low- and moderate-income taxpayers were paying the bill.

A major objective of the Reagan administration's social welfare policy is to restore fairer standards of eligibility so that the available resources can be focused on those least able to take care of themselves.

The extent to which this has been achieved is still unclear, but there are some signs it is working. Last year *New York Times* reporters interviewed state welfare officials in all fifty states in an effort to ascertain the consequences of the Reagan administration's adjustments to the social welfare budget. They were expecting reports of "protests, demonstrations, and lobbying campaigns in behalf of the poor." What they found was silence— no protests, no demonstrations, and no lobbying campaigns. And the major reason for this may be found in the explanation given by John T. Dempsey, director of the Michigan Department of Social Services, who was reported to have "said that he thought Mr. Reagan had cut benefits in a way that minimized the effect on the poorest people, by reducing welfare benefits for those who could work or who had income exceeding 150 percent of the subsistence income level set by each state."

FRAUD, WASTE, AND EXTRAVAGANCE

While past studies by the General Accounting Office, the Department of Health and Human Services, and various state governments have shown massive amounts of fraud and mismanagement in social welfare programs, there has been very little rigorous analysis by social welfare scholars of the extent and causes of this phenomenon. But this has done little to deter the problem from continuing in the real world.

One of the major objectives of the social welfare policy of the Reagan administration is to reduce and some day eliminate the massive fraud and abuse that characterizes so many of those programs. There are two basic reasons for doing so. The obvious one is to save a considerable amount of money, money that could be given to those who qualify and money that would not have to be spent at all. Another reason is to remove the stigma that attaches to all people receiving social welfare benefits, because those who are cheating and getting away with it have convinced the vast majority of the American public that fraud is widespread in social welfare programs. Not knowing which recipients are fraudulent, the public tends to be suspicious of them all. If there is anything that infuriates the American taxpayer it is the idea that someone is getting his tax money who should not be.

THE NEW FEDERALISM

The question of the proper division of responsibility for government social welfare programs between the federal government and the states and localities is one that has been with us for a long time. What has been called the *New Federalism* of the Reagan administration is, for the most part, an old federalism concept that has been discussed for decades. Over thirty years ago President Eisenhower established the Commission on Intergovernmental Relations. The commission, which included such distinguished Americans as Marion B. Folsom, Oveta Culp Hobby, Clark Kerr, Wayne Morse, and Hubert Humphrey, deliberated for two years and delivered a far-reaching report that concluded that we should:

1. Leave to private initiative all the functions that citizens can perform privately.
2. Use the level of government closest to the community for all public functions it can handle.
3. Utilize cooperative intergovernmental arrangements where appropriate to attain economical performance and popular approval.
4. Reserve National action for residual participation where State and local governments are not fully adequate, and for the continuing responsibilities that only the National Government can undertake.

A major objective of the Reagan administration is to systematically transfer authority and responsibility for some social welfare programs to the states and localities along with the tax resources necessary to finance them. This is the thrust of the New Federalism.

The objective is not to eliminate the programs.

The objective is not to dump the programs on the states and localities, forcing them to raise taxes to whatever extent they can in order to continue programs.

The objective is to improve the operation of those social welfare programs, and to reduce their costs, by returning responsibility and resources to a level of government that is more appropriate for these programs. There is a good deal of sympathy for the view that Dan Lufkin expressed after serving for two years as Connecticut's first commissioner of environmental protection: "The more the administration of policies and programs is brought down to the state and local level, the better the people will be able to judge who is fair, who is honest, who is creative, and who is productive and efficient."

OPPOSITION TO A GUARANTEED INCOME

Sometimes what is not said or done is just as important as what is said and what is done. Before President Reagan took office there had been a string of administration efforts—both Republican and Democratic—to radically change the existing welfare system and to establish guaranteed income for all Americans. President Nixon proposed the Family Assistance Plan. President Ford explored the Income Supplementation Plan. And President Carter tried the Program for Better Jobs and Income.

All these programs were spawned by a small, largely liberal, intellectual elite, some of whom were well aware that what they were trying to foist on an unsuspecting public was a guaranteed income. Unfortunately for the programs, the public, which has a keen abhorrence of any guaranteed income scheme, sensed the true nature of these programs and our elected representatives thoroughly drubbed those proposals when they reached the Congress.

One of the more important social policy objectives of the Reagan administration is to *not* propose any disguised guaranteed income programs. This deliberate neglect of one of the hallowed canons of social welfare policy in this country for the last twenty years or so is, and I believe will continue to be, a major social policy objective of the Reagan administration.

Comments

Stuart E. Eizenstat

Now I will briefly describe what I believe constitutes the Reagan social welfare program. First, the administration, more fundamentally than any of its predecessors, believes that the government should have a markedly reduced social role. David Stockman's contention that the people are not "entitled" to any services from the federal government provides the philosophical underpinning of this policy. FY 1983 domestic spending was reduced by $43 billion below that needed to maintain programs at their current levels. By FY 1986 the president's budget would reduce outlays for these domestic programs from 65 percent of the total budget to about 55 percent. The FY 1984 budget proposes reducing grants to states and localities by $5 billion below the amount necessary to provide the same services as offered in FY 1983. Income security programs such as AFDC, Medicaid, Food Stamps, Low Income Energy Assistance, and child nutrition programs will be cut to $2.3 billion below their projected maintenance costs. The president has called for a FY 1984 budget freeze for all areas except defense and interest payments, which in real terms would mean a 5 percent reduction in all other spending. Sixty percent of the proposed budget reductions affect programs for low-income people. One study indicated that two-thirds of the federal savings from budget cuts devolves upon those making $20,000 or less, compared to 10 percent upon those with incomes over $40,000.

This first element of the Reagan program is a celebration of the private marketplace over government. While cutting funds for public education, Reagan favors tuition tax credits to provide parents with incentives to send their children to private schools. While sharply reducing public enforcement of environmental programs, Reagan gives private companies more latitude in complying with environmental requirements. He has systematically cut or eliminated federally supported alternate energy and conservation programs, while opening public lands for private development. He has eliminated public service jobs and public subsidies for legal services, training of physicians, and health maintenance organizations.

A second element of the Reagan agenda is a major shift in national priorities from domestic to defense programs. In 1981 the president proposed an increase of 9 percent in real terms for defense, or $1.6 trillion over five years. Defense spending would rise from 5.6 percent of the Gross National Product (GNP) to 7 percent. Defense outlays would rise from 24 percent of the budget to 36 percent in five years, while at the same time large

SOURCE: Stuart Eizenstat, in *The Social Contract Revisited: Aims and Outlines of President Reagan's Welfare Policy* (conference volume), ed. D. Lee Bawden (Washington, D.C.: Urban Institute Press, 1984), pp. 15–32.

real declines are proposed for discretionary nondefense programs. Grants to state and local governments and other federal operations would experience real declines of 30 to 50 percent over prior levels. From 1981 to 1986 all areas not dominated by entitlement programs—including education, social services, employment and training, and transportation—will be reduced from 16 to 63 percent, depending on the program.

A third element of the Reagan program is a massive shift in responsibilities from the national government to state and local governments. This would be accomplished under the president's New Federalism in two ways. First, President Reagan proposed a swap of major programs. The federal government would assume Medicaid costs in exchange for states taking over Food Stamps and AFDC; in addition, the federal government would turn some forty other programs over to the states at lower rates of spending. Second, President Reagan proposed that seventy-seven specific federal programs be abolished and consolidated into nine block grants. In 1980 federal funding constituted about 25 percent of state and local expenditures. The administration's goal is to reduce this to the 4 to 5 percent level by 1991, as low a share of state and local budgets as existed in 1933.

Lastly, the administration has sharply departed from Keynesian economics. Reagan's tax cuts were not only mammoth, but heavily weighted to benefit the wealthy. In 1983, persons earning less than $10,000 will pay $120 less than last year in taxes, while those making over $80,000 will pay on the average $15,000 less. By 1985 the tax reduction as a percentage of income will be 2.3 percent for those earning less than $10,000, 5.0 percent for those earning from $20,000 to $40,000, and 8.5 percent for those earning $80,000 or more. As a percentage of income, those in the highest bracket have a tax cut five times as large as those in the lowest bracket. The combined impact of the budget cuts and tax cuts represents a significant shift of resources from public to private ends, from lower- to upper-income taxpayers, from poorer states and regions (e.g., the East and South) to richer states and regions (e.g., the West and Southwest). Households earning less than $10,000 will suffer an annual net loss from budget and tax cuts of $240, while those making $80,000 or over will have a net benefit of more than $15,000. In other words, the Reagan program offers no significant benefits for those making less than $15,000, modest benefits for those in the middle class, and substantial gains for higher-income families.

In addition to benefiting the rich, the tax cuts play another critical function in the Reagan revolution—namely, to deprive the federal government of money that might otherwise go toward new social programs. These tax cuts are seen not only as an economic necessity to stimulate growth, but as an ideological imperative as well. Federal tax receipts as a percentage of GNP will decline in only four years (1981–1985) from 21 to 18.5 percent, resulting in a growth in the federal deficit from 2 to 6.5 percent of GNP. President Reagan intends to use these deficits to push Congress to cut still more in social spending.

Franklin Delano Roosevelt's revolution long outlived him. It institutionalized a relationship between the American people and the federal government which persists to this day; it created a set of responsibilities for the federal government in areas of economic management, social services, and income support. It has been a durable foundation, the policy of Republican and Democratic administrations alike. In contrast to the legacy of FDR, President Reagan—if he is reelected in 1984—will outlive his own revolution. This is not to denigrate Reagan's accomplishments. He has caused the rethinking of basic assumptions and changed the entire framework of the social welfare debate. But his revolution has been essentially a counterrevolution, one which has run its course. It constitutes a significant midcourse correction, but not a basic underlying change. His social and economic programs have been unable to accomplish all that they promised but, more fundamentally, their impact will be shortlived because of their fundamental dissidence from mainstream Democratic and Republican thought.

Government has certain unavoidable roles in a complex modern industrial democracy. Americans have come to expect a certain level of service. Tax cuts cannot be used to explain away massive deficits. There are limits to prudent defense spending. The goals of reduced taxes, greater defense spending, and a balanced budget were inconsistent. The 1983 agreement by Republicans in the Senate and Democrats in the House on a budget which fundamentally departs from the Reagan administration program demonstrates that the public will not tolerate any further reorientation of public resources.

*****

Remarks on Private Sector Initiatives at a White House Luncheon for National Religious Leaders April 13, 1982

Ronald Reagan

We just celebrated the happiest and holiest holidays of the Christian faith, and we're in the sixth day of the eight days of Passover, a reminder of our nation's Judeo-Christian tradition. Today America's in the midst of a period of reevaluation about the role of our fundamental institutions, what functions are within the proper sphere of government, which of those should be left at State and local levels, how much can government tax before it infringes on our citizens' freedom and damages the economy's ability to grow and prosper.

For some time now I've been convinced that there is a great hunger on the part of our people for a spiritual revival in this land. There is a role for churches and temples—just as there has been throughout our history. They were once the center of community activity, the primary source of help for the less fortunate, with the churches that ran orphanages, homes for the elderly, other vital services. As late as 1935, at the depth of the Great Depression, a substantial portion of all charity was sponsored by religious institutions. And today, as we all know, the field seems to have been co-opted by government.

The story of the Good Samaritan has always illustrated to me what God's challenge really is—the injured pilgrim lying by the roadside, those who passed by, and then the one man, the Samaritan, who crossed over to help him. He didn't go running into town and look for a caseworker to tell him that there was a fellow out there that needed help. He took it upon himself. Today, we've become so used to turning to government rather than taking the personal time and effort required to help those in need. Some even confuse charity as being the money that is given for lobbying to get more social programs passed.

I realize there is apprehension in the religious community about budget cuts, fear that we're trying to dump responsibility on others, including the churches, and I understand that concern. While we've quite justly, and out of economic necessity, cut some budgets, we have not, contrary to what seems to be the perception, abandoned America's commitment to the poor.

Critics notwithstanding, overall social spending on the part of govern-

SOURCE: Ronald Reagan, *Public Papers of the Presidents: Ronald Reagan* I (Washington, D.C.: U.S. Government Printing Office, 1982), pp. 454–56.

ment is up. For example, the budget for Health and Human Services will total $274.2 billion in 1983, an increase of 8 percent or $20 billion over 1982. And that's $53 billion more than the defense budget. Our budget for Health and Human Services alone is larger than the national debts of all the countries in the world—or any other country in the world, except the United States and the Soviet Union. It provides increases for Head Start, Social Security, Medicare, and other safety net programs.

By and large, when people speak about budget cuts, what they're actually referring to is the trimming of projected increases in spending. Well, there've been some cuts in some programs, programs that were inefficient, top-heavy with bureaucracy, or not coming close to accomplishing what they set out to do. Government spending, in general, and social spending, in particular, got out of hand during the last decade. The Federal budget tripled, even though defense spending, in real dollars, was decreasing. I mention defense, because most of the critics of the budget seem to want to draw that comparison as to what we're doing in that regard. But with this growth in government came double-digit inflation, economic stagnation, and high levels of unemployment. Something had to be done.

If you just take inflation; if it had kept running at the rate it was in 1980, rather than what we brought it down to, a family of four on a fixed income of $15,000 would now be about $1,000 poorer in purchasing power. Inflation, which was 12.4 percent in 1980, has been averaging $4\frac{1}{2}$ percent for the last six months. To lay the groundwork for economic recovery, we had to make some changes. But we're maintaining our fundamental commitment to the poor.

We must recapture the spirit of brotherhood, however, of family and community that once was the hallmark of this country. We're trying to get people, once again, to help others directly. Accomplishing this is not simply a matter of raising money; it's not just reaching into our pockets but reaching into our hearts. I've established a Task Force on Private Sector Initiatives, chaired by Bill Verity, who is with us here today. It's coordinating a broad-range program that's beginning to have a tangible impact.

I appreciate that your presence here represents something of a commitment to provide the leadership necessary to build stronger working partnerships to tackle community problems throughout the country. But I'm not suggesting, nor have I ever suggested, that churches and other voluntary groups should pick up the dollar-for-dollar cost of reduced Federal programs. I just believe it would be a good thing for the soul of this country to encourage people to get involved and accept more direct responsibility for one another's health, happiness, and well-being, rather than leaving it to the bureaucracy.

When someone starts talking about accepting more responsibility, I know that many in organizations whose budgets are already pinched get a queasy feeling. Well, we all know the study of the 5,000 who were fed from what today would probably have been called a brown paper bag lunch—a few loaves and fishes. But somehow, God can take our limited resources and solve larger problems if we're willing to share and to have faith. Today I'm convinced that with God's help the American people are capable of great things and that we'll be blessed beyond all expectation if we only try.

George Bush's wife, Barbara, told me of a church that she visited in Atlanta, St. Luke's Episcopal Church. In the early seventies this church was in decline. It was losing membership and attendance. And then a few members realized that you only gain your life by giving it away. So, some of them started a food program. At first, it was just sandwiches at lunch for the needy of the neighborhood. Now it runs seven days a week and serves up to 600 people a day. The church has also opened a building to an educational program for high school dropouts, which is jointly run by a nonprofit organization, the local school system, and members of the community. The church, incidentally, has grown tremendously in membership.

At this time of Passover we can be reminded of the wisdom of the Talmud, which says, "These are the things for which there are no prescribed limitations: the corner of the field for gleaners, the giving of the first fruits and the deeds of loving kindness. The fruit of these deeds is for them in this world, while the principle remains in the world to come." God's treasures surround us and are waiting for those willing to do His work.

Our task force on private initiatives, chaired by Bill Verity, has challenged the corporate community to double its philanthropic contributions. Today, while private citizens and corporations contribute $47 billion annually, 94 percent of U.S. corporations do not contribute more than $500 annually.

Now, contributions need not be in money. Companies can sponsor volunteer programs for their management and employees or even volunteer the use of their equipment. Prudential Insurance Company, for example, has the largest corporate van-pool system in the United States to bring their employees to and from work. Between office runs, their fleet of vans in Union County, New Jersey, is used to transport the elderly and the underprivileged. The potential for community projects like Prudential's van fleet is limited only by our imagination.

I suspect that those who manage corporations would be pleased to speak with the delegation of the local clergy with an idea of bettering the community. We must remember that many of those who run America's business do sit each week in church or synagogue here and there in the country.

If not the churches, whose job is it to touch the hearts of those who are not already involved? Pardon me if this sounds familiar, but: If not us, who? If not now, when?

Two years ago a Catholic nun, Sister Ruth Haney, and a Southern Baptist lady, Mrs. Janice Webb, discovered something in their town of

Jefferson City, Missouri, that cried out for action. There are four prisons located in that city, and when families of the prisoners came to visit, many had to sleep in the park or under bridges. These two women of different faiths mobilized churches across the State, headed up a committee, and raised $46,000 from churches and individual members to buy an old rooming house three blocks from one of the prisons.

Individual churches took responsibility for renovating and furnishing the dozen rooms in the house and for the continued support of its operation. Mrs. Webb says, "Our sole purpose is to provide"—and I hope I'm pronouncing this right; I realized when I read the word I had never said it aloud—"agape, God's unconditional love to prisoners and their families." And so they named it the Agape House. They provide a bed and bath, but something deeper—the certainty that someone cares. This is the kind of spirit we need to draw upon.

In Chicago, Father Clements started the one-church–one-child program aimed at finding adoptive parents for minority children with special needs, handicapped children, children with learning disabilties, older children. The program, as its name suggests, asked each church to take responsibility to help one lost and lonely child find a home. In a year's time, 159 churches have responded to Father Clements' challenge, and he's taking the idea out of Chicago and going nationwide.

A few weeks ago, I met here in the White House with a group of 75 black ministers. It was a warm and inspiring meeting. Yes, they were concerned about our budget cuts. And we talked about that.

The black clergymen represent a noble tradition in this country. Their struggle to aid the poor, help the sick, and counsel the troubled has always been a real part of their ministry. I sincerely believe they have much to teach all of us about what can be accomplished. But today many black churches need a helping hand. If nothing else, I would hope that we see more religious organizations—black and white, Christian and Jewish—working together.

There is, for example, expertise in America's churches that could be put to use teaching the unemployed skills that would change their lives. Your churches and synagogues can be the catalyst to convene a strong community partnership that can and will make the difference.

It's time for me to sit down, but I'd like to end with this thought. We have problems in our country, and many people are praying and waiting for God to do something. I just wonder if maybe God isn't waiting for us to do something. And while no one else is capable of doing everything, everyone is capable of doing something.

This is the spirit that built and preserved our freedom, made us a humane and God-fearing people. It lives among us still, here in this house and across the land, and as long as it lives, so too will the America that we cherish.

CHAPTER 12

Postscript

INTRODUCTION

The issue of work presents a dominant theme in discussions of welfare from the nineteenth century through today. In pointing to the persistence of work values in welfare policy, the issue is not whether work and self-reliance are good or bad in themselves. Most believe that work is fundamental to the dignity of the individual and basic to a humane and liberal society. The focus on work, however, has meant the larger issues concerning income redistribution, full employment, and structural reform have been given less attention in policy discussions. The persistence of work values in discussions concerning welfare policy suggests that middle-class values have continued to set a context for debates over welfare in modern America. And, as historian William O'Neill observed, "The Protestant Ethic never really died among middle-class Americans, who continued to think their prosperity, however slight, was the reward of virtue, and others' poverty, however great, the penalty of vice."

The final essay in this volume examines the welfare state and its future. Mickey Kaus, in "The Work Ethic State," argues that welfare reform will present a major challenge in the next decade. A proponent of "workfare" programs, Kaus critically examines programs in California and Massachusetts, which offer a variety of services designed to help those on welfare to find work. These services include job appraisals, career planning, remedial education, job training, and placement services. He concludes, "Workfare should not be a short-term program to help existing welfare clients, but a long-term program to destroy the culture of poverty."

Workfare proposals have created a good deal of controvesy. Many experts in social policy have criticized workfare programs as misreading the problems of the poor in America. Critics point out that many of the poor are unable to work, or are with young children, or remain on welfare only a short time as it is. However accurate or fair these criticisms are, it remains clear that the welfare debate is far from finished.

Further Readings:

Important perspectives on poverty in America are offered by David T. Ellwood, *Poor Support: Poverty in the American Family* (New York: Basic Books, 1988); William J. Wilson, *The Truly Disadvantaged: The Inner City, the Underclass, and Public Policy* (Chicago: University of Chicago Press, 1987).

The Work Ethic State

Mickey Kaus

"The most important analytic point . . . is the fact that poverty in America forms a culture, a way of life and feeling, that makes it a whole."

Who said that? Here's a hint—he wrote in the early '60s. Here's another: he dramatically portrayed the breakdown of family life in the black ghetto, the tendency of young men to move from one woman to another without forming marital bonds, and the disastrous rise in the number of families headed by women. This new culture, he said, was different from the culture of other poor ethnic immigrants—more isolated, more dispiriting, more self-perpetuating.

Give up? Did you guess Daniel Patrick Moynihan, author of a famous government report on the topic in 1965? Well, you're wrong. If you guessed Kenneth Clark, the black sociologist whose book *Dark Ghetto* anticipated much of Moynihan's report—you're also wrong. Those are both good guesses. But the quote is from the socialist Michael Harrington—from his 1962 book, *The Other America*, generally credited with prodding a Democratic administration into launching the War on Poverty.

Today it's Ronald Reagan who warns of "a permanent culture of poverty . . . a second and separate America." Reagan conservatives blame the growth of this underclass on the antipoverty war Harrington started. The mere existence of this underclass is considered a refutation of liberalism, and many liberals seem to react as if that were true. But as Harrington's quote shows, we really haven't come very far since 1962, when the War on Poverty hadn't even begun.

In the intervening years much of America's policy establishment fled from the underclass problem. Black leaders caught up in the enterprise of building ethnic pride ("black is beautiful") and worried in part that an unflattering description of ghetto life would reflect on all blacks, reacted against Moynihan's report, enforcing an etiquette of silence on the subject. Liberal whites, frustrated by the failure of the "hand-up-not-handout" programs of the early Great Society, nevertheless were reluctant to "blame the victim." Instead, they gravitated toward a bland redistributionism which held that if the poor couldn't or wouldn't earn their way out of poverty, the government should simply give them cash in the form of a guaranteed income.

Now we're back at the beginning. The government is not about to try to end poverty by simply mailing out checks. More important, there is justified doubt that cash in itself can end the pathology. No one who has watched Bill

SOURCE: Mickey Kaus, *The New Republic* (July 7, 1986), pp. 22–32. Reprinted by permission of *The New Republic* ©1986, The New Republic, Inc.

Moyers's "CBS Reports" on the black family's decline, or read Leon Dash's series on black teenage pregnancy in the *Washington Post*, or Nicholas Lemann's recent *Atlantic* articles on "The Origins of the Underclass," or Ken Auletta's book on the same subject, can doubt that there is a culture of poverty out there that has taken on a life of its own. Right and left now recognize that neither robust economic growth nor massive government transfer payments can by themselves transform a "community" where 90 percent of the children are born into fatherless families, where over 60 percent of the population is on welfare, where the work ethic has evaporated and the enterpreneurial drive is channeled into gangs and drug-pushing. In the District of Columbia ghetto, "getting paid" is slang for mugging somebody.

The underclass embraces only a minority of the poor. It doesn't even include most who go on welfare. (A majority get off the welfare rolls within two years.) On the other hand, about 10 to 15 percent of single mothers who go on welfare stay there for eight years or more, and they account for about half the money spent on welfare at any one time, according to a study by David Ellwood and Mary Jo Bane of Harvard. These people, who are poor on a more or less permanent basis, are part of who we're talking about.

Is the underclass black? Certainly it does not include most blacks, two-thirds of whom live above the poverty line. And it has become fashionable for conservatives to downplay the significance of race in the poverty culture, the better to lay the blame squarely on liberal welfare programs. "The focus on blacks cripples progress," writes Charles Murray, author of *Losing Ground* and the most prominent neocon underclass theorist. Murray claims to have found a town in Ohio where white mothers are producing illegitimate babies at Moynihan-report levels (25 percent of all births), presumably encouraged by the same welfare system that ensnares blacks.

But it is simply stupid to pretend that the culture of poverty isn't largely a black culture. Lemann's recent *Atlantic* essay effectively debunks the idea that we can treat the underclass as a color-blind phenomenon. Lemann stresses a fairly direct connection between those blacks who worked in the sharecropping system in the South and those who formed the lower class of the ghettoes after the great migration North. When desegregation allowed middle- and upper-class blacks to escape the ghetto, Lemann argues, they left behind the black lower class that had always been there. Only now that isolated lower-class culture was free from the restraints the black middle class had quite self-consciously imposed on it.

A large ongoing survey at the University of Michigan shows that although blacks compose only 12 percent of the population, they make up 62 percent of those who stay poor for a long time and 58 percent of the "latent poor"—that is, those who would be poor but for welfare. In this respect the old stereotype that most of the poor are black is accurate. The statistics are equally striking on the question of family breakup. Black illegitimacy rates have always been many times higher than white rates. Then, starting around 1965, the black rate rose dramatically from its already high Moynihan-report level of 25 percent to close to 60 percent today. White illegitimacy rates have been rising too, but the white rate is still only about 13 percent. That Murray could find one poor town where the white rate reaches less than half the average rate for *all* blacks only proves how vast the gap is. Even if whites were a majority of the long-term poor, it would be hard for them to create a poverty "culture" because poor whites have never been confined to segregated communities.

So yes, the problem I am talking about is the culture of our largely black, largely urban ghettos. It is only part of the broader problem of poverty, although it is the most intractable part. It is only part of the problem facing black Americans, although all blacks are unfairly stigmatized by the behavior of the underclass minority. Today, when most liberal black leaders are finally speaking frankly about the crisis in the ghettoes, the important question is no longer whether there is a culture of poverty, but what we are going to do to change it.

'ONLY BLACK PEOPLE CAN DO THIS'

One possible solution is "self-help," which means efforts by the black middle and upper classes to perform what William Raspberry calls "an unprecedented and enormously difficult salvage operation" in the ghetto. This strategy accords with both the hesitancy of liberal whites to tell blacks how to behave and the interest of bootstrapping black neocons in shifting the focus away from a "civil rights" strategy that relies on government intervention. "Only blacks can effectively provide moral leadership for their people," says Glenn Loury of Harvard, a prime spokesman for self-help. More successful blacks, especially, "are strategically situated to undertake" this task. Even Loury's liberal black critics, such as Roger Wilkins, accept both the need for changing underclass culture and the assumption that "only black people can do this." Let-Blacks-Do-It is the new left-right consensus.

When you get to just how the black community itself is going to accomplish a "massive cultural turnaround," however, things get vague. Loury talks about "discussion of values" and "building constructive, internal institutions." Wilkins admits he has only "the sketchiest of ideas." The "local Urban League," he says, could "assemble a roster of role models and present them as a package of assembly speakers for inner-city schools."

Good luck to such efforts, but let's be realistic: today's underclass infants will be great-great-grandparents before these well-intentioned and pathetically limited schemes accomplish any "massive cultural turnaround." The "luckier blacks" can't do it themselves. I'm not even sure it's *fair* to expect middle-class blacks to bear the load of reshaping the underclass simply because they share the same skin color.

Nor is it clear that all the black talk of "self-help"—tinged as it often is with an element of separatism—will push in the right direction. Blacks are more likely to make it by integrating with mainstream economic culture than by selling each other toothpaste. But self-helpers from Louis Farrakhan to Republican heroes such as conservative community activist Robert Woodson seem to be promising inherently limited bootstrapping operations that restrict the arena for black enterprise to the nation's poorest community.

Above all, the Let-Blacks-Do-It boom tempts non-blacks to avoid thinking with any urgency about solutions to the problem that everyone is so proud to have reacknowledged. The biggest disappointment was Moynihan's recent book *Family and Nation*, an effort long on elegantly posed questions and short on answers. Moynihan was once a bold social reformer, but here he was talking about the "limits of government." Likewise, former Virginia governor Charles Robb recently attracted a lot of attention with a speech referring to "self-defeating patterns of [black] behavior." The *New York Times* praised Robb's willingness to face up to "hard truths." But when it came to hard solutions, Robb's most concrete suggestion was that "young mothers, as a condition of receiving welfare," be required to let "visiting teachers come to their homes periodically, to teach learning games and encourage language development. . . . " Learning games!

The alternative is to search for the sort of sweeping government effort that has helped solve our other problems—not new civil rights laws, but efforts that might have the same beneficial effect as the early civil rights laws. As Moynihan says, in the best two sentences in his book, "The central conservative truth is that it is culture, not politics, that determines the success of a society. The central liberal truth is that politics can change a culture and save it from itself."

THE UMBILICAL CORD THEORY

That brings us to the subject of welfare reform. If you are looking for a political handle on the culture of poverty, there is none bigger. Welfare reform is a hot topic in Washington these days, next on the National Agenda once tax reform is out of the way. Task forces are springing up all over the place. Reagan has commissioned three. Mario Cuomo has one. Bruce Babbitt has one designed to keep Reagan's honest from the left, while Michael Novak chairs one to horn in from the right. The mood is early War on Poverty, but in Reagan's Washington the eager young antipoverty warriors are carrying copies of *Losing Ground* rather than *The Other America*. They are going to break the culture of poverty by replacing the Great Society with a "conservative vision of the welfare state."

What's wrong with the current welfare state, anyway? The basic features of our current system for the poor are these: Fairly generous benefits are available to those who are deemed totally and permanently disabled.

Very little in the way of benefits (mainly Food Stamps and stingy state "general relief" money) is available to able-bodied men and women, single or married. But if you are a single parent (almost always a mother) responsible for taking care of a child, you qualify for Aid to Families with Dependent Children (AFDC), which is what most people mean by welfare. In California and New York the AFDC benefit, combined with other benefits, is high enough to bring a welfare mother close to the poverty line. In most Southern states the AFDC benefit is much lower.

The central dilemma of our welfare state, then, is not the age-old general tension between "compassion" and "dependency." For most of the able-bodied, Americans have decided against much cash compassion. Ours is a more specific and modern dilemma: what about a single able-bodied woman who must also care for a child? If we give her no more aid than we give able-bodied men, we may be punishing the child. But to aid the child, we must aid the mother, as AFDC does—and then we risk the "social hazard" of encouraging women to put themselves in that disastrous position. To women, the AFDC system seems to say, "Have a kid and the state will take care of you—as long as you don't live with the father." To men, it says, "Father children and the state will take care of them."

This can't *help*. But the current attack on welfare by conservatives mixes up two quite distinct theories as to how it might hurt. In theory #1, prospective mothers and fathers are influenced directly by the economic blandishments of AFDC, much as if by bribes. A mother might have a baby "to go on welfare." A father might leave his wife or girlfriend so she qualifies for the program. Believers in this theory are apt to say that welfare *caused* the growth of the underclass. This is the theory behind Charles Murray's notorious "Harold and Phyllis" story, which compares in minute detail the financial prospects of a fictitious ghetto couple on and off welfare, concluding that between 1960 and 1970 benefit increases and eased eligibility rules had tipped the balance and made welfare an appealing option.

As "absent father" cases grew from 30 percent of AFDC homes in 1940 to 64 percent in 1960, even many liberals were quite willing to denounce AFDC's "discrimination" against intact families. The preferred liberal solution, however, was not to take benefits away from broken families but to extend them to intact ones. The guaranteed-income concept was the logical conclusion of this line of thought.

But once the guaranteed income was politically dead, liberals took off after the Bribe Theory. And it turns out the theory doesn't hold up very well. For one thing, as Lemann points out, the Bribe Theory doesn't account for black exceptionalism. Welfare certainly couldn't have caused the black family patterns that W. E. B. DuBois noted in Philadelphia in 1899, 35 years before welfare existed. For another, the impact of marginal Harold-and-Phyllis style calculations on the decision of women to have a child out of wedlock does not appear to be great. The illegitimacy problem got worse in the mid to late 1970s, even though AFDC benefits were falling in real dollars. And, in a much-cited study, Ellwood and Bane compared family structures in states with varying benefit levels and concluded that high benefits have no effect on the decision to have a baby. Ghetto teenagers don't have children to go on welfare, these experts tell us. They have babies to increase their self-esteem, to give themselves "something to love" in a world where delayed gratification seems pointless. Teenage men seek to prove their masculinity, while girls, as Dash's series described in horrifying detail, are often ridiculed *by other girls* if they remain virgins too long into their teens.

But there is a second, and far more plausible, theory that implicates welfare in this cultural catastrophe. It holds that although welfare might not *cause* the underclass, it *sustains* it. With AFDC in place, young girls look around them and recognize, perhaps unconsciously, that girls in their neighborhood who have had babies on their own are surviving, however uncomfortably (but who lives comfortably in the ghetto?). Welfare, as the umbilical cord through which the mainstream society sustains the isolated ghetto society, permits the expansion of this single-parent culture. It is its economic life support system, much as the entertainment deduction is the life support system of the culture of the $45 business lunch. No businessmen goes into an overpriced restaurant *in order* to run up a big deduction. But without the deduction, businessmen would quickly change their lifestyle and such restaurants would disappear.

The Umbilical Cord Theory doesn't talk of families being directly "pulled apart" by welfare, but of families that are never formed in the culture welfare subsidizes. Once AFDC benefits reach a certain threshold that allows poor single mothers to survive, the culture of the underclass can start growing as women have babies for all the various non-welfare reasons they have them. Indeed, precisely *because* nobody has babies in order to go on welfare, marginally lowering welfare benefits won't affect them.

If the Bribe Theory is the basis of Murray's "Harold and Phyllis" example, the Umbilical Cord Theory underlies his equally notorious "thought experiment." What would happen, he asks, if there were no welfare *at all*? Answer: things would have to change. "You want to cut illegitimate births among poor people? . . . I know how to do that," Murray told Ken Auletta in a *Washington Monthly* interview. "You just rip away every kind of government support there is. What happens then? You're going to have lots of parents talking differently to daughters, and you're going to have lots of daughters talking differently to their boyfriends. . . . " If the daughters didn't, their plight trying to raise kids without welfare would serve as an example to their neighbors.

The implications of this second view of welfare are far nastier than those of the Bribe version. If the Umbilical Cord Theory is correct, it isn't enough to *extend* welfare benefits so that intact families are well off in comparison to single-parent families. You have to deny benefits to the single-parent families, to unplug the underclass culture's life support system.

Those of us who don't have the stomach to go through with Murray's "experiment" (and Murray himself waffles) are compelled to come up with a more humane way of changing the welfare culture. And there remains the possibility that something less than Murray's "let-them-starve" solution might work—something that doesn't cause pain exactly, but that does impose upon individuals the consequences of their choices, at the same time that it offers them a way out. Something like work.

This is the promise of "workfare," right now the hottest thing in the hot field of welfare reform. Workfare holds out the hope of achieving the ends of Murray's "experiment," without the intolerable toll of human suffering, simply by exposing welfare recipients to the necessity that has been the fate of mankind since Eden: the necessity of labor.

THE SIX PERCENT SOLUTION

In 1969, when Nixon proposed the ambitious guaranteed income scheme for families with children, his domestic adviser, one Daniel Patrick Moynihan, threw in a token "work requirement" to placate conservatives. This gave William Safire, Nixon's speechwriter, the excuse he needed to label the entire concoction "workfare," thus permanently confusing the meaning of that term. The Nixon plan, in reality, offered the poor money with no strings attached. As such it was the opposite of what most people mean by workfare, and what I mean by workfare, which is what Ronald Reagan meant by workfare when he first proposed in 1967 that welfare recipients in California be required to work, in government public service jobs if necessary, in exchange for their welfare checks.

Workfare drove liberals berserk back then. Thanks in part to liberal opposition, Reagan's California program never really got off the ground. But he persisted, and when he got to Washngton in 1981 he proposed requiring all states to make welfare recipients work off their grants at the minimum wage. Congress didn't give him that, but it did allow states to experiment with workfare if they wanted.

The result is one of those bipartisan movements that seems to herald a genuinely productive marriage of liberalism with the more authoritarian wing of conservatism. *Time* magazine reports: "In statehouses across the country, Democrats and Republicans have joined forces to support legislation that combines the job programs traditionally favored by liberals with efforts to pare the welfare rolls advocated by conservatives." Some 28 states have run experiments, most of them small, with one or another variety of workfare. More important, three of the five biggest states in the union—

California, New York, and Illinois—all recently announced ambitious plans to apply workfare precepts to their entire caseloads.

The appearance of a new bipartisan toughness can be deceiving, however. Virtually everybody by now agrees that, as Cuomo put it, "work is better than welfare"—that welfare recipients, mothers included, should be in the labor force (something neither liberals nor conservative women's-place-is-at-home types would have agreed on a few years ago). Beyond that, "workfare"—like "industrial policy"—is vague enough to mean quite different things to different people.

On one extreme is Massachusett's touted Employment and Training Choices program, ET for short. But ET is not really workfare at all. There is nothing mandatory about it. True, welfare mothers with no children under six must *register* for the program, but registration for work has been a federal welfare requirement since 1967. (It's "nothing other than filling out a form," says Massachusetts Welfare Commissioner Charles Atkins.) Everything else about ET is voluntary and upbeat. Welfare mothers are offered a variety of services designed to help them find work—job appraisals, career planning workshops, remedial education, job training, placement services. Those who find jobs get transportation allowances and free day care for a year after they start work, plus Medicaid for up to 15 months if their employers don't provide health insurance.

But welfare recipients don't have to do any of this. If they prefer they can still stay home and collect a check. If "clients" decline ET's "invitation" to participate, they are placed on an automated "future participation" list and targeted for "special marketing campaigns." As for mandatory programs—that is to say, workfare—Atkins has a simple answer: "I think workfare is slavery."

The most important criticism of ET, however, is that it doesn't come close to "solving the problem" of the culture of poverty. ET is about as good a voluntary job-training program as we are likely to get. It is competently run, well funded, skillfully marketed. It operates in the hottest regional economy in the country. But of 112,983 welfare cases in 1985, about 7,660 or 6.8 percent, actually got full-time jobs through ET. Even if all of those people wouldn't have found work otherwise, that isn't a big enough percentage to transform the underclass. "What we did in ET is pick off the people who are most motivated to go to work," Atkins admits. Those remaining are the least motivated, the hardest to "seduce." ET offers those willing to work their way out of the culture of poverty a way to do it, no small thing. But it leaves the culture itself largely unscathed.

THE POVERTY LAWYERS' PLAYPEN

If George Deukmejian, California's Republican governor, could talk like Mario Cuomo, we would all have heard more than enough about GAIN (Greater Avenues for INdependence), the welfare reform plan that sailed through his state's legislature early this year. But Deukmejian's a bore, so the most important welfare reform in decades went largely unnoticed in the Eastern press.

GAIN is big. It tries to impose a mandatory program on the largest welfare caseload in the country. GAIN is also complicated. Democrats added so many options, protections, and furbelows to Deukmejian's basic work-off-your-grant proposal that the GAIN flow chart resembles a diagram of the Chernobyl nuclear plant. As finally adopted, California's plan offers a generous menu of training and education "options" to welfare recipients in addition to "work experience," here relabeled "pre-employment preparation" (PREP). Welfare recipients (who get free day care if necessary) can choose to take vocational education, remdeial education, English-as-a-second-language, among others, instead of working for their checks. This smorgasbord approach is the latest workfare fashion. Attribute it to ET's influence.

But unlike ET, under GAIN recipients must do *something*. No welfare recipient will be forced to work off her grant right away. If she doesn't get a job after training in a specific job skill, then the state may require her to work off her grant—but it must offer her a workfare job that uses the skill she has learned. Welfare mothers trained as nurses' aides may not be required to work as secretaries, etc. Only if the recipient screws up in some way—drops out of school or falls out of the training program—may she be required to take a long-term public service job unrelated to her training. These "long-term PREP" cases are reviewed every six months, and may then be recycled through the system.

As a hard workfare strategy to destroy the poverty culture, GAIN suffers from the two major structural flaws common to most such programs. First, it requires nothing of welfare mothers until their oldest child reaches the age of six. This one restriction excuses two-thirds of the welfare caseload in California. If the sight of other teenagers living on welfare after having babies is a bad influence on their contemporaries, workfare programs limited to those with school-age children may not dramatically change those background conditions. And if anyone wants to avoid the workfare obligation, one way out is obvious—she can "go home and have another baby," as California State Senator Diane Watson threatened her inner-city constituents would do when confronted with "forced labor." Hard workfare advocates such as New York's Blanche Bernstein worry privately about this have-a-kid loophole. Bernstein would extend workfare to mothers with no children younger than three, which would bring 62 percent of the national welfare caseload into the program. Beyond that, Bernstein says she is "depending on physiological constraints"—i.e., there are only so many babies a woman can have.

Even more important, neither GAIN nor any mere "workfare" plan does much to employ those in the underclass who have few welfare benefits to "work off," namely able-bodied men. The welfare mother whose ET session I observed asked if there were any way the program could find a job for her "friend." That was the third such request the caseworker had had that day. It will be hard to break the culture of single motherhood as long as among non-whites aged 20–24 there are only 48 employed civilian—i.e., "marriageable"—men for every 100 women (as William Julius Wilson and Kathryn Neckerman of the University of Chicago estimate). In fact, the absolute number of illegitimate black births has not been increasing, but the rate at which legitimate black families are formed has plummeted. No program is apt to arrest this decline unless it puts more men into jobs. By offering women who head fatherless families a way out of poverty, while failing to offer it to potential fathers (or childless women), work and training programs may reinforce whatever incentives in favor of single-parent families the AFDC system generates ("Have a Kid, Get Job Training").

ONLY WORK WORKS

What would a program that had a real chance of undermining the underclass look like? The deficiencies in the efforts currently underway give us some idea. First, it would be a program that expects women to work even if they have young children. Second, it would offer work to ghetto men and single women as well as to the welfare mothers. Third, it will have to deal with the related Take Away and Low Wage dilemmas: how can you require welfare recipients to accept private jobs if they pay less than welfare? How can you avoid making workfare or training more lucrative than private sector work?

Solving these problems will take something more radical than any existing workfare plan. It must be far bigger, in order to offer jobs to men, and far tougher in its dealings with young mothers. Above all, the program must unambiguously announce the cultural norm it seeks to promote in place of the culture of welfare.

What is required, I think, is something like this: replacing all cash-like welfare programs that assist the able-bodied poor (AFDC, general relief, Food Stamps, and housing subsidies, but not Medicaid) with a single, simple offer from the government—an offer of employment for every American citizen over 18 who wants it, in a useful public job at a wage slightly below the minimum wage. If you could work, and needed money, you would not be given a check (welfare). You would not be given a check and then cajoled, instructed, and threatened into working it off or "training it off" (workfare). You would be given the location of several government job sites. If you showed up, and worked, you would be paid for your work. If you don't show up, you don't get paid. Simple.

Unlike "workfare" jobs, these jobs would be available to everybody, men as well as women, single or married, mothers and fathers alike. No perverse "anti-family" incentives. No "means test" either. If David Rockefeller showed up, he could work too. But he wouldn't. Most Americans wouldn't. The low wage itself would "ration" the jobs to those who needed them most, and preserve the incentive to look for better work in the private sector. Instead of paying what in effect are high workfare "wages" and then relying on the stigma of welfare to encourage people to leave, this program would pay low wages but remove the stigma. Those who worked in the jobs would be earning their money. They could hold their heads up. They would also have something most unemployed underclass members desperately need: a supervisor they could give as a job reference to other employers. Although the best workers could be promoted to higher paying public service positions, for most workers movement into the private sector would take care of itself. If you have to work anyway, why do it for $3 an hour?

Those who didn't take advantage of these jobs, however, would be on their own. No cash doles. Mothers included. (Remember, we're only talking here about those able to work.) People who show up drunk for their jobs, who show up high, or who pick a fight with their supervisor could be fired (though they could show up again after a decent interval). There would be no need to "require" work. Work would be all that was offered. The problem of having to take away high benefits to force low-wage work would be solved by simply not providing those benefits in the first place.

This is not a new idea. Similar proposals have been advanced in the past by Russell Long and (of all people) Arthur Burns. Basically, it makes the same decision Franklin Roosevelt made in 1934, when he decided to replace a system of cash relief for the able-bodied with the Work Projects Administration, the WPA. Liberals who invoke Roosevelt's "compassionate" legacy tend to forget this anti-dole decision. Meanwhile, Reagan gleefully quotes Roosevelt's description of the dole as "a narcotic," somehow failing to mention that FDR said it in the speech where he proposed the largest government jobs program in the nation's history. In fact, FDR's anti-dole and pro-WPA opinions were of a piece, a decision in favor of work-welfare and against cash-welfare.

Of course, Roosevelt's WPA was designed to combat general unemployment at a time when most of those needing "relief" were veteran workers and nobody imagined that the tiny AFDC program, nestled unnoticed in the New Deal structure, would one day sustain millions of husbandless mothers. Our goal, in contrast, is to break the culture of poverty by providing jobs for ghetto men and women who may have no prior work habits, at the same time as we end the option of a life on welfare for single mothers. It is the transformation of the welfare state into the Work Ethic State, in which status, dignity, and government benefits flow only to those who work, but in which the government steps in to make sure work is available to all. There are a number of obvious objections to so simple a solution.

Will the wage be enough to support a family? No. This is the Low Wage dilemma. The poverty line for a family of three is $8,570. A full-time, minimum-wage job brings in only $7,000, and the government jobs proposed here would pay less than that. But there are ways to supplement the incomes of low-wage workers outside the welfare system (while preserving an incentive to seek better pay). The current Earned Income Tax Credit is one, the innovative Wage Rate Subsidy system of Brandeis professor Robert Lerman (which would pay half the difference between the family breadwinner's wage and $6 an hour) is another. Even Ronald Reagan once proposed this approach while testifying against the guaranteed income in 1972.

A subsidized wage would, in effect, be a guaranteed income *for those who work* (a far more affordable proposition than an income guarantee that doesn't have a base of wages to start from). There is no objection, in the Work Ethic State, to the government sending out checks as long as able-bodied people only get them if they work. Supplementing wages is a much better solution to the Low Wage problem than pretending the underclass can get "good jobs" that pay enough in themselves to support a family.

Will people be allowed to starve? The state's basic obligation, in this scheme, is to provide dignified work for all who can work, and a decent income for the disabled. There will be those who refuse work. Many ghetto men, at least initially, will prefer the world of crime, hustle, and odd jobs to working for "chump change." One advantage of the Work Ethic State is that criminals can be treated as criminals, without residual guilt about the availability of jobs. Others—the addled and addicted—will simply fail at working, or not even try. Even a fraction of welfare mothers, the most employable underclass group, will have trouble. "The workplace is so foreign to so many people who are second- and third-generation dependents," says Tom Nees, a Washington, D.C., minister whose Community of Hope works with welfare families poor enough to be homeless.

The first underclass generation *off* welfare will be the roughest. Those people who fail at work will be thrown into the world of austere public, in-kind guarantees—homeless shelters, soup kitchens, and the like—and the world of private charitable organizations like Nees's. This aid would be stigmatizing (as it must be if work is to be honored), but it could be compassionate. Nobody would starve. Counseling, therapy, training, could be offered, even subsidized by the government, in order to help these people back on their feet. The one thing the government would not offer them is cash.

What about mothers with young children? The government would announce that, after a certain date, single mothers would no longer qualify for cash welfare payments. The central ambiguity of our welfare system—whether single mothers should work—would be resolved cleanly and clearly in favor of work. This hard choice is a key way the Work Ethic State would hope to break the self-perpetuating culture of poor, single-parent families. Teenage mothers who had babies could no longer count on welfare to sustain them. They would have to work like everyone else, and the prospect of juggling motherhood and a not-very-lucrative job would make them think twice, although it would also offer a way out of poverty that Charles Murray's starvation solution would deny.

What would the children do when their mothers were working? If the government is going to expect mothers to work, then it will have to provide day care for all those who need it. This will be expensive (Massachusetts pays $2,800 a year for each day-care slot). But it won't be as prohibitively expensive as many who raise the day-care issue seem to believe. In every state in which free day care has been offered to AFDC mothers, demand has fallen below predictions. "It is never utilized to the extent people thought it would be," says Barbara Goldman of MDRC. Most mothers, it seems, prefer to make their own arrangements. Whether those arrangements are any good is another question. The government might actually have to take steps to encourage day care, as part of the general trend toward getting kids out of underclass families and into school at an early age.

What about mothers with very young children, two years and under? A destitute mother with a newborn infant presents the basic AFDC dilemma in the starkest form. It *is* a dilemma, meaning there are arguments on both sides. One alternative is to allow temporary cash welfare for the first two years of a child's life, with a three-year limit to avoid the have-another-kid loophole. A two-year free ride is better than a six-year free ride. Teenagers are likely to be friends with someone in their community who has a two-year-old kid and is "up against it," as Murray puts it. On the other hand, no free ride at all (except for in-kind nutritional assistance during pregnancy and infancy to avoid disastrous health problems) would clearly have stronger impact. It would also put mothers into the world of work without letting them grow accustomed to dependency. Oklahoma applies its soft workfare requirement to mothers as soon as their kids are born, with no apparent ill effects.

And if a mother refuses? The short, nasty answer is that if a mother turns down the state's offer of a job with which she might support her children, and as a result her children live in squalor and filth, then she has neglected a basic task of parenthood. She is subject to the laws that already provide for removal of a child from an unfit home.

What about teenagers who haven't even finished high school? They could receive free day care while finishing, and in-kind nutritional assistance, but no cash. To obtain any extra cash necessary to support a baby, they would have to work, in one of the guaranteed government jobs if necessary. Again, the government could offer as many free training programs as it wanted, but without cash entitlements. Since training would no longer be an alternative to working, trainees would have every incentive to make the most of it.

Will there be enough jobs these people can do? As noted above, the objection can't be that there aren't enough worthwhile jobs to be done. The crumbling "infrastructure" that pre-occupied Washington three years ago hasn't been patched up overnight. All around the country governments have stopped doing, for financial reasons, things they once thought worthwhile, like opening libraries on Saturday and picking up trash twice a week. Why not do them again?